Modeling Monetary Economies

The approach of this text for upper-level undergraduates is to teach monetary economics using the classical paradigm of rational agents in a market setting. Too often monetary economics has been taught as a collection of facts about existing institutions for students to memorize. By teaching from first principles instead, the authors aim to instruct students not only in the monetary policies and institutions that exist today in the United States but also in what policies and institutions may or should exist tomorrow and elsewhere. The text builds on a simple, clear monetary model and applies this framework consistently to a wide variety of monetary questions. The authors have added in this second edition new material on speculative attacks on currencies, social security, currency boards, central banking alternatives, the payments system, and the Lucas model of price surprises. Discussions of many topics have been extended, presentations of data greatly expanded, and new exercises added.

Bruce Champ is an economist at the Federal Reserve Bank of Cleveland. Earlier he taught at Virginia Polytechnic Institute, the Universities of Iowa and Western Ontario, and Fordham University. Dr. Champ's research interests focus on monetary economics, and his articles have appeared in the *American Economic Review, Journal of Monetary Economics, Canadian Journal of Economics*, and the *Journal of Money, Credit, and Banking*, among other leading academic publications.

Scott Freeman is Professor of Economics at the University of Texas, Austin. He previously taught at Boston College and the University of California, Santa Barbara. Professor Freeman specializes in monetary theory, and his articles have appeared in the *Journal of Political Economy, American Economic Review, Journal of Monetary Economics*, and the *Journal of Money, Credit, and Banking*, among other eminent academic journals.

Advance Praise for *Modeling Monetary Economies*

"This is simply the best book on monetary theory with which I am familiar. I cannot emphasize strongly enough how this book belongs in the curriculum of advanced undergraduates. There is no acceptable alternative. Former students have told me that the best favor that they did for themselves, before going to graduate school in economics, was reading the earlier version of Champ and Freeman, cover to cover. In a better world, this would be the standard undergraduate macro text; and with the improvements in the new version, particularly the inclusion of the seminal Lucas model of price surprises, it may yet become so. The ideal course is based on Champ and Freeman, and on Russell W. Cooper, *Coordination Games: Complementarities and Macroeconomics* (Cambridge University Press, 1999). If you cannot do this for your intermediate students, do it for your advanced students."

– John Bryant, *Rice University and CentER, Tilburg University*

"This is without a doubt the best text on the market in advanced undergraduate or masters-level monetary economics. Champ and Freeman provide a unified theoretical treatment of all the important topics in money and banking, and their second edition adds important new and topical material on central banking and the payments system."

– Stephen D. Williamson, *University of Iowa*

"This is an absolutely outstanding textbook. The authors are able to communicate at a very basic but rigorous level many of the complex and subtle issues being tackled by monetary theorists at the frontier of the discipline. The text is easy to read and the theoretical analysis is applied to many real-world issues and phenomena, which made it a big hit with my students."

– David Andolfatto, *Simon Fraser University*

Modeling Monetary Economies

Second Edition

BRUCE CHAMP
Federal Reserve Bank of Cleveland

and

SCOTT FREEMAN
University of Texas at Austin

CAMBRIDGE
UNIVERSITY PRESS

PUBLISHED BY THE PRESS SYNDICATE OF THE UNIVERSITY OF CAMBRIDGE
The Pitt Building, Trumpington Street, Cambridge, United Kingdom

CAMBRIDGE UNIVERSITY PRESS
The Edinburgh Building, Cambridge CB2 2RU, UK
40 West 20th Street, New York, NY 10011-4211,
10 Stamford Road, Oakleigh, VIC 3166, Australia
Ruiz de Alarcón 13, 28014 Madrid, Spain
Dock House, The Waterfront, Cape Town 8001, South Africa

http://www.cambridge.org

First published 2001

Printed in the United States of America

Typeface Times 11/14 pt.   *System* LATEX 2$_\varepsilon$ [TB]

A catalog record for this book is available from the British Library.

Library of Congress Cataloging in Publication Data
Champ, Bruce.
Modeling monetary economics / by Bruce Champ and Scott Freeman. – 2nd ed.
p.   cm.
Includes bibliographical references and index.
ISBN 0-521-78354-2 – ISBN 0-521-78974-5 (pb)
1. Money – Mathematical models.   I. Freeman, Scott.   II. Title.
HG221 .C447   2000
332.4′01′5118 – dc21
00-040343

ISBN 0 521 78354 2 hardback
ISBN 0 521 78974 5 paperback

For Brian, Julie, and Stacy;
Lauren and Tyler

Contents

Preface

WE OFFER THIS book as an undergraduate-level exposition of lessons about monetary economics gleaned from overlapping generations models of money. Assembling recent advances in monetary theory for the instruction of undergraduates is not a quixotic goal; these models are well within the reach of undergraduate students at the intermediate and advanced levels. These elegantly simple models strengthen our fundamental understanding of the most basic questions in monetary economics: How does money promote exchange? What should serve as money? What causes inflation? What is the cost of inflation?

This approach to teaching monetary economics follows the profession's general recoginition of the need to build the microeconomic foundations of monetary and other macroeconomic topics – that is, to explain aggregate economic phenomena as the implications of the choices of rational individuals who seek to improve their welfare within their limited means. The use of microeconomic foundations makes macroeconomics easier to understand because the performance of abstract economic processes such as gross national product and inflation is linked to something intuitively understood by all – rational individual behavior. It also brings powerful microeconomic tools familiar to undergraduates, such as indifference curves and budget lines, to bear on the questions of interest. Finally, the joining of micro- and macroeconomics introduces an element of consistency across undergraduate studies. Certainly, students will be puzzled if taught that people are rational and prices clear markets when studied by microeconomists but not when studied by macroeconomists.

Inertia and tradition, however, have mired the teaching of monetary economics in a swamp of institutional details, as if monetary economics were only an unchanging set of facts to be memorized. The rapid pace of change in the financial world belies this view. Undergraduates need a way to analyze a wide variety of monetary events and institutional arrangements because the events and institutions of the future will not be the same as those that the students studied in the classroom. The teaching of analysis, the heart of a liberal education, is best accomplished by having the students analyze clear, explicit, and internally consistent models. In this way, the students may uncover the links between the assumptions underlying the models and the performance of these model economies and thus may apply their lessons to new events or changes in government priorities and policies.

This book implements our goals by starting with the simplest model of money – the basic overlapping generations model – which we analyze for its insights into the most basic questions of monetary economics, including the puzzling demand for useless pieces of paper and the costs of inflation. Of course, such a simple model will not be able to discuss all issues of monetary economics. Therefore, we proceed in successive chapters by asking which features of actual economies the simple model does not address. We then introduce these neglected features into the model to enable us to discuss these more advanced topics. We believe this gradual approach allows us to build, step by step, an integrated model of the monetary economy without overwhelming the students.

The book is organized into three parts of increasing complexity. Part I examines money in isolation. Here we take up the questions of the demand for fiat money, a comparison of fiat and commodity monies, inflation, and exchange rates. In Part II, we add capital, to study money's interaction with other assets, banking, the intermediation of these assets into substitutes for fiat money, and alternative arrangements of central banking. In Part III, we look at the effects of money on saving, investment, and output through its effect on nonmonetary government debt.

This book is written for undergraduate students. Its mathematical requirements are no more advanced than the understanding of basic graphs and algebra; calculus is not required. (Those who want to use calculus can find a basic exposition of this approach in the appendix to Chapter 1.) Although we hope the book may also prove useful to graduate students as a primer in monetary theory, the main text is pitched at the undergraduate level. This pitch has held us back from a few demanding topics, such as nonstationary equilibria, but we hope the reader will be satisfied by the large number of topics we present in simple, clear models within a single basic framework. Material that is difficult but within the grasp of advanced undergraduates is set apart in appendices and thus easily skipped or inserted. The appendices also contain extensions, like the model of credit, that many instructors may want to use but that are not essential to the exposition of the main topics.

The references display the most tension between the needs of undergraduates and the technical base in which this approach originated. Whenever possible we reference related material written for undergraduates or general audiences; these references are marked by asterisks. We also reference the works from which our models and data have been drawn. Finally, where undergraduate-level references were not available, we have inserted references to a few academic articles and surveys to offer graduate and advanced undergraduate students some places to start with more advanced work. These are not intended to be a full survey of the advanced literature.

The choice of topics to be covered was also difficult. We make no claim to encyclopedic coverage of every topic or opinion related to monetary economics. We limited coverage to the topics most directly linked to money, covering banking (but not finance in general) and government debt (but not macroeconomics in general). We insisted on ideas consistent with fully rational people operating in explicitly specified environments to promote the unity and consistency of our approach across topics. We also selected topics tractably teachable in the basic framework of the overlapping generations model. Finally, we offer what we best know and understand. We hope individual instructors will build on our foundations to fill any gaps.

To reduce these gaps, in this second edition we have added new material on speculative attacks, the not-very-monetary topic of social security, currency boards, central banking alternatives, the payments system, and the Lucas model of price surprises. We have greatly expanded our presentations of data and have added new exercises.

Many have contributed to the development of this book. We owe Neil Wallace a tremendous intellectual debt for impressing upon us the importance of microeconomic theory in monetary economics. Many others have provided helpful suggestions, criticisms, encouragement, and other assistance during the writing of this book, including David Andolfatto, Leonardo Auernheimer, Robin Bade, Valerie Bencivenga, Mike Bryan, John Bryant, Douglas Dacy, Silverio Foresi, Christian Gilles, Paul Gomme, Joseph Haslag, Dennis Jansen, David Laidler, Kam Liu, Mike Loewy, Helen O'Keefe, John O'Keefe, Michael Parkin, Dan Peled, Tom Sargent, Pierre Siklos, Bruce Smith, Ken Stewart, Dick Tresch, François Velde, Paula Hernandez Verme, Warren Weber, and Steve Williamson. We thank the large number of students at Boston College, the University of California at Santa Barbara, the University of Western Ontario, Fordham University, and the University of Texas at Austin, who persevered through the various preliminary versions of this book. We are grateful for their patience and suggestions. The views stated in this book are those of the authors and not necessarily those of the Federal Reserve Bank of Cleveland or of the Board of Governors of the Federal Reserve System.

Bruce Champ
Scott Freeman

Part I

Money

IN PART I we develop and learn to work with our most basic model of money, applying it to the study of fiat and commodity monies, inflation, and international monetary systems. In studying each of these topics, we will examine how money can facilitate trade and we will ask which form of money or system of exchange does so most efficiently.

Chapter 1 begins with a simple model of money designed to answer the most basic question in monetary economics: Why do people use money? Why do people value pieces of paper that cannot be consumed? With this model, we discover that intrinsically worthless pieces of paper can have value by providing a means by which individuals can acquire goods that they do not possess. Because of this, we also find that the introduction of money into an economy improves welfare. The model of Chapter 1 serves as the foundation on which we later build more complex models.

Chapter 2 considers two alternatives to the paper money of Chapter 1 – barter and commodity money. This chapter first presents a model that demonstrates, in a multiple good model, why barter, the direct trade of goods owned for goods desired, may be more costly than monetary exchange, the trade of goods owned for money and the subsequent trade of money for goods desired. Chapter 2 also demonstrates that commodities may be exchanged as monies. We will ask which commodities make the best monies and we will compare the efficiency of exchange with commodity money to exchange with fiat money.

Chapter 3 uses the basic model of money of Chapter 1 to analyze the effects of the expansion of the money supply on prices, the willingness of people to use money, and the welfare of individuals. We also see how the printing of fiat money can be used to raise revenue for government expenditures. We compare the efficiency of this revenue device with that of taxes.

Chapter 4 examines international monetary systems. We discover some of the important determinants of exchange rates, we discuss floating versus fixed exchange rate regimes and speculative attacks, and we compare alternative international monetary systems.

Chapter 5 looks at some effects of price surprises on labor and output. We introduce the concept of rational expectations and show that a positive correlation between price surprises and output may not imply that the monetary authority is able to increase output in any systematic way. More generally, the chapter is intended to demonstrate the pitfalls of giving policy advice based on purely statistical correlations without understanding the workings of the economy that generated those correlations.

Chapter 1

A Simple Model of Money

Building a Model of Money

IN THIS BOOK we will try to learn about monetary economies through construction of a series of model economies that replicate essential features of actual monetary economies. All such models are simplifications of the complex economic reality in which we live. They may be useful, however, if they are able to illustrate key elements of the behavior of people who choose to hold money and to predict the reactions of important economic variables such as output, prices, government revenue, and public welfare to changes in policies that involve money. We start our analysis with the simplest conceivable model of money. We will learn what we can from this simple model and then ask how the model fails to represent reality adequately. Throughout the book we will try to correct the model's oversights by adding, one by one, the features that it lacks.

To arrive at the simplest possible model of money, we must ask ourselves what features are essential to monetary economies. The demand for money is distinct from the demand for the goods studied elsewhere in economics. People want goods for the utility received from their consumption. In contrast, people do not want money in order to consume it; they want money because money helps them get the things they want to consume. In this way, money is a **medium of exchange** – something acquired to make it easier to trade for the goods whose consumption is desired.

A model of this distinction in the demand for money therefore requires two special features. First, there must be some "friction" to trade that inhibits people from directly acquiring the goods they desire in the absence of money. If people could costlessly trade what they have for what they want, there would be no role for money.

Second, someone must be willing to hold money from one period to the next. This is necessary because money is an asset held over some period of time, however short, before it is spent. Therefore, we will look for models in which there is always someone who will live into the next period.

Two possible frameworks meet this second requirement. People (or households) could live infinite lives or could live finite lives in generations that overlap (so that some but not all people will live into the next period). For many of the topics we study, life span does not matter. We identify where it does matter in Appendix B of Chapter 15, where infinitely lived households are studied in detail.

With the exception of that appendix, we concentrate on the second framework – the **overlapping generations model**. This model, introduced by Paul Samuelson (1958), has been applied to the study of a large number of topics in monetary theory and macroeconomic theory. Among its desirable features are the following:

- Overlapping generations models are highly tractable. Although they can be used to analyze quite complex issues, they are relatively easy to use. Many of their predictions may be described on a simple two-dimensional graph.
- Overlapping generations models provide an elegantly parsimonious framework in which to introduce the existence of money. Money in overlapping generations models dramatically facilitates exchange between people who otherwise would be unable to trade.
- Overlapping generations models are **dynamic**. They demonstrate how behavior in the present can be affected by anticipated future events. They stand in marked contrast to **static** models, which assume that only current events affect behavior.

We begin this chapter with a very simple version of an overlapping generations model. As we proceed through the book, we introduce extensions to this basic model. These extensions allow us to analyze a variety of interesting issues. For now, let us turn to the development of the basic overlapping generations model.

The Environment

In the basic overlapping generations model, individuals live for two periods. We call people in the first period of life **young** and those in the second period of life **old**.

The economy begins in period 1. In each period $t \geq 1$, N_t individuals are born. Note that we index time with a subscript. For example, N_2 is our notation for the number of individuals born in period 2. The individuals born in periods 1, 2, 3, ... are called the **future generations** of the economy. In addition, in period 1 there are N_0 members of the **initial old**.

Hence, in each period t, there are N_t young individuals and N_{t-1} old individuals alive in the economy. For example, in period 1, there are N_0 initial old individuals and N_1 young individuals who were born at the beginning of period 1.

For simplicity, there is only one good in this economy. The good cannot be stored from one period to the next. In this basic setup, each individual receives an **endowment** of the consumption good in the first period of life. The amount of this

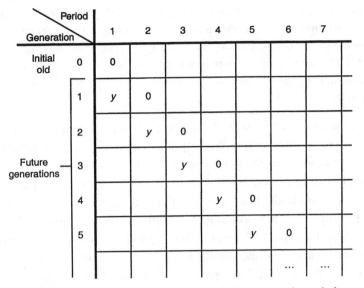

Figure 1.1. The pattern of endowments. In each period t, generation t is born. Each individual lives for two periods. Individuals are endowed with y units of the consumption good when young and 0 units when old. In any given period, one generation of young people and one generation of old people are alive. The name of this model, the overlapping generations model, follows from this generational structure.

endowment is denoted as y. Each individual receives no endowment in the second period of life. This pattern of endowments is illustrated in Figure 1.1.

We can also interpret the endowment as an endowment of labor – the ability to work. By using this labor endowment (by working), the individual is able to obtain a real income of y units of the consumption good.

Preferences

Individuals consume the economy's sole commodity and obtain satisfaction or, in the economist's jargon, utility from having done so.

Future Generations

Members of future generations in an overlapping generations model consume both when young and when old. An individual member's utility therefore depends on the combination of personal consumption when young and when old. We make the following assumptions about an individual's preferences about consumption:

1. For a given amount of consumption in one of the periods, an individual's utility increases with the consumption obtained in the other period.

2. Individuals like to consume some of this good in both periods of life. An individual prefers the consumption of positive amounts of the good in both periods of life over the consumption of any quantity of the good in only one period of life.
3. To receive another unit of consumption tomorrow, an individual is willing to give up more consumption today if the good is currently abundant than if it is scarce relative to consumption tomorrow.

With these assumptions, we are assuming that individuals are capable of ranking combinations (or bundles) of the consumption good over time in order of preference. We denote the amount of the good that is consumed in the first period of life by an individual born in period t with the notation $c_{1,t}$. Similarly, $c_{2,t+1}$ denotes the amount the same individual consumes in the second period of life. It is important to note that $c_{2,t+1}$ is consumption that actually occurs in period $t+1$, when the person born at time t is old. When the time period is not crucial to the discussion, we denote first- and second-period consumption as c_1 and c_2.

Suppose we offer an individual the following consumption choices:

- Bundle A, which consists of 3 units of the consumption good when young and 6 units of the consumption good when old. We denote this bundle as $c_1 = 3$ and $c_2 = 6$.
- Bundle B, which consists of 5 units of the consumption good when young and 4 units of the consumption good when old ($c_1 = 5, c_2 = 4$).

By assuming that an individual can rank these bundles, we are saying that this individual can state a preference for bundle A over bundle B, for bundle B over bundle A, or equal happiness with either bundle. The individual can rank any number of bundles of the consumption good that we might offer in this manner.

It will be extremely useful to portray an individual's preferences graphically. We do this with indifference curves. An **indifference curve** connects all consumption bundles that yield equal utility to the individual. In other words, if offered any two bundles on a given indifference curve, the individual would say, "I do not care which I receive; they are equally satisfying to me." In the preceding example, if the individual were indifferent to bundles A and B, then those two bundles would lie on the same indifference curve. Figure 1.2 displays a typical indifference curve.

On this indifference curve we show the two points A and B from our earlier example. We also illustrate a third point, C, representing the bundle $c_1 = 11$ and $c_2 = 2$. Because C lies on the same indifference curve as points A and B, point C yields the same level of utility as points A and B for the individual. In fact, any point along the illustrated indifference curve represents a bundle that yields the same utility level.

Note some features of the indifference curve. The first feature is that the curve gets flatter as we move from left to right. This is how indifference curves represent assumption 3. This property of indifference curves is called the assumption of **diminishing marginal rate of substitution**. To illustrate this assumption, start

Figure 1.2. An indifference curve. Individual preferences are represented by indifference curves. The figure portrays an indifference curve for a typical individual. Along any particular indifference curve, utility is constant. Here, the individual is indifferent between points A, B, and C.

at point A, where $c_1 = 3$ and $c_2 = 6$. Suppose we reduce the individual's second period consumption by 2 units. The indifference curve tells us that, to keep the individual's utility constant, we must compensate the individual by providing 2 more units of first-period consumption. This places the individual at point B on the indifference curve. Now suppose we reduce second-period consumption by another 2 units. To remain indifferent, 6 more units of first-period consumption must be given to the individual. In other words, we must compensate the individual with ever-increasing amounts of first-period consumption as we successively cut second-period consumption. This should make intuitive sense; individuals are more reluctant to give up something they do not have much of to begin with.

Take food and clothing as an example. A person who has a large amount of clothing and very little food would be willing to give up a fairly large amount of clothing for another unit of food. Conversely, this person would be willing to give up only a small amount of food to obtain another unit of clothing.

This assumption of diminishing marginal rate of substitution is captured by drawing an indifference curve so that it becomes flatter as we move downward and to the right along the curve.

We also assume that the indifference curves become infinitely steep as we approach the vertical axis and perfectly flat as we approach the horizontal axis. The curves never cross either axis. This might be justified by saying that consuming nothing in any one period would mean horrible starvation, to which consuming even a small amount is preferable. This is assumption 2.

It is also important to keep in mind that the indifference curves are dense in the (c_1, c_2) space. This means that if you pick a combination of first- and second-period

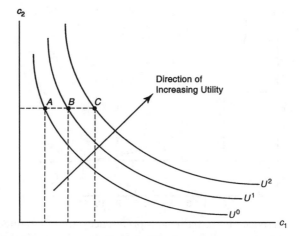

Figure 1.3. An indifference map. An indifference map consists of a collection of indifference curves. For a constant amount of consumption in one period, individuals prefer a greater amount of consumption in the other period. For this reason, individuals prefer point C to point B and point B to point A. Utility increases in the general direction of the arrow.

consumption, there is an indifference curve running through that point. However, to avoid clutter, we normally show only a few of these indifference curves. A group of indifference curves shown on one graph is often called an **indifference map**. Figure 1.3 illustrates an indifference map that obeys our assumptions.

Note that utility is increasing in the direction of the arrow. How do we know this? Compare points A, B, and C. Each of these bundles gives the individual the same amount of second-period consumption. However, moving from point A to B to C, the individual receives more and more first-period consumption. Hence, the individual will prefer point B to point A. Likewise, point C will be preferable to both points A and B. This is assumption 1.

It is often useful to draw an analogy between an indifference map and a contour map that shows elevation. On a contour map, the curves represent points of constant elevation; on an indifference map, the curves represent points of constant utility. Extending the analogy, if we think of traversing the indifference map in a northeasterly direction, we would be going uphill. In other words, utility would be increasing. In fact, an indifference map, like a contour map, is merely a handy way to illustrate a three-dimensional concept on a two-dimensional drawing. The three dimensions here are first-period consumption, second-period consumption, and utility.

One other important concept about our individual's ranking of preferences is that they are transitive. If an individual prefers bundle B to bundle A and bundle C to bundle B, then that individual must also prefer bundle C to bundle A. Graphically, this implies that indifference curves cannot cross. To do so would violate this property of transitivity and assumption 1. To see this, refer to Figure 1.4. In this figure, we have

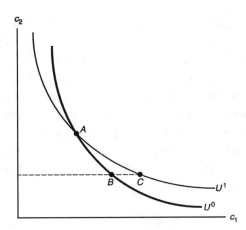

Figure 1.4. Indifference curves cannot cross. By our first assumption about preferences, the individual whose preferences are represented by these indifference curves prefers bundle C over bundle B because bundle C consists of more first-period consumption and the same amount of second-period consumption compared with bundle B. However, because the individual must be indifferent between all three bundles, A, B, and C, a contradiction arises. Our assumptions rule out the possibility of indifference curves that cross.

portrayed two indifference curves that cross at point A. We know that indifference curves represent bundles that give an individual the same level of utility. In other words, the individual whose preferences are represented by Figure 1.4 is indifferent between bundles A and B, because they lie on the same indifference curve U^0. Similarly, the individual must be indifferent between bundles A and C on indifference curve U^1. We see, then, that the individual is indifferent between all three bundles. However, if we compare bundles B and C, we also observe that they consist of the same amount of second-period consumption, but C contains more first-period consumption than B. By assumption 1, the individual must prefer C to B. But this contradicts our earlier statement about indifference between the three bundles. For this reason, indifference curves that cross violate our assumptions about preferences.

The Initial Old

The preferences of the initial old are much easier to describe than those of future generations. The initial old live and consume only in the initial period and thus simply want to maximize their consumption in that period.

The Economic Problem

The problem facing future generations of this economy is very simple. They want to acquire goods they do not have. Each has access to the nonstorable consumption good only when young but wants to consume in both periods of life. They must therefore find a way to acquire consumption in the second period of life and then decide how much they will consume in each period of life.[1]

We will examine, in turn, two solutions to this economic problem. The first, a centralized solution, proposes that an all-knowing, benevolent planner will allocate the economy's resources between consumption by the young and by the old. In the second, decentralized solution, we allow individuals to use money to trade for what they want. We will then compare the two solutions and ask which is more likely to offer individuals the highest utility. The answer will help to provide a first illustration of the economic usefulness of money.

Feasible Allocations

Imagine for a moment that we are central planners with complete knowledge of and total control over the economy. Our job is to allocate the available goods among the young and old people alive in the economy at each point in time.

As central planners, under what constraint would we operate? Put simply, it is that at any given time we cannot allocate more goods than are available in the economy. Recall that only the young people are endowed with the consumption good at time t. There are N_t of these young people at time t. We have

$$\text{(total amount of consumption good)}_t = N_t y. \tag{1.1}$$

Suppose that every member of generation t is given the same lifetime allocation $(c_{1,t}, c_{2,t+1})$ of the consumption good (our society's view of equity). In this case, total consumption by the young people in period t is

$$\text{(total young consumption)}_t = N_t c_{1,t}. \tag{1.2}$$

Furthermore, total old consumption in period t is

$$\text{(total old consumption)}_t = N_{t-1} c_{2,t}. \tag{1.3}$$

Let us make sure the notation is clear. Recall that the old people at time t are those who were born at time $t - 1$. There were N_{t-1} of these people born at time $t - 1$. Furthermore, recall that $c_{2,t}$ denotes the second period (time t) consumption by someone who was born at time $t - 1$. This implies that total consumption by the old at time t must be $N_{t-1} c_{2,t}$.

---

[1] We could make this model more complex by assuming that there are many types of goods and many periods in which to consume them. A model with many types of goods is introduced in Chapter 2. We will see, however, that this simple model is all that is needed to illustrate a demand for money.

Total consumption by young and old is the sum of the amounts in Equations 1.2 and 1.3. We are now ready to state the constraint facing us as central planners: total consumption by young and old cannot exceed the total amount of available goods (Equation 1.1) . In other words,

$$N_t c_{1,t} + N_{t-1} c_{2,t} \leq N_t y. \tag{1.4}$$

For simplicity, we assume for now that the population is constant ($N_t = N$ for all t). In this case, we rewrite Equation 1.4 as

$$N c_{1,t} + N c_{2,t} \leq N y.$$

Dividing through by N, we obtain the per capita form of the constraint facing us as central planners:

$$c_{1,t} + c_{2,t} \leq y. \tag{1.5}$$

For now, we are also concerned with a stationary allocation. A **stationary allocation** is one that gives the members of every generation the same lifetime consumption pattern. In other words, in a stationary allocation, $c_{1,t} = c_1$ and $c_{2,t} = c_2$ for every period $t = 1, 2, 3, \ldots$. However, it is important to realize that a stationary allocation does not necessarily imply that $c_1 = c_2$. With a stationary allocation, the per capita constraint becomes

$$c_1 + c_2 \leq y. \tag{1.6}$$

This represents a very simple linear equation in c_1 and c_2, which is illustrated in Figure 1.5.

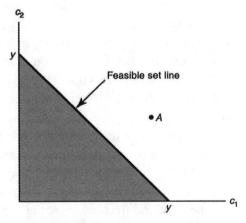

Figure 1.5. The feasible set. The feasible set, the gray triangle, represents the set of possible allocations that can be attained given the resources available in the economy. Points outside the feasible set, such as point A, are unattainable given the resources of the economy.

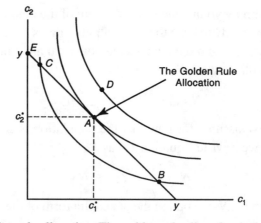

Figure 1.6. The golden rule allocation. The golden rule allocation is the stationary, feasible allocation of consumption that maximizes the welfare of future generations. It is located at a point of tangency between the feasible set line and an indifference curve (point A). This is the highest indifference curve in contact with the feasible set. As drawn, the golden rule allocation A allocates more goods to people when old than when young ($c_2^* > c_1^*$), but this is arbitrary. The tangency can just as easily have been drawn at a point where $c_2^* < c_1^*$.

The set of stationary, feasible, per capita allocations – the feasible set, for short – is bounded by the triangle in the diagram. We refer to the triangular region as the **feasible set**. The thick diagonal line on the boundary of the feasible set is called the **feasible set line**. The feasible set line represents Equation 1.6, evaluated at equality.

The Golden Rule Allocation

If we now superimpose a typical individual's indifference map on this diagram, we can identify the preferences of future generations among feasible stationary allocations. This is done in Figure 1.6.

The feasible allocation that a central planner selects depends on the objective. One reasonable and benevolent objective is the maximization of the utility of the future generations, an objective we call the **golden rule**. The golden rule in Figure 1.6 is represented by point A, which offers each individual the consumption bundle (c_1^*, c_2^*). This combination of c_1 and c_2 yields the highest feasible level of utility over an individual's entire lifetime. Note that the golden rule occurs at the unique point of tangency between the feasible set boundary and an indifference curve. Any other point that lies within the feasible set yields a lower level of utility. For example, points B and C are feasible because they lie on the boundary of the feasible set. However, they lie on an indifference curve that represents a lower level of utility than the one on which point A lies. Point D is preferable to point A, but it is unattainable. The endowments of the economy simply are not large enough to support the allocation implied by point D.

The Initial Old

It is important to consider the welfare of all participants in the economy – including the initial old – when considering the effects of any policy. Although the golden rule allocation maximizes the utility of future generations, it does not maximize the utility of the initial old. To see this, recall that the initial old's utility depends solely and directly on the amount of the good they consume in their second period of life. The goal of the initial old is to get as much consumption as possible in period 1, the only period in which they live. (You may want to imagine that the initial old also lived in period 0; however, because this period is in the past, it cannot be altered by the central planner, who assumes control of the economy in period 1.) If the central planner's goal were to maximize the welfare of the initial old, the planner would want to give as much of the consumption good as possible to the initial old. This would be accomplished among stationary feasible allocations at point E of Figure 1.6, which allocates y units of the good for consumption when old (including consumption by the initial old) and nothing for consumption when young.

This stationary allocation, which implies that people consume nothing when young, would not maximize the utility of the future generations. They prefer the more balanced combination of consumption when young and old represented by (c_1^*, c_2^*). Faced with this conflict in the interests of the initial old and the future generations, an economist cannot choose among them on purely objective grounds. Nevertheless, the reader will find that, on subjective grounds (influenced by the fact that there are an infinite number of future generations and only a single generation of initial old), we tend to pay particular attention to the golden rule in this book.

Decentralized Solutions

In the previous section, we found the feasible allocation that maximizes the utility of the future generations. However, to achieve this allocation, in each period the central planner would have to take away c_2^* from each young person and give this amount to each old person. Such a redistribution requires that the central planner have the ability to reallocate endowments costlessly between the generations. Furthermore, in order to determine c_1^* and c_2^*, this central planner also must know the exact utility function of the subjects.

These are strong assumptions about the power and wisdom of central planners. This leads us to ask if there is some way we can achieve this optimal allocation in a more decentralized manner, one in which the economy reaches the optimal allocation through mutually beneficial trades conducted by the individuals themselves. In other words, can we let a market do the work of the central planner?

Before we answer this question, we need to define some terms that are used throughout the book. First, we discuss the notion of a competitive equilibrium. A

competitive equilibrium has the following properties:

1. Each individual makes mutually beneficial trades with other individuals. Through these trades, the individual attempts to attain the highest level of utility that he can afford.
2. Individuals act as if their actions have no effect on prices (rates of exchange). There is no collusion between individuals to fix total quantities or prices.
3. Supply equals demand in all markets. In other words, markets clear.

Equilibrium Without Money

Let us consider the nature of the competitive equilibrium when there is no money in our economy of overlapping generations. Recall that agents are endowed with some of the consumption good when young. Their endowment is zero when old. Their utility can be increased if they give up some of their endowment when they are young in exchange for some of the goods when they are old. Without the presence of an all-powerful central planner, we must ask ourselves if there are trades between individuals in the economy that could achieve this result.

No such trades are possible. Refer to Figure 1.1, which outlines the pattern of endowments. A young person at period t has two types of people with whom to trade potentially in period t – other young people of the same generation or old people of the previous generation. However, trade with fellow young people would be of no benefit to the young person under consideration. They, like him, have none of the consumption good when they are old. Trade with the old would also be fruitless; the old want the good the young have, but they do not have what the young want (because they will not be alive in the next period). The source of the consumption good at time $t + 1$ is from the people who are born in that period. However, in period t, these people have not yet come into the world and so do not want what young people have to trade. This lack of possible trades is the manner in which the basic overlapping generations model captures the "absence of double coincidence of wants" [a term introduced by the nineteenth century economist W. S. Jevons (1875) to explain the need for money]. Each generation wants what the next generation has but does not have what the next generation wants.[2]

The resulting equilibrium is **autarkic** – individuals have no economic interaction with others. Unable to make mutually beneficial trades, each individual consumes his entire endowment when young and nothing when old. In this autarkic equilibrium, utility is low. Both the future generations and the initial old are worse off than they would be with almost any other feasible consumption bundle. A member of the future generations would gladly give up some of his endowment when young in order to consume something when old. A member of the initial old would also like to consume something when old.

---

[2] People cannot trade directly in this model because they are separated in time. The same absence of trade would result if they were separated in space, as in the models of Robert Townsend (1980).

Equilibrium with Money

To open up a trading opportunity that might permit an exit from this grim autarkic equilibrium, we now introduce fiat money into our simple economy. **Fiat money** is a nearly costlessly produced commodity that cannot itself be used in consumption or production and is not a promise to anything that can be used in consumption or production.

For the purposes of our model, we assume the government can produce fiat money costlessly but that it cannot be produced or counterfeited by anyone else. Fiat money can be costlessly stored (held) from one period to the next and it is costless to exchange. Pieces of paper distinctively marked by the government generally serve as fiat money.

Because individuals derive no direct utility from holding or consuming money, fiat money is valuable only if it enables individuals to trade for something they want to consume.

A **monetary equilibrium** is a competitive equilibrium in which there is a valued supply of fiat money. By valued, we mean that the fiat money can be traded for some of the consumption good. For fiat money to have value, its supply must be limited and it must be impossible (or very costly) to counterfeit. Obviously, if everyone has the ability to print money costlessly, its supply will rapidly approach infinity, driving the value of any one unit to zero.

We begin our analysis of monetary economies with an economy with a fixed stock of M perfectly divisible units of fiat money. We assume that each of the initial old begins with an equal number, M/N, of these units.[3]

The presence of fiat money opens up a trading possibility. A young person can sell some of his endowment of goods (to old persons) for fiat money, hold the money until the next period, and then trade the fiat money for goods (with the young of that period).

Finding the Demand for Fiat Money

Of course, this new trading possibility exists only if fiat money is valued – in other words, if people are willing to give up some of the consumption good in trade for fiat money and vice versa. Because fiat money is intrinsically useless, its value depends on one's view of its value in the future, when it will be exchanged for the goods that do increase an individual's utility.

If it is believed that fiat money will not be valued in the next period, then fiat money will have no value in this period. No one would be willing to give up some of the consumption good in exchange for it. That would be tantamount to trading something for nothing.

---

[3] Because the government is the creator of fiat money, we are implicitly assuming that the government has made a gift of the initial money stock to the initial old.

Extending this logic, we can predict that fiat money will have no value today if it is known with complete certainty that fiat money will be valueless at any future date T. To see this, first ask what the value of fiat money will be at time $T - 1$; in other words, ask how many goods you would be willing to give for money at $T - 1$ if it is known that it will be worthless at time T. The answer, of course, is that you would not be willing to give up any goods at time $T - 1$ for money. In other words, fiat money would have no value at time $T - 1$. Then what must its value be at time $T - 2$? By similar reasoning, we see that it will also be valueless at time $T - 2$. Working backward in this manner, we can see that fiat money will have no value today if it will be valueless at some point in the future.

Now let us consider a more interesting equilibrium where money has a positive value in all future periods. We define v_t as the value of 1 unit of fiat money (let us call the unit a dollar) in terms of goods; that is, it is the number of goods that one must give up to obtain one dollar. It is the inverse of the dollar price of the consumption good, which we write as p_t. For example, if a banana costs 20 cents, $p_t = 1/5$ dollars and the value of a dollar, v_t, is five bananas. Note also that because our economy has only one good, the price of that good p_t can be viewed as the price level in this economy.

An Individual's Budget

Let us now examine how individuals will decide how much money to acquire (assuming that fiat money will have a positive value in the future). To answer, we must first establish the constraints on the choices of the individual – why he cannot simply enjoy infinite consumption both when young and when old. As it was for the entire society, the constraints on an individual are that he cannot give up more goods than he has. We will refer to the limitations on an individual's consumption as his **budget constraints**.

In the first period life, an individual has an endowment of y goods. The individual can do two things with these goods – consume them and/or sell them for money. Notice that no one in the future generations is born with fiat money. To acquire fiat money, an individual must trade. If the number of dollars acquired by an individual (by giving up some of the consumption good) at time t is denoted by m_t, then the total number of goods sold for money is $v_t m_t$. We can therefore write the budget constraint facing the individual in the first period of life as

$$c_{1,t} + v_t m_t \le y. \tag{1.7}$$

The left-hand side of Equation 1.7 is the individual's total uses of goods (consumption and acquisition of money). The right-hand side of Equation 1.7 represents the total sources of goods (the individual's endowment).

In the second period of life, the individual receives no endowment. Hence, when old, an individual can acquire goods for consumption only by spending the money acquired in the previous period. In the second period of life (period $t + 1$), this money will purchase $v_{t+1}m_t$ units of the consumption good. The only use for these goods is second-period consumption. This means that the constraint facing the individual in the second period of life is

$$c_{2,t+1} \leq v_{t+1}m_t. \tag{1.8}$$

In a monetary equilibrium where, by definition, $v_t > 0$ for all t, we can rewrite this constraint as $m_t \geq (c_{2,t+1})/(v_{t+1})$ and substitute it into the first-period constraint (Equation 1.7) to obtain

$$c_{1,t} + \frac{v_t c_{2,t+1}}{v_{t+1}} \leq y, \tag{1.9}$$

or

$$c_{1,t} + \left[\frac{v_t}{v_{t+1}}\right] c_{2,t+1} \leq y. \tag{1.10}$$

Equation 1.10 expresses the various combinations of first- and second-period consumption that an individual can afford over a lifetime. In other words, it is the individual's **lifetime budget constraint**.

We can graph this budget constraint as shown in Figure 1.7. We can easily verify that the intercepts of the budget line are as illustrated. The budget line represents

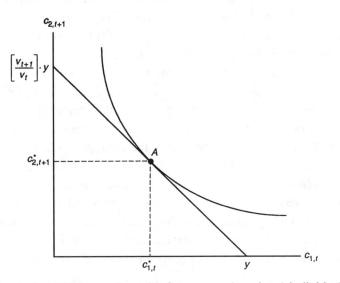

Figure 1.7. The choice of consumption with fiat money. At point A individuals maximize utility given their lifetime budget set in the monetary equilibrium. Point A is found by locating a point of tangency between an indifference curve and the individual's lifetime budget set line. The rate of return on fiat money determines the slope of the budget set line.

Equation 1.10 at equality. If nothing is consumed in the second period of life $(c_{2,t+1} = 0)$, then the constraint implies that $c_{1,t} = y$. This is the horizontal intercept of the budget line. On the other hand, if nothing is consumed in the first period of life $(c_{1,t} = 0)$, so that the entire endowment of y is used to purchase money, the constraint implies that $[(v_t)/(v_{t+1})]c_{2,t+1} = y$ or $c_{2,t+1} = [(v_{t+1})/(v_t)]y$. This represents the vertical intercept of the budget line.

Note that $(v_{t+1})/(v_t)$ can be considered as the (real) **rate of return of fiat money** because it expresses how many goods can be obtained in period $t + 1$ if one unit of the good is sold for money in period t.[4]

For a given rate of return of money, $(v_{t+1})/(v_t)$, we can find the $(c_1^*, c_{2,t+1}^*)$ combination that will be chosen by individuals who are seeking to maximize their utility. This point is shown in Figure 1.7. It is the point along the budget line that touches the highest indifference curve. This must occur at a point where the budget line is tangent to an indifference curve.

Finding Fiat Money's Rate of Return

But how can we determine the rate of return on intrinsically useless fiat money? The value that individuals place on a unit of fiat money at time t, v_t, depends on what people believe will be the value of one unit of money at $t + 1$, v_{t+1}. By similar logic, the value of a unit of fiat money at time $t + 1$ depends on people's beliefs about the value of money in period $t + 2$, v_{t+2}. And so on. We see that the value of fiat money at any point in time depends on an infinite chain of expectations about its future values. This indefiniteness is not due to any peculiarity in our model but rather to the nature of fiat money, which, because it has no intrinsic value, has a value that is determined by views about the future.

Whatever the views of the future value of money, a reasonable benchmark is the case in which these views are the same for every generation. This is plausible because in our basic model every generation faces the same problem; endowments, preferences, and population are the same for every generation. If views about the future are also the same across generations, then individuals will react in the same manner in each period, choosing $c_{1,t} = c_1$ and $c_{2,t} = c_2$ for each period t. We call such equilibria **stationary equilibria**. Notice that because individuals face different circumstances, depending on whether they are young or old, c_1 will not in general be equal to c_2 in a stationary equilibrium. People may choose to consume more when young or more when old. It turns out that the relative mix of first- and second-period consumption depends on preferences and on the rate of return on fiat money.

---

[4] Note that v_{t+1}/v_t is the gross rate of return of fiat money. The *net* rate of return of fiat money is equal to $[(v_{t+1})/(v_t)] - 1$.

We also assume that individuals in our economy form their expectations of the future rationally. In this nonrandom economy, where there are no surprises, **rational expectations** means that individuals' expectations of future variables equal the actual values of these future variables. In this special case, we say that people have **perfect foresight**. With perfect foresight, there are no errors in individuals' forecasts of the important economic variables that affect their decisions. In the context of our model, this assumption means that an individual born in period t will perfectly forecast the value of money in the next period, v_{t+1}. The individual's expectation of this value will be exactly realized. This assumption would be less credible in an economy buffeted by random shocks than in our model economy, where preferences and the environment are unchanging and therefore are perfectly predictable.[5]

To see the importance of perfect foresight, consider the alternative in a nonrandom economy – that individuals always expect a value of money greater or less than the value of money that actually occurs. Individuals with wrong beliefs about the future value of money will not choose the money balances that maximize their utility. They therefore have an incentive to figure out the value of money that will actually occur.

Let us now employ the assumptions of stationarity and perfect foresight to find an equilibrium time path of the value of money. In perfectly competitive markets, the price (or value) of an object is determined as the price at which the supply of the object equals its demand. This applies to the determination of the price (value) of money as well as the price of any good.

The demand for fiat money of each individual is the number of goods each chooses to sell for fiat money, which equals the goods of the endowment that the individual does not consume when young, $y - c_{1,t}$. The total money demand by all individuals in the economy at time t is therefore $N_t(y - c_{1,t})$.

The total supply of fiat money measured in dollars is M_t, implying that the total supply of fiat money measured in goods is the number of dollars multiplied by the value of each dollar, or $v_t M_t$. Equality of supply and demand therefore requires that

$$v_t M_t = N_t(y - c_{1,t}). \tag{1.11}$$

This in turn implies that

$$v_t = \frac{N_t(y - c_{1,t})}{M_t}, \tag{1.12}$$

---

[5] We examine individuals' formations of expectations in a random economy in Chapter 5.

which states that the value of a unit of fiat money is given by the ratio of the real demand for fiat money to the total number of dollars. Similarly, at time $t + 1$,

$$v_{t+1} = \frac{N_{t+1}(y - c_{1,t+1})}{M_{t+1}}. \tag{1.13}$$

Using Equations 1.12 and 1.13 together, we have

$$\frac{v_{t+1}}{v_t} = \frac{\frac{N_{t+1}(y - c_{1,t+1})}{M_{t+1}}}{\frac{N_t(y - c_{1,t})}{M_t}}. \tag{1.14}$$

To simplify this, we look for a stationary solution, where $c_{1,t} = c_1$ and $c_{2,t} = c_2$ for all t. Because all generations have the same endowments and preferences and anticipate the same future pattern of endowments and preferences, it seems quite reasonable to look for a stationary equilibrium. Then, after some cancelation, Equation 1.14 becomes

$$\frac{v_{t+1}}{v_t} = \frac{\frac{N_{t+1}(y - c_1)}{M_{t+1}}}{\frac{N_t(y - c_1)}{M_t}} = \frac{\frac{N_{t+1}}{M_{t+1}}}{\frac{N_t}{M_t}}. \tag{1.15}$$

Because we are assuming a constant population ($N_{t+1} = N_t$) and a constant supply of money ($M_{t+1} = M_t$), the terms in Equation 1.15 cancel out and we find that

$$\frac{v_{t+1}}{v_t} = 1 \quad \text{or} \quad v_{t+1} = v_t, \tag{1.16}$$

implying a constant value of money. Because the price of the consumption good p_t is the inverse of the value of money, it too is constant over time.

Notice that the rate of return on fiat money is also a constant (1) in the stationary equilibrium. Identical people who face the same rate of return will choose the same consumption and money balances over time, a stationary equilibrium. Therefore, the stationary equilibrium is internally consistent.

Using the information that $(v_{t+1})/(v_t) = 1$ and recalling that the budget line in a stationary monetary equilibrium is represented by $c_1 + [(v_t)/(v_{t+1})]c_2 = y$, we determine that $c_1 + c_2 = y$. Our graph of the budget line therefore becomes the one depicted in Figure 1.8.

Be aware that the stationary equilibrium may not be a unique monetary equilibrium. There also may exist more complicated nonstationary equilibria. In this text, however, we confine our attention to stationary equilibria because there is much that can be learned from these easy-to-study cases.[6]

---

[6] Nonstationary equilibria have been studied by Azariadas (1981) and by Cass and Shell (1983).

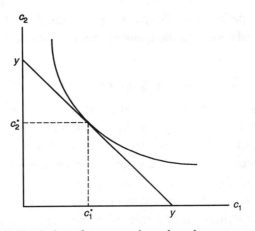

Figure 1.8. An individual's choice of consumption when the money supply and population are constant. With a constant money supply and population, the rate of return on fiat money is 1, implying the lifetime budget constraint of the diagram.

The Quantity Theory of Money

The simplest version of the **quantity theory of money** predicts that the price level is exactly proportional to the quantity of money in the economy. We would like to investigate whether this theory holds in our basic overlapping generations model.

Recall that, in Equation 1.12, we found that the value of money is determined by

$$v_t = \frac{N_t(y - c_{1,t})}{M_t}.$$

In a stationary equilibrium with a fixed population and a fixed stock of fiat money, this equation simplifies to

$$v_t = \frac{N(y - c_1)}{M}. \tag{1.17}$$

As we have seen, the value of money is constant in this simple economy. This is evident from the lack of time subscripts on the right-hand side of Equation 1.17.

Because the price level is the inverse of the value of money ($p_t = 1/v_t$), we can write an expression for the price level as

$$p_t = \frac{1}{v_t} = \frac{M}{N(y - c_1)}. \tag{1.18}$$

This illustrates that the price level in our model is, in fact, proportional to the stock of fiat money, M. As an example, suppose that the initial stock of fiat money in the economy M is doubled but remains constant from then on. (This is referred to as a *once-and-for-all increase* in the fiat money stock.) Equation 1.18 tells us that the price level in every period will also be twice as high. This demonstrates that our model is indeed consistent with the quantity theory of money.

The Neutrality of the Fiat Money Stock

The nominal (measured in dollars) size of the stock of fiat money M has no effect on the real (measured in goods) values of consumption or money demand ($y - c_1$) of this monetary equilibrium. We see from Figures 1.7 and 1.8 that an individual's choices of consumption and real money balances do not depend on the total number of dollars but do depend on the rate of return of money. The rate of return of money is unaffected by the size of the constant stock of fiat money (notice in Equation 1.15 that the money stock terms canceled each other out). This property of the monetary equilibrium is referred to as the **neutrality of money**.[7]

The Role of Fiat Money

The introduction of valued fiat money into the basic overlapping generations model improves the welfare of the individuals of the economy. Why is this the case? All we have done is to introduce intrinsically worthless pieces of paper into an economy. How can this improve welfare? We hinted at the answer earlier. Without fiat money, people are unable to trade for the goods they desire (c_2) because they do not own anything that the owners of these goods, the next generation, desire. With fiat money, however, people are able to trade for the goods they desire despite this absence of a double coincidence of wants. People sell some of the goods they have for fiat money and then use the money to buy the goods they want. In this model economy, therefore, fiat money serves as a medium of exchange. It is not consumed nor does it produce anything that can be consumed. It is valued nevertheless because it helps people acquire goods they otherwise could not have acquired.

Second-period consumption is a market good in the sense that an individual must trade to obtain more of it. In contrast, first-period consumption is a nonmarket good; individuals already possess first-period consumption without needing to trade for it. We can say then that fiat money provides a means for individuals to purchase market goods.[8]

Is This Monetary Equilibrium the Golden Rule?

We have seen that fiat money can provide for second-period consumption, improving the welfare of individuals otherwise unable to trade. We would like to make the

---

[7] Keep in mind that we are discussing here the size of a constant stock of money. We will allow the stock of money to change over time in Chapter 3.

[8] The interpretation of the model as one in which people save for old age is not especially helpful here but is taken more seriously in later chapters.

individuals in our economy not just better off but as well off as possible. It remains to ask, therefore, whether the monetary equilibrium results in the best possible allocation of goods. In particular, we would like to see whether the stationary monetary equilibrium we have just found maximizes the welfare of future generations. In other words, does the monetary equilibrium reach the golden rule?

Compare the budget line of Figure 1.8 with the feasible set line of Figure 1.6. They are identical. The choice of consumption in this monetary equilibrium will be identical to the one we found when we were looking at the stationary allocation that was dictated by a central planner who wanted to maximize the utility of the future generations. This implies that the stationary monetary equilibrium obeys the golden rule. The introduction of fiat money allows the future generations not only to increase their utility through trade but, in this case, actually allows them to reach their maximum feasible utility. This will not always be the case. The budget set and the feasible set answer different economic questions. The budget set depicts the constraint on an individual, whereas the feasible set describes the constraint on the society as a whole. We will later find cases in which these two constraints differ and the monetary equilibrium does not obey the golden rule.

The initial old are also better off in the monetary equilibrium than they were with the autarkic equilibrium. In the monetary equilibrium, each person among the initial old will receive $v_1 m_0 = (v_1 M)/(N)$ units of the consumption good when they trade their initial holdings of money for goods with the young of period 1. This means their consumption will be positive. In the autarkic equilibrium, their consumption would be zero. They are certainly better off in the monetary equilibrium.

Because we concentrate on stationary monetary equilibria in this book, it may be useful to summarize the features of such equilibria. A stationary consumption bundle of a monetary equilibrium satisfies two basic properties:

- It provides the maximum level of utility given the individual's budget set. It is found where an indifference curve lies tangent to the individual's budget set.
- It lies on the feasible set line, with the boundary of the set representing all feasible per capita allocations.

A Monetary Equilibrium with a Growing Economy

In the example we just considered, we found that a constant value of money (constant prices) led to an equilibrium that maximized the welfare of future generations. Is this always the case? Are there cases in which a changing value of money maximizes the utility of future generations? To answer these questions, we now complicate our example by allowing the economy to grow over time. We accomplish this by assuming that the population is increasing over time. This implies that the total amount of the consumption good available in the economy will grow over time.

In a monetary equilibrium, the assumption of a growing population also implies a growing demand for fiat money.

Specifically, we will assume that the population of this economy is growing so that $N_t = nN_{t-1}$ for every period t, where n is a constant greater than 1. This says that the number of people born in any period is always n times the number born in the previous period. For example, if $n = 1.05$, then the number of people born in each period is growing by 5 percent from generation to generation. Five percent is the **net rate** of population growth; $n = 1.05$ is the **gross rate**. The gross rate is the net rate plus 1. To test your understanding of population growth rates, try Example 1.1.

Example 1.1 Suppose there are 100 initial old in an economy ($N_0 = 100$) and that the number of young born in the economy is changing according to $N_t = nN_{t-1}$ in each period t, where $n = 1.2$. Trace out the number of young and old people alive in periods 1 and 2. What is the growth rate of the total population?

The Feasible Set with a Growing Population

First, as before, consider the case of an all-powerful central planner who determines allocations of the available goods in each generation. We consider the case of a monetary equilibrium later. As we determined earlier, the total amount of goods available for allocation in period t is $N_t y$. Assuming that all persons within a generation will have identical consumption, total consumption in each period t consists of aggregate consumption by the young ($N_t c_{1,t}$) and aggregate consumption by the old ($N_{t-1} c_{2,t}$). We will consider the stationary case where $c_{1,t} = c_1$ and $c_{2,t} = c_2$. The constraint describing feasible allocations is the same as before

$$N_t c_1 + N_{t-1} c_2 \leq N_t y. \tag{1.19}$$

When we considered the case of a constant population ($N_t = N_{t-1}$), the N terms canceled out in the previous expression. Although this will not occur here, we can simplify Equation 1.19 by dividing through both sides of the inequality by N_t.

$$\left[\frac{N_t}{N_t}\right] c_1 + \left[\frac{N_{t-1}}{N_t}\right] c_2 \leq \left[\frac{N_t}{N_t}\right] y. \tag{1.20}$$

If we recall that $N_t = nN_{t-1}$, we can simplify this expression to

$$c_1 + \left[\frac{N_{t-1}}{nN_{t-1}}\right] c_2 \leq y,$$

or

$$c_1 + \left[\frac{1}{n}\right] c_2 \leq y. \tag{1.21}$$

Figure 1.9. The golden rule allocation with a growing population. When the population grows at the rate n, the feasible set line has a horizontal intercept of y and a vertical intercept of ny. As before, the golden rule allocation is determined at a point of tangency between the feasible set line and an indifference curve.

We can easily graph this constraint, as is done in Figure 1.9. You should verify that the intercepts are as shown in the diagram.

Note that if the two axes are scaled the same, then because $n > 1$, the vertical intercept lies farther from the origin than does the horizontal intercept. Why is this vertical intercept greater than it was in the case of a constant population? With a growing population, there are n young people for each old person. Therefore, if we divide the entire endowment of the young equally among the old, there will be ny goods for each old person. It is easier for the planner to provide for consumption by the old because they are relatively few in number.

If we superimpose a typical individual's indifference curves on the graph with the feasible allocations line, we can find the stationary allocation that maximizes the utility of future generations. As always, this occurs at a point of tangency between the feasible allocations line and an indifference curve. This yields the point (c_1^*, c_2^*), which is illustrated in Figure 1.9. If the central planner were to give this combination of c_1 and c_2 to each member of future generations, his welfare would be maximized.

The Budget Set with a Growing Population

Now that we have determined the optimal allocation for future generations, let us turn to the case of a stationary monetary equilibrium. As before, we will eliminate the central planner and introduce fiat money into the economy. We again require that markets clear. In particular, the total demand for money must equal the aggregate supply. Earlier we found that this condition implies (see Equation 1.12) that

$$v_t = \frac{N_t(y - c_{1,t})}{M_t}. \tag{1.22}$$

Note that the numerator of Equation 1.22 is the total real demand for fiat money and the denominator is the total fiat money stock. The equation tells us that the value of fiat money in any period is determined by the relative demand for fiat money and its supply. A higher real demand for fiat money will raise its value, and a higher supply of fiat money will lower its value.

If we update the time subscripts in Equation 1.22 one period, we find that an expression for the value of fiat money in period $t + 1$ is

$$v_{t+1} = \frac{N_{t+1}(y - c_1)}{M_{t+1}}. \tag{1.23}$$

If we now look at the rate of return on money $(v_{t+1})/(v_t)$ we have

$$\frac{v_{t+1}}{v_t} = \frac{\frac{N_{t+1}(y - c_1)}{M_{t+1}}}{\frac{N_t(y - c_1)}{M_t}} = \frac{\frac{N_{t+1}}{M_{t+1}}}{\frac{N_t}{M_t}}. \tag{1.24}$$

If we assume a constant money supply, the M terms cancel. Previously, with a constant population, the N terms also canceled. However, with a growing population, we know that $N_{t+1} = nN_t$, so that Equation 1.24 becomes

$$\frac{v_{t+1}}{v_t} = \frac{N_{t+1}}{N_t} = \frac{nN_t}{N_t} = n. \tag{1.25}$$

The rate of return on money is merely equal to the rate of population growth n. Because $n > 1$, the value of money is increasing over time. This implies that the price of the consumption good is falling over time. Note that our earlier constant-population example is merely a special case of the one just considered. With a constant population, n is equal to 1. We therefore conclude that the rate of return on money is also equal to 1 in that case.

Now if we recall the individual's lifetime budget constraint (Equation 1.10), we find that

$$c_1 + \left[\frac{v_t}{v_{t+1}}\right]c_2 \le y \Rightarrow c_1 + \left[\frac{1}{n}\right]c_2 \le y. \tag{1.26}$$

This turns out to be the same constraint that faced our central planner (Equation 1.21) . Therefore, the best allocation in the budget sets of future generations must also be the golden rule, the best allocation in the feasible set for future generations. This implies that an omnipotent, omniscient, and benevolent central planner could do no better than individuals acting within their budget sets.

You should note that our analysis also applies to a shrinking economy, where $n < 1$. In such a case, the value of money falls over time, implying a rising price level. However, much of the previous analysis would still apply. The monetary equilibrium with a constant fiat money stock would still attain the golden rule.

Summary

In this chapter, we introduced the basic overlapping generations model. We found that fiat money, intrinsically worthless pieces of paper, can have value by providing a means for individuals to acquire goods that they do not possess. In addition, we saw that the introduction of a fixed stock of fiat money into an economy enables future generations to attain the maximum possible level of utility given the resources available.

So far, we have concentrated on factors that affect the demand for money. We found that, in a growing economy where the demand for money increases over time, a constant fiat money stock enables individuals to attain the golden rule. We might also be interested in knowing what effects a growing supply of fiat money has on an economy. We turn our attention to the case of an increasing fiat money stock in Chapter 3. Before doing so, in Chapter 2 we consider two alternative trading arrangements to using fiat money – the use of barter and the use of commodity money.

Exercises

1.1 Consider an economy with a constant population of $N = 100$. Individuals are endowed with $y = 20$ units of the consumption good when young and nothing when old.

  a. What is the equation for the feasible set of this economy? Portray the feasible set on a graph. With arbitrarily drawn indifference curves, illustrate the stationary combination of c_1 and c_2 that maximizes the utility of future generations.

  b. Now look at a monetary equilibrium. Write down equations that represent the constraints on first- and second-period consumption for a typical individual. Combine these constraints into a lifetime budget constraint.

  c. Suppose the initial old are endowed with a total of $M = 400$ units of fiat money. What condition represents the clearing of the money market in an arbitrary period t? Use this condition to find the real rate of return of fiat money.

For the remaining parts of this exercise, suppose preferences are such that individuals wish to hold real balances of money worth

$$\frac{y}{1 + \frac{v_t}{v_{t+1}}} \text{ goods.}$$

[In the appendix to this chapter, it is verified that this demand for fiat money comes from the utility function $(c_{1,t})^{1/2} + (c_{2,t+1})^{1/2}$.]

   d. What is the value of money in period t, v_t? Use the assumption about preferences and your answer in part c to find an exact numerical value. What is the price of the consumption good p_t?

   e. If the rate of population growth increased, what would happen to the rate of return of fiat money, the real demand for fiat money, the value of a unit of fiat money in the initial period, and the utility of the initial old? Explain your answers. *Hint:* Answer these questions in the order asked.

   f. Suppose instead that the initial old were endowed with a total of 800 units of fiat money. How do your answers to part d change? Are the initial old better off with more units of fiat money?

1.2 Consider two economies, A and B. Both economies have the same population, supply of fiat money, and endowments. In each economy, the number of young people born in each period is constant at N and the supply of fiat money is constant at M. Furthermore, each individual is endowed with y units of the consumption good when young and zero when old. The only difference between the economies is with regard to preferences. Other things being equal, individuals in economy A have preferences that lean toward first-period consumption; individual preferences in economy B lean toward second-period consumption. We will also assume stationarity. More specifically, the lifetime budget constraints and typical indifference curves for individuals in the two economies are represented in the following diagram.

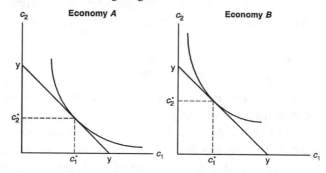

   a. Will there be a difference in the rates of return of fiat money in the two economies? If so, which economy will have the higher rate of return of fiat money? Give an intuitive interpretation of your answer.

   b. Will there be a difference in the value of money in the two economies? If so, which economy will have the higher value of money? Give an intuitive interpretation of your answer.

1.3 Consider an economy with a growing population in which each person is endowed with y_1 when young and y_2 when old. Assume that y_2 is sufficiently small that everyone wants to consume more than y_2 in the second period of life. Bear in mind that under the new assumptions the equations and graphs you find may differ from the ones found previously.

a. Apply the steps taken in Equations 1.1 to 1.6 to find the feasible set.

b. Assume that all individuals within a generation will be treated alike and graph the set of stationary per capita feasible allocations. Draw arbitrarily located, but correctly shaped, indifference curves on your graph and point out the allocation that maximizes the utility of the future generations.

c. Turning now to the monetary equilibrium, find the equation representing the equality of supply and demand in the market for money.

d. Assume a stationary solution and a constant money supply. Use the equation in (c) to find v_{t+1}/v_t.

e. Draw the budget set for an individual in this monetary equilibrium. Does this monetary equilibrium maximize the utility of future generations? Explain.

1.4 In this chapter, we modeled growth in an economy by a growing population. We could also achieve a growing economy by having an endowment that increases over time. To see this, consider the following economy. Let the number of young people born in each period be constant at N. There is a constant stock of fiat money, M. Each young person born in period t is endowed with y_t units of the consumption good when young and nothing when old. The individual endowment grows over time so that $y_t = \alpha y_{t-1}$ where $\alpha > 1$. For simplicity, assume that in each period t individuals desire to hold real money balances equal to one-half of their endowment, so that $v_t m_t = y_t/2$.

a. Write down equations that represent the constraints on first- and second-period consumption for a typical individual. Combine these constraints into a lifetime budget constraint.

b. Write down the condition that represents the clearing of the money market in an arbitrary period, t. Use this condition to find the real rate of return of fiat money in a monetary equilibrium. Explain the path over time of the value of fiat money.

Appendix: Using Calculus

With the use of simple calculus we can derive mathematical representations of the demand for fiat money from specific utility functions. In the main body of the text we have simply assumed certain demand-for-money functions to illustrate monetary equilibria. In this appendix, we demonstrate that these functions can be derived from utility functions that satisfy our basic assumptions about preferences. The appendix also serves as an illustration of a way to solve explicit examples of monetary equilibria. Following similar steps, advanced students may be able to solve examples of their own creation based on the simple model of this chapter or on the more complex economies of succeeding chapters.

If you do not know calculus, simply skip this appendix. It is not a prerequisite for any material in the succeeding chapters.

The problem facing a young person born at t is to maximize utility, which is a function, $U(c_{1,t}, c_{2,t+1})$, of consumption in each period of life. We assume that the function is continuous in each argument. The individual is constrained by his budget constraints

$$c_{1,t} + v_t m_t \leq y, \qquad (1.27)$$

$$c_{2,t+1} \leq v_{t+1} m_t. \qquad (1.28)$$

We want to solve for a young person's real demand for fiat money $v_t m_t$, which we write as q_t. We can now write the person's budget constraints (solved at equality) as

$$c_{1,t} + q_t \leq y, \qquad (1.29)$$

$$c_{2,t+1} \leq v_{t+1} m_t = \frac{v_{t+1}}{v_t}[v_t m_t] = \frac{v_{t+1}}{v_t}[q_t]. \qquad (1.30)$$

If we use the budget constraints to substitute for $c_{1,t}$ and $c_{2,t+1}$ in the utility function, we can write utility as the following function of q_t:

$$U\left(y - q_t, \frac{v_{t+1}}{v_t}[q_t]\right). \qquad (1.31)$$

If we graph utility as a function of q_t, we find a function, like that in Figure 1.10, with a single peak. (That there is a single peak is ensured by our assumption of a diminishing marginal rate of substitution.) Maximum utility is reached at q_t^*, where the slope of the utility function is zero.

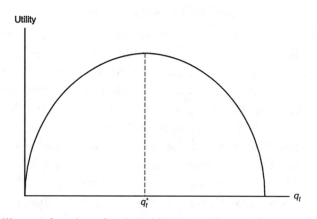

Figure 1.10. Utility as a function of an individual's real demand for fiat money. An individual's utility can be expressed as a function of real fiat money holdings. Utility is maximized by holding real fiat money balances of q_t^*.

The derivative of a function is its slope. Therefore, we find maximum utility at the value of q_t where the derivative of $U(y - q_t, [v_{t+1}/v_t]q_t)$ with respect to q_t equals zero. Let U_i denote the derivative of utility with respect to c_i. Then the utility-maximizing demand for money, q_t^*, is defined by

$$\frac{\partial U\left(y - q_t, \left[\frac{v_{t+1}}{v_t}\right][q_t]\right)}{\partial q_t}\Bigg|_{q_t = q_t^*} = 0$$

$$\Rightarrow -U_1\left(y - q_t^*, \frac{v_{t+1}}{v_t}[q_t^*]\right) + \left[\frac{v_{t+1}}{v_t}\right]U_2\left(y - q_t^*, \frac{v_{t+1}}{v_t}[q_t^*]\right) = 0 \qquad (1.32)$$

$$\Rightarrow \frac{U_1\left(y - q_t^*, \frac{v_{t+1}}{v_t}[q_t^*]\right)}{U_2\left(y - q_t^*, \frac{v_{t+1}}{v_t}[q_t^*]\right)} = \frac{v_{t+1}}{v_t}.$$

Equation 1.32 states that the utility-maximizing demand for money occurs where the marginal rate of substitution between first- and second-period consumption equals the rate of return on money.

The marginal rate of substitution U_1/U_2, which is the ratio of the marginal utilities in the two periods of life, represents -1 times the slope of the indifference curve at the combination of $c_{1,t}$ and $c_{2,t+1}$ that corresponds to a given value of q_t. Because the slope of the budget set is -1 times the rate of return of fiat money, Equation 1.32 is simply a mathematical expression of the statement that utility is maximized where an indifference curve is tangent to the budget line.

An Example

Suppose that utility is given by $(c_{1,t})^{1/2} + (c_{2,t+1})^{1/2}$. If we use the budget constraints to substitute for $c_{1,t}$ and $c_{2,t+1}$, we can find utility as the following function of q_t:

$$(y - q_t)^{1/2} + \left(\frac{v_{t+1}}{v_t}[q_t]\right)^{1/2}. \qquad (1.33)$$

Now differentiate this function with respect to q_t and set the derivative equal to zero:

$$-\frac{1}{2}(y - q_t^*)^{-1/2} + \frac{1}{2}\left[\frac{v_{t+1}}{v_t}\right]^{1/2}(q_t^*)^{-1/2} = 0. \qquad (1.34)$$

Now solve this for q_t^*. (To start, take the first term over to the right-hand side and square both sides.) You should find the money demand function that we used in Exercise 1.1.

$$q_t^* = \frac{y}{1 + \frac{v_t}{v_{t+1}}}.$$ (1.35)

Appendix Exercise

1.1 Suppose utility equals $\ln(c_{1,t}) + \beta \ln(c_{2,t+1})$ where $\ln(c)$ represents the natural logarithm of c, whose derivative equals $1/c$. The parameter β is a positive number.

a. Prove that real money balances are

$$q_t^* = \frac{\beta y}{1 + \beta}.$$

b. Derive expressions for the lifetime consumption pattern $c_{1,t}^*$ and $c_{2,t+1}^*$.

c. What effect does an increase in β have on real money balances and the lifetime consumption pattern? Give an intuitive interpretation of the parameter β.

Chapter 2

Barter and Commodity Money

THE NEED FOR exchange is derived from the problem that the goods a person produces may not be the goods that person wants to consume. In Chapter 1 we modeled this problem by assuming that people had goods when young but also wanted to consume when old. Because of the model's simplicity we use it as the foundation on which we build more complicated models.

The simple model, however, allows no alternatives to fiat money – fiat money is used in exchange because there is no other way to trade what one has for what one wants. The model has only a single type of good in every period, so trading goods for goods is ruled out. In this chapter we consider models of two historically important alternative trading possibilities – direct barter and commodity money. In a fiat monetary system, goods trade for fiat money, but goods trade directly for goods in an economy with barter or commodity money. We distinguish between the two in the following way. In a direct barter economy, the goods one owns are exchanged for the goods one desires. In a commodity money economy, the goods one owns may be traded for a good that is not consumed but is traded, in turn, for the good one desires.

In each case, we compare the performance of the model economy using fiat money with the alternative trading device. The first model illustrates how direct barter may be more costly than monetary exchange, the trading of goods for money and, subsequently, money for goods. In the second model, real commodities (not just pieces of paper) serve as money; people trade for commodities they do not want to consume in order to trade later for the goods they do want to consume. We then compare economies using commodity monies to those using fiat money to determine whether one is preferred to the other.

A Model of Barter

If we look at primitive economies, we find that they were typically barter economies. A **barter economy** is one in which the goods one owns are traded directly for the goods one wants to consume. In a barter economy, no particular good is used as a medium of exchange. For small economies with few goods, barter does not present many problems for the typical trader. However, once an economy begins to produce a greater variety of goods and specialization in production develops, barter becomes increasingly inefficient. This is because trade in barter economies requires a **double coincidence of wants**. For a successful trade in a barter economy, the person with whom you wish to trade must not only have what you want but also want what you have. The inefficiency is apparent; a great deal of time is spent merely finding someone with whom to trade.

We turn now to a model that will illustrate the advantages of using fiat money to facilitate trades when there exist many types of goods.[1] Consider a model economy like the overlapping generations model of the Chapter 1, but in which there are J different types of goods. Each person is endowed with y units of one type of good when young and with nothing when old. Equal numbers of the young are endowed with each type of good. When young, individuals wish to consume the type of good with which they are endowed. When old, they will wish to consume one of the other types of goods. However, young people do not know what type of good they will want to consume when old.

There exists a fixed stock of M units of fiat money, which is also costlessly stored. In the first period, the stock of fiat money is owned by the initial old. To allow an alternative to fiat money, we assume that goods can be stored costlessly over time.

People live on a large number of spatially separated islands. Everyone on a given island has the same endowment and tastes. Hence, all young people on a given island will be endowed with the same type of good. For example, a large number of islands will have young people endowed with good 1 when young and similarly for the remaining goods. When old, all the people on a given island will again desire to consume the same type of good, a good with which they were not endowed.

People who want to trade must travel in a group to a trading area, where a group from one island is matched at random with a group from another island seeking to trade. When the people from a pair of islands meet, they can reveal to each other the type of good they are carrying and the type of good they want. If the groups agree to trade, they do so and go home. If they do not both wish to trade, they split and each is matched again with some other island. We assume that islands searching for trading partners can choose to search among the young or the old.

---

[1] The model is taken from Freeman (1989). Kiyotaki and Wright (1989) and Maeda (1991) offer other recent, interesting models of the use of money when there are many different goods.

Exchange is costly in the following way. Each time a group from one island is matched with a group from another island, each person in the group loses α units of utility. This represents the bother of searching for a suitable trading partner.

Let us now identify patterns of trade through which people in this economy may acquire the goods they desire.

Direct Barter

The most direct way for these people to get what they want is to store some of their endowment until they are old and then trade what they have for what they want to consume. Recall that, until they are old, they do not know what they want to consume.[2] When they know what they want, they can go out and seek a trade.

Let us now determine the probability on any given attempt that they will meet someone who has what they want and wants what they have. Figure 2.1 presents every possible combination of the good with which a person is endowed and the good that person wants to consume for $J = 3$, labeling the goods a, b, and c. The asterisks in Figure 2.1 represent the possible combinations of endowments and desires. If it were possible to desire when old the good with which one is endowed, there would be $J^2 = 9$ possible combinations. Because those three combinations are ruled out, there are $J^2 - J = 6$ possible combinations. Assuming that each group is equally likely to meet any of the possible combinations at any given meeting, the probability of finding a match in which your trading partner has what you want and wants what you have is only $1/(J^2 - J)$ on any given attempt. If there are many types of goods (if J is large), $1/(J^2 - J)$ is a small number. For example, if there are 100 goods, the probability of a successful trade for a given encounter is only $1/(10,000 - 100) = 1/(9,900)$.

Endowment Good desired	a	b	c
a		*	*
b	*		*
c	*	*	

Figure 2.1. Endowments and desired goods. When old, individuals do not wish to consume the same good with which they are endowed. Only those combinations of endowments and goods desired marked by asterisks are possible.

---

[2] These people will not want to barter when young because they do not yet know what they will want to consume.

The small probability of finding someone who has what you want and wants what you have is a good illustration of Jevons' absence of a double coincidence of wants. The average (mean) number of attempts before finding a double coincidence of wants is $J^2 - J$, the inverse of the probability of success on any single try.[3] Given that each search costs α units of utility, the average of search costs under barter is therefore $\alpha(J^2 - J)$.

Monetary Exchange

An alternative pattern of trade uses fiat money as a medium of exchange. Suppose young people seek to trade their goods to the old for fiat money and then, when old, use the fiat money to buy the goods they want.

In this pattern of trade, people undertake two searches and exchanges over their lifetimes. Nevertheless, average lifetime search costs may be less with monetary exchange. In a single try, a young person's probability of finding an old person who wants what he is selling is $1/J$. The young person wants fiat money and does not care which type of old person is encountered, because all old people carry what the young person wants, fiat money. Therefore, the probability of a match on any given attempt is only $1/J$, which is greater than the probability of a match under barter, $1/(J^2 - J)$, where each side of the transaction cared about the type of good carried by the other side. With fiat money, it takes J searches on average for a successful trade.[4] Because each person undertakes two such searches, one when young and one when old, lifetime search costs will average $2\alpha J$ when people use money.

We would like to compare the search costs associated with using barter [$\alpha(J^2 - J)$] with those when money is used ($2\alpha J$). We find that the search costs when using

---

[3] Students of statistics know that the number of attempts before a success follows a geometric distribution. The mean of the geometric distribution is the probability of failure on any single trial [here, $1 - 1/(J^2 - J)$] divided by the probability of success on any one try, $1/(J^2 - J)$. Hence, in this problem, the average number of failures before a success is

$$\frac{1 - \frac{1}{J^2 - J}}{\frac{1}{J^2 - J}} = \left[1 - \frac{1}{J^2 - J}\right](J^2 - J) = (J^2 - J) - 1.$$

Because this number represents the average number of failures before a success, success will occur in the next search. Hence, the average number of searches (including the last successful one) is $J^2 - J$. In this problem the number of attempts before a success approximates a geometric distribution because the probability of finding a match will rise once almost everyone else has found a match. However, the difference is small in a large population of people seeking matches.

[4] As in the previous footnote, we compute the mean of the geometric distribution (mean number of failures before a success) as

$$\frac{\text{probability of failure}}{\text{probability of success}} = \frac{1 - \frac{1}{J}}{\frac{1}{J}} = \left(1 - \frac{1}{J}\right)J = J - 1.$$

Hence, on average, the first successful search occurs on the Jth attempt.

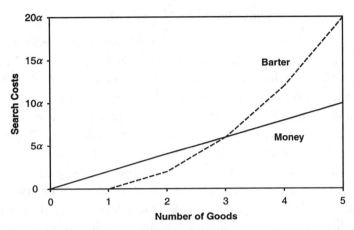

Figure 2.2. Search costs for barter and money. When there are fewer than three goods in an economy, the search costs associated with barter are less than those associated with using fiat money. With three goods present, the search costs are identical for both methods of exchange. When more than three goods exist, fiat money has a clear advantage relative to barter in terms of search costs. The search costs associated with barter rise exponentially with the number of goods.

barter are greater than those when using money if

$$\alpha(J^2 - J) > 2\alpha J \quad \Leftrightarrow \quad J > 3.$$

If there are more than three types of goods (if $J > 3$), average lifetime search costs are lower using money than barter. Although people must trade twice when using money, average search costs are lower (if $J > 3$) for monetary exchange because people do not have to search until they find a double coincidence of wants. It is easier to find someone who wants to buy the endowment good with money, and then, when old, find someone who has the desired good and will accept money. The key to money's usefulness is that everyone accepts money in trade, whereas people who barter accept only the goods they desire.

Notice that the search cost advantage of money grows with the complexity of the economy. Figure 2.2 graphs the search costs associated with barter and money for different numbers of goods. As the number of types of goods J increases, search costs increase faster for barter $[\alpha(J^2 - J)]$ than for money $(2\alpha J)$; with barter, it becomes more and more difficult to find someone who has what you want and wants what you have. If goats and spears are the only two tradable commodities in a primitive village economy, it does not take very long for a goatherd to find a hungry spear maker with whom to trade. In contrast, in a complex modern economy, it may take some time for a hungry economist to find a restaurant owner who wants a lesson in monetary economics.

What Should be Used as Money?

Nothing in our model of money and barter requires that the medium of exchange be fiat money. A commodity also can be used as a medium of exchange. Note that, as economies develop and a greater variety of goods are produced, the search costs associated with barter rise exponentially. As the number of wants and goods expands, an individual might come to accept one particular good in exchange for others even if the person did not wish to consume that good. This can occur if the individual believes that it will then be possible to trade that good for one the person wants to consume. Once most people in the economy come to accept this special good, these barter economies essentially become monetary economies – more specifically, commodity money economies. An often cited modern example of a commodity money is the cigarettes that circulated in prisoner-of-war camps in World War II.[5] Lacking any government currency, even nonsmoking prisoners of war came to accept cigarettes in trade, aware that the cigarettes could be used later to bribe guards or to trade for desired goods. The example demonstrates that money is a natural economic phenomenon not dependent on government for its existence.

A good that everyone accepts in payment for goods is called a commodity money. More precisely, a **commodity money** is a good with intrinsic value (at least some people derive utility from consuming this good directly) that is used as a medium of exchange. A commodity money stands in contrast to fiat money, which has no intrinsic value.

In humankind's long history, the use of fiat monies is a rarity. Most economies either have used some valuable commodity as their medium of exchange or have backed their paper currency with a promise that it can be exchanged for some specified amount of a valuable commodity.

Which commodities will surface as media of exchange? The usefulness of a commodity or fiat money as a medium of exchange depends on its exchange costs.

Exchange Costs

Monetary exchange involves two trades – goods for money, then money for goods – whereas barter requires only one trade. If a money is costly to exchange, its advantage in reducing search costs may be offset by the costs of the second trade.

To be more precise, assume that there is an exchange cost of λ units of utility per person each time goods are accepted. This represents the bother of verifying the quantity and quality of goods exchanged or some other cost of transferring the goods from one island to another. Let λ denote the exchange cost of goods

---

[5] This example was introduced to economists by Radford's (1945) "The Economic Organization of a P.O.W. Camp." This nontechnical article still makes interesting reading.

Table 2.1. *Search and Exchange Costs for Barter and Money*

	Search cost	Exchange cost	Total cost
Barter	$\alpha(J^2 - J)$	λ	$\alpha(J^2 - J) + \lambda$
Money	$2\alpha J$	$\lambda + \lambda_m$	$2\alpha J + \lambda + \lambda_m$

per person, and let λ_m denote the exchange cost associated with using money. An exchange cost is incurred whenever goods or money are accepted.

The lifetime exchange costs of barter equal λ because each person accepts delivery of goods once in a lifetime. The exchange costs of monetary exchange equal $\lambda_m + \lambda$ because each person accepts money when young and goods when old. The average costs associated with money and barter are summarized in Table 2.1.

When the exchange cost of money λ_m is zero, barter and monetary exchange have the same lifetime exchange costs. Monetary exchange is then superior to barter because of money's lower search costs (if $J > 3$). If, however, money has an exchange cost, its advantage over barter in search costs may be offset by the extra cost of exchange incurred by making two trades instead of one.

It follows that people will want to use something easy to exchange as money. What makes something easy to exchange? It must be easy to recognize and measure. Fiat money tends to possess these properties. Hence, exchange costs for fiat money λ_m are approximately zero.

However, exchange costs with a commodity money system are typically not equal to zero. In fact, exchange costs with commodity money systems may be quite high. For example, early examples of commodity money took the form of chunks of precious metals called *bullion*.[6] Individuals typically accepted these chunks of metal in payment for goods or services. A merchant who accepted bullion in exchange for goods had to assay the quality of the metal. Furthermore, accurate scales were needed to determine the weight of the metal. This process of verifying the quality of the money was costly. In the context of our model, λ_m, the exchange costs associated with using bullion as money were quite high relative to those that would be associated with using fiat money. This, as stated before, at least partially offset the lower search costs associated with the use of metals as money.

In an attempt to lower the exchange costs associated with commodity money, governments soon entered the picture by assaying metals and stamping them with their own insignia. This led to the minting of the metals into regular shapes (coins) stamped with their value.[7] The value that was stamped on the face of the coin was appropriately called the *face value* of the coin.

---

[6] For example, the Babylonians began using silver bullion as money around 2000 B.C.

[7] Herodotus attributes the origin of coinage to the kings of Lydia in the eighth century B.C., although evidence exists that suggests coinage may have existed in India prior to this time.

A Model of Commodity Money

We have seen that exchange costs may be higher in a commodity money system than in a fiat money system. Are there other advantages or disadvantages of using commodity money versus fiat money?

To answer this question, we introduce into the basic overlapping generations model of Chapter 1 a commodity money, which we will call *gold*.[8] We assume that the consumption good is not storable, but gold can be stored costlessly without physically changing. In other words, there is no depreciation or appreciation associated with gold storage in that 1 unit of gold stored at time t is still 1 unit of gold at time $t + 1$. At any point in time, gold can be consumed. When consumed, each unit of gold gives an individual as much utility as the consumption of $\tilde{v}$ more units of the consumption good. We say that the **intrinsic value** of gold is $\tilde{v}$ in this economy, because an individual is indifferent between consuming 1 unit of gold or $\tilde{v}$ units of the consumption good. In contrast, the fiat money of Chapter 1 had an intrinsic value of zero.

Each member of the initial old is endowed with m_0^g units of gold, so that the total initial gold stock is $M^g = Nm_0^g$. There is no source of gold other than this initial stock. Furthermore, no fiat money is present in the economy at any point in time.

As before, each member of the future generations is endowed with y units of the (nongold) consumption good when young and with nothing when old. These people are not endowed with any gold. We assume a constant population in which N individuals are born in each period. We define m_t^g to be the number of units of gold purchased by an individual at time t and v_t^g as the value of a unit of gold in units of the consumption good.

A Commodity Money Equilibrium

Gold has two possible uses in this economy – consumption and trade. It follows that there are two possible equilibria – one in which gold is traded and not consumed and another in which gold is consumed. Let us look first at an equilibrium in which gold is traded but never consumed.

In each period, the young individuals consume a portion of their endowment and use the remainder to purchase gold. In this way, gold will be used as money to trade for second-period consumption. Given our notation, the number of units of the consumption good that will be used to purchase gold will be $v_t^g m_t^g$. This implies that the constraint facing each individual in the first period of life is

$$c_{1,t} + v_t^g m_t^g \leq y. \tag{2.1}$$

---

[8] The model is taken from Sargent and Wallace (1983). Commodity money could also be studied in the multiple good model of this chapter. We return to the model of Chapter 1, however, because it is simpler.

When old, each individual will trade holdings of gold for some of the consumption good. Therefore, the constraint facing each individual in the second period of life is

$$c_{2,t+1} \leq v_{t+1}^g m_t^g. \tag{2.2}$$

Substituting Equation 2.2 into Equation 2.1, we find the combined budget constraint for an individual born at time t:

$$c_{1,t} + \left[\frac{v_t^g}{v_{t+1}^g} \right] c_{2,t+1} \leq y. \tag{2.3}$$

We know that the market for gold must clear in each period. Recall that the supply of gold in each period is fixed at M^g. From Equation 2.1, we can see that each young individual's demand for gold in period t is

$$m_t^g = \frac{y - c_{1,t}}{v_t^g}, \tag{2.4}$$

so that the total demand for gold is $[N(y - c_{1,t})]/v_t^g$. Equating the total supply of gold to the total demand for gold, we see that

$$M^g = \frac{N(y - c_{1,t})}{v_t^g} \quad \Rightarrow \quad v_t^g = \frac{N(y - c_{1,t})}{M^g}. \tag{2.5}$$

As usual, we restrict our attention to the stationary case where $c_{1,t} = c_1$ and $c_{2,t+1} = c_2$ for all t. In this case, we find that the value of gold in each period is

$$v_t^g = \frac{N(y - c_1)}{M^g}. \tag{2.6}$$

Note that in this stationary equilibrium the value of gold is constant over time. This means that the rate of return of gold is 1 in every period ($v_{t+1}^g/v_t^g = 1$ for all t).

We have assumed in this equilibrium that gold is not consumed; the entire initial stock of gold is used as a medium of exchange. For this to represent the behavior of rational people, there must be no incentive for any individual to consume gold. What condition ensures that this gold consumption does not take place? If individuals can obtain greater utility by trading gold for the consumption good, then they will not choose to consume their gold. In this case, the trading value of a unit of gold exceeds $\tilde{v}$, which is its intrinsic value. In other words, we must have that

$$v_t^g = \frac{N(y - c_1)}{M^g} > \tilde{v}. \tag{2.7}$$

In this case, trading 1 unit of the gold will give an individual v_t^g units of the consumption good, which will generate a certain amount of utility. If people consumed the gold, they would obtain the amount of utility associated with consuming $\tilde{v}$ units of the consumption good. Clearly, then, if $v_t^g > \tilde{v}$, the amount of utility obtained by trading gold for the consumption good is higher than that obtained by consuming the gold. This, in turn, implies that individuals will choose to trade their gold, utilizing it as a medium of exchange.

The Consumption of Gold

The other possibility is worth noting. Suppose that the trading value of gold is less than $\tilde{v}$. This would occur if

$$v_t^g = \frac{N(y - c_1)}{M^g} < \tilde{v}. \tag{2.8}$$

In this case, the initial old will choose to consume gold rather than trade it. If they sell their gold for some of the consumption good, their utility will be less than if they consume gold for its intrinsic value.

Will they consume all the gold? As they consume gold, the total stock of gold in the economy begins to fall. From Equation 2.6, we see that the price of gold will begin to rise. As long as the price of gold is less than $\tilde{v}$, this process will continue and the price of gold will increase. Eventually, the price of gold must rise to its intrinsic value. At this point, the consumption of gold will stop and we will be in the situation described in the first scenario. The remaining gold will then be used as a medium of exchange from that point forward in time. If we denote the amount of gold used for monetary purposes (not consumed) as M^{g^*}, this variable is determined by

$$v_t^g = \frac{N(y - c_1)}{M^{g^*}} = \tilde{v} \quad \Rightarrow \quad M^{g^*} = \frac{N(y - c_1)}{\tilde{v}}. \tag{2.9}$$

The amount of gold in monetary use will be equal to the initial stock of gold minus the amount demanded for personal use (the amount consumed). More precisely, the real value (in units of the consumption good) of gold used as a medium of exchange, $\tilde{v}M^{g^*}$, will be a quantity that will just equal $N(y - c_1)$. The amount of gold consumed by the initial old will be $M^g - M^{g^*}$.

Because commodity money may be consumed, the quantity theory of money may not hold in quite the same way for commodity money as it did for fiat money. Recall that the quantity theory predicts that if two economies are identical except that the fiat money stock in one is twice as large as in the other, the price level will be twice as high (the value of money will be half as high) in the economy with the larger money stock. Prices adjust to the stock of money. Now consider two economies that are identical except that the gold stock in one is twice as large as in the other. If gold is never consumed but serves solely as a commodity money, prices will simply be twice as high in the economy with the larger stock of gold, just as it was in the case of fiat money. But if gold is consumed at the margin in both countries, with a trading value just equal to its intrinsic value, then the economy with a larger gold stock will consume gold until gold's trading value equals gold's intrinsic value. After the consumption of gold, the amount of gold used as money will be the same in the two economies. The intrinsic value of gold sets a minimum value for the trading value of gold, preventing higher nominal prices. If we consider the *initial* stock of gold in the two economies, the quantity theory does not hold because the price level in the economy with the larger initial stock of gold is not twice as high as the economy with the smaller gold stock. However, if we consider the stocks of gold actually *used as money* in the two economies, then the quantity theory does hold. In this case, the quantity theory holds because the stock of gold used as money adjusts to the price level and not because the price level adjusts to the stock of gold.

We see then that the price of gold will equal or exceed its intrinsic value if it is used as a medium of exchange – in other words, as a commodity money. This is a general feature of monetary systems, including commodity money systems; the trading value of a money may exceed its intrinsic value. This is not puzzling in light of the conclusions of Chapter 1. In the monetary equilibrium of that chapter, we saw that fiat money is valued even though it has an intrinsic value of zero. Like gold, fiat money, when used as a medium of exchange, may also have a price in excess of its intrinsic value. Money – whether it be fiat money or commodity money – may have value in excess of its intrinsic value because it provides a means of trading for goods desired (c_2) but otherwise unattainable.

Because the use of a commodity as money may raise its value, what serves as a medium of exchange in an economy has implications for the distribution of wealth. For example, if a commodity money system with $v_t^g > \tilde{v}$ were replaced with a fiat money system, the price of gold would fall to its intrinsic value of $\tilde{v}$. For this reason, owners of gold or other possible commodity monies are very interested in the medium of exchange used in their economy.

The Inefficiency of Commodity Money

Economists have often stated that commodity monies are inefficient.[9] What is meant by this statement? From the development of this chapter, we can gain useful insights into this claim.

---

[9] See, for example, Friedman (1960).

It is useful to compare the economy developed in this chapter with the fiat money economy of Chapter 1. In that chapter, we considered a monetary equilibrium where there was a constant population and a constant money supply. Hence, that environment was similar to the environment of the commodity money economy of this chapter.

Recall the combined budget constraint governing individual choices in our commodity money economy (Equation 2.3, with stationarity imposed):

$$c_1 + \left[\frac{v_t^g}{v_{t+1}^g} \right] c_2 \le y. \tag{2.10}$$

We found that, in this economy, the price of gold is constant over time, which implies a rate of return on gold of 1 ($v_{t+1}^g / v_t^g = 1$). Substituting this result, we find

$$c_1 + c_2 \le y. \tag{2.11}$$

This represents the budget set available to future generations. Reference to Figure 1.8 shows that the budget set in the commodity money economy is identical to that in the comparable fiat money economy. The choices open to individuals of future generations are the same. Given identical preferences between the two economies, we expect individuals to choose the same (c_1^*, c_2^*) combination. With regard to future generations, the commodity money regime provides no advantages (or disadvantages) relative to the fiat money regime. All consumption possibilities that are attainable in the commodity money economy are also available in the fiat money economy. From the viewpoint of future generations, the inefficiency of commodity money systems is not apparent.

It is the initial old who are better off if our commodity money economy switches to the use of fiat money as a medium of exchange. The initial old could use their holdings of fiat money to purchase some of the consumption good. The amount of the consumption good they could purchase with fiat money would be identical to the amount that could be purchased in the commodity money regime. In addition, they could consume all their holdings of gold, which gives them even more utility. Clearly, then, the consumption and utility of the initial old are higher in the fiat money regime than in the commodity money regime. It is important to keep in mind that this is accomplished without diminishing the welfare of future generations.

The intuition is that with a commodity money system, resources that have intrinsic value are tied up in order to provide a medium of exchange. The fiat money system utilizes intrinsically worthless resources to provide the same services. In the case of a gold standard, precious metal that could be used to make jewelry or aeronautical equipment is used as money and is unavailable for these purposes. In this way, commodity money systems are inefficient. A fiat money system allows the same trading patterns while freeing up a commodity that is useful for nonmonetary purposes.

Summary

The major goal of this chapter was to compare the efficiency of trade using barter or commodity money with that of trade using fiat money. This analysis is interesting because of the historical importance of barter and commodity money.

We found that search costs of barter exceed those of money when many types of goods are present in the economy. Intuitively, money facilitates trade by solving the double coincidence of wants problem that is inherent in barter. The search cost advantage of using money expands as the number of types of goods becomes larger.

It is important to remember that the search cost advantage of money over barter holds whether the money we are considering is fiat money or commodity money. However, search costs are only part of the story. The use of money (trading goods for money and money for goods) requires twice as many exchanges as barter (trading goods for goods). Therefore, the exchange costs associated with using money may be higher than those associated with barter, partially offsetting money's lower search costs. To minimize exchange costs, a medium of exchange should be easily recognized and measured.

In the last part of this chapter, we compared welfare under two different monetary standards – a commodity money system and a fiat money system – assuming identical costs of search and exchange. We found that a commodity money system needlessly reserves as a medium of exchange goods that would give people utility if consumed. The switch to a fiat money system improves welfare by freeing those goods for individual consumption.

Exercises

2.1 Consider a fiat money/barter system like that portrayed in this chapter. Suppose that the number of goods J is 100. Each search for a trading partner costs an individual 2 units of utility.

    a. What is the probability that a given random encounter between individuals of separate islands will result in a successful barter?

    b. What are the average lifetime search costs for an individual who relies strictly on barter?

    c. What are the average lifetime search costs for an individual who uses fiat money to make exchanges?

Now let us consider exchange costs. Suppose that it costs 4 units of utility to verify the quality of goods accepted in exchange and 1 unit of utility to verify that money accepted in exchange is not counterfeit.

d. What are the total exchange costs of someone utilizing barter?

e. What are the total exchange costs of someone utilizing money?

2.2 Consider a commodity money model economy like the one described in this chapter but with the following features. There are 100 identical people in every generation. Each individual is endowed with 10 units of the consumption good when young and nothing when old. To keep things simple, let us assume that each young person wishes to acquire money balances worth half of his endowment, regardless of the rate of return. The initial old own a total of 100 units of gold. Assume that individuals are indifferent between consuming 1 unit of gold and consuming 2 units of the consumption good.

a. Suppose the initial old choose to sell their gold for consumption goods rather than consume the gold. Write an equation that represents the equality of supply and demand for gold. Use it to find the number of units of gold purchased by each individual, m_t^g, and the price of gold, v_t^g.

b. At this price of gold, will the initial old actually choose to consume any of their gold?

c. Would the initial old choose to consume any of their gold if the total initial stock of gold were 800? In this case, what would be the price of gold and the stock of gold after the initial old consume some of their gold? Compare your answer in this part with your answer in part a. Does the quantity theory of money hold?

d. Suppose it is learned that a gold discovery will increase the stock of gold from 100 to 200 units in period t^*. Assume the government uses the newly discovered gold to buy bread that will not be given back to its citizens. Find the price of gold at $t^* - 1$ and at t^*. Find also the rate of return of gold acquired at $t^* - 1$.

2.3 (**advanced**) Suppose the consumption of gold offers people a marginal utility that diminishes as that person consumes more gold. Assume also that gold can be mined in unlimited amounts at the constant marginal cost, χ, units of the nongold consumption good.

a. Can the trading value of gold exceed χ in equilibrium? Explain. What is the effect on gold consumption and mining of an increased use of gold as money?

b. Suppose instead that the marginal mining cost increases with the amount mined. What is now the effect on gold consumption and mining of an increased use of gold as money?

2.4 (**advanced**) Consider again the model economy described in Exercise 2.2, but suppose there is a second storable good, silver. Silver is as easy to exchange and store as gold. The initial old own a total of 50 units of silver. There can be no additions to the stock of silver. Individuals are indifferent between consuming 1 unit of silver and 1 unit of the consumption good. Let v_t^s denote the trading value of a unit of silver.

a. Find the market clearing condition if both silver and gold are used as money. Can there be an equilibrium in which both silver and gold are used only as money (are not consumed) and $v_t^s = 1.5? \ldots v_t^s = 2$? In each case use the market-clearing condition to find the corresponding equilibrium trading value of gold. For what range of values of v_t^s is there an equilibrium in which both silver and gold are used only as money (are not consumed)?

b. What would happen to the value of silver if the government passed a law banning the use of gold as money?

c. If one member of the initial old owned the entire stock of silver, would that person prefer that gold alone, silver alone, or both gold and silver be used as money? Explain.

d. If each member of the initial old owned 1/2 unit of silver and 2 units of gold, would the initial old prefer that gold alone, silver alone, or both gold and silver be used as money? Explain.

Chapter 3

Inflation

IN CHAPTER 1, where the basic overlapping generations model was presented, we concentrated on factors that affected the demand for fiat money. For example, we considered a case in which the population was growing at a constant rate and analyzed the effects of such a situation. In this chapter, we focus on the supply of fiat money.

What are the consequences of an increasing stock of fiat money? What effect does such a policy have on the welfare of individuals in the economy? Can a government raise revenue merely by printing money at a faster rate? These are some of the questions we address in this chapter.

We have seen that we can find a role for money with either the simple, single-good model of Chapter 1 or the more complex multiple-good model of Chapter 2. It can be verified that both models have essentially the same implications for the subject of this chapter, inflation, and for the subjects of later chapters.[1] If two models have the same implications for a topic of interest, then it is generally preferable to work with the simpler model. For this reason, we use the single-good model of Chapter 1 as the framework for this and following chapters.

A Growing Supply of Fiat Money

Let us now study the effects of an expansion of the supply of fiat money. First we consider money supply expansion in the simplest overlapping generations model with a constant population and a nonstorable consumption good. Contrary to Chapter 2, no commodity money is present in the economy.

Let the money supply growth be such that

$$M_t = zM_{t-1} \tag{3.1}$$

---

[1] See Freeman (1989).

for each period t where z, the gross rate of money supply expansion, is greater than 1. This implies that

$$M_t - M_{t-1} = M_t - \frac{M_t}{z} = \left(1 - \frac{1}{z}\right)M_t \tag{3.2}$$

units of new fiat money are printed each period. This new money is introduced into the economy by means of lump-sum subsidies (transfers) to each old person in every period t worth a_t units of the consumption good; that is,

$$N_{t-1}a_t = \left(1 - \frac{1}{z}\right)v_t M_t$$

or

$$a_t = \frac{\left(1 - \frac{1}{z}\right)v_t M_t}{N_{t-1}}. \tag{3.3}$$

(To find a_t we multiplied the newly created money by the value of money to find its real value and then divided it by the number of old people among whom it will be distributed to find its value per old person.)

Equation 3.3 is our first example of the **government budget constraint**, an equilibrium condition that will prove essential in the analysis of government policy. The government budget constraint simply says that the government (like an individual) cannot spend more than it takes in. In this case, the expenses of government are its gifts to old people and its revenue is the new fiat money it has printed.

It is important that these subsidies be made in a lump-sum fashion so that we can study the effect of money supply expansion in isolation. A subsidy (or tax) is **lump sum** if the amount given to (or taken from) any individual does not depend on any decision made by that particular individual. The subsidy returns the new money to the public. In this way, we ensure that the expansion of the money stock does not represent a transfer of resources from the public to the government, a case we will consider later in this chapter.

The budget constraints of the individual are now

$$c_{1,t} + v_t m_t \leq y, \tag{3.4}$$

and

$$c_{2,t+1} \leq v_{t+1}m_t + a_{t+1}. \tag{3.5}$$

The resulting budget line is now

$$c_{1,t} + \left[\frac{v_t}{v_{t+1}}\right]c_{2,t+1} \leq y + \left[\frac{v_t}{v_{t+1}}\right]a_{t+1}. \tag{3.6}$$

The equality of supply and demand in the market for money is

$$v_t M_t = N_t(y - c_{1,t}). \tag{3.7}$$

Using stationarity,[2] we can solve this for v_t to get

$$v_t = \frac{N_t(y - c_1)}{M_t}. \tag{3.8}$$

Then the rate of return of fiat money is given by

$$\frac{v_{t+1}}{v_t} = \frac{\frac{N_{t+1}(y - c_1)}{M_{t+1}}}{\frac{N_t(y - c_1)}{M_t}} = \frac{M_t}{M_{t+1}} = \frac{M_t}{z M_t} = \frac{1}{z}. \tag{3.9}$$

Because the population is constant, the N terms in Equation 3.9 cancel out.

Equation 3.9 tells us that when $z > 1$ the value of money declines over time. Furthermore, the larger the value of z, the lower the rate of return on money. In other words, expansion of the money supply creates inflation as more dollars (for example) bid for the same number of goods. The resulting inflation is easily seen by recalling that $p_t = 1/v_t$ and analyzing how the price level evolves over time. This is done by looking at the ratio of next period's price level to this period's price level (this ratio is the **gross inflation rate**) and using the results of Equation 3.9:

$$\frac{p_{t+1}}{p_t} = \frac{\frac{1}{v_{t+1}}}{\frac{1}{v_t}} = \frac{v_t}{v_{t+1}} = z, \tag{3.10}$$

$$\Rightarrow p_{t+1} = z p_t. \tag{3.11}$$

When $z > 1$, Equation 3.11 predicts that the price level increases over time at the same rate as the fiat money stock. For example, if $z = 1.05$, the price level grows at the same 5 percent net rate at which the fiat money stock is growing. In this way, the price level remains proportional to the size of the fiat money stock, as predicted by the quantity theory of money.

The Budget Set with Monetary Growth

We found in Equation 3.9 that the rate of return of fiat money (v_{t+1}/v_t) in a stationary equilibrium is $1/z$. Substituting this into the lifetime budget set (Equation 3.6), we find

$$c_1 + z c_2 \leq y + z a. \tag{3.12}$$

---

[2] In Equation 3.33 of the appendix, it is verified that a stationary equilibrium is consistent with a constant subsidy, a.

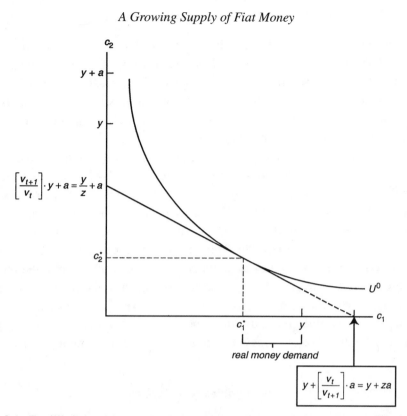

Figure 3.1. Equilibrium with growth of the money supply. The lifetime budget line is drawn for the case in which the fiat money stock is growing at the rate z and the newly printed money is introduced in the form of a lump-sum transfer to the old. Individuals will choose the consumption bundle where the budget line is tangent to the indifference curve labeled U^0. The individual's real money demand is marked in the diagram.

In Figure 3.1, the budget set with inflation is graphed with a typical indifference curve that indicates the monetary equilibrium (c_1^*, c_2^*). Note that inflation $(z > 1)$ has altered our graph of the budget set in two ways. First, the budget line is flatter. This means that to get a unit of goods when old, an individual must give up more units when young than when there was no inflation. This reflects the lower rate of return offered by money when new money is being created. Second, the budget set intercepts the horizontal axis at $y + za$ instead of y, because an individual's income now includes both the endowment and the subsidy.[3]

Common sense tells us that in order to make gifts (subsidies) to individuals, a government that owns no goods can raise revenue for the gifts only by taking goods from private citizens (i.e., through taxation). Money creation may seem to be a way

---

[3] Note that the budget line from $c_1 = y$ to $c_1 = y + za$ (the intercept) is dashed. For people to consume more than y when young ($c_1 > y$), they must hold no money balances and also borrow from others, promising to repay the loan from the subsidy they will receive when old. Although any single person has this choice, no one is willing to lend when everyone is alike, so this option is never actually used. Therefore, although we mention this option here for completeness, we hereafter ignore it when presenting the budget equations and lines.

to raise revenue without taxation. Is this really so? The government can create fiat money out of thin air (or cheap paper), but the real value of the government subsidy must come from somewhere. The feasible set is not magically expanded when the government decides to print additional intrinsically useless pieces of paper. Because the total number of goods in the economy is fixed at the total endowment $(N_t y)$, the gifts to old people can come only from losses sustained by them or by others.

Who loses goods when the government expands the fiat money stock? When the government expands the stock of fiat money, the stock of money currently held by private citizens falls in value. The new money competes with the old money to purchase the goods of the young and drives down the value of all money. The loss sustained by the owners of the old money works as a tax on their money holdings.

Note that the value lost to the "tax" effected by the expansion of the money stock is proportional to the amount of money held (the more money held, the more one loses through inflation). In other words, the expansion of the money stock lowers the rate of return on fiat money. To reduce one's exposure to this tax on money balances, one can reduce one's use of money. In this way, inflation induces people to conserve on their use of money; the incentive for holding money is reduced.

The Inefficiency of Inflation

Let us return to the question of the optimality of expanding the money stock. To judge whether the equilibrium with inflation is optimal, we must compare it with the other possible alternatives. As in Chapter 1, this translates into comparing the budget set, which shows the options available to individuals in a monetary equilibrium, with the feasible set, which details the consumption allocations that are feasible for the economy. If the budget set coincides with the feasible set, as it did in Chapter 1, then the golden rule allocation is attainable under the monetary equilibrium.

The government's expansion of the fiat money stock should have no effect on what is feasible in this economy. Merely printing more pieces of paper does not alter the stock of goods available for distribution between the consumption of the young and old. The feasible set is therefore exactly the one we found in Equations 1.4 to 1.6 of Chapter 1:

$$N_t c_{1,t} + N_{t-1} c_{2,t} \leq N_t y,$$

which, for a constant population and a stationary allocation, simplifies to

$$N c_1 + N c_2 \leq N y,$$

or

$$c_1 + c_2 \leq y.$$

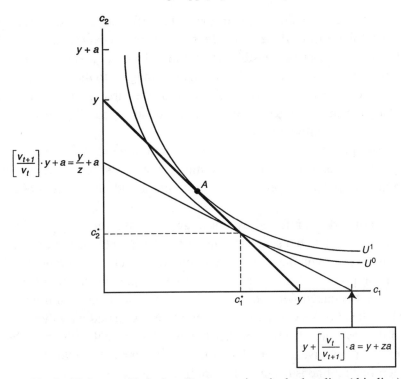

Figure 3.2. The inefficiency of inflation. By comparing the budget line (thin line) and the feasible set line (thick line), we discover that the monetary equilibrium is inefficient when there is inflation. Point A yields a higher level of utility for both future generations and the initial old than the monetary equilibrium (c_1^*, c_2^*). Point A is feasible but unattainable in the inflationary equilibrium; it lies outside the budget set. Point A could be attained in a monetary equilibrium by keeping the fiat money stock constant.

To compare the monetary equilibrium with its feasible alternative allocations, in Figure 3.2 we superimpose the feasible set line on the monetary equilibrium graphed in Figure 3.1.[4] In this diagram, the feasible set line is represented by the thick line and the budget line is represented by the thin line. The feasible set line starts at y on the vertical axis and intersects the budget line at (c_1^*, c_2^*) as shown in Figure 3.2. If (c_1^*, c_2^*) lay in the interior of the feasible set, it would imply that someone was throwing goods away, an action not consistent with utility maximization. If it lay outside the feasible set, people would be consuming more goods than exist, which is impossible. Therefore, the equilibrium consumption bundle (c_1^*, c_2^*) must lie on the edge of the feasible set; that is, the feasible set line passes through (c_1^*, c_2^*).[5]

In examining Figure 3.2, recall that, because (c_1^*, c_2^*) represents the maximum utility possible in the budget set, the consumption bundle (c_1^*, c_2^*) is located where some indifference curve (U^0 in Figure 3.2) is tangent to the budget line at (c_1^*, c_2^*).

[4] This graph and its proof of the inefficiency of inflation are taken from Wallace (1980).
[5] See the appendix of this chapter for a formal proof of this statement.

Note also that the absolute value of the slope of the budget line is $1/z$ and that the absolute value of the slope of the feasible set is 1. Given that $(1/z) < 1$, the budget line is flatter than the feasible set. Because the feasible set line goes through (c_1^*, c_2^*) but at a different slope, it cannot also be tangent to the indifference curve U^0 but must intersect it. This tells us that in the feasible set there are points of higher utility for the future generations than the monetary equilibrium (c_1^*, c_2^*). One such point is A on indifference curve U^1.

Point A is preferred by the future generations over (c_1^*, c_2^*) because it lies on a higher indifference curve. Furthermore, because second-period consumption is higher at point A than at (c_1^*, c_2^*), the initial old also prefer point A over (c_1^*, c_2^*).

Because point A is preferred by future generations over (c_1^*, c_2^*), why did the future generations not choose it? The answer is that point A is not in their budget set. The rate of return on fiat money is too low for the future generations to be able to consume at point A. If individuals were to consume the amount of first-period consumption associated with point A, their money holdings would be too small to afford the level of second-period consumption associated with that point. This is due to the low rate of return on fiat money. We know that the best the future generations can do, given this policy of monetary expansion, is to choose (c_1^*, c_2^*) where their budget line is tangent to an indifference curve.

Recall from Chapter 1 (Figure 1.8) that, in the absence of money creation, the budget set was identical to the feasible set. To see this, realize that if there is no expansion of the money stock, $z = 1$ and $a = 0$. For these values of z and a the budget set is identical to the feasible set, as drawn in Figure 3.2. Therefore, when the fiat money stock is fixed, individuals are free to choose A, the best feasible point for future generations. It follows that future generations prefer the monetary equilibrium without an expanding money supply.

Figure 3.2 can help us uncover the welfare cost of expanding the money stock. The inflation caused by money creation does not destroy any goods; individuals still consume at the boundary of the feasible set. However, they consume a different combination of c_1 and c_2 with inflation than they would consume without it. They choose to consume less of the good c_2, whose purchase requires the use of fiat money (and more of the other good, c_1) because of the lower rate of return on fiat money. In other words, the tax on money balances induces future generations to reduce their demand for money $(y - c_1)$ to a level below the optimum. Moreover, the drop in the demand for fiat money reduces the value of the initial money balances owned by the initial old, thus also reducing their utility.

We should be careful about interpreting this model. A literal interpretation may lead us to conclude that the cost of inflation is that people are induced to consume too much when young and not enough when old.

What, then, is the cost of inflation? People are induced by fiat money's low rate of return to consume needlessly less of goods that require the use of money. In our model, c_2 represents a market good, whose acquisition requires the use of fiat money and c_1 is a nonmarket good that can be acquired without the use of money (leisure is a good real-world example).

To make this clearer, one can interpret the model as follows. Let the endowment in the first period of life be an endowment of time, which can be spent in any combination of leisure or labor. Leisure is that part of the time endowment consumed immediately, c_1 in the notation we have been using. Each unit of labor produces 1 unit of goods, which can be sold to the old for fiat money. The worker then spends the money in the second period of life. In this interpretation, the key economic decision of the model is not one of an individual saving for retirement but one of an individual who works during the week to acquire money to spend on the weekend.

What is the cost of inflation under this interpretation of the model? Inflation discourages the consumption of the market good c_2 in favor of the consumption of leisure c_1, which an individual can acquire without the use of money. By discouraging the use of money, inflation also discourages the supply of labor to be exchanged for money. In this way inflation may affect aggregate output in addition to the timing of consumption.

More generally, we might say that inflation causes people to economize needlessly on the benefits offered by the use of money to conduct transactions. Therefore, inflation will reduce welfare in any model or real economy where money offers benefits of any sort to those who use it and people face a nontrivial choice of how much money to hold.[6]

The Golden Rule Monetary Policy in a Growing Economy

Up to this point in the chapter, we have held the population constant. We would like to see how the results of this chapter change if we allow for a growing population. With such a modification of the environment, we can then analyze an economy where fiat money supply and demand both change over time.

Consider our basic overlapping generations model when the consumption good cannot be stored and the economy is growing so that $N_t = nN_{t-1}$ for every period t, where n is a constant greater than 1. Let $M_t = zM_{t-1}$. Any increases in the fiat money stock will finance a lump-sum gift of a_{t+1} goods to each old person in period $t + 1$. Hence, this setup will be identical to the one just covered, except that we now allow for a growing population. What will be the rate of return on fiat money in this economy?

---

[6] The literature's first formal discussion of the welfare cost of inflation was by Bailey (1956). For a more modern survey, see Abel (1987).

If we set the supply of money equal to its demand in periods t and $t + 1$, we find the expression for the real rate of return of money like those we found previously in Equations 1.24 and 3.9:

$$\frac{v_{t+1}}{v_t} = \frac{\frac{N_{t+1}(y-c_1)}{M_{t+1}}}{\frac{N_t(y-c_1)}{M_t}} = \frac{\frac{N_{t+1}}{M_{t+1}}}{\frac{N_t}{M_t}} = \frac{N_{t+1}}{N_t}\frac{M_t}{M_{t+1}} = \frac{nN_t}{N_t}\frac{M_t}{zM_t} = \frac{n}{z}. \tag{3.13}$$

As before, we are making use of the fact that in a stationary equilibrium $a_{t+1} = a$ and $c_{1,t} = c_1$ for all t. The other cancelations occur because of assumptions about how the fiat money stock and the population change over time.

Because we restrict ourselves to stationary equilibria, in which money demand per person is the same in every period, the only source of change in total money demand in our model is the growth in population.

The budget line in this economy is the same one we found in Equation 3.6:

$$c_{1,t} + \left[\frac{v_t}{v_{t+1}}\right]c_{2,t+1} \leq y + \left[\frac{v_t}{v_{t+1}}\right]a_{t+1}, \tag{3.14}$$

but with $v_t/v_{t+1} = z/n$ and stationarity:

$$c_1 + \left[\frac{z}{n}\right]c_2 \leq y + \left[\frac{z}{n}\right]a. \tag{3.15}$$

Again, we must compare the budget set with the feasible set. The printing of money does not alter what is feasible, so the feasible set remains

$$N_t c_{1,t} + N_{t-1}c_{2,t} \leq N_t y, \tag{3.16}$$

which, in a stationary allocation with a growing population, simplifies to

$$c_1 + \left[\frac{1}{n}\right]c_2 \leq y. \tag{3.17}$$

Again, note that the expansion of the money stock does nothing to alter what is feasible (neither z nor a appears in Equation 3.17).

To compare the monetary equilibrium with the feasible set, we graph the two together (the feasible set line is the thick line). As before, we take advantage of our knowledge that the point of maximum utility in the budget set (point B in Figure 3.3) must lie on the edge of the feasible set.

In Figure 3.3 we see that there are many feasible points (such as A) that offer greater utility to both the future generations and the initial old than does the monetary equilibrium (point B). Point A lies on a higher indifference curve, indicating that the future generations prefer it, and it offers more c_2, indicating that the initial old prefer it.

Figure 3.3. An economy with a growing population and monetary expansion. The monetary equilibrium when the fiat money stock grows at the rate of z is represented by point B in the diagram. The monetary equilibrium is inefficient because an allocation like that represented by point A is attainable and is preferred by all to the monetary equilibrium.

The expansion of the money stock ($z > 1$) distorts the budget set by changing its slope from n to n/z. In this way the budget set is no longer the same as the feasible set. This means that the budget set no longer offers an individual a choice of all feasible allocations. In Figure 3.3, for example, we can see that, although allocation A is feasible and is preferred to allocation B, it is not available within the individual's budget set. People cannot choose allocation A because the expansion of the money stock lowers the rate of return of fiat money below n, taxing people's money balances. A person who holds more money in an effort to get to allocation A would find himself not at A but at a point below A on the budget line. He does not get to A because the more money he holds, the more value he loses to the newly printed money.

A Government Policy to Fix the Price Level

In the case just analyzed, the population grew at the rate n, implying that the total endowment of the economy also grew at this rate. We saw in Chapter 1 that the value of a unit of money rises with time when the economy is growing but the money stock is fixed. Many economists[7] have suggested that if the economy is growing, the money supply should grow at the same rate in order to keep the value

---

[7] Notably, Friedman (1960). Friedman (1969) no longer supported this view in "The Optimum Quantity of Money."

of money constant. Let us examine this policy suggestion in two steps. First, let us ask what rate of fiat money creation will maintain constant prices. Second, let us ask whether such a policy will make individuals better off.

From Equation 3.13 we see that, to keep the value of money (and thus the price level) constant, the rate of expansion of the fiat money stock z must be set to equal the rate of growth of money demand, which is the rate of growth of the population n. Speaking more generally, we will maintain a constant value of money when the stock of fiat money expands at the same rate as the demand for fiat money.

The question that remains is whether it is desirable to increase the money stock at the same rate at which money demand is growing. To answer this question, we must compare the monetary equilibrium with $z = n$ to the feasible set when $n > 1$. When z is equal to n, the lifetime budget set in a stationary monetary equilibrium (Equation 3.15) becomes

$$c_1 + c_2 \leq y + a. \tag{3.18}$$

This budget set, along with the feasible set (which is still given by Equation 3.17), is displayed in Figure 3.4. As we can see from the diagram, there are many points, like point A, that everyone prefers to the monetary equilibrium (represented by point B). Point A is attainable and is preferred to point B by both the future

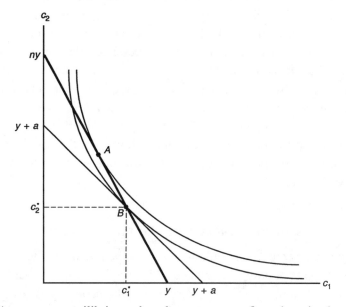

Figure 3.4. A monetary equilibrium when the government fixes the price level. When the government sets the growth rate of the money supply equal to the growth rate of the economy, the monetary equilibrium is at point B. The monetary equilibrium is inefficient because an allocation like point A is feasible and preferred by all.

generations and the initial old. Future generations prefer point A because it lies on a higher indifference curve. The initial old prefer point A because it represents more second-period consumption.

What is wrong with this policy of setting z equal to n? When the price level is fixed, an individual's budget set has a slope equal to -1. This tells the individual that, by consuming one less good today, he will receive one more good in the next period. In other words, the budget set tells the individual that goods are equally available in every period. However, this is not the true state of the economy. The economy is growing. Therefore, if in each generation young people consume one less good when young, there will be n extra goods available for old people in each generation. In other words, the economy can provide n goods for old people for each single good not consumed by young people. For this reason, the feasible set has the slope $-n$.

The message that the economy can offer n goods to the old for each good not consumed by the young is not conveyed through the budget set if prices are constant over time. Because the rate of return on money is 1, people see instead that giving up one good when young will get them only one good when old. As a result, at the monetary equilibrium B, people consume more when young and less when old than at the best feasible allocation A.

How, then, can we convey to individuals the message of the extra availability of goods for the old? The budget set faced by individuals must be identical to the feasible set. We saw in Chapter 1 that the budget and feasible sets (Equations 1.26 and 1.21, respectively) are identical when there is no expansion of the fiat money stock. When there is no change in the fiat money stock, fiat money offers the rate of return n, which signals to people the true state of the growing economy; for each good not consumed by a young person, an old person can consume n goods. In this case, the budget set is identical to the feasible set, so that people who choose the highest level of utility afforded by their budget are selecting the point with the highest feasible utility. For this reason, the golden rule monetary policy is to maintain a fixed stock of fiat money, whatever the growth rate of the economy. Although the policy prescription that the growth rate of the money supply should be set equal to the growth rate of the economy (here, $z = n$) keeps the price level constant, this policy does not maximize the utility of future generations.

Financing Government Purchases

In the preceding section, we found that the government was able to print costlessly new units of fiat money that were valued by the public. It follows that a government that needs to raise revenue for government purchases of goods may do so by printing new units of fiat money. The use of money creation as a revenue device is called **seigniorage**. Let us examine the welfare effects of such a policy.

Again, let $M_t = zM_{t-1}$ for every period t, where z is a constant greater than 1. This implies that

$$M_t - M_{t-1} = (z - 1)M_{t-1} = \left(1 - \frac{1}{z}\right)M_t \qquad (3.19)$$

units of new fiat money are created each period. This rate of money creation can finance the government's acquisition of

$$G_t = \left[1 - \frac{1}{z}\right]v_t M_t \qquad (3.20)$$

goods per period. Denote (constant) government purchases per old person as $g = G_t/N_{t-1}$. Equation 3.20 is the government's budget constraint when the revenue from printing money is used to finance government purchases of goods (in contrast to the government subsidies already studied).

We assume that the goods the government acquires from its seigniorage revenue are used in such a way as not to affect an individual's consumption bundle choice. We might think of such an expenditure as foreign aid or defense expenditures, which may be necessary or desirable but have no direct effect on the relative desirability of c_1 and c_2. For simplicity, we could even think of the government as merely dumping the acquired goods into the ocean. We make this assumption so that we may study the effects of acquiring revenue for the government in isolation from the benefits of the government purchases.

The problem of the individual is the same as it was in the case with no subsidy in that the budget line is still $c_{1,t} + (v_t/v_{t+1})c_{2,t+1} = y$ as in Equation 1.10.

We can again use the equality of supply and demand in the money market $v_t M_t = N_t[y - c_{1,t}]$ (Equation 1.11) and stationarity to get an equation for v_t,

$$v_t = \frac{N_t(y - c_1)}{M_t} \qquad (3.21)$$

Assume, for now, that the population is constant ($N_t = N$ for every period t). Then

$$\frac{v_{t+1}}{v_t} = \frac{\frac{N_{t+1}(y-c_1)}{M_{t+1}}}{\frac{N_t(y-c_1)}{M_t}} = \frac{M_t}{M_{t+1}} = \frac{1}{z}. \qquad (3.22)$$

Note that because the money supply increases at the same rate in each period, we again looked at the stationary solution ($c_{1,t} = c_1$ for all t). Through cancelation of terms, we learned that the value of money declines when money is created in a

Figure 3.5. A monetary equilibrium with seigniorage revenue. The monetary equilibrium when a growing fiat money stock is used to finance government expenditures is represented by (c_1^*, c_2^*). The rate of fiat money creation z determines the slope of the budget line.

nongrowing economy. In other words, money creation causes inflation because an increasing number of dollars bid for the same number of goods.

Given that the rate of return on fiat money is $1/z$, the individual's lifetime budget constraint becomes

$$c_1 + zc_2 \le y. \tag{3.23}$$

In Figure 3.5 the resulting budget set is graphed with an arbitrarily drawn indifference curve indicating the monetary equilibrium (c_1^*, c_2^*). Note two effects of an increase in z. As before, the slope of the budget line has been made flatter, which implies that an individual must give up more of c_1 to get a unit of c_2 in the presence of inflation because money has a lower rate of return. In addition, we now find that the budget set has shrunk; it lies inside the budget set without inflation. This occurs because the goods acquired by the expansion of the money stock are now being used up by the government instead of being returned to individuals as a subsidy.

Is Inflation an Efficient Tax?

As before, to discuss the optimality of this monetary equilibrium, we need to find the feasible set to see if any feasible allocations are preferred to the monetary equilibrium (c_1^*, c_2^*). To find the feasible set, we look at the total resources available and require that they not be exceeded by the goods used up. However, now we must be sure to include the goods used up by the government so that we compare the utility of individuals given the same level of government purchases G_t. Therefore, the feasible set for stationary allocations is now given by

$$N_t c_1 + N_{t-1} c_2 + G_t \leq N_t y. \tag{3.24}$$

To get the per capita form, divide through by N_t:

$$c_1 + \left[\frac{N_{t-1}}{N_t} \right] c_2 + \frac{G_t}{N_t} \leq y$$

$$\Rightarrow c_1 + \frac{c_2}{n} + g \leq y. \tag{3.25}$$

For $N_t = N$ (constant population so that $n = 1$),

$$c_1 + c_2 + g \leq y. \tag{3.26}$$

From Equation 3.26 we see that the new feasible set touches the horizontal axis at $c_1 = y - g$. We also know that the monetary equilibrium (c_1^*, c_2^*) lies on the line defining the feasible set because, after the government has taken its share, no consumer will elect to throw goods away.

We can use this information to add the feasible set to Figure 3.5, as we do in Figure 3.6. Note that, because the indifference curve is tangent to the budget line with a slope of $-1/z$, the feasible set line going through (c_1^*, c_2^*) with a slope of -1 must intersect the indifference curve if $z \neq 1$. This implies that the feasible set can reach a higher indifference than can the budget set. Therefore,

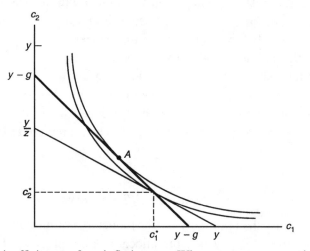

Figure 3.6. The inefficiency of an inflation tax. When a government raises seigniorage revenue to finance government purchases, the monetary equilibrium is (c_1^*, c_2^*). As we have seen before, this equilibrium is inefficient because there exist many points, such as point A, which are feasible, provide the same level of government revenue, and are preferred to (c_1^*, c_2^*).

a move from (c_1^*, c_2^*) to A, as shown in Figure 3.6, benefits the current young and future generations. Also, because this move increases second-period consumption c_2 it also benefits the initial old. Therefore, the monetary equilibrium in this case is not optimal because point A, among other allocations, will make everyone better off.

A Nondistorting Tax

Can we get a budget set of a monetary equilibrium to reflect the feasible set and so make point A attainable? Yes. Consider a fixed tax of τ goods collected from each old person. We refer to such a tax as a *lump-sum tax* because the amount paid to the government is not affected by any actions the individual may undertake. The equations defining this budget when young and old become

$$c_{1,t} + v_t m_t = y \quad \text{and} \quad c_{2,t+1} = v_{t+1} m_t - \tau, \tag{3.27}$$

or, combined,

$$c_{1,t} + \left[\frac{v_t}{v_{t+1}}\right] c_{2,t+1} = y - \left[\frac{v_t}{v_{t+1}}\right]\tau. \tag{3.28}$$

If the entire amount of government purchases is raised through lump-sum taxation ($\tau = g$), the money supply can be held constant. As we found before, the rate of return on money (v_{t+1}/v_t) in a stationary equilibrium will equal 1 when both population (i.e., money demand) and the stock of money are fixed over time. (You will be asked to study the case of a growing population in Example 3.1.) The budget set for $\tau = g$ and $z = 1$,

$$c_1 + c_2 = y - g, \tag{3.29}$$

is identical to the per capita feasible set. Therefore, the point of the maximum feasible utility for the future generations (point A) also lies within the budget set and is thus attainable by individuals. By using lump-sum taxes, the government raised the desired revenue with no distortion of the budget set – that is, without inducing people to reduce their money balances in an effort to avoid inflation's implicit tax on those money balances. Moreover, with lump-sum taxation, the demand for fiat money is greater than when revenue is raised through inflation, implying a greater real value of the money balances owned by the initial old. This, in turn, implies an improvement in the welfare of the initial old.

We see from the previous work that money creation is inferior to lump-sum taxation as a revenue device. Indeed, any tax on an economic activity (unless the activity is socially undesirable) is inferior to a lump-sum tax because it reduces the incentive to undertake that activity. Given that we do not see lump-sum taxes in the real world (perhaps because societies want the rich to pay more than the poor), seigniorage may just be one of many imperfect taxes in an imperfect world.

An obvious advantage of printing money to raise revenue is the ease with which it may be done. It requires no army of accountants or police; the only administrative costs are the costs of printing the notes. It costs pennies to produce a $1000 bill (or a $1 bill). This may explain the heavy use of money creation in poorer nations that may be lacking the extensive informational infrastructure required to enforce income taxes.

The burden of seigniorage falls on those who hold currency. Although everyone uses currency to make purchases, most U.S. currency is held by nonresidents or by people engaged in illegal activities, who do not want their transactions observed.[8] Seigniorage may then be desirable as a way to tax these groups.[9]

The use of seigniorage as a source of government revenue varies from country to country.[10] For most developed countries during normal times, seigniorage contributes very little to government revenue. In the United States, during the period 1948–89, on average seigniorage accounted for less than 2 percent of total federal government revenues and for around 0.3 percent of gross national product (GNP). On the other hand, Fischer (1982) found significant reliance on seigniorage in high-inflation countries like Argentina, Uruguay, Chile, and Brazil. As an example, seigniorage accounted for around 46 percent of Argentinian government revenues (6.2 percent of GNP) for the period 1960–75. Figure 3.7 presents data on seigniorage revenue as a percentage of total government revenue for several countries.

An extreme case in point is provided by Germany during its hyperinflation of the early 1920s. To help finance subsidies to workers in the French-occupied Ruhr and other government expenditures after World War I, Germany turned to the printing press. As a result, seigniorage revenue was eventually 10 to 15 percent of GNP.[11]

Example 3.1 Let $N_t = nN_{t-1}$ and $M_t = zM_{t-1}$ for every period t, where z and n are both greater than 1. The money created in each period is used to finance government purchases of g goods per old person. Prove that the monetary equilibrium does not maximize the utility of future generations. *Hint:* Follow the steps of the example just completed. Explain but do not formally prove why the feasible set line goes through the monetary equilibrium (c_1^*, c_2^*).

---

[8] See Avery et al. (1987).

[9] The case for seigniorage is made by Aiyagari (1990).

[10] For an excellent cross-country accounting of revenue from seigniorage, see Fischer (1982). See Barro (1982) for seigniorage estimates for the United States.

[11] Barro (1982).

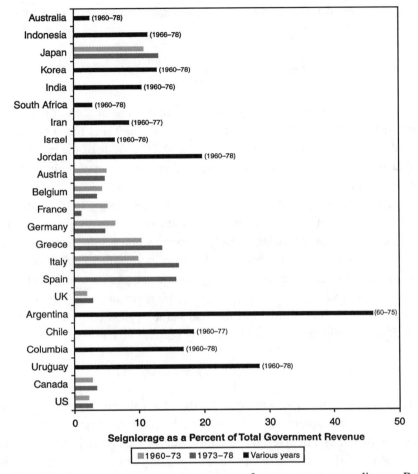

Figure 3.7. Seigniorage revenue as a percentage of government expenditures. Reliance on seigniorage as a source of government revenue varies dramatically across countries. Although the use of seigniorage varies most significantly across regions of the world, substantial variation exists within regions. For example, within Europe during the period 1973–78, seigniorage as a percentage of government revenue ranged from to 1 (France) to 16 (Italy) percent. *Source:* Fischer (1982, Tables A1 and A2, pp. 308–12).

The Limits to Seigniorage

Does seigniorage represent an unlimited source of government revenue? Can the government simply print enough money to pay all its bills without the bother of direct taxation? Although the government is able to print any number of dollars, the value of those dollars shrinks as the government prints more fiat money. Therefore, government revenue in terms of real goods is limited by the real value of the fiat money stock.

To see this, recall that real government revenue from seigniorage at t can be written as

$$(M_t - M_{t-1})v_t = \left[1 - \frac{1}{z}\right]v_t M_t. \tag{3.30}$$

The term $v_t M_t$ in Equation 3.30 represents the real value of the fiat money stock. Because this is the object being taxed, we may consider this the seigniorage **tax base**. The term $1 - (1/z)$ represents the fraction of the value of the real fiat money stock that winds up as government revenue; therefore, it may be considered the seigniorage **tax rate**.

Assume for a moment that the real value of the fiat money stock $v_t M_t$ remains constant as the rate of money creation z is increased. This assumes that people desire the same level of real balances of fiat money whatever the rate of inflation. If this is the case, real seigniorage revenue is always increasing in z. It is nevertheless bounded. As z is driven to infinity, the seigniorage tax rate goes to $1 - (1/\infty) = 1$ and the entire real value of money balances $v_t M_t$ is acquired by the government. But this quantity is finite, limited to the real value of desired money balances by the equality of supply and demand for money (Equation 1.11):

$$v_t M_t = N_t[y - c_{1,t}]. \tag{3.31}$$

There is in fact a more severe limit on the real value of seigniorage revenue. Suppose that a fixed amount of government expenditure is raised through some combination of lump-sum taxes and seigniorage. As the rate of inflation increases, each individual will choose to reduce the real balances of money held ($y - c_{1,t}$) in an attempt to reduce the amount of goods lost to the government through inflation.

To see this reduction in the demand for fiat money, let us examine the budget set when a fixed amount of government purchases is raised through some combination of lump-sum taxes and seigniorage. (You are asked to find this budget set in Exercise 3.6.) Figure 3.8 graphs the budget set and the monetary equilibrium for two alternative policies raising the same government revenue: policy A, in which all revenue is raised through lump-sum taxes ($\tau = g; z = 1$) and policy B, in which some revenue is raised through an expansion of the fiat money supply ($z > 1$). It illustrates how the seigniorage tax base $N_t(y - c_1^*)$ falls as the rate of money creation z increases. The reduction of the demand for fiat money reduces the real value of fiat money balances and thus the real value of the fiat money the government is printing.

The effect of the rate of fiat money creation on the real demand for fiat money can be seen by looking at data from the hyperinflationary episodes after World War

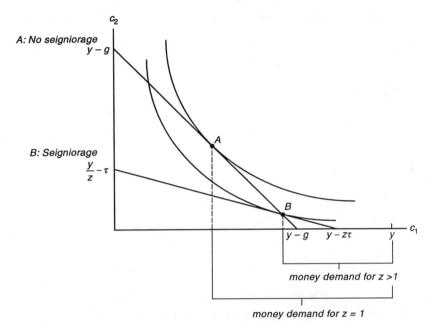

Figure 3.8. The decline in real money balances resulting from an increase in the rate of monetary expansion. Policy B, where the government provides for some of its purchases by printing fiat money, results in a smaller real demand for fiat money than policy A, where the government provides for its expenditures through a lump-sum tax. This illustrates the reduction in the seigniorage tax base from an increase in the rate of monetary growth.

I studied by Sargent (1986a). Austria, to illustrate such a case, printed fiat money at extremely high rates during the early 1920s in order to finance government deficits. For example, Austrian notes in circulation increased by over 70 percent from July to August 1922. This rapid increase in fiat money creation led to annual inflation rates that approached 10,000 percent per year. As shown in Figure 3.9, data from this episode demonstrate the tendency for real money balances to fall as the inflation rate increases.

We see from Figure 3.8 that, for a given level of government purchases, there is a more severe limit on the real value of seigniorage revenue. An increase in the rate of fiat money expansion discourages people from using money, which reduces the demand for fiat money $(y - c_1)$. In this way, an increase in the rate of fiat money expansion reduces the seigniorage tax base as it increases the seigniorage tax rate. It follows that, if the government inflates the stock of fiat money too rapidly, it may raise less revenue in real terms than it could raise with a lower rate of money creation. Although the exact shape of the revenue function depends on

Figure 3.9. Real money balances during the Austrian hyperinflation. During this hyperinflationary episode of the 1920s, real currency balances tended to fall as the rate of inflation
increased. *Source:* Authors' calculations using data from Young (1925) as published by
Sargent (1986a, Tables 3.2 and 3.3, pp. 49 and 51).

the utility function of individuals and anything else that affects the demand for fiat
money, the general shape of the revenue function may be something like that in
Figure 3.10.[12]

Such a relationship between tax rates and tax revenues may sound familiar.
The Laffer curve hypothesizes a similar relationship between income tax rates
and income tax revenue.[13] The notion that a government might increase tax revenues by cutting income tax rates is analogous to the possibility that the government might increase seigniorage revenue by decreasing the rate of money
creation.

In Chapter 6, we will see that the introduction of alternative forms of saving
will place additional limitations on the amount of seigniorage revenue that can be
generated by the government.

As shown in Figure 3.11, data from the Austrian hyperinflation show that after a certain point real seigniorage revenue declines at higher rates of fiat money
creation.

---

[12] See Bailey (1956).

[13] Economists discussed this relationship between tax rates and tax revenue long before its popularization by
Arthur Laffer during the promotion of *supply-side economics* by the Reagan administration.

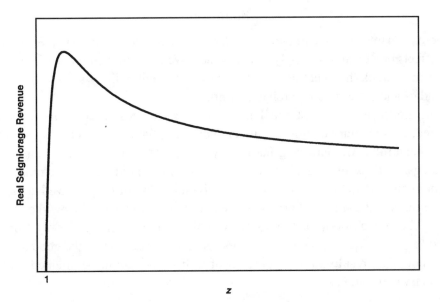

Figure 3.10. Seigniorage revenue and the growth rate of the money supply. As the government increases the rate of monetary expansion above 1, seigniorage revenue increases as the seigniorage tax rate increases. However, as shown in Figure 3.8, the seigniorage tax base falls as z increases. Eventually, this effect may dominate so that seigniorage revenue actually falls as z continues to increase.

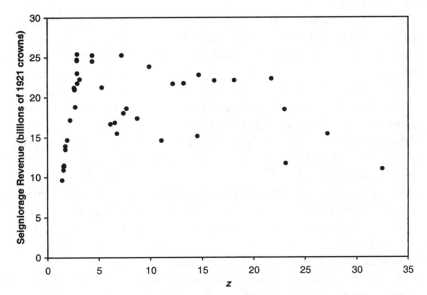

Figure 3.11. Seigniorage revenue during the Austrian hyperinflation. Continual increases in the rate of fiat money creation eventually correspond to lower levels of real seigniorage revenue. *Source:* Authors' calculations using data from Young (1925) as published by Sargent (1986a, Tables 3.2 and 3.3, pp. 49 and 51).

Summary

Whereas Chapter 1 concentrated on the demand for fiat money, this chapter analyzed the effects of a changing supply of fiat money. We concentrated on increases in the fiat money stock that were used to finance government policies such as lump-sum subsidies and government purchases of goods.

The models of this chapter had one overriding theme. In each of the cases considered, the monetary equilibria with an increasing fiat money stock did not attain the golden rule. An increasing fiat money stock acts as an implicit tax on money holdings, causing individuals to economize on their holdings of fiat money. By economizing on their money holdings, individuals do not fully take advantage of the benefits that fiat money provides. Real money holdings fall below the optimal level. The consumption pattern of individuals is altered, tilting it away from the good (c_2) that requires fiat money for its acquisition and toward the good (c_1) that does not. This results in a lower level of utility than could be attained without monetary expansion.

Exercises

3.1 Let $N_t = nN_{t-1}$ and $M_t = zM_{t-1}$ for every period t, where z and n are both greater than 1. The money created each period is used to finance a lump-sum subsidy of a_t^* goods to each *young* person.

    a. Find the equation for the budget set of an individual in the monetary equilibrium. Graph it. Show an arbitrary indifference curve tangent to the budget set and indicate the levels of c_1 and c_2 that would be chosen by an individual in this equilibrium.

    b. On the graph you drew in part a, draw the feasible set. Take advantage of the fact that the feasible set line goes through the monetary equilibrium (c_1^*, c_2^*). Label your graph carefully, distinguishing between the budget and feasible sets.

    c. Prove that the monetary equilibrium does not maximize the utility of the future generations. Support your assertion with references to the graph you drew of the budget and feasible sets.

3.2 Consider an economy with a shrinking stock of fiat money. Let $N_t = N$, a constant, and let $M_t = zM_{t-1}$ for every period t, where z is positive but less than 1. The government taxes each old person τ goods in each period, payable in fiat money. It destroys the money it collects.

    a. Find and explain the rate of return in a monetary equilibrium.

    b. Prove that the monetary equilibrium does not maximize the utility of the future generations. *Hint:* Follow the steps of the equilibrium with a subsidy, noting that a tax is like a negative subsidy.

    c. Do the initial old prefer this policy to the policy that maintains a constant stock of fiat money? Explain.

3.3 Consider an overlapping generations model with the following characteristics. Each generation is composed of 1,000 individuals. The fiat money supply changes according to $M_t = 2M_{t-1}$. The initial old own a total of 10,000 units of fiat money ($M_0 = \$10,000$). Each period, the newly printed money is given to the old of that period as a lump-sum transfer (subsidy). Each person is endowed with 20 units of the consumption good when born and nothing when old. Preferences are such that individuals wish to save 10 units when young at the equilibrium rate of return on fiat money.

   a. What is the gross real rate of return on fiat money in this economy?

   b. How many goods does an individual receive as a subsidy?

   c. What is the price of the consumption good in period 1, p_1, in dollars?

3.4 Consider the following economy. Individuals are endowed with y units of the consumption good when young and nothing when old. The fiat money stock is constant. The population grows at rate n. In each period, the government taxes each young person τ goods. The total proceeds of the tax are then distributed equally among the old who are alive in that period. (The tax is less than the real balances people would choose to hold in the absence of the tax.)

   a. Write down the first- and second-period budget constraints facing a typical individual at time t. (*Hint:* Be careful; remember that more young people than old people are alive at time t.) Combine the constraints into a lifetime budget constraint.

   b. Find the rate of return on fiat money in a stationary monetary equilibrium.

   c. Does the monetary equilibrium maximize the utility of future generations?

   d. Does this government policy have any effect on an individual's welfare?

   e. Does your answer to part d change if the tax is larger than the real balances people would choose to hold in the absence of the tax?

   f. Suppose that tax collection and redistribution are (very) costly, so that, for every unit of tax collected from the young, only 0.5 unit is available to distribute to the old. How does your answer to part d change?

3.5 Describe the essential features of a model economy of rational people for which each of the following statements is true. These features might include the pattern of population growth, monetary growth, endowments, and government policies. Note that there may be more than one model that yields the given results.

   a. The gross rate of return on fiat money is 1. The monetary equilibrium also maximizes the utility of the future generations.

   b. The price level doubles from period to period. The monetary equilibrium also maximizes the utility of the future generations.

   c. The gross rate of return on fiat money is 1. The monetary equilibrium does not maximize the utility of future generations.

3.6 Assume that people face a lump-sum tax of τ goods when old and a rate of expansion of the fiat money supply of $z > 1$. The tax and the expansion of the fiat money stock are used to finance government purchases of g goods per young person in every period. There are N people in every generation.

   a. Find the individual's budget constraints when young and when old. Combine them to form the individual's lifetime budget constraint and graph this constraint.

b. Find the government's budget constraint.

c. Graph together the feasible set and the stationary monetary equilibrium.

d. Find the stationary monetary equilibrium when $z = 1$ and add it to the graph in part c.

e. Use a ruler on your graph to compare the real balances of fiat money when $z > 1$ to the values when $z = 1$.

3.7 (advanced, requires calculus) Assume that the utility function of people in the economy described in Exercise 3.6 is $\log(c_{1,t}) + \log(c_{2,t+1})$.

a. Find the real demand for money ($q = v_t m_t$) in a stationary equilibrium as a function of z and τ. *Hint:* See the appendix to Chapter 1 for a discussion of solution techniques.

b. Find the government budget constraint in a stationary equilibrium. Solve it for τ as a function of z. (The expression will also involve y and g.)

c. Substitute your expression for τ from the government budget constraint (part b) into the demand for money (part a). Use this to find seigniorage as a function of z alone. Graph seigniorage as a function of z. For the graph, use the following parameter values: $N = 1,000$, $y = 100$, and $g = 10$.

3.8 Consider an economy with a constant population of $N = 1,000$. Individuals are endowed with $y = 20$ units of the consumption good when young and nothing when old. All seigniorage revenue is used to finance government expenditures. There are no subsidies and no taxes other than seigniorage. Suppose that preferences are such that each individual wishes to hold real balances of fiat money worth

$$\frac{y}{1 + \frac{v_t}{v_{t+1}}} \text{ goods.}$$

a. Use the equality of supply and demand in the money market to find the total real balances of fiat money in a stationary equilibrium as a function of the rate of fiat money creation z.

b. Use your answer in part a to find total seigniorage revenue as a function of z. Graph this function and explain its shape.

3.9 (advanced) Suppose the monetary authority prints fiat money at the rate z but now does not distribute the newly printed money as a lump-sum subsidy. Instead, the government distributes the newly printed money by giving each old person α new dollars for each dollar acquired when young. Assume that there is a constant population of people endowed only when young.

a. Use the government budget constraint to find α as a function of z.

b. Find the individual's budget constraints when young and old. Combine them to form the individual's lifetime budget constraint.

c. What is the rate of inflation p_{t+1}/p_t? What is the real rate of return on fiat money? *Hint:* The real rate of return on a unit of fiat money is not simply v_{t+1}/v_t in this case.

d. Compare the individual's lifetime budget constraint with the feasible set. Demonstrate that the monetary equilibrium satisfies the golden rule regardless of the rate of inflation. Explain why inflation does not induce people to reduce their real balances of fiat money in this case.

Appendix: Equilibrium Consumption Is at the Edge of the Feasible Set

We wish to prove algebraically that all goods are consumed in equilibrium – i.e., that the monetary equilibrium consumption bundle (c_1^*, c_2^*) is on the line defining the feasible set. From the work done previously, we know that the following equations – the lifetime budget constraint, the definition of the subsidy a, and the market clearing condition – describe the stationary monetary equilibrium:

$$c_1^* + \left[\frac{z}{n}\right] c_2^* = y + \left[\frac{z}{n}\right] a, \tag{3.32}$$

$$a = \frac{\left[1 - \frac{1}{z}\right] v_t M_t}{N_{t-1}}, \tag{3.33}$$

$$v_t M_t = N_t (y - c_1^*). \tag{3.34}$$

From Equations 3.33 and 3.34 we have that

$$a = \frac{\left[1 - \frac{1}{z}\right] v_t M_t}{N_{t-1}} = \frac{\left[1 - \frac{1}{z}\right] v_t M_t n}{N_t} = \left(1 - \frac{1}{z}\right) n[y - c_1^*]. \tag{3.35}$$

Substituting Equation 3.35 into the lifetime budget constraint, Equation 3.32, we find

$$c_1^* + \left[\frac{z}{n}\right] c_2^* = y + \left[\frac{z}{n}\right] \left(1 - \frac{1}{z}\right) n[y - c_1^*]. \tag{3.36}$$

Collecting and canceling terms, we find

$$z c_1^* + \left[\frac{z}{n}\right] c_2^* = z y. \tag{3.37}$$

Dividing through by z, we find that

$$c_1^* + \left[\frac{1}{n}\right] c_2^* = y, \tag{3.38}$$

proving that (c_1^*, c_2^*) is on the line defining the feasible set.

Chapter 4

International Monetary Systems

UP TO THIS point, we have examined only closed monetary economies – economies that operate entirely in isolation with a single fiat money. Trade and financial links between countries are increasingly important in the modern world, raising the importance of monetary links. Therefore, in this chapter we examine the role of money in economies that encompass more than one country and currency. We examine how exchange rates are determined and seek to explain observed exchange rate changes, especially the dramatic fluctuations of recent decades. We then go on to ask what kind of international monetary system should be in place. In particular we ask the question now facing the European Community: Should trading partners agree to fix their exchange rates or, going even further, adopt a single currency?

A Model of International Exchange

To address these international issues we assume that there exist two countries, a and b, each with its own fiat money. As in Chapter 3, people live two-period lives in overlapping generations. They are endowed with goods when young but not when old, yet they want to consume in both periods of life. The endowments in each country consist of the same goods (a good in country a is indistinguishable from a good in country b). People are indifferent to the origin of the goods they purchase. We use superscripts a and b to identify the parameters and variables of each country; for example, countries a and b have population growth rates n^a and n^b and money growth rates z^a and z^b, respectively. Assume that all changes in the fiat money stock are used to purchase goods for the government. We assume there is free international trade in goods.

The monies of the two countries can be traded at the **exchange rate** e_t, which is defined to be the units of country b money that can be purchased with one unit of

Table 4.1. *Options available to an owner of 1 unit of country* a *money*

Option A	Option B
Keep the country a money Buy v_t^a goods	Trade for e_t units of country b money Buy $e_t v_t^b$ goods

Options available to an owner of 1 unit of country b *money*

Option A	Option B
Trade for $1/e_t$ units of country a money Buy v_t^a/e_t goods	Keep the country b money Buy v_t^b goods

country a money. For example, suppose country a is the United States and country b is Japan. Then the exchange rate is

$$e_t = \frac{\text{Japanese yen}}{\text{U.S. dollar}},$$

the number of Japanese yen per U.S. dollar or, alternatively, the number of yen that can be bought with a dollar. (There is, of course, a second exchange rate, the number of U.S. dollars that can be bought with a Japanese yen, which is simply the inverse of the first exchange rate. It does not matter which one we study.)

As in our single country model, old people seek to trade their fiat money for the goods owned by young people. Naturally, the old people wish to purchase the most goods possible with the money they have. By definition, the owner of a unit of country a money at time t can buy v_t^a goods and the owner of a unit of country b money at time t can buy v_t^b goods. If people are free to trade monies at the exchange rate e_t, then the owner of a unit of country a money has the option of purchasing v_t^a goods with country a money or trading a unit of country a money for e_t units of country b money, which will buy $e_t v_t^b$ goods. Similarly, an owner of a unit of country b money has the option of purchasing v_t^b goods with country b money or trading a unit of country b money for $1/e_t$ units of country a money, which will buy v_t^a/e_t goods. These options are depicted in Table 4.1.

If $v_t^a > e_t v_t^b$, everyone prefers country a money (option A). Owners of country b money will want to trade for country a money to make their purchases, but owners of country a money will not want to trade their money for country b money. Because owners of country b money are not content with the form of their money balances, this cannot be an equilibrium in which both fiat monies are valued. The exchange rate e_t must be higher or v_t^a/v_t^b must be lower. Similarly, if $v_t^a < e_t v_t^b$, everyone prefers country b money (option B). Owners of country a money will want to trade for country b money to make their purchases, but owners of country b money will not want to trade their money for country a money. This also is not an equilibrium in which both fiat monies are valued because the owners of country a money are not content with the form of their money balances.

Only if $v_t^a = e_t v_t^b$ will owners of both countries' monies be indifferent between their two options and thus satisfied with the form of their money balances. Therefore, if both fiat monies are valued, in equilibrium it must be that

$$v_t^a = e_t v_t^b \quad \text{or} \quad e_t = \frac{v_t^a}{v_t^b}. \tag{4.1}$$

We wish to determine the behavior of this exchange rate under alternative international monetary arrangements.

Foreign Currency Controls

The first international monetary system we will study is one that completely separates the monetary sectors of the two countries through a policy of **foreign currency controls** and flexible exchange rates. By foreign currency controls, we mean that the citizens of each country are permitted to hold over time only the fiat money of their own country. Foreign currency controls do not rule out the possibility of trade between the two countries. An old citizen who wishes to buy goods from another country may exchange his money for the foreign currency and then make the purchase. However, the young of each country can hold only their country's money from one period to the next.

The imposition of foreign currency controls implies that each country has its own money supply and demand that independently determine the value of its fiat money:

$$v_t^a M_t^a = N_t^a \left(y^a - c_{1,t}^a \right), \tag{4.2}$$

$$v_t^b M_t^b = N_t^b \left(y^b - c_{1,t}^b \right), \tag{4.3}$$

The exchange rate $e_t = v_t^a / v_t^b$ is therefore

$$e_t = \frac{v_t^a}{v_t^b} = \frac{\dfrac{N_t^a \left(y^a - c_{1,t}^a \right)}{M_t^a}}{\dfrac{N_t^b \left(y^b - c_{1,t}^b \right)}{M_t^b}} = \frac{N_t^a \left(y^a - c_{1,t}^a \right)}{N_t^b \left(y^b - c_{1,t}^b \right)} \frac{M_t^b}{M_t^a}. \tag{4.4}$$

Note that the exchange rate, the value of country a money in terms of country b money, depends simply on the relative values of the demand for money and the supply of money in the two countries. The greater the demand for country a money relative to the demand for country b money, the higher the value of country a money (the exchange rate). The greater the supply of country a money relative to the supply of country b money, the lower the value of country a money.

Following the steps described in Equation 3.13, we can use Equations 4.2 and 4.3 to find the rates of return of the two monies to be

$$\frac{v^a_{t+1}}{v^a_t} = \frac{n^a}{z^a} \quad \text{and} \quad \frac{v^b_{t+1}}{v^b_t} = \frac{n^b}{z^b}. \tag{4.5}$$

Essentially, everything here is just what we found in the one-country case of Chapter 3 (but with superscripts now attached for each country).

Let us now determine the path of the exchange rate over time. The rate of change of the exchange rate is e_{t+1}/e_t. Using the definition of the exchange rate (Equation 4.1), we can express this in terms of the values of the two countries' monies at t and $t+1$,

$$\frac{e_{t+1}}{e_t} = \frac{\frac{v^a_{t+1}}{v^b_{t+1}}}{\frac{v^a_t}{v^b_t}}, \tag{4.6}$$

at which point we can make use of the expressions for the rates of return of the two monies (Equation 4.5) to find

$$\frac{e_{t+1}}{e_t} = \frac{\frac{v^a_{t+1}}{v^b_{t+1}}}{\frac{v^a_t}{v^b_t}} = \frac{v^a_{t+1}}{v^a_t} \frac{v^b_t}{v^b_{t+1}} = \frac{n^a}{z^a} \frac{z^b}{n^b} = \frac{n^a}{n^b} \frac{z^b}{z^a}. \tag{4.7}$$

From Equation 4.7 we can determine how the exchange rate will change over time: the greater the growth rate of country a's population relative to country b's, the greater the rate of growth of the exchange rate, the relative value of country a money. This happens because the growth of a country's population causes an increase in its demand for fiat money. Indeed, any increase in the demand for money in a country will drive up its relative value. An increase in a country's endowments (in y, the output of young people), for example, would have the same effect. If both countries expand the money stock at the same rate ($z^a = z^b$) but country a grows faster (in output or population), the relative value of country a's money will increase over time; country a will experience an **appreciation** of its exchange rate.

We can also see from Equation 4.7 that the greater the growth rate of country a's money supply relative to country b's, the lower the rate of growth of the exchange rate, the relative value of country a money. Suppose, for example, that the two countries have equal rates of growth in the demand for money ($n^a = n^b$); then if country a expands its money at a faster rate than does country b, the value of country a's money will fall relative to country b's money; country a will experience a **depreciation** of its exchange rate.

Fixed Exchange Rates

We see from Equation 4.7 that the exchange rate will not change over time $(e_{t+1} = e_t)$ if

$$z^a = \frac{n^a}{n^b} z^b. \tag{4.8}$$

A commitment to fix the exchange rate therefore requires that one or both of the countries choose rates of fiat money creation that satisfy Equation 4.8. Of course, a monetary authority committed to a fixed exchange rate can no longer freely set the rate of money creation in order to raise a chosen level of seigniorage revenue. A country can choose the rate of money creation to fix the exchange rate or to acquire its preferred level of seigniorage revenue, but it cannot meet both objectives.

Suppose, for example, that country a desires to keep a fixed exchange rate with country b. It will then set its growth rate of fiat money creation according to Equation 4.8. If country b now increases its fiat money creation growth rate, country a will be forced to follow suit and increase z^a if it wants to keep the exchange rate fixed.

Note also that Equation 4.8 implies that the fiat monies of both countries will have the same rate of return $(n^a/z^a = n^b/z^b)$ under fixed exchange rates. Alternatively stated, they will have the same inflation rates. If country a wishes to maintain a fixed exchange rate and the monetary authority of country b inflates, country a's monetary authority will be forced to inflate too. Country a loses its independence in monetary policy by following its fixed exchange rate policy.[1]

Example 4.1 Suppose that the United States (country a) and Great Britain (country b) have foreign currency controls in effect. The demand for money is growing at 10.25 percent in the United States and at 2 percent in Great Britain (net rates) each period. The fiat money supplies in the United States and Britain are growing at 5 percent and at 6.25 percent net rates in each period, respectively.

a. Defining the exchange rate (e_t) as in the text, what are the units in which the exchange rate is measured, U.S. dollars per British pound or British pounds per U.S. dollar?
b. What is the rate of return on fiat money in the United States? In Great Britain?
c. In a system of flexible exchange rates, what is the time path of the exchange rate between the United States and Great Britain (e_{t+1}/e_t)?

---

[1] Countries with a history of overusing seigniorage may actually choose to fix their exchange rate with respect to a country that is not likely to inflate. Chapter 16 examines why countries may need to make commitments that limit their ability to print money at will.

d. Suppose the United States desires to fix the exchange rate. How can the United States government set its gross rate of fiat money creation z^a to accomplish this goal?

Example 4.2 Suppose that the (gross) rate of return on fiat money in the United States (country a) is 2.0 and that of Canada (country b) is 1.0. The (gross) growth rate of the Canadian population (n^b) is 1.2. Foreign exchange controls are in effect.

a. What is the time path of the exchange rate (e_{t+1}/e_t)?
b. Suppose that Canada wishes to maintain a fixed exchange rate with the United States. To accomplish this goal Canada must set its gross rate of fiat money creation (z^b) to what value?

The Costs of Foreign Currency Controls

We have assumed that people don't care where goods come from. Suppose instead that people want to consume at least some goods from another country. Foreign currency controls require that when an old person of country a buys a good from a young person of country b, the young person of b cannot simply keep the country a money and use it to make a purchase in old age. Because he is allowed to hold only his own country's money, he must either require that the country a person exchange his country a money and pay in country b money, or accept the country a money and immediately exchange it himself. In either case, an exchange of monies occurs that would not be necessary in the absence of foreign currency controls.

In the model of an international economy just described, there seems to be little cost to the money changing that results from the imposition of foreign currency controls. It was assumed that people could exchange one money costlessly for another in order to purchase goods from another country. Anyone who has traveled abroad, however, knows that the exchange of one money for another is not costless. Money changers incur expenses in providing the offices and labor required to conduct the exchanges and charge for this service.[2]

The Indeterminacy of the Exchange Rate[3]

Because foreign currency controls force people to exchange money in order to buy the goods of another country, they impose extra costs on international trade in a

---

[2] There is a second reason for the inefficiency of foreign currency controls. If the monies of the two nations have different rates of return, their citizens differ in their willingness to trade c_1 for c_2 (have different marginal rates of substitution). This is inefficient because the separation of the two economies prevents citizens from making mutually beneficial trades. See Kareken and Wallace (1977).

[3] The ideas expressed in this section are drawn from the work of Kareken and Wallace (1981). The exposition owes much to Wallace's (1979) article "Why Markets in Foreign Exchange Are Different from Other Markets."

world of costly money exchange. Therefore, let us consider our two-country model economy when people are free to hold and use the money of any country.

To find the exchange rate in such a world, we will turn, as before, to the equality of money supply and demand. Because people are now allowed to hold the money of either country, we can no longer determine the money supply and demand of each country separately but must examine the world's supply of and demand for money. The world supply of fiat money, measured in goods, is $v_t^a M_t^a + v_t^b M_t^b$ and the world demand for fiat money is $N_t^a(y^a - c_{1,t}^a) + N_t^b(y^b - c_{1,t}^b)$. Setting supply equal to demand, we have that

$$v_t^a M_t^a + v_t^b M_t^b = N_t^a\left(y^a - c_{1,t}^a\right) + N_t^b\left(y^b - c_{1,t}^b\right). \tag{4.9}$$

A serious problem now appears in our effort to find the exchange rate. We have the single Equation 4.9 with which to determine two variables, v_t^a and v_t^b. Such an equation has an infinite number of solutions. Because $e_t = v_t^a/v_t^b$, this means that we can find an equilibrium in which world money supply equals world money demand for any positive exchange rate e_t.

This indeterminacy of the exchange rate did not appear when foreign currency controls limited citizens to their own country's money. In that case, the equality of money supply and money demand determined the value of fiat money in each country; the two market-clearing equations, Equations 4.2 and 4.3, determined the two variables v_t^a and v_t^b, which, in turn, determined the exchange rate.

Now, however, we have only a single market-clearing condition with which to try to determine the value of two monies. The right-hand side of Equation 4.9 tells us the total world demand for money, but it cannot tell us whether the dollars of country a are worth more or less than the yen of country b.

Substitute $e_t v_t^b$ for v_t^a in Equation 4.9. We find

$$e_t v_t^b M_t^a + v_t^b M_t^b = N_t^a\left(y^a - c_{1,t}^a\right) + N_t^b\left(y^b - c_{1,t}^b\right)$$

or

$$v_t^b\left[e_t M_t^a + M_t^b\right] = N_t^a\left(y^a - c_{1,t}^a\right) + N_t^b\left(y^b - c_{1,t}^b\right). \tag{4.10}$$

The term $[e_t M_t^a + M_t^b]$ in Equation 4.10 is the world money supply (measured in units of country b money), and $v_t^b[e_t M_t^a + M_t^b]$ is therefore the real value of the world money supply.

Note that, because people are free to hold either country's money, the size of one nation's money demand affects the real value of the world money supply. However, it no longer determines the rate of exchange because a nation is no longer restricted to using only its own money. Similarly, the supply of money printed by any one country does not determine the exchange rate because this money can be used in any country.

To understand this indeterminacy better, suppose that a single government issued two types of currency (say, green and blue) in a single, unified economy but neglected to put any numbers on the bills, choosing instead to let the free market determine the rate of exchange between the two. What would be the exchange rate? Would people value the green bills more or less than the blue? It is impossible to say. Either bill could be worth more than the other. There is nothing to pin down the rate at which people will exchange two intrinsically useless fiat currencies.

Now suppose that the green bills are printed in New York and the blue bills are printed in Des Moines, Iowa. Does this change our answers? No. If the two bills can be traded freely in all parts of the country, their rate of exchange is still undetermined. Printing the bills in two different locations does not end the indeterminacy as long as they are acceptable in trade everywhere. Note that neither the size of the city nor the number of bills printed in the city matters to the exchange rate.

Finally, suppose the blue bills are printed in Toronto, but the United States and Canada allow the holding and use of both colors of money. The political border should not make any difference to our answer. If the two colors of bills are perfect substitutes for each other within North America, nothing pins down their rate of exchange.[4]

Exchange Rate Fluctuations

In the absence of the government determination of the exchange rate, the exchange rate in a unified world economy can be whatever people believe it to be. It follows that, if these beliefs fluctuate, the exchange rate will also fluctuate because there is nothing to pin it down. These fluctuations need not be tied to changes in real economic conditions. Therefore the dollar may fall against another currency simply because everyone believes it will fall, regardless of whether U.S. output or some other real factor has changed.

Since 1971, when President Richard Nixon announced the abandonment of all U.S. efforts to control exchange rates, the world has seen tremendous volatility in exchange rates. It has become common for a currency to gain or lose 20 percent or more of its value in a matter of months. This volatility is clearly shown in Figure 4.1, which displays the U.S. exchange rate against six major currencies for the past four decades.

---

[4] On both sides of the U.S.–Canadian border, the currencies of both countries do circulate, but there remain some exchange controls that make the currencies less than perfect substitutes – for example, the restriction that only U.S. dollars can be used as reserves for U.S. bank deposits. (Reserve requirements are studied in Chapter 7.)

Figure 4.1. The U.S. exchange rate against six major currencies. Since the United States abandoned efforts to stabilize exchange rates in 1971, there has been marked volatility in the exchange rates between major currencies. This is seen in the U.S. exchange rates with Canada, France, former West Germany, Italy, Japan, and the United Kingdom. Shaded regions portray the period when the United States attempted to stabilize exchange rates. *Source:* Exchange rate data are from the Federal Reserve Bank of St. Louis FRED database (http://www.stls.frb.org/fred/index.html).

Table 4.2. *Exchange rate fluctuations*

Country	Months	Exchange Rate Movement
France	Dec 1973–Jan 1974	9.4% depreciation of the franc
Germany	Jun 1973–Jul 1973	9.4% appreciation of the mark
Italy	Sep 1992–Oct 1992	11.3% depreciation of the lira
Japan	Sep 1998–Oct 1998	10.0% appreciation of the yen
United Kingdom	Sep 1992–Oct 1992	11.7% depreciation of the pound

For a sense of the volatility of the data presented in Figure 4.1, we could calculate month to month changes in the exchange rates. Table 4.2 presents the extreme values for these calculations and the month in which they occurred.

The fluctuations in exchange rates cannot be readily traced to changes of similar magnitude in a country's money supply or its demand for money. None of the countries in Table 4.2 printed or destroyed over 9 percent of its money stock in a single month, nor did it have a one-month change in real economic activity of that magnitude, nor did the combination of one-month changes in money supply and demand across the two countries reach the magnitude of these changes in the exchange rates. A possible explanation for this exchange rate volatility may be the existence of sufficiently large sectors of the world economy that are free to hold multiple currencies. Although you or I may not be part of this group, there exist multinational institutions that certainly are.

International Currency Traders

Is there a cost to large random fluctuations in exchange rates? An individual can hedge against the fluctuations if he were able to costlessly hold a perfectly balanced portfolio of different currencies. In real life this option, although open to multinational institutions, does not seem to be costlessly open to ordinary people with small money balances (at least, we do not observe the holding of balanced money portfolios). The nuisance and costs of determining and acquiring a balanced portfolio of monies may be the reason or it may be that people are subject to government regulations that force them to use the local currency. As a result, fluctuations in the exchange rate put the value of people's money balances at risk.

To make this point more precisely, consider a model economy suggested by King, Wallace, and Weber (1992), in which there are three types of people:

1. citizens of country a, forced by law to hold only country a's money;
2. citizens of country b, forced by law to hold only country b's money;
3. multinational people, free to hold either currency.

Let N_t^a, N_t^b, and N_t^c, respectively, represent the number of people of each type in a generation born in period t. (We use superscripts to indicate a person's type for all variables.)

As always, the value of each country's currency (and thus the exchange rate) is affected by the demand for it. Each country's money is held by its own citizens and perhaps by multinational people as well. Let's let λ_t represent the fraction of the multinational people's money balances that is held in the form of country a's money. We can now write the two equations that represent the markets for the currencies of countries a and b, respectively,

$$v_t^a M_t^a = N_t^a \left(y^a - c_{1,t}^a\right) + \lambda_t N_t^c \left(y^c - c_{1,t}^c\right), \tag{4.11}$$

$$v_t^b M_t^b = N_t^b \left(y^b - c_{1,t}^b\right) + (1 - \lambda_t) N_t^c \left(y^c - c_{1,t}^c\right). \tag{4.12}$$

It is obvious from Equations 4.11 and 4.12 that, the more the multinational people (type c) want to hold country a's money (i.e., the greater the value of λ_t), the greater will be the value of country a's money and the lower will be the value of country b's money. This, in turn, implies that the greater the value of λ_t, the greater will be the exchange rate e_t. However, because the multinational people are free to hold any fraction of their money balances in each country's money, there are many possible equilibrium exchange rates. To see this point, note that from Equations 4.11 and 4.12, the exchange rate in this world economy is

$$e_t = \frac{v_t^a}{v_t^b} = \frac{\dfrac{N_t^a \left(y^a - c_{1,t}^a\right) + \lambda_t N_t^c \left(y^c - c_{1,t}^c\right)}{M_t^a}}{\dfrac{N_t^b \left(y^b - c_{1,t}^b\right) + (1 - \lambda_t) N_t^c \left(y^c - c_{1,t}^c\right)}{M_t^b}}. \tag{4.13}$$

As an illustration, consider a simple case in which the total real demand for currency is identical across the different types of people. In other words, suppose that $N_t^a(y^a - c_{1,t}^a) = N_t^b(y^b - c_{1,t}^b) = N_t^c(y^c - c_{1,t}^c)$. We can then factor those terms out of Equation 4.13. We find that the exchange rate is

$$e_t = \frac{v_t^a}{v_t^b} = \frac{\dfrac{1 + \lambda_t}{M_t^a}}{\dfrac{1 + (1 - \lambda_t)}{M_t^b}} = \frac{\dfrac{1 + \lambda_t}{M_t^a}}{\dfrac{2 - \lambda_t}{M_t^b}}. \tag{4.14}$$

Equation 4.14 illustrates that, for given stocks of fiat money in countries a and b, changes in λ_t will cause fluctuations in the exchange rate. An increase in λ_t will cause the exchange rate to rise and a decrease in λ_t will cause the exchange rate to fall. As an example, verify to yourself that, if the two countries issue the same nominal number of notes (i.e., $M_t^a = M_t^b$), the exchange rate can take on any value between $1/2$ and 2. (Hint: What is the range of values for λ_t?)

Example 4.3 Suppose there are three types of people in our model of two countries and two currencies. Type *a* people can hold only the money of country *a*, type *b* can hold only the money of country *b*, and type *c* can hold the money of either country. Every person wants to hold 10 goods worth of money. There are 300 type *a* people, 200 type *b* people, and 100 type *c* people. There are 100 units of country *a* money and 200 units of country *b* money.

a. Find the range of stationary equilibrium values for v^a, v^b, and e.
b. Now suppose that 100 type *a* people and 100 type *b* people become type *c* people (able to hold the money of either country). Now find the range of stationary equilibrium values for v^a, v^b, and e. Has the range of equilibrium exchange rates expanded or contracted? Explain this change.

As we saw earlier, the multiplicity of exchange rates that satisfy the conditions for a stationary equilibrium suggests that exchange rates may fluctuate dramatically as multinationals change the composition of their money balances. These fluctuations make each currency a risky asset.[5] Those who have access to only a single currency, however, will see the real value of their money balances, and thus their consumption, rise or fall with the exchange rate. Multinationals can free themselves from this risk if they hold a balanced portfolio of both monies so that if the exchange rate changes, the decreased value of one currency is offset by the increased value of the other. Although this balancing of currency balances may free multinationals from risk, it may be bothersome or otherwise costly to hold perfectly balanced stocks of both countries' currency.

Monetary authorities may therefore wish to stabilize the exchange rate to free their citizens from the risk of a decline in the value of their money balances or from the bother of perfectly balancing their money balances.

Fixing the Exchange Rate

Cooperative Stabilization

How can we organize the world to provide a stable exchange rate? For a solution to the indeterminacy of the exchange rate in the absence of foreign currency controls, let us take a cue from the monetary organization of national economies. What determines the exchange rate between two different bills in a single national economy? Quite simply, the government tells us the rate of exchange by printing the denomination on each bill and standing ready to exchange the bills at that rate. In the United States a bill with a picture of Alexander Hamilton trades for 10 bills with pictures of Washington because the monetary authority of the United States, the

---

[5] Fluctuating exchange rates also make risky the real value of any contract denominated in a single country's currency.

Federal Reserve, will exchange the bills at a rate of ten to one. This exchange rate does not depend on how many pictures of Washington have already been printed.

The exchange rate in a national economy also fails to depend on where the bills are printed. Each piece of U.S. currency carries the name of one of the 12 Federal Reserve banks, but the bills always trade one for one. No merchant in California sells goods for a higher dollar price if the dollars happen to be marked with the name of the Boston Federal Reserve Bank. No bank trades two pictures of Washington marked "Federal Reserve Bank of New York" for one picture of Washington marked "Chicago." When the Texas economy is in a slump, the value of bills marked "Dallas" does not fall.[6]

What is true for a single national economy is also true for a world economy unified in its use of currencies. If the two governments stand ready to exchange currencies at some given rate, they may determine the exchange rate. If the central banks of all countries stood ready to give $2 whenever presented with a British pound, people would be indifferent between £1 and $2. In this way the exchange rate would become determined.[7]

The exchange rate would also be fixed over time. In the absence of foreign currency controls, fiat currencies are held voluntarily. However, no currency will be held voluntarily if its value will fall over time relative to the value of other currencies. Such a currency offers a lower rate of return than the others, inducing everyone to switch to other currencies.

This solution seems so easy that one wonders why we rarely see fixed exchange rates. The European Economic Community (EEC), for example, although an advanced and integrated international economy, had tremendous difficulties in maintaining fixed exchange rates despite the pledges of the European governments.[8] During 1992, several countries in the EEC encountered difficulties maintaining fixed exchange rates with one another. As one example, after attempts to fix the value of the British pound relative to the German mark, Britain abandoned such measures in September 1992, allowing the pound to fall more than 10 percent in value relative to the mark. We will now examine two major impediments to the stabilization of exchange rates – speculative attacks on currencies and the strong incentive to inflate when exchange rates are fixed.

A key part of fixing the exchange rates among different forms of a national money is the willingness of the monetary authority to accept any amount of one

---

[6] Rolnick and Weber (1989) discuss the notion that Federal Reserve notes are distinct currencies trading at fixed exchange rates. See their paper for an excellent comparison of fixed and floating exchange rates.

[7] A recent example of fixing the exchange rate in this way came during the reunification of Germany, when the German central bank announced that it would accept East German marks at a one-for-one rate of exchange with West German marks, despite the fact that they were trading well below that rate of exchange before the announcement.

[8] Actually, the members of the European Monetary System agreed to keep exchange rates between pairs of member countries within narrow bands (±2.25 percent) of a fixed exchange rate. These bands were increased to ±15 percent after several countries abandoned attempts to maintain the narrow bands during September 1992.

form of money in exchange for money at a different form at the fixed rate. No matter how many Hamiltons you wish to trade for Washingtons, the Federal Reserve will exchange them at the rate of 10 Washingtons per Hamilton. And no matter how many bills with the stamp of Dallas you wish to trade for bills with the stamp of Boston, they can be had at the rate of one for one. How can the monetary authority make such an unbounded promise? What if they run out of Washingtons or bills with the stamp of Boston?

No one worries about a scarcity of Washingtons or bills with the stamp of Boston. If for any reason people want more of any type of bill, the Federal Reserve can simply have more printed. There is no limit to the exchanges the Federal Reserve can make; and if they burn the bills turned in, there is no inflationary consequence. Because people know this, no one ever worries about a shortage of any particular bill or believes that a bill stamped with one city's name will sell at a premium relative to that with another city's name. As a result there is never any reason to avoid any type of bill. Indeed most people never even look at the stamp indicating a city's name.

So why might there be any problem with fixing the exchange rates of any two fiat monies, such as those of two different countries? They are just bills with the names of countries instead of cities. If there is a monetary authority that can print any amount of one nation's currency for that of another, there is indeed no problem in maintaining a fixed exchange rate between the currencies of the two countries.

Unilateral Defense of the Exchange Rate

But does such an unlimited commitment exist between sovereign nations? Suppose that every holder of the British pound decided to turn in his pounds for German marks. Will the central bank of Germany (the Bundesbank) actually print all the marks necessary? Might they not be afraid that the United Kingdom would later decide to reimpose foreign currency controls that would send all those marks back to Germany in an inflationary tidal wave?[9]

How can the fixed exchange rate be supported without the full cooperation of foreign central banks? Is there another manner in which a government can keep its promise to exchange foreign currency for the domestic currency at a fixed exchange rate? One option is a government commitment to tax its citizens to acquire goods that may be sold in order to purchase the foreign currency demanded.[10]

---

[9] See Exercise 4.2.

[10] Another option is to dedicate a stockpile of storable goods like gold as reserves for the defense of the currency. Government stockpiles, of course, do not materialize out of thin air; they come from an earlier taxation of the people or an earlier decision not to distribute the stocks among the people. Interest-bearing assets may also function as reserves, as we will see in Chapter 10.

If such a commitment is believed and no foreign currency controls are imposed, there will be little incentive for anyone to turn in one form of money for the other. Both currencies can be used and held in either country (because of the absence of foreign currency controls) and neither loses value relative to the other (because of the fixed exchange rate). The two "national" currencies function essentially as two denominations of a single internationally accepted currency. People will be indifferent between the two types of currencies. Thus, if the commitment is believed, the government may never be obliged to actually tax its citizens or spend its stockpile.

To be believable in all circumstances, the government commitment to tax must be large enough to acquire enough goods to redeem all its money that might be turned in to it – all of that nation's money in the hands of those who are free to exchange one currency for another. This quantity could be quite large.[11] One must ask if it is believable that the government would actually tax its citizens to defend a fixed exchange rate in the circumstance in which a large number of people are trying to exchange the domestic currency for another.

Consider our two-country model economy with no foreign currency controls and no cooperation between central banks. The government of country a pledges to tax the old in order to defend a fixed exchange rate. (The tax is levied on the old because they are the citizens who will lose if the nation's money loses value.) Because of the absence of foreign currency controls we will assume that some of each country's currency is held by the old of each country. Recall that the world market for currency is given by

$$v_t^a M_t^a + v_t^b M_t^b = N_t^a \left(y^a - c_{1,t}^a \right) + N_t^b \left(y^b - c_{1,t}^b \right),$$

or

$$\bar{e} v_t^b M_t^a + v_t^b M_t^b = N_t^a \left(y^a - c_{1,t}^a \right) + N_t^b \left(y^b - c_{1,t}^b \right). \tag{4.15}$$

where $\bar{e}$ denotes the fixed exchange rate.

Now suppose that the entire world arbitrarily decides to exchange a large part of its holdings of country a money for country b money. If the government honors these requests, M_t^a falls, increasing the value of all currency by reducing the world's nominal stock of currency. (Note that M_t^b does not rise as a consequence of this action because no additional country b money is printed. The government of country a purchases the country b money from people currently holding it.) This increases the wealth of all holders of this money, whatever their citizenship.

---

[11] Restricting our attention to currency, we find an extreme example in the United States, whose currency is used worldwide in official and unofficial transactions. Porter and Judson (1996) estimate that two-thirds of the stock of U.S. currency is held abroad.

Where does this wealth come from? The government of country a is obliged under its pledge to tax its old citizens in order to acquire the foreign currency demanded by those turning in country a money. Thus the reduction of country a money comes from the taxation of the old citizens of country a. In this way the taxpayers of a alone pay for an increase in the value of money that benefits moneyholders in all countries. The net effect of the policy is therefore to transfer wealth from citizens of a to citizens of b. Although the people of a may want a fixed exchange rate, they will be made worse off if the government must actually tax them to defend the currency.

To better understand the differences between cooperative stabilization versus unilateral defense of the exchange rate, let us consider a specific example. Suppose countries a and b are identical. In each country, the population of every generation is 100 ($N_t^a = N_t^b = 100$), and each young person wants real money balances worth 10 goods. This implies that aggregate real money balances in each country are

$$N_t^a \left(y^a - c_{1,t}^a \right) = N_t^b \left(y^b - c_{1,t}^b \right) = (100)(10) = 1{,}000.$$

Also assume that the total fiat money stock of country a is \$800 and that of country b is £600. We assume that there are no foreign currency controls in effect and that each money is held in both countries. In particular we assume that the fiat money stocks are equally dispersed among the initial old of both countries. Because there are 100 individuals born in each generation, there are 200 initial old people across the two countries. This implies that each member of the initial old holds \$4 (=\$800/200) and £3 (=£600/200), regardless of citizenship. Finally, assume that the exchange rate is fixed at $\bar{e} = 1/2$; \$1 trades for £0.5.

From the world money market-clearing condition (Equation 4.13), we can find the value of each country's fiat money in a stationary equilibrium.

$$\bar{e} v_t^b M_t^a + v_t^b M_t^b = N_t^a \left(y^a - c_{1,t}^a \right) + N_t^b \left(y^b - c_{1,t}^b \right)$$

$$\left(\frac{1}{2} \right) v_t^b (800) + v_t^b (600) = 1{,}000 + 1{,}000$$

$$1{,}000 v_t^b = 2{,}000$$

$$v_t^b = 2.$$

Because the exchange rate is fixed at $1/2$, we can derive the value of country a money:

$$v_t^a = \bar{e} v_t^b = \frac{1}{2}(2) = 1.$$

The consumption by each old person in both countries is equal to the real value of that person's total money holdings. In other words,

$$c_2^a = c_2^b = v_t^a(4) + v_t^b(3) = (1)(4) + (2)(3) = 10 \text{ goods.}$$

Now suppose that every member of the initial old of both countries decides to cut their real balances of country a money in half. Each member of the initial old therefore turns in $2 to the monetary authority of country a in order to acquire country b money. Assume that the monetary authority of country b has agreed to cooperate by printing as much of its currency as demanded. This is an example of cooperative stabilization. Because the exchange rate is fixed at $1/2$, this means that country b must print £0.5 for every dollar turned in by the old, or £1 per old person. At the end of the currency exchange, the stock of dollars has shrunk by $400 and the stock of pounds has grown by £200. In this situation, the total fiat money stocks of each country have become $400 and £800.

As we did earlier, when we solve the world money market-clearing condition for the value of country b money, we find that its value is unchanged:

$$\bar{e}v_t^b M_t^a + v_t^b M_t^b = N_t^a\left(y^a - c_{1,t}^a\right) + N_t^b\left(y^b - c_{1,t}^b\right)$$

$$\left(\frac{1}{2}\right)v_t^b(400) + v_t^b(800) = 1,000 + 1,000$$

$$1,000v_t^b = 2,000$$

$$v_t^b = 2.$$

With the exchange rate fixed at $1/2$, we see that v_t^a is still equal to 1. The consumption of each old person is equal to

$$c_2^a = c_2^b = v_t^a(2) + v_t^b(4) = (1)(2) + (2)(4) = 10 \text{ goods.}$$

We see that the consumption by each old person is unchanged under a policy of cooperative stabilization. Each is unaffected in real terms by holding fewer dollars and more pounds.

Now let us see how the results differ when cooperative stabilization is absent and country a attempts a unilateral defense of the exchange rate. Suppose country b refuses to print fiat money to accommodate the desires of the old to trade in their dollars for pounds. Assume that the government of a decides to honor its pledge to exchange currency through an equal tax on every old citizen of its country. To do this, the government of country a must raise tax revenue sufficient to honor its pledge to provide all the country b money demanded. With 200 individuals across the two countries exchanging $2 for pounds at the exchange rate of $1/2$, the total number of pounds that must be acquired by country a is equal to $(200)\$2\bar{e} = (200)£1 = £200$.

The real value of the tax on the old is $v_t^b(£200)$ goods. Because country a can tax only its own citizens, each old person of country a will be required to pay a tax of

$$\frac{200v_t^b}{100} = 2v_t^b.$$

To completely see the impact of this tax, we need to determine the new value of country b money. Since each of 200 old people has turned in \$2 of his initial holding of \$4, the total fiat money stock of country a has fallen to

$$M_t^a = \left(N_t^a + N_t^b\right)\$2 = (100 + 100)\$2 = \$400,$$

which is half its previous level. However, unlike the case of cooperative stabilization, the fiat money stock of country b is unchanged, because country b refuses to print additional money. Country b's total fiat money stock remains at £600. Using the world money market-clearing condition, we find that the value of country b money is

$$\bar{e}v_t^b M_t^a + v_t^b M_t^b = N_t^a\left(y^a - c_{1,t}^a\right) + N_t^b\left(y^b - c_{1,t}^b\right)$$

$$\left(\frac{1}{2}\right)v_t^b(400) + v_t^b(600) = 1,000 + 1,000$$

$$800v_t^b = 2,000$$

$$v_t^b = 2.5.$$

Given the fixed exchange rate of $1/2$, the value of country a money rises to 1.25. This verifies our earlier statement that the value of all currency will increase under a unilateral defense of the exchange rate. This stands in marked contrast to the cooperative stabilization solution, where we found that the value of each currency remained unchanged.

Now that we have found the value of country b money, we can see that to pay for the defense of its currency each old person of country a must be taxed

$$2v_t^b = 2(2.5) = 5 \text{ goods.}$$

Now let us see the effect of this policy on the consumption by each old person the two countries. After each person has traded \$2 to get £1, each person owns \$2 and £4 before taxes. The old of country b have no taxes to pay, permitting them to consume

$$c_2^b = v_t^a(2) + v_t^b(4) = (1.25)(2) + (2.5)(4) = 12.5 \text{ goods.}$$

The old of country b benefit from the unilateral defense policy because the real value of their currency holdings increases and they are not subject to a tax.

Because the old of country a must pay a tax to defend their currency, their consumption is equal to the real value of their money holdings less the tax:

$$c_2^a = v_t^a(2) + v_t^b(4) - (\text{tax}) = (1.25)(2) + (2.5)(4) - 5 = 7.5 \text{ goods.}$$

Because of the tax, the old of country a are made worse off by this policy of unilateral defense than they were under the cooperative stabilization policy, where their consumption was 10.

In effect, the unilateral defense policy has resulted in a transfer of 2.5 goods from each old person of country a to each old person of country b. Only the citizens of country a pay the tax that increases the value of all moneyholders, transferring wealth from the taxpayers of the country defending the exchange rate to the moneyholders of the other country.

Example 4.4 Consider two identical countries in our standard overlapping generations model. In each country the population of every generation is 100 and each young person wants money balances worth 18 goods. Each member of the initial old starts with $3 of country a money and £3 of country b money regardless of citizenship. The exchange rate is fixed at 2: $1 is worth £2. There are no foreign currency controls.

a. Find the value (measured in goods) of a unit of each country's money in a stationary equilibrium with unchanging money stocks. [Use the world money market-clearing condition (Equation 4.13).] What is the consumption of each old person? (Remember that each old person owns currency from both countries.)
b. Suppose each member of the initial old of both countries decides to cut his real balances of country a money by one-third (to 8 goods). He turns in $1 to the monetary authority of country a in order to acquire more country b money. Assume that the monetary authority of country b has agreed to cooperate by printing as much of its currency as is demanded. What will be the total nominal stock of the each country's money? What will be the value of a unit of each country's money?
c. Suppose each member of the initial old turns in $1 to the monetary authority of country a in order to acquire more country b money at the fixed exchange rate, but the monetary authority of country b refuses to cooperate. Assume that the government of country a decides to honor its pledge through an equal tax on every old citizen. What is the value of a unit of each country's money? How many goods must each old citizen of a be taxed? What is the consumption of the old in each country? (Remember to include the tax.) Who prefers this policy to the policy in part b? Who does not?
d. Suppose each member of the initial old decides to cut his real balances of country a money by one-third (to 8 goods), and the government decides not to intervene to fix the exchange rate. What is the new exchange rate? What is the consumption of each old person? Why doesn't the exchange rate change hurt anyone? Who prefers this policy to the policy in part c? Who does not?

Speculative Attacks on Currencies

A unilateral policy of fixing the exchange rate relies on the government's willingness to take actions (taxation) that make its citizens worse off. People may quite rationally question the government's commitment to follow through with a policy that hurts its own citizens. If the government lacks the will to take any of the actions it promises, people will rationally anticipate the promise of a fixed exchange rate as meaningless, returning the economy to an equilibrium of undetermined exchange rates.

It may be, however, that the government is prepared to take limited action to defend the exchange rate. Suppose, for example, that the government is willing to tax its citizens a limited amount – say F goods, where F is less than the total value of the country's stock of currency. The government is committed to exchange foreign for domestic currency until the tax bill of this policy has reached F goods, at which point it will abandon its efforts and let the exchange rate fluctuate. If fewer than F goods worth of domestic currency are turned in for exchange, the fixed exchange rate is maintained.

As pointed out by Salant and Henderson (1978) and Krugman (1979),[12] a limited government commitment may encourage speculative attacks in foreign currency markets in a way that does not occur when the government commitment is total. European countries (e.g., Britain and Sweden) in 1992–93 and East Asian countries (e.g., South Korea and Indonesia) in 1997 experienced recent waves of such speculative attacks.

Suppose you are holding some currency balances of a country with a limited commitment to defend its exchange rate. You decide to exchange that currency for the money of another country. If the commitment of that country is sufficient to meet the entire demand for foreign exchange, the exchange rate does not change and you are no worse off than before. If that country's commitment is too small to meet the entire demand for foreign exchange, its currency will fall in value, and the foreign currency will gain in value. If you are one of the lucky ones who arrive at the foreign exchange window before the government's limit is reached, you will profit by acquiring the currency that is about to gain in value. This is a can't-lose proposition for speculators: they either win or are not hurt.[13] Faced with these possible outcomes, every holder of that country's currency will want to rush to the foreign exchange window.[14]

This is also a can't-win policy for taxpayers. If a speculative attack occurs and the commitment proves sufficient, taxpayers have still been taxed to meet the attack.

---

[12] See also Krugman and Rotemberg (1991).

[13] Of course there is a chance of a loss if the currency they purchase is also subject to a speculative attack.

[14] Your only cost is the cost of making the transaction, which may be small for large traders of foreign currency.

If the commitment proves insufficient, the taxpayers are taxed and the currency depreciates nevertheless.

Inflationary Incentives

In the absence of foreign currency controls, the exchange rate is independent of national money stocks. Look again at the world money market-clearing condition (Equation 4.13). The value of a unit of money is determined by the total world money supply and not the money supply of the issuing nation. Therefore, an increase in the stock of one money reduces the value of all money and not just the money whose supply is expanded.

Let us examine this implication of the absence of foreign currency controls in the context of a national economy. If the monetary authority prints and distributes a large number of new \$1 bills, the real (goods) value of the \$1 bills will fall, but the real (goods) value of \$10 bills will also fall. Why? The two are perfect substitutes for each other and have a fixed rate of exchange. Therefore, if inflation reduces the real value of \$1 bills, it also reduces the real value of \$10 bills. Similarly, an increase in the number of Federal Reserve notes marked Boston will reduce the value of all Federal Reserve notes in every part of the United States.

For the same reasons, in an international economy of perfectly substitutable currencies trading at a fixed exchange rate, an increase in the stock of one country's money reduces the real value of all monies. This can occur because people, indifferent between currencies in the absence of foreign currency controls, treat the different currencies as simply different denominations of a world money free to circulate in all nations. Therefore, it does not matter which denomination (which nation's money) is increased during an expansion of the world stock of money; all currencies will fall in real value.

The expansion of one nation's money stock does not affect the real value of other currencies when foreign currency controls are in effect because the currencies are not perfect substitutes and do not trade at a fixed exchange rate. Citizens hold only their own country's money and thus are not affected by the inflation of some other country.

The transmission of inflation across countries in the absence of foreign currency controls raises an important political problem. We learned in the previous chapter that a nation that expands its money stock acquires revenue by lowering the value of the outstanding money stock, in effect by taxing moneyholders. In the presence of foreign currency controls, a nation willing to see the value of its money fall by half can raise seigniorage equal to half the value of the nation's money balances. In the absence of foreign currency controls, however, a nation willing to see the value of its money fall by half can raise seigniorage equal to half the value of the world's money balances; the seigniorage tax base is greatly expanded, and with it, seigniorage revenue. In this way, seigniorage can be collected from the citizens of other countries.

The political incentives created by a single world demand for currency in the absence of foreign currency controls are obvious. Imagine the inflation that would result if local governments were free to issue nationally accepted money. If any tax is favored by politicians, it's a tax collected in large part from people unable to vote against them in the next election. The same logic applies to the international case. Because every national government will wish to inflate to collect seigniorage from the citizens of other countries, a large inflation of the world's money stock will result.

This inflation can be prevented if governments are willing to agree to limit the rate at which each is allowed to expand its fiat money stock. Such coordination may work if each government wishes to rely on seigniorage to roughly the same degree. If, however, some countries want to rely on seigniorage far more than others, it may be difficult to reach an agreement.

If it is not possible to coordinate monetary policies, a nation can avoid the politically induced inflation only by separating the demand for its currency from that of the others – that is, by imposing foreign currency controls that prevent the currency of other countries from substituting for their own currency. Of course, under foreign currency controls, the citizens incur the costs of exchanging money whenever they trade with the people of another nation.

The Optimal International Monetary System

If political coordination were not a problem, what sort of international monetary system would we want? Let us answer this by first asking what monetary system we would want within a nation (a politically coordinated entity). Would we want each city and town to have its own money? If they did, imagine the costs of learning the current exchange rate and changing money as one makes purchases in different towns. The obvious way to eliminate these transaction costs and facilitate trade is to have only a single money for the entire nation. This is the monetary system selected by every nation.

How do these nations prevent their cities from issuing money to tax each other through seigniorage? They simply authorize a single national authority as the only issuer of fiat money. This means that the cities within any nation are not free to pursue distinct seigniorage policies. Nevertheless, cities seem willing to yield their sovereignty over monetary policy in order to reduce the costs of trade among themselves.

The same solution suggests itself to the world economy. The costs of conducting trade between nations would be minimized if a single money were used worldwide. People would not have to exchange their money to make purchases from other countries, nor would they have to fear that their money would suddenly lose its value because of an exchange rate change. A single world money would require that nations surrender their sovereignty over monetary policy to some trusted nation[15] or international institution, preferably with strict instructions about the rate of money expansion and the disposition of the revenue from seigniorage. This solution, in the form of a single European currency with a single European monetary authority, is currently being implemented by the European Economic Community (EEC). Adoption of the U.S. dollar, long established in Panama, has been considered in Argentina and is commonly discussed in other countries in the Americas.

If a world money is too much to ask, most of the benefits of a world money can be acquired if there are multiple currencies trading at fixed exchange rates with no currency controls. In this case, the different currencies function as different denominations of the world money supply, freely traded everywhere. This requires that monetary policies be coordinated to prevent speculative attacks and also to prevent the temptation for each national government to tax the entire world through inflation.

In actuality, political coordination may not be a trivial prerequisite. If countries considering a monetary union differ greatly over whether seigniorage is an important source of government revenue or over some other aspect of monetary policy, the gains to reducing the costs of international trade may not be worth foregoing an independent monetary policy. It follows that monetary union is more likely among countries with similar economies, like the countries of the EEC. Even these, however, differ significantly in their reliance on seigniorage. Seigniorage as a percentage of tax revenue ranged from 1 to 16 percent during the period 1973–1978.[16] Figure 3.7 of Chapter 3 presents data on seigniorage revenue for the countries of the EEC.

Summary

The goal of this chapter has been to understand the implications of different international monetary systems. This study is important in today's world, where countries

---

[15] At the close of World War II, the Western nations and others pledged at Bretton Woods, New Hampshire, to conduct their monetary policies in a way that maintained a fixed rate of exchange with the U.S. dollar, which pledged to redeem dollars in gold. Although this era is not strictly an example of a world money, its political implications are similar because the fixed exchange rates required that nations maintain rates of money creation compatible with that of the United States. The agreement broke down in the Vietnam War era when the United States effectively printed dollars to help finance the war. In 1971, President Nixon announced that the United States would no longer maintain a fixed exchange rate or its commitment to redeem dollars for gold.

[16] See Fischer (1982). See Canzoneri and Rogers (1990) for a discussion of the trade-off faced by the EEC.

are considering adopting widespread reforms of the systems under which they operate.

We first looked at a system in which currency controls are in effect. We found that the exchange rate between two countries' currencies is determined by the factors affecting the relative supply and demand of those currencies. With floating exchange rates and currency controls, the value of each country's money is unaffected by the other country's money supply or demand.

Currency controls require a potentially costly exchange of money in order to make a purchase in another country. These costs of the exchange of currencies can be avoided if people are free to hold and use any country's money. In this case, however, the exchange rate becomes indeterminate. This indeterminacy may give rise to erratic fluctuations in exchange rates, fluctuations that expose moneyholders to the risk of a sudden drop in the value of the money they hold.

The indeterminacy problem can be solved if countries agree to fix the exchange rate. When all monies are perfect substitutes, however, there exists the temptation to tax the citizens of other countries through seigniorage. This implies that countries fixing their exchange rate must also coordinate their monetary policies.

Exercises

1. Suppose that Germany (country a) and France (country b) do not have foreign currency controls in effect. The total demand for money is always 2,000 goods in Germany and 1,000 goods in France. The fiat money supplies are 100 marks in Germany and 300 francs in France.
   a. Find the value of each country's money if the exchange rate e_t (as defined in the text) is 3. Do the same if $e_t = 1$. Is one exchange rate more likely than the other? Explain.
   b. Suppose the exchange rate is 3 and that France triples its fiat money stock, whereas Germany prints no new money. How many goods will France gain in seigniorage? What fraction of this seigniorage comes from German citizens?

4.2 Consider two identical countries in our standard overlapping generations model. In each country the population of every generation is 100 and each young person wants money balances worth 10 goods. There are $400 of country a money and £100 of country b money. The exchange rate is fixed at 1. There are no foreign currency controls and the monetary authorities do not cooperate. Each country is willing to raise up to 500 goods in taxes on their old citizens in order to defend the exchange rate.
   a. What is the value in goods of a dollar? Of a pound?
   b. Find the value of a dollar if people abandon use of the pound and the value of a pound if people abandon use of a dollar.
   c. To be free from a speculative attack, a country's commitment to defend the exchange rate must be sufficient to purchase all its currency if it is offered for foreign exchange.

Which of these two countries is subject to a speculative attack? (*Hint:* In answering you will need to use your answers to part b, not to part a.)

4.3 Consider two identical countries, *a* and *b*, in our standard overlapping generations model. In each country the population of every generation is 200 and each young person wants money balances worth 50 goods. Assume that the money of country *a* is the only currency that currently circulates in the two countries. There is $800 of country *a* money split equally among the initial old of both countries.

a. Find the value of a country *a* dollar and the consumption of the initial old.

b. Suppose country *b* issues its own money, giving £10 to each of the initial old of country *b*. To ensure a demand for this currency, country *b* imposes foreign exchange controls. Find the value of a pound and the value of a dollar. Find the consumption of the initial old in country *a* and in country *b*. Who has been made better off by this policy switch?

Chapter 5

Price Surprises

TO THIS POINT we have examined only anticipated increases in the fiat money stock. In this chapter we examine the effects of monetary surprises – unanticipated fluctuations in the fiat money stock – on output, in particular. As we do so, we also study the more general question of how data correlations resulting from policy surprises may mislead naive policy makers about the effects of the sustained implementation of their policies.

The Data

The Phillips Curve

In 1958, A.W. Phillips discovered a significant statistical link between inflation and unemployment for the United Kingdom over a century.[1] Subsequent work uncovered the same correlation for many other economies. Although it was not understood why such a correlation existed, this discovery excited many in the economics profession by suggesting that there may be an exploitable trade-off between inflation and unemployment – that by increasing inflation, the government might achieve lower unemployment and greater output. The apparent inverse relationship between inflation and unemployment rates that existed in the United States data between 1948 and 1969 is illustrated in Figure 5.1.

In the next decades, many governments tried to use monetary policy to stimulate the economy. Suddenly, the Phillips curve, a stable relation over a century, disappeared. Inflation occurred with no gains in output or employment. The disappearance of the stable relationship between the inflation rate and the unemployment

---

[1] Actually, Phillips investigated a relationship between *wages* and the unemployment rate. Although the statistical correlation between the inflation rate and the unemployment rate bears Phillips' name, Fisher (1926) originally pointed out such a relationship.

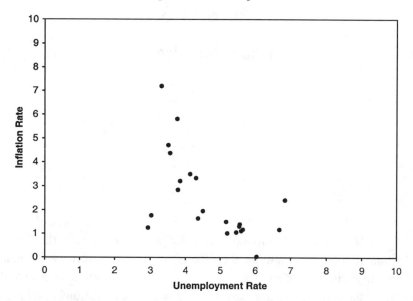

Figure 5.1. The Phillips curve (1948–1969). Before the 1970s, there appeared to be a stable inverse relationship between the inflation rate and the unemployment rate, often referred to as the Phillips curve. *Source:* The Federal Reserve Bank of St. Louis FRED database (http://www.stls.frb.org/fred/index.html).

rate becomes obvious when we look at U.S. data on these variables for the period from 1970 to the present, as in Figure 5.2.

What happened? Did some malevolent god, in order to frustrate the progress of humanity, suddenly alter the "laws" of economics at the very moment we discovered the way to end recessions?

Cross-Country Comparisons

Comparisons across countries add to the puzzle. Lucas (1973), for example, found that, if anything, inflation rates are on average higher in countries with lower average real growth rates as shown in Figure 5.3. How can these seemingly contradictory correlations come from a single world?

Expectations and the Neutrality of Money

In "Expectations and the Neutrality of Money," Lucas (1972) addressed this puzzle, proposing a model economy consistent with

- a positive short-run correlation between inflation and output,
- the disappearance of that correlation when policy makers attempt to exploit it, and
- a negative correlation between long-run inflation and output across countries.

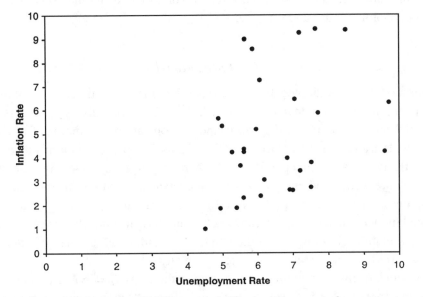

Figure 5.2. The Phillips curve (1970–present). Data on the unemployment rate and the inflation rate from the period after the 1960s display no apparent relationship between these two variables. *Source:* The Federal Reserve Bank of St. Louis FRED database (http://www.stls.frb.org/fred/index.html).

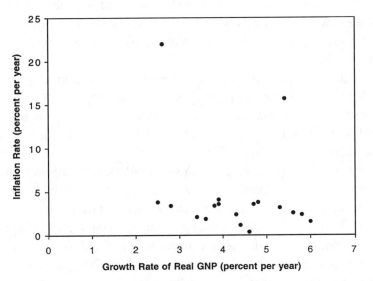

Figure 5.3. Inflation rate versus real output across countries. Data on inflation rates and real output demonstrate the weak tendency for average inflation to be high in countries with low average growth rates of real output. *Source:* Lucas (1973).

With this model as an illustration, Lucas revolutionized the methods of modern macroeconomic theory and practice.

The Lucas Model

For his model, Lucas adopted the standard overlapping generations model of money, adding the assumption that individuals live on two spatially separated islands. The total population across the two islands is constant over time. Half of the old individuals in any period live on each of the islands. The old are randomly distributed across the two islands, independently of where they lived when young. The young, however, are distributed unequally across the islands, with two-thirds of the young living on one island (and one-third on the other), in our simplified version of the original model.[2] In any single period, each island has an equal chance of having the large population of young. The outcome of this random assignment of population in any period has no effect on the outcome in any other period.

The stock of fiat money grows according to the rule $M_t = z_t M_{t-1}$. As in Chapter 3, increases in the fiat money stock are effected through lump-sum subsidies to each old person in every period t worth $a_t = [1 - (1/z_t)](v_t M_t / N)$ units of the consumption good.[3]

Informational assumptions are critical to individual behavior in this model. In any period, the young can directly observe neither the number of young people on their island nor the size of the subsidies to the old. The nominal stock of fiat money balances is known with a delay of one period. The price of goods on an island is observed but only by the people on that island. No communication between islands is possible within a period.

Although individuals are assumed to be unable to observe directly the realization of a variable of importance, the population of young people on their island, we do not assume that these people are stupid or irrational. They are assumed to know the possible outcomes they face and the probability of each outcome. They are free to infer whatever they can from the price they observe. We assume they make the most correct inference possible given the explicitly specified limits on what they can observe. The assumption that people understand the probabilities of outcomes important to their welfare was introduced by Muth (1961) as **rational expectations.**

While working with the overlapping generations model in this chapter, we will reinterpret an individual's problem to better reflect the difference between market and nonmarket goods. People are endowed when young with y units of time, which can be used in leisure, c_1, or as labor. The young work (give up leisure)

---

[2] We draw some of our exposition from a similarly simplified version of the Lucas model presented by Wallace (1980).

[3] Lucas (1972) assumes subsidies proportional to an individual's balances of fiat money.

to produce goods to sell to the old. We will let $l_t^i = l(p_t^i)$ represent the choice of labor by an individual born in period t for a given price of goods p_t^i on island i. Each unit of labor produces one unit of goods, implying that $l(p_t^i)$ also represents the individual's production of goods. Note that the amount of labor supplied by an individual depends on the price the individual receives on the goods produced. The individual's budget constraint when young in period t on island i can now be written as

$$c_{1,t}^i + l_t^i = c_{1,t}^i + v_t^i m_t^i = y. \tag{5.1}$$

The notation is that used in previous chapters, but with i superscripts to denote the island on which the individual was born. A young individual's holdings of fiat money (in units of the consumption good $v_t^i m_t^i$) is equal to the amount of goods that individual produces and sells on the market l_t^i. This represents the individual's real demand for fiat money. These holdings of fiat money, along with the lump-sum government transfer, will serve to finance consumption when old. In terms of notation, the budget constraint of an old person in period $t + 1$ may be represented by

$$c_{2,t+1}^{i,j} = v_{t+1}^j m_t^i + a_{t+1} = \left[\frac{v_{t+1}^j}{v_t^i} \right] l_t^i + a_{t+1} = \left[\frac{p_t^i}{p_{t+1}^j} \right] l_t^i + a_{t+1}. \tag{5.2}$$

Note second-period consumption depends on the island i where the individual is born and on the island j where the individual is randomly assigned when old. People choose their work effort l_t^i to maximize their expected utility for a given local price, p_t^i. Preferences are restricted to the case in which the young will choose to work more the greater the rate of return to their work. For a given future price of goods, the greater the current price of goods, the greater the rate of return to labor p_t^i / p_{t+1}^j. Therefore, we are assuming that an increase in the current price of goods, *other things equal*, will induce the young to work more.[4] In the words of standard microeconomic theory, the *substitution effect* of an increase in price (a high relative price of goods encourages output) is assumed to dominate the *wealth*, or *income*, *effect* (a high relative price of goods makes people wealthier and thus more desirous of reducing work in order to consume more leisure).

Nonrandom Inflation

Let us start by examining the behavior of individuals when the money stock grows at a fixed rate $z_t = z$ in all periods. In this case rational individuals can easily determine the current money stock by multiplying last period's money stock, which they are assumed to know, by z.

---

[4] See Lucas (1972) for the exact restrictions assumed on preferences.

Now we examine the market-clearing condition on an island with N^i young people. In period t, each young person's demand for fiat money is $l_t^i = l(p_t^i) = v_t^i m_t^i$ goods. Because there are N^i young people on island i, the total demand for fiat money is $N^i l(p_t^i)$. Because the old people are equally distributed across islands regardless of their island of birth, half the fiat money stock is brought to each island. Equating the total real supply of fiat money in period t, $v_t^i (M_t/2)$, we obtain the following condition clearing the market of fiat money for goods

$$N^i l\left(p_t^i\right) = v_t^i \frac{M_t}{2}. \tag{5.3}$$

Because the value of fiat money v_t^i is equal to the inverse of the price level p_t^i, we can rewrite Equation 5.3 as

$$N^i l\left(p_t^i\right) = \frac{M_t/2}{p_t^i}. \tag{5.4}$$

N^i is either $(1/3)N$ or $(2/3)N$, depending on whether island i has a small or large number of young people, respectively. Rearranging Equation 5.4, we find that

$$p_t^i = \frac{M_t/2}{N^i l\left(p_t^i\right)}. \tag{5.5}$$

Because the population of the young on each island is the only random variable, the market-clearing condition implicitly expresses the price level as a function of the population of the young (N^i). Therefore, observing the price of goods p_t^i allows all of the young to infer the number of the young on their island. Letting p_t^A and p_t^B denote the price of goods when the population is small $[N^A = (1/3)N]$ and large $[N^B = (2/3)N]$, respectively, we find from Equation 5.5 that on island A

$$p_t^A = \frac{M_t/2}{N^A l\left(p_t^A\right)} = \frac{M_t/2}{\frac{1}{3}Nl\left(p_t^A\right)}, \tag{5.6}$$

and on island B

$$p_t^B = \frac{M_t/2}{N^B l\left(p_t^B\right)} = \frac{M_t/2}{\frac{2}{3}Nl\left(p_t^B\right)}. \tag{5.7}$$

We can see that $p_t^A > p_t^B$, revealing that the price of goods is high when the population is low. The price of goods is driven up by the scarcity of young people producing goods. (We present a proof that $p_t^A > p_t^B$ in the appendix of this chapter.) Because the price of goods in the next period is independent of the price of goods this period, the greater the price this period, the greater the rate of return to producing goods, p_t^i/p_{t+1}^j. In sum, when the population on an island is low, people want to work more because the price of their goods and thus the rate of return on their labor is greater.

Put another way, those young people on an island with plenty of young people face a relatively low demand for their product; there are many young people available to produce for the old. A low price of goods results. Those young people on an island with few young people face a relatively high demand for their product; there are few young people available to produce for the old. A high price of goods results.

Our assumption that the substitution effect dominates the wealth effect ensures that the young respond to favorable rates of return by working more. This means that when there are few young people to produce for the old, each young person produces more; where there are many young people, each produces less. Of course, because there is always one island with $(2/3)N$ people and another with $(1/3)N$ young people, aggregate output does not depend on which of the islands has the larger number of young.

Prices here do the job we expect of them in market economies. They signal the true state of the world so that people can choose the quantity of their output that maximizes their well-being, given their true situation.

Will the young react to high prices in the same way if they know the high prices are caused by a once-and-for-all higher level of the fiat money stock? No. Look at the rate of return to work when the money stock is higher in both this period and the next.

$$\frac{v_{t+1}^j}{v_t^i} = \frac{p_t^i}{p_{t+1}^j} = \frac{\frac{M_t/2}{N^i l(p_t^i)}}{\frac{M_{t+1}/2}{N^j l(p_{t+1}^j)}} = \frac{N^j l(p_{t+1}^j)}{N^i l(p_t^i)} \frac{M_t}{M_{t+1}}. \tag{5.8}$$

A permanent increase in the money stock raises both M_t and M_{t+1} by the same portion and so fails to affect the relative price of goods in this period and the next. Therefore, a high current price caused by a permanent increase in the money stock does not at all affect the rate of return to labor and thus the desire to work. As we saw in Chapters 1 and 3, money is neutral in this economy.

What is the effect of anticipated inflation on work? Is money superneutral? No. Look again at Equation 5.8, this time with $M_{t+1} = zM_t$. As z increases, $M_t/M_{t+1} = M_t/zM_t = 1/z$ decreases, and the rate of return to work falls, discouraging work because the money balances earned from labor are taxed by the expansion of the money stock.[5] The decline in work effort as z increases translates into lower output.

---

[5] Lucas (1972) assumed subsidies proportional to an individual's money balances. In this case, output is unaffected by rate of expansion z of the fiat money stock.

Figure 5.4. Inflation and output across economies in the Lucas model. This figure illustrates the output predicted by the Lucas model for two economies, one with a high rate of expansion of the fiat money stock and one with a low rate.

Let us now construct a graph comparing output as a function of the (steady) rate of expansion z of the fiat money stock.

Figure 5.4 shows a negative correlation between inflation and output, the opposite of the Phillips curve correlation. [Not exactly having unemployment rates in this model, we use total labor supplied (denoted by L in the diagram), or equivalently aggregate output, which we expect to be negatively correlated with the unemployment rate.] It is important to keep in mind that Figure 5.4 represents a *cross section*, a comparison of two distinct economies, each with a different fixed inflation rate. In this way Figure 5.4 is better compared with Lucas's (1973) study of the correlation of average inflation and output across countries, which, like Figure 5.4, shows a negative correlation between inflation and output.

In contrast, the Phillips curve was a *time-series* comparison of inflation and unemployment in different periods of the same economy. Therefore, to judge whether our model is also consistent with the Phillips curve, we must introduce variations in the inflation rate over time.

Random Monetary Policy

Now let us consider a single two-island economy with the following random monetary policy:

$$M_t = \begin{cases} M_{t-1} & \text{with probability } \theta \quad (z_t = 1) \\ 2M_{t-1} & \text{with probability } 1 - \theta \ (z_t = 2) \end{cases} . \qquad (5.9)$$

The realization of monetary policy (the realized value of z_t) is kept secret from the young until all purchases have occurred – i.e., individuals do not learn M_t until period t is over.

As before, in order to determine their preferred work effort, the young wish to know whether they live with many or few other young people. Prices are the only thing directly observable by the young. Can they still deduce the population of young on the island by observing prices as they were able to do in the case in which z was nonrandom? Look again at the market clearing condition (Equation 5.3):

$$N^i l(p_t^i) = v_t^i(M_t/2), \tag{5.10}$$

or

$$p_t^i = \frac{M_t/2}{N^i l(p_t^i)} = \frac{z_t(M_{t-1}/2)}{N^i l(p_t^i)}. \tag{5.11}$$

Because both the island population N^i and the money stock are unknown to individuals, it is no longer always possible to infer the number of young just by looking at the price of goods. A high price, for example, may result from either a low population of young workers or a high fiat money stock. The distinction is important to the young. If the high price comes from a small number of young people, all of the young will want to work hard because they anticipate a good average return to their labor. On the other hand, if the high price comes from an increase in the fiat money stock, there is no reason to work especially hard. A high current money stock does not affect the anticipated rates of return to money and labor because it does not affect expectations of the future rate of money printing M_{t+1}/M_t; the monetary shocks are independent over time ("serially uncorrelated").

Is there anything about N^i that the young can learn from the price of goods? In our simplified version of the model with two possible population sizes and two possible rates of money printing, there are four possible states of the world represented by the various combinations of young people on the island and the realized value of z. Making use of Equation 5.11, let us look at what happens to the price level in each of those four cases.

Note from Table 5.1 that (for a given l) $p_t^a < p_t^b = p_t^c < p_t^d$. Therefore two of the four possible prices are unique: each can have occurred in only one particular combination of events. The price p_t^a can occur only when the money stock is small and the population is large, and the price p_t^d can occur only when the money stock is large and the population is small.

Therefore, if the young observe the price p_t^d, they can infer that the population on their island must be small. This implies that on average they can expect a good return to work, which encourages them to work hard, supplying l_t^d units of labor. Note that the price p_t^d is observed only when the fiat money stock is large ($z_t = 2$).

Table 5.1. *The four possible prices when the money stock is random*

	Number of Young People	
Growth Rate of Fiat Money Stock	$\frac{2}{3}N$	$\frac{1}{3}N$
$z_t = 1$	$p_t^a = \dfrac{M_{t-1}/2}{\frac{2}{3}Nl(p_t^a)}$	$p_t^b = \dfrac{M_{t-1}/2}{\frac{1}{3}Nl(p_t^b)}$
$z_t = 2$	$p_t^c = \dfrac{2(M_{t-1}/2)}{\frac{2}{3}Nl(p_t^c)}$	$p_t^d = \dfrac{2(M_{t-1}/2)}{\frac{1}{3}Nl(p_t^d)}$

Note: With a random money stock and population, there are four possible values for the price of output, only two of which are unique. The low price p_t^a can occur only when the growth rate of money is low and the population is large. The high price p_t^d can occur only when the growth rate of money is large and the population is small. However, when the intermediate price $p_t^b = p_t^c$ is observed, individuals cannot infer the particular values of the population and the growth rate of the money.

Similarly, if the young observe the price p_t^a, they can infer that the population on their island must be large. This implies that on average they can expect a poor return to work, which encourages them to work little, supplying l_t^a units of labor. Note that the price p_t^a is observed only when the fiat money stock is small ($z_t = 1$).

What happens in cases b and c? In these two cases the young are unable to infer the number of young on their island. They cannot tell if they are on an island with a small number of young people and a small money stock (case b) or on an island with a large number of young people but also a large money stock (case c). Unable to infer anything about the number of young on their island, each young worker in this situation will produce l^*, less than he would if he knew the population to be small and more than if he knew the population to be large. This will result in an intermediate price level, p^*, which is higher than p^a and lower than p^d.

Note that this randomized monetary policy does not always increase output. Although in case c people produce more than they would have if they knew their actual situation, in case b they produce less, imagining that the price they see may signal an increase in the money stock instead of an increase in the demand for their product.

This output behavior is summarized in Figure 5.5.

In an economy, there is always one island with a large population of young and another with a small population of young. Therefore, in periods when the money stock is large ($z_t = 2$), one island will be in case c and another will be in case d, and total output will be a weighted average of l^c and l^d. Similarly, in periods when the money stock is small ($z_t = 1$), one island will be in case a and another will be in case b, and total output will be a weighted average of l^a and l^b. A graph of total output L will look something like Figure 5.6. This results in a relationship similar

Figure 5.5. Inflation and output across islands. This figure illustrates the output predicted by the Lucas model for islands in a single economy with randomly high and low rates of expansion of the fiat money stock.

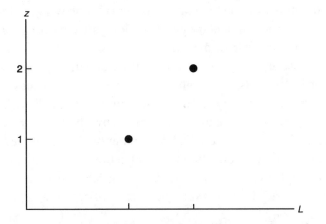

Figure 5.6. Inflation and aggregate output. This figure illustrates the total output predicted by the Lucas model in a single economy with randomly high and low rates of expansion of the fiat money stock.

to the Phillips curve. Output is high (unemployment is low), when the inflation rate is high (a high value of z).

The Lucas Critique of Econometric Policy Evaluation

Suppose that economists look at the time series plotted in Figure 5.6, the economy's experience over, say, 100 years, with no understanding of the model economy that generated it. The historical record clearly demonstrates that output is higher in the periods in which the fiat money stock is expanded. What might the economists be tempted to infer? . . . that money printing causes increased output?

The government controls the fiat money stock. Does this historical correlation suggest that the government can control aggregate output through its control of the money stock? If economists believe their government always to be more concerned with achieving high output than low rates of inflation, what policy might they then be tempted to propose? Print money to stimulate output in every period?

Will this policy work? What happens to output in this economy if the money stock is expanded in every period? We have already worked out the answer in Figure 5.4. Output is reduced, not increased. When the government inflates the fiat money stock in every period, people will no longer be confused about the state of the world. They know that cases *a* and *b* will no longer occur. Therefore, if they see the price p^c they will know there is a large number of people on their island, leading them to work less and create less output. Because they observe that the government always inflates, no longer will they imagine that they might be in case *b*, with a small number of young people and a small money stock. Inflation's boost to output under a random monetary policy no longer works because people are no longer fooled about the state of the world.

[Inflating almost always will not do the trick either. Suppose the government inflates in 99 of 100 periods. Although it is possible that people may find themselves in case *a* and *b* under this policy, anyone observing an intermediate price, p^*, knows that there is a 99 percent chance that this is caused by a high money stock and only a 1 percent chance that it is caused by a low number of young people. Although they may shade their labor decision a tiny bit to reflect the 1 percent chance of being in case *b*, young people observing p^* will base their labor reaction to the far likelier possibility that the price is almost surely the result of case *c*, a large population and a large stock of money.]

Our atheoretical economists have egg on their faces. They went to the monetary authorities with a well-intentioned policy designed to permanently stimulate output and wound up reducing it instead. A correlation stable for 100 years changed the very moment the government tried to exploit it. What went wrong? Why did the inflation/output curve change the sign of its slope?

The correlation of money and output, or indeed any set of variables, results from the reaction of decision makers to the environment they face. An important feature of this environment is government policies. In particular, the relation between money and output depends on the monetary policy being followed. When in this economy the policy changed from one of random inflation to one of steady inflation, the reactions of producers also changed.

A correlation between variables that is the result of the equilibrium interactions of an economy can be called a reduced-form correlation. In our example this would be represented by the slope of a line connecting the points in Figure 5.6. The "Lucas critique" points out that these reduced-form correlations are subject to change when the government changes its policies and thus the rules under which decision makers operate. The example we have studied is particularly startling in that when the government changes from a policy of random inflation to a policy of steady inflation, the correlation (slope) not only changes, it also changes sign – from positive to negative.

How then can we evaluate policies? We need some understanding about how people will react to the new policy: we need a theory. If we understand people's motives (preferences) and constraints (physical limitations, informational restrictions, government policies), we can predict how people will react to changes in a policy. Lucas's point is not that econometric policy evaluation is impossible, but that it cannot be done without a theory, an understanding of how the economy works. It is not sufficient just to look at the data. The correlations found in the data are subject to change when government policy changes.

Optimal Policy

What is the best policy? Should the government play dice with the economy? Let us look at the welfare consequences of a randomized monetary policy.

By randomizing the rate of expansion of the fiat money stock, the government creates confusion about the meaning of prices. In essence, isn't the government withholding information about the true state of the world? People are not always sure whether a price increase signals an increase in the demand for their product, in which case they benefit by producing more, or an increase in the money stock, in which case they will not make themselves better off by increasing production. The more often the government expands the money stock, the more people believe that any observed price increase is just the government playing with the money stock. It follows that a major cost of randomizing the money stock is that people fail to take advantage of actual increases in the demand for their output.

Even if the government could fool people, should it? Why should the government want to fool people into producing more than they would choose to produce if they knew their actual situation? A baseball pitcher or a soccer player will randomize the location of the ball to fool the batter or goalie, but these players are on opposing teams. Isn't the government on the same team as the public it represents? Is the proper goal of a government manipulation of output or the welfare of its citizens?

Summary

We began this chapter by noting the observed relationship between the unemployment rate and the inflation rate and the subsequent breakdown of that relationship. This chapter presented a model consistent with these observations – a simplified version of Lucas's 1972 model.

In this model, young people cannot directly observe a real variable important to their output decision, the number of other young people producing on the island on which they were born. We first considered a case of nonrandom inflation, where the monetary authority adheres to a fixed growth rate of the fiat money stock. In this case, agents could infer the number of young people producing on their island by observing the price of goods. An increase in inflation, which in this case is always known, lowers the rates of return on labor, discouraging work effort and lowering output. This is consistent with Lucas's observation that average inflation rates and output are negatively correlated across countries.

When we examined random inflation in this model, the relation of inflation to output dramatically changed, generating a Phillips curve. Random inflation complicated an individual's work effort decision because agents could no longer always infer the number of young people on their island by observing the price of the good. If, for example, a high price was caused by a small number of young people on the island, the young would want to work hard because they expect a high average return to their labor. On the other hand, if a high price is caused by an increase in the fiat money stock, there is no incentive to work hard. Because of the randomness of the money stock, prices are less informative about the true state of the world. This inability of individuals to determine the true state of the world causes them, at times, to work harder and produce more output than they would choose to do if they were able to determine their true situation. At other times, they mistakenly work less than they would choose to do if they were able to determine their true situation. When we observe this economy over time, we find that high inflation rates are associated with high levels of output (low unemployment rates) – the Phillips curve.

This relation between output and inflation depends crucially on the assumption of random inflation. A government attempting to exploit this relation by inflating in any systematic way will find that the positive correlation between inflation and output disappears.

The importance of the Lucas model lies not primarily in its explanation of the money/output correlation, as interesting as it may be. There are certainly other explanations, some of which we will study in later chapters, that may or may not do a better job of explaining that correlation.

Lucas's paper changed macroeconomics by demonstrating that the correlations among macroeconomic aggregates are subject to change when economic policy changes. This showed macroeconomists the pitfalls in evaluating policy by looking simply at correlations in the data, without a working theory of how people may react to policy changes. Those macroeconomists who open their eyes to Lucas's critique are thereafter compelled to fully specify the environment in which the economic agents studied make their decisions. It is with the Lucas critique in mind that this book endeavors to present only explicit models, specifying all our assumptions about people's preferences and constraints.

Exercises

5.1 Consider the following version of the model of this chapter. The number of young individuals born on island i in period t, N_t^i, is random according to the following specification:

$$N_t^i = \begin{cases} \frac{4}{5}N & \text{with probability } 0.5 \\ \frac{1}{5}N & \text{with probability } 0.5 \end{cases}.$$

Assume that the fiat money stock grows at the fixed rate $z_t = z$ in all periods.

a. Set up the budget constraints of the individuals when young and when old in terms of l_t^i. Also set up the goverment budget constraint and money market-clearing condition. Find the lifetime budget constraint (combine the budget constraints of the young and old by substituting for l_t^i).

b. On which island would you prefer to be born? Explain with reference to the rate of return to labor.

c. Show how the rate of return to labor and the individual's labor supply depend on the value of z.

For the following parts, assume that the growth rate of the fiat money stock z_t is random according to

$$z_t = \begin{cases} 1 & \text{with probability } \theta \\ 4 & \text{with probability } 1 - \theta \end{cases}.$$

The realization of z_t is kept secret from the young until all purchases of goods have occurred (individuals do not learn M_t until period t is over). Given these changes in assumptions, answer the following questions.

d. How many states of the world would the agents be able to observe if information about every variable were perfectly available? Describe those possible states.

e. How many states of the world are the agents able to distinguish when there is limited information (they do not know the value of z_t)?

f. Draw a graph of labor supply and the growth rate of the fiat money stock in each possible state of the world when there is limited information. What is the correlation observed between money creation and output?

g. Suppose the government wanted to take advantage of the relation between money creation and output. If it always inflates ($\theta = 1$), will the graph you derived in part f remain the same? Explain fully.

Appendix: A Proof by Contradiction

After presentation of Equations 5.6 and 5.7, we claimed that $p_t^A > p_t^B$. This appendix offers a proof of that claim. We utilize a common technique in mathematics whereby a proof is established by assuming the opposite conclusion and by then showing this assumption leads to a contradiction.

We assume the opposite of our conclusion: $p_t^A \leq p_t^B$. From the assumption that individuals supply a greater amount of labor the larger the price they obtain for their output, this implies that

$$l\left(p_t^A\right) \leq l\left(p_t^B\right). \tag{5.12}$$

Multiplying both sides of Equation 5.12 by $(1/3)N$, we obtain

$$\frac{1}{3}Nl\left(p_t^A\right) \leq \frac{1}{3}Nl\left(p_t^B\right), \tag{5.13}$$

which in turn implies

$$\frac{1}{3}Nl\left(p_t^A\right) \leq \frac{1}{3}Nl\left(p_t^B\right) < \frac{2}{3}Nl\left(p_t^B\right). \tag{5.14}$$

Rearranging Equation 5.14 yields

$$\frac{1}{\frac{1}{3}Nl\left(p_t^A\right)} > \frac{1}{\frac{2}{3}Nl\left(p_t^B\right)}. \tag{5.15}$$

By multiplying both sides of Equation 5.15 by $M_t/2$, we find that

$$\frac{M_t/2}{\frac{1}{3}Nl\left(p_t^A\right)} > \frac{M_t/2}{\frac{2}{3}Nl\left(p_t^B\right)}. \tag{5.16}$$

Comparing Equation 5.16 with our expressions for p_t^A and p_t^B in Equations 5.6 and 5.7, we see that the left-hand side of Equation 5.16 is p_t^A and the right-hand side is p_t^B. This implies that $p_t^A > p_t^B$. This contradicts our original assumption that $p_t^A \leq p_t^B$. The original assumption must be wrong, proving that in fact $p_t^A > p_t^B$.

Part II

Banking

UNTIL NOW we have confined our attention to model economies where fiat or commodity money was the only asset. Although this was useful while we learned some basic features of monetary economies, it is hardly realistic. Therefore let us now study the demand for money in the presence of another asset. The introduction of alternative assets will also provide a framework in which to study banking (the intermediation of other assets into money) and central banking (the management of the monetary system). We also introduce some basic concepts that will be useful in later chapters: a diminishing marginal product of capital, rate of return equality, and risk aversion.

Chapter 6 begins with a model of capital, an alternative asset to money. Among assets, capital has particular importance because its level affects output. We discover conditions under which individuals are willing to hold money and capital (or other assets) simultaneously. In the appendices to Chapter 6, we supplement our discussion of alternative assets to fiat money. Appendix A presents a model of a credit economy, in which private loans are used to finance consumption. Appendix B discusses the determination of the socially optimal level of capital in an economy.

A central question in the study of monetary economics is why people hold fiat money when there are alternative assets that pay higher rates of return. Chapter 7 investigates one possible answer to that question by noting that money is more liquid than other assets. In the course of the investigation, we also discover important relationships between real and nominal interest rates and inflation rates. Chapter 7 also introduces a model of banking whereby banks help to correct the mismatch between the maturities of various assets and aid in the formation of capital. We also demonstrate in the appendix to Chapter 7 that banks can fill another role by serving as monitors of risky ventures.

Chapter 8 provides a first glimpse of an important institution of modern economies – the central bank. We explore the macroeconomic effects of the reserve requirements that central banks often impose on financial institutions. We also see how central banks affect economies by their lending policies.

Chapter 9 studies another central puzzle in monetary economics – the observed correlation between money and output. This chapter presents a model that displays this important correlation and other observed facts. We also examine whether monetary aggregates are useful guides for determining monetary policy.

Chapter 10 analyzes a monetary arrangement in which a central bank uses the return from assets that it owns to pay interest on the money it issues. Monetary policy will be seen to work very differently under this arrangement than it does under a system of fiat (unbacked) money. The appendix to Chapter 10 studies one possible consequence of paying interest on money – price level indeterminacy – and shows how this potential problem can be solved.

Chapter 11 examines how banks play a role in the payments system through which private debt is repaid. To perform their role as the clearinghouses of private debt, banks may need to temporarily issue additional liquid assets. The needed liquidity can be provided by issuing private bank notes or by establishing a central bank discount window where banks may borrow currency.

A common problem in modern economies is the failure of financial institutions. Chapter 12 investigates bank risk by presenting a model in which bank runs occur. We also make some suggestions about how to minimize the exposure of financial institutions to runs and failure. An important topic that arises in this discussion is the provision of deposit insurance by the government.

Chapter 6

Capital

SO FAR, INDIVIDUALS in our model have had only one way to acquire consumption at a later time – by holding fiat money. In the real world, however, there are many other assets. In this chapter, we concentrate on one particular alternative asset, capital. We focus on capital here and in later chapters because capital produces goods and thus affects an economy's output. Nevertheless, our basic conclusions are applicable to other assets. We will see how the presence of an alternative asset affects people's willingness to hold fiat money. We begin by looking at the simplest model of capital.

Capital

Consider the following production technology: if k_t units of the consumption good are converted into capital goods at time t, at time $t + 1$ you will receive $x k_t$ consumption goods, where x is some positive constant. This implies that the gross real rate of return on capital is x. We will assume that the capital goods produce only once before disintegrating (the depreciation rate is 100 percent).[1]

As in previous models, individuals in the single-country economy are endowed with y units of the consumption good when young and zero units when old. Population grows at the gross rate n. Each member of the initial old begins with a stock of capital that produces $x k_0$ goods in the first period.

Let us first analyze an equilibrium without fiat money. The capital technology enables the young to use some of today's consumption good to produce the consumption good at a later date. When young, individuals can convert part of their endowment into capital and consume the rest. This implies that in the first period

---

[1] This linear capital production technology was introduced into the overlapping generations model by Cass and Yaari (1966). See also Wallace (1980). A production technology that uses capital and labor together is described by Diamond (1965).

of life the budget constraint facing individuals born in period t is

$$c_{1,t} + k_t \leq y. \tag{6.1}$$

When old, the individual will consume the goods produced by the capital xk_t. The second period constraint is then

$$c_{2,t+1} \leq xk_t. \tag{6.2}$$

We can combine Equations 6.1 and 6.2 into a lifetime budget constraint. Equation 6.2 tells us that $k_t \geq c_{2,t+1}/x$. Substituting this into Equation 6.1, we obtain the lifetime budget constraint

$$c_{1,t} + \frac{c_{2,t+1}}{x} \leq y. \tag{6.3}$$

We can see that x determines the slope of the budget line. If, for example, $x > 1$, then the vertical intercept of the budget line will lie farther from the origin than the horizontal intercept. How much capital will an individual desire? As before, the answer is derived by superimposing the individual's indifference map on the budget set. This is done in Figure 6.1.

This simple model of capital assumes that the output from each unit of capital is the same regardless of how much capital already exists. The rate of return of capital is simply assumed to be some number unaffected by any economic forces. Although the assumption of a fixed rate of return of capital makes the model very easy for us to

Figure 6.1. The individual's choice of capital. This figure portrays the budget line when capital pays the gross rate of return x. Individuals will maximize utility by choosing the consumption pattern (c_1^*, c_2^*). Individual capital holdings will be $k^* = y - c_1^*$.

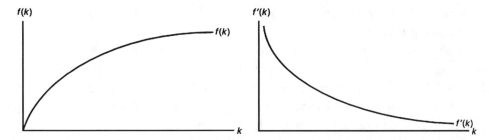

Figure 6.2. The total and marginal product of capital. The left-hand figure represents the amount of output that is created as the amount of capital varies. We assume that the quantity of output increases as the amount of capital increases. However, the slope of the total product curve diminishes as capital increases. This is reflected in the right-hand diagram, which plots the slope of the total product curve. The slope of the total product curve is the marginal product of capital.

use, we sometimes need a more general model, especially to answer questions about how economic forces or government policies may affect the rate of return on capital.

Consider then the alternative assumption that capital exhibits a **diminishing marginal product**; as capital is increased, the added output from an extra unit of capital gets smaller (total output will still rise as long as the marginal product of capital is positive). We will write output from capital as a function, $f(k)$, of capital per person k. Then the **marginal product of capital**, the added output resulting from the addition of one extra unit of capital, can be written as $f'(k)$. The case of a diminishing marginal product of capital is graphed in the right frame of Figure 6.2.

Figure 6.2 also plots $f(k)$ (the upward-sloping curve, left frame), which represents the amount of output (or total product) generated in period $t + 1$ from the purchase of k units of capital in period t. Diminishing marginal product of capital is portrayed by the fact that the slope of the $f(k)$ curve decreases as k increases. In fact, the marginal product curve $f'(k)$ is merely the slope of the $f(k)$ curve.[2] The first model of this chapter considered a case in which the marginal product of capital $f'(k)$ was equal to a constant, x.

Rate-of-Return Equality

Capital is not the only alternative to fiat money. People can store value over time in many other ways. They might purchase land and sell it when they want to consume. They might make loans to people who want to borrow against future income.

What are the implications of the presence of alternative assets? Consider, for example, an economy with both capital and private debt (loans) that offers the rate

---

[2] For those students familiar with calculus, the marginal product function $f'(k)$ is the derivative of the function $f(k)$.

of return r. Is there a relationship that must hold between the rates of return on capital and private debt?

Suppose that the rate of return on private debt r is less than the rate of return on capital x. Would people be willing to make loans to other people who wish to borrow? No. To do so would imply accepting a lower rate of return than can be obtained by creating capital. In this case, people would prefer to put all their savings into the creation of capital and would make no loans.

But what if borrowers must obtain loans? Consider, for example, someone with an endowment of goods when old but nothing when young. This person must borrow if he is to have any consumption when young. (Recall that we have assumed that individuals in our models will go to great lengths to avoid situations where their consumption is zero in any period.) This implies that borrowers are placed in the position in which they must entice people to make them loans. How can they do so? By offering at least as good a rate of return on loans as an individual could obtain by creating capital.

Suppose, on the other hand, that r exceeds x – that the rate of return on private loans exceeds that on capital. Would anyone choose to save in the form of capital? Again, the answer is no. In such a circumstance, people would choose to save solely in the form of loans to borrowers.

From our discussion here, it is clear that, for people to be willing to hold both capital and loans as assets, the rates of return on these two assets must be identical ($r = x$). Any imbalance between these two rates of return will imply that people will gravitate to the asset, loans or capital, that pays the highest rate of return.

However, it is important to realize that we have been implicitly assuming that private debt and capital are perfect substitutes from the viewpoint of people willing to save. Either asset can provide for second-period consumption just as well as the other. In such a circumstance, to observe both assets being held, their rates of return must be identical.

Consider more general versions of the preceding model in which there are many assets available to individuals. Furthermore, suppose there is no uncertainty about returns and no government restrictions that interfere with individuals' holdings of assets. If individuals are willing to hold all the available assets simultaneously, the rates of return on these assets must be identical. We refer to this as the principle of **rate-of-return equality**.

Can Fiat Money Coexist with Another Asset?

Now suppose that we introduce fiat money into our economy with capital and private loans, so that we now have three potential ways for lenders to save. People who want to save will view capital, loans, and fiat money as perfect substitutes. Extending our previous discussion, it should be obvious that, for lenders to be willing to hold all three assets as a form of saving, their rates of return must be equal. We know that the rate of return on fiat money is n/z when the population and the stock of fiat money are growing at the gross rates n and z, respectively. Therefore, if all three assets are held, rate-of-return equality requires that $n/z = r = x$.

If the rate of return on fiat money is less than that on loans or capital, then lenders will not choose to use fiat money as a form of saving. So for fiat money to be valued, its rate of return must be at least as large as those of the alternative assets, capital and loans.

Example 6.1 Consider an overlapping generations economy with two assets – capital and money. Suppose the number of young people born in period t is determined by $N_t = 1.5N_{t-1}$. Capital pays the gross rate of return $x = 1.25$. For what values of z will fiat money be valued?

The Tobin Effect

We have seen that, in a model economy where capital and fiat money coexist as perfect substitutes, we will observe rate-of-return equality between these two assets. Let us further explore the implications of this result in a situation in which capital displays a diminishing marginal product.

When capital and fiat money are both valued, the desired capital stock is determined by the condition that the rate of return on capital equals the rate of return on fiat money n/z. What is the rate of return on capital in the case of a diminishing marginal product? This is given by capital's marginal product, $f'(k)$, which tells us how much additional output is produced when the capital stock increases by 1 unit. Hence, rate-of-return equality implies that $f'(k)$ must be equal to n/z. From this condition, we can determine an individual's desired capital stock. When the rate of return on fiat money equals n/z, the capital stock is k^*, as shown in Figure 6.3.

Let us now consider a permanent increase in the anticipated rate of fiat money creation from z to z'. This increase in z generates inflation and lowers the anticipated rate of return on fiat money from n/z to n/z'. The lower rate of return on fiat money induces people to hold capital instead of fiat money. This switch to capital increases the capital stock, which lowers the marginal product of capital. People will stop switching from fiat money to capital either when fiat money balances have fallen to zero or when the rate of return on capital falls to the new lower rate of return on fiat money (when capital reaches $k^{*'}$ in Figure 6.3). The substitution of private capital for fiat money in reaction to an increase in anticipated inflation is called the **Tobin effect**, described in Tobin (1965).

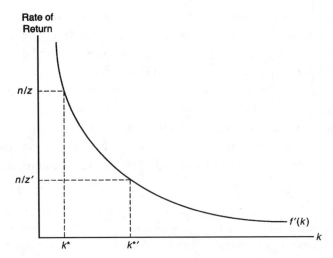

Figure 6.3. An individual's choice of capital in the presence of fiat money. When fiat money and capital coexist as perfect substitutes, an individual invests in capital up to the point where the marginal product of capital $f'(k)$ is equal to the rate of return on fiat money n/z. A permanent increase in the anticipated rate of fiat money creation lowers the rate of return on fiat money, inducing individuals to create more capital.

We conclude that, when capital and fiat money are substitutes, an increase in the rate of fiat money creation leads to an increase in the capital stock. Given that capital generates output in the following period, the larger capital stock implies a subsequent increase in output. In period t, total real output (**gross domestic product**, or **GDP**) in this economy equals the total endowment ($N_t y$) plus output generated by capital that was created in the previous period. Because in period $t-1$ each individual created k_{t-1} units of capital and there were N_{t-1} of those individuals, real GDP in period t equals

$$\text{GDP}_t = N_t y + N_{t-1} f(k_{t-1}). \tag{6.4}$$

If we live in a world in which capital and money are substitutes, should we use anticipated inflation, brought about by an increase in z, as a tool to increase output? The answer may be no – for two distinct reasons.

First, we must remember not to confuse output with welfare. The goal of a benevolent government is to increase the welfare (utility) of its citizens and not solely the output. The increase in z caused people to increase their holdings of capital, with the result being a decline in the rate of return on capital. As a consequence, the economy's capital stock may not be at its optimal level. As we show in Appendix B of this chapter, an economy's capital stock is optimal when the marginal product of capital is equal to n, the growth rate of the economy. A government policy of inflation would lead to capital formation above the optimal level.

Second, it is important to note that this effect is not large in the real world. Relative to the capital stock, the size of the fiat money stock in an economy is minuscule. At the end of 1997, the total net private capital stock in the United States was $17,316 billion. At the same time, the total fiat money stock was $490 billion.[3] Even if the entire fiat money stock were replaced by capital, the capital stock would increase by less than 3 percent.

When Fiat Money and Other Assets Are Not Substitutes

Let us now take a closer look at the effects of anticipated inflation on interest rates, capital, and output when fiat money and other assets are not substitutes. In particular we will examine the case in which the rate of return of capital and other assets exceeds that of fiat money. This certainly seems to be the case in most economies, where most debt pays (nominal) interest and fiat money pays none. This raises an obvious question: why would fiat money still be valued? We will postpone this important question for later chapters. For now let us simply assume that each young person is required by law to acquire real balances of fiat money worth a fixed number of goods, q^*. This requirement is a simple way to ensure that fiat money is valued even if another asset has a better rate of return. This will let us take a first look at the effects of anticipated inflation when the rate of return of fiat money is dominated by that of other assets.[4]

Nominal Interest Rates

The interest rates cited by financial intermediaries and the press in the real world are nominal rates, describing the number of dollars paid in interest for each dollar lent. In times of inflation these nominal rates do not reflect the real rate of return, the number of goods paid in interest for each good lent. Because utility depends on real consumption, it is important to learn the connection between real and nominal rates.

Let us write the **nominal interest rate** in period t, the rate of return in units of money, as R_t and the **real interest rate**, the rate of return in goods, as r_t. As always, we refer to gross rates of return. Remember that to find net rates of return, just subtract 1 from the gross rate. Let p_t denote the price of a good in fiat money, the inverse of the value of a unit of fiat money, v_t. The gross nominal rate on a one-period loan made at t (R_t) is the dollars received at $t + 1$ divided by the dollars lent at t. Therefore, to find the real rate from a given nominal rate, we must divide

---

[3] The capital stock data is from the *Survey of Current Business* (August 1999, Table B.12, p. D-35). It is the amount of fixed private capital (nonresidential and residential). The value of the fiat money stock is series bogambns from the Federal Reserve Bank of St. Louis FRED database (http://www.stls.frb.org/fred/index.html).

[4] We take a more serious look at required holding of money in Chapter 8.

each dollar value by the price level at that time (or multiply by the value of a dollar at that time). This is done in Equation 6.5 for a loan of d dollars.

$$r_t = \frac{\frac{R_t d}{p_{t+1}}}{\frac{d}{p_t}} = \frac{R_t p_t}{p_{t+1}}. \tag{6.5}$$

By the definition of these terms this relation must always hold between the gross rates of nominal interest, real interest, and inflation. Rearranging terms, we can express this relation in the following way:

$$R_t = r_t \left(\frac{p_{t+1}}{p_t} \right). \tag{6.6}$$

If we subtract 1 from each side of Equation 6.6, we can express this relationship in terms of net rates:

$$
\begin{aligned}
R_t - 1 &= r_t \left(\frac{p_{t+1}}{p_t} \right) - 1 \\
&= [(r_t - 1) + 1]\left[\left(\frac{p_{t+1}}{p_t} \right) - 1 + 1 \right] - 1 \\
&= (r_t - 1) + \left(\frac{p_{t+1}}{p_t} - 1 \right) + (r - 1)\left(\frac{p_{t+1}}{p_t} - 1 \right).
\end{aligned}
\tag{6.7}
$$

Equation 6.7 states that the **net nominal rate of interest** $(R_t - 1)$ equals the **net real rate** $(r_t - 1)$ plus the **net inflation rate** $[(p_{t+1}/p_t) - 1]$ plus the product of the two. For low values of the real interest rate and inflation rate, this last term is small and is often ignored.

What is the net inflation rate, according to the results of our model? From Chapter 3, we learned that the gross rate of return on fiat money (v_{t+1}/v_t) in the case of a growing economy and an expanding fiat money stock is n/z. We also know that the price level in every period t is related to the value of fiat money in the same period by

$$p_t = \frac{1}{v_t}. \tag{6.8}$$

From the relationship $v_{t+1}/v_t = n/z$ and Equation 6.8, we find that the net inflation rate is

$$\frac{p_{t+1}}{p_t} - 1 = \frac{v_t}{v_{t+1}} - 1 = \frac{z}{n} - 1. \tag{6.9}$$

Example 6.2 Suppose the fiat money stock changes according to the rule $M_t = 1.5M_{t-1}$ and the number of young people born in each generation evolves according to $N_t = 1.25N_{t-1}$.

Let the gross real interest rate be 1.1.

a. Calculate the gross and net inflation rates.
b. Calculate the gross and net real rates of return of fiat money.
c. Calculate the gross and net nominal interest rates.
d. Calculate the net nominal interest rate using the approximation $R - 1 = (r - 1) + (p_{t+1}/p_t - 1)$. Compare your answer here with the one in part c.

Anticipated Inflation and the Nominal Interest Rate

If we return to Equation 6.7, we can examine the effect of inflation on real and nominal rates of interest. In particular, we want to ask if the nominal rate fully adjusts to an anticipated change in the inflation rate so that the real interest rate remains unchanged. The predicted full adjustment of the nominal interest rate to anticipated inflation is called the **Fisher effect**, after Irving Fisher, an American economist of the early part of this century.

Assume that capital pays the constant gross rate of return x. By rate-of-return equality, the real interest rate in this economy must equal the real rate of return on capital, a parameter given by the physical environment. No one would make a loan unless it paid at least this real return. A loan must therefore offer a nominal rate of return, R, so that

$$x = \frac{\frac{R}{p_{t+1}}}{\frac{1}{p_t}} = \frac{R v_{t+1}}{v_t} = \frac{R n}{z} \tag{6.10}$$

or

$$R = x\left(\frac{z}{n}\right). \tag{6.11}$$

Therefore, the nominal interest rate rises with anticipated inflation to keep the real interest rate constant at x.

As shown in Figure 6.4, there is a tendency for nominal interest rates and inflation rates to move together in accordance with the Fisher effect. However, because of changes in the real interest rate, the gap between the nominal interest rate and the inflation rate is not constant. It is not possible to tell from this graph whether real interest rate changes are influenced by the rate of inflation or by some other factor. The following section suggests one way inflation may affect real interest rates.

Anticipated Inflation and the Real Interest Rate

An exception to the Fisher effect may occur if two conditions are met. If fiat money and capital are substitutes, a rise in the anticipated inflation rate will encourage

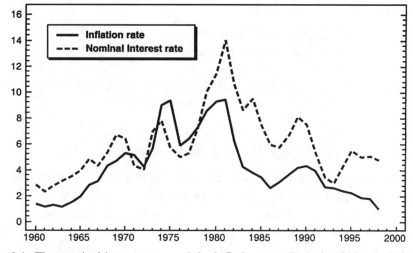

Figure 6.4. The nominal interest rate and the inflation rate. Periods of high inflation rates are typically associated with high nominal interest rates. *Source*: The inflation rate is the annual inflation rate according to the GNP deflator. The interest rate is the 90-day Treasury bill rate. Both series come from the Federal Reserve bank of St. Louis FRED database (http://www.stls.frb.org/fred/index.html).

people to reduce their holdings of fiat money and increase their holdings of capital.[5] This is the Tobin effect.

If we also assume that capital has a diminishing marginal product, the increase in capital described by the Tobin effect can occur only with a reduction in the marginal product of capital. This represents a reduction in the real rate of return on capital and thus, by rate-of-return equality, a reduction in the real rate of interest. In this case, the increase in anticipated inflation will still lead to a rise in the nominal interest rate, but, because of the simultaneous decrease in the real interest rate, the nominal rate will not rise by the full amount of the rise in anticipated inflation.

Risk

In studying rate-of-return equality, we have assumed that all assets pay a rate of return that is known with complete certainty. What would happen to rate-of-return equality if instead we assumed that one asset had a random rate of return? For example, what happens if we modify our assumption about the perfect repayment of loans? Suppose there is some positive probability that a loan will not be repaid by the borrower – the borrower may **default** on a loan. This means there is an element of risk in making a loan. As before, suppose that capital always pays the rate of return x. Here, capital and loans are not viewed as perfect substitutes. One of the

---

[5] Freeman (1985) shows that a fixed fiat money stock is optimal in this economy, just as it was in the economy without capital.

assets (loans) pays an unknown rate of return, and the other (capital) pays a return that is certain.

If people do not care about risk (are **risk neutral**), we would expect rate-of-return equality to hold on average. For lenders to be willing to make a loan they would have to receive on average a rate of return on loans that equaled the rate of return on capital. By an asset's average or expected rate of return we mean the expected value of its rate of return. If there are a finite number of possible rates of return, the expected rate of return can be calculated as the sum of each rate of return multiplied by the probability it will occur. Suppose an asset pays n possible rates of return, $r_1, r_2, \ldots, r_n$. The probabilities of paying each rate of return $r_1, r_2, \ldots, r_n$ are $\pi_1, \pi_2, \ldots, \pi_n$, respectively. The **expected rate of return** on this asset is measured by the expected value of its rate of return, which we denote as $E(r)$. We calculate this expected value by

$$E(r) = \pi_1 r_1 + \pi_2 r_2 + \cdots + \pi_n r_n. \tag{6.12}$$

Consider, for example, a loan paying a 15 percent net interest rate (a gross rate of return of 1.15) with a 10 percent chance of a default returning only half the principal. This loan offers two possible rates of return. With a probability of 0.9, the loan pays a gross rate of return of 1.15, When there is a default, the loan pays a gross rate of return of 0.5, with a probability of 0.1. To calculate the expected gross rate of return of this loan, we add together the possible rates of return multiplied by their respective probabilities,

$$E(r) = (0.9)(1.15) + (0.1)(0.5) = 1.085,$$

or an expected net rate of return equal to $1.085 - 1 = 0.085 = 8.5$ percent.

Example 6.3 Find the expected rate of return of farm machinery that costs 10 goods but produces 18 goods in normal weather, 8 goods in rainy weather, and 5 goods in a drought. There is a one-fourth chance of rainy weather occurring and a 10 percent chance of drought. Find the expected rate of return. Note that the gross rate of return is the total return divided by the amount invested.

Are people risk neutral? Suppose you were offered this bet: A fair coin will be tossed. If it lands heads, you will lose all your possessions; if it lands tails, your possessions will be doubled. Will you take this bet? If not, you are **risk averse**. Most people are likely to refuse this bet because the drop in utility from losing the bet exceeds the gain in utility from winning the bet even though the potential loss and potential gain are equal when measured in goods.

If people are risk averse, it does not mean they will never accept a risky asset. As a risk-averse person, you may not wager $1,000 on the toss of a fair coin if you stand to win only another $1,000. You may, however, take the chance of losing

$1,000 if you will gain $100,000 by winning the toss. If people dislike risk (are risk averse), they will not hold a risky asset if its expected rate of return only equals that of the risk-free asset. They will hold a risky asset only if its expected rate of return exceeds that of the risk-free asset, compensating for the risk. The extra average rate of return that is necessary to entice people to hold a risky asset is called a risk premium. The greater the potential loss and the greater the probability of the loss, the larger the risk premium must be.

Suppose a risky asset pays an expected rate of return equal to $E(r_{risky})$ and that a risk-free asset always pays the rate of return r_{safe}. Then the risk premium on the risky asset is defined by

$$\text{risk premium} = E(r_{risky}) - r_{safe}. \tag{6.13}$$

Summary

In earlier chapters, money was the only asset available to individuals in our model economies. However, in the real world, many alternative assets to fiat money exist. The goal of this chapter has been to understand the effects that the presence of these alternative assets might create.

To begin, we introduced a simple model of capital, an important alternative asset to money because capital produces goods. At first, we considered capital in isolation in a model without fiat money.

We then asked what might happen if we introduced other assets into the model, so that these alternative assets competed with capital. It is here that we encountered the important principle of rate-of-return equality. This principle states that, if assets are viewed as perfect substitutes, then for individuals to be willing to hold all the assets simultaneously, their rates of return must be equal.

However, we must keep in mind the strong assumptions behind the principle of rate-of-return equality. It is important that all of the assets be viewed as perfect substitutes for one another. If, for example, one of the assets is risky and the others are not, we would not expect rate-of-return equality to hold. Because it is easily observed that, in the real world, fiat money does not pay the same rate of return as capital and many other assets, we must look for reasons that fiat money is not a perfect substitute for other assets. We will study this topic in the next chapter.

Exercises

6.1 Suppose people in our overlapping generations model have the opportunity either to hold fiat money with complete safety or to lend to someone who may never repay the loan. The chance of such a default is 10 percent. Assume a stationary monetary equilibrium in which the population grows at a net rate of 8 percent and the fiat money stock is fixed. What real interest rate will be charged the borrower if people are risk neutral? What can you say about the level of the real interest rate if people are instead risk averse?

6.2 Suppose capital is risky and pays gross real rates of return of 1.2, 1.1, and 0.9 with probabilities 0.1, 0.7, and 0.2, respectively. A risk-free asset pays a safe gross real rate of return of 1.04. What is the expected rate of return on capital? What is the risk premium of capital?

Appendix A: A Model of Private Debt

In Chapter 6, we introduced a model in which individuals held capital. We also discussed the implications of introducing private loans into that model. In this part of the appendix, we develop a formal model of private debt, IOUs issued by individuals.

Private Debt

To introduce IOUs into our simple model with two-period lives, let there be two types of people – borrowers, endowed with nothing when young and y when old, and lenders, endowed with y when young and nothing when old.[6] For simplicity, there is no fiat money or capital in the economy (we will introduce capital later in the appendix).

The Lender Problem

A lender in the first period of life divides her endowment between consumption $(c_{1,L})$ and loans to borrowers (l). When old, her consumption $(c_{2,L})$ is limited by the amount received from loans repaid with interest (rl). (To reduce the notational burden, we drop the time subscripts and consider only stationary equilibria.) Note that r is the gross real rate of interest on private loans. This is the return from both principal and interest, which is 1 plus the net rate of interest. If, for example, the net rate of interest is 9 percent, the gross rate of interest is 1.09. We write a lender's constraints at equality as

$$c_{1,L} + l = y, \tag{6.14}$$

and

$$c_{2,L} = rl. \tag{6.15}$$

---

[6] For more formal undergraduate-level treatments of the interaction of fiat money with loans, see Wallace (1984).

Figure 6.5. The lender problem. Changes in the real interest rate will alter a lender's choice of consumption and loans. With preferences represented by the indifference map portrayed in the diagram, the lender chooses to increase loans as the real interest rises.

Combining these constraints, we obtain the lifetime budget constraint for a lender:

$$c_{1,L} + \frac{c_{2,L}}{r} = y. \tag{6.16}$$

In Figure 6.5 we graph this budget line for various levels of the real interest rate r. If we knew the individual's exact preferences, we could learn the number of goods lent by individuals for each value of r. One such function is graphed in Figure 6.6. Note that this relationship does not have to be positively sloped everywhere, although a typical assumption is that higher interest rates lead to a greater supply of loans.

The Borrower Problem

A borrower, when young, can consume ($c_{1,B}$) only what he borrows (b). When old, he may consume ($c_{2,B}$) what is left of his endowment after he repays his loan. These

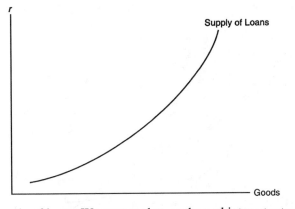

Figure 6.6. The supply of loans. We assume that, as the real interest rate rises, the amount of loans made by a typical lender also increases. When we aggregate across all individuals in the economy, the total supply of loans will also vary directly with the real interest rate.

constraints can be written as

$$c_{1,B} = b, \tag{6.17}$$

and

$$c_{2,B} = y - rb. \tag{6.18}$$

These constraints can be combined to get the borrower's lifetime budget line:

$$c_{1,B} + \frac{c_{2,B}}{r} \leq \frac{y}{r}. \tag{6.19}$$

This budget line is graphed in Figure 6.7 for $r > 1$, $r = 1$, and $r < 1$.

Note that, for typical indifference curves, as r decreases, $c_{1,B}$ increases. Because $c_{1,B} = b$, the amount borrowed also increases as r decreases. This gives us an individual demand curve for loans that is negatively sloped. Aggregating across all borrowers in the economy, we will obtain a total demand for loans curve that is also negatively sloped. We can combine this demand curve with the supply curve for loans to find the equilibrium quantity of loans L^* and the equilibrium interest rate r^* as done in Figure 6.8.

Private Debt and Capital

Now suppose that we introduce capital into our model of borrowing and lending. For simplicity, we assume that capital pays the constant gross rate of return x. Now lenders have two assets from which to choose – capital and loans. Let us also assume that there is no risk inherent in either of the two assets. Our discussion

Figure 6.7. The borrower's problem. As the real interest rate falls, a typical borrower will desire to increase first-period consumption. Because first-period consumption is financed by borrowing, the individual's demand for loans also increases as the real interest rate falls.

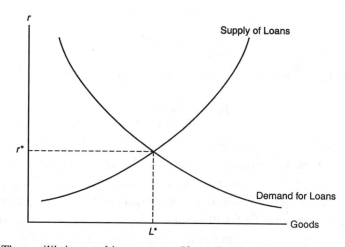

Figure 6.8. The equilibrium real interest rate. If we plot the total demand for loans and the total supply of loans on the same graph, we can determine the equilibrium quantity of loans (L^*) and the equilibrium real interest rate (r^*).

of the principle of rate of return equality will help us to discover which asset the borrowers will choose.

Suppose the rate of return on capital x is less than r^*. Lenders will choose the asset that pays the greater rate of return. So if $x < r^*$, lenders will only make loans;

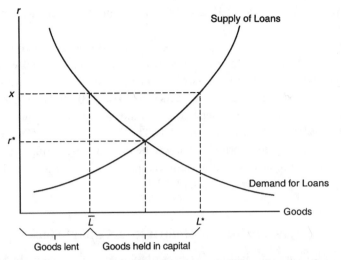

Figure 6.9. Holdings of capital and loans when $x > r^*$. When the rate of return on capital exceeds r^*, lenders will hold a mixed portfolio of capital and loans. The total amount of loans made is equal to $\bar{L}$ and the total amount of capital held by lenders is $L^* - \bar{L}$.

their holdings of capital will be zero. People will choose to hold capital only if $x \geq r^*$.

Now suppose that $x > r^*$. We know that lenders can be enticed to make loans to borrowers only if the real interest rate on loans is equal to x. This means that the real interest rate will exceed r^*. Such a case is illustrated in Figure 6.9.

Note from Figure 6.9 that at the rate of return x, borrowers want to borrow only $\bar{L}$, but lenders want to save L^*. The difference is held in the form of capital.

Appendix Exercises

6.1 Use the graph in Figure 6.9 to answer the following questions.
   a. Suppose the government restricts total borrowing to an amount less than $\bar{L}$. What would be the effect on capital holdings?
   b. Find the effect of an increase in the supply of loans on capital and the interest rate. What would be the effect on the interest rate if there were no capital?
   c. Find the effect of a decrease in capital's rate of return on the amount borrowed and the stock of capital.
6.2 Consider an economy of three-period-lived people in overlapping generations. Each person is endowed with y goods when young and old and nothing when middle-aged. The population of each generation born in period t is N_t, where $N_t = nN_{t-1}$. There are no assets other than loans. Explain how credit can be used to provide for consumption when middle-aged. Point out who lends to whom and write the condition for the equality of supply and demand for loans in period t. Write the budget constraints

for the young, the middle-aged, and the old. Be sure to define any notation that you introduce.

6.3 Consider an overlapping generations model with 200 lenders and 100 borrowers born in every period. Everyone lives for only two periods. Each lender is endowed with 20 goods when young and nothing when old. Each borrower is endowed with nothing when young and 40 goods when old. The lenders want to save 10 goods each, regardless of the rate of return on their savings. Each borrower wants to borrow $10/r$ goods each, where r is the gross real interest rate on private IOUs. The lending market is free and competitive.

    a. In a nonmonetary equilibrium, what will be the market-clearing value of r?

    b. Now turn to a monetary equilibrium. Suppose $z = 0.5$. What will be the real fiat money holdings of a typical lender?

Appendix B: The Golden Rule Capital Stock

Is more capital always desirable? At first glance, it may appear that more capital is always desirable, because it leads to higher output in the future. However, we must realize that, to create capital, individuals must give up consumption today. With this realization, we may also wish to ask the following questions: What is the optimal level of capital? Will a free market necessarily induce the optimal level of capital?

We will answer these questions in the context of a model in which capital created at t pays the return $f(k_t)$ at $t + 1$, with the diminishing marginal product $f'(k_t)$.[7] To determine the optimal capital stock, we must first learn what combinations of consumption and capital are feasible in an economy with capital; that is, we must find the feasible set for economies with capital. With the addition of capital to our model, we now have a source of goods in addition to endowments. The goods available for use in period t now include the output from capital created in the previous period $N_{t-1}f(k_{t-1})$ as well as the endowments of the current young $N_t y$. There is also a new use for goods, investment. The total use of the consumption good in period t is for consumption by the young ($N_t c_{1,t}$), consumption by the old ($N_{t-1}c_{2,t}$), and investment in capital ($N_t k_t$). Hence, the feasible set can be written as

$$N_t c_{1,t} + N_{t-1}c_{2,t} + N_t k_t \le N_t y + N_{t-1}f(k_{t-1}). \tag{6.20}$$

As before, we will divide through by N_t to find the feasible set in per-young-person terms. If we also restrict ourselves to stationary solutions, we can eliminate the time subscripts. These simplifications result in

$$c_1 + \frac{c_2}{n} + k \le y + \left[\frac{f(k)}{n}\right], \tag{6.21}$$

---

[7] This is a slightly simplified version of Diamond's (1965) original analysis.

or

$$c_1 + \frac{c_2}{n} \leq y + \left[\frac{f(k)}{n} - k \right]. \tag{6.22}$$

Equation 6.22 reveals the conditions under which capital is desirable in a stationary allocation. The right-hand side of this equation represents output net of the costs of investment, or **net domestic product**, per young person. These are the goods available for consumption. The optimal stationary capital stock maximizes the goods available for consumption in a stationary allocation.

Consider first the case for a constant population ($n = 1$). A 1-unit increase in capital per young person in each generation, k, has two effects on output net of investment. It increases output from capital $[f(k)]$ by its marginal product $f'(k)$ but increases the cost of investment by 1. As long as a unit of capital produces more than it costs, it will increase the goods available for consumption in stationary allocations.

The case of a growing population ($n > 1$) is only slightly different. The marginal benefit per young person from an increase in k is the marginal product of capital divided by n because the output from capital comes from a smaller number of people; there are only $1/n$ old people for each young person. Therefore, a 1-unit increase in capital per old person increases the goods available for consumption by $f'(k)/n$. It follows that extra capital is desirable in a stationary allocation as long as its benefits, $f'(k)/n$, exceed its cost, 1. The golden rule for capital accumulation is therefore to increase capital until its marginal product just equals the rate of population growth, as depicted in Figure 6.10.

Recall that the principle of rate-of-return equality requires that interest rates must equal the marginal product of capital. It is simple therefore to learn whether a stationary economy is at the golden rule: simply compare its interest rate with its growth rate. If its growth rate exceeds its interest rate, an economy has too much capital, or **capital overaccumulation**; if the interest rate exceeds the growth rate, an economy has too little capital relative to the golden rule, or **capital underaccumulation**.

Once capital is at the level ($\hat{k}$) that maximizes net output, it remains to find the golden rule allocation of consumption between c_1 and c_2. Graphing the feasible set at $\hat{k}$, we find a line of slope $-n$, as graphed in Figure 6.11. As before, we find the golden rule allocation of consumption at the unique tangency between the feasible set and an indifference curve (point A in Figure 6.11).

Nothing guarantees that a free market will lead to an interest rate that equals the economy's growth rate. The stock of capital is determined by the amount that people wish to save for later in life. If this amount is smaller than the golden rule capital stock (capital underaccumulation), the marginal product of capital will be

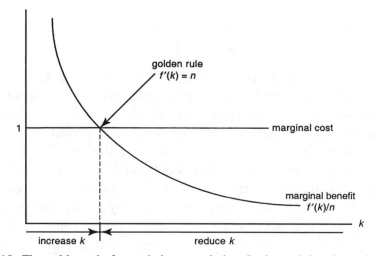

Figure 6.10. The golden rule for capital accumulation. In determining the optimal capital stock, we compare the marginal benefits of creating capital with the marginal cost. As long as the marginal benefit exceeds the marginal cost, the capital stock should be increased. On the other hand, too much capital is being created if the marginal benefit is less than the marginal cost. The optimal capital stock is where the marginal product of capital is equal to the growth rate of the economy.

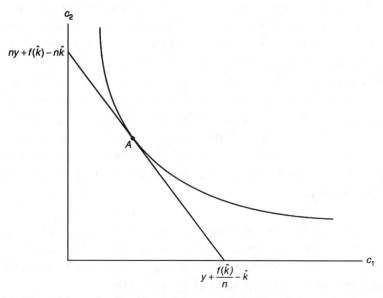

Figure 6.11. The golden rule allocation of consumption. If capital creation is at its golden rule level, the feasible set is as illustrated. The golden rule consumption allocation, point A, can be found at the tangency of the feasible set line and the highest attainable indifference curve.

higher than n. If this amount is larger than the golden rule capital stock (capital overaccumulation), the marginal product of capital will be lower than n.

When the interest rate is n, both conditions for the golden rule are met:

1. Capital is at the level that maximizes output (its marginal product equals the interest rate n).
2. Consumption is distributed among young and old in the way that maximizes stationary utility.

When capital is overaccumulated, one way to get to the golden rule is to issue a constant stock of fiat money, which pays the golden rule rate of return n. With this asset as an alternative, no one will choose to invest in any capital whose marginal product is less than n. Moreover, at the golden rule rate of return, individuals will also choose the combination of c_1 and c_2 that maximizes steady-state utility.

Another way to alter the accumulation of capital in equilibrium is through intergenerational transfers, like social security in the United States and social insurance in Canada. Taxing young people to pay old people reduces the amount that people will save on their own to provide for retirement, reducing the need for capital as a form of saving. This can help an economy out of an overaccumulation of capital. If the economy faces instead an underaccumulation of capital, the transfer must go in the opposite direction, with old people taxed to fund subsidies to young people. This will increase private saving through capital as young people have more available for savings and a greater need for savings because of the taxes they will face when old. The effects on capital, consumption, and savings of taxes and subsidies involving the young and the old are more carefully studied in Chapter 15.

Appendix Exercise

6.4 (advanced) Consider an economy of two-period-lived people in overlapping generations. Each person produces from labor y goods when young but nothing when old. The number of people born doubles every period. There is the following capital technology: if k_t goods per young person are turned into capital at t, the capital produces $f(k_t)$ goods at $t + 1$. The diminishing marginal product of capital is $f'(k_t)$. After production takes place, δ units of capital are lost to depreciation. However, the remaining units of capital can be consumed.

    a. Find an equation that represents the set of feasible stationary allocations and explain it in words.

    b. Find the equation that describes the golden rule capital stock for this economy. You may use either calculus or a marginal cost and marginal benefit analysis.

Chapter 7

Liquidity and Financial Intermediation

WE SAW IN Chapter 6 that if the rate of return on other assets is greater than that of fiat money, fiat money is not valued in these model economies. We observe, however, that fiat money is valued in many real economies where other assets have a greater rate of return than fiat money. Why do people choose to hold fiat money when many alternative assets appear to offer greater rates of return? Chapter 6 gave us one possible answer. Risky assets would have to display a risk premium for risk-averse individuals to be willing to hold them. In this chapter we consider the additional possibility that fiat money is valued because it is more liquid than alternative assets.

Our study of liquidity will lead us to a study of financial intermediation. It may be that a private entity can arrange to offer people a liquid substitute for fiat money. Why might it wish to do so? The difference in the rates of return of liquid and illiquid assets opens up an opportunity for profits through arbitrage – by borrowing at the low rate of return of money while investing at the high rate of return of the illiquid asset.

Money as a Liquid Asset

As we saw in Chapter 6, if fiat money and other assets were perfect substitutes, people would value only the asset with the greater rate of return. To explain why fiat money is valued despite offering a lower rate of return than other assets, it may help to note evidence that fiat money and capital are held for different motives. Fiat money changes hands much more frequently than other assets (is held for shorter periods of time), and it (with other moneylike assets) is used in the bulk of all transactions. Money's acceptance despite its low rate of return may therefore be linked to its usefulness in exchange.

Whenever an exchange takes place, there may be **transaction costs** incurred that would not have been incurred if the owners had simply held on to the items exchanged. It is generally accepted that money is less costly to exchange than other assets. Consider the cost incurred when a house changes hands compared with the negligible cost of exchanging fiat money. It comes to thousands of dollars.

If held for over 20 years, a house pays a much better return (including both its resale value and the value of the shelter it provides) than does fiat money. Is this true for a shorter period? Approximate the rate of return, net of transaction costs, on a house owned for a week. Which asset now offers the greater rate of return? Note that the notion that people value an asset for its rate of return is not violated by the example of liquid assets so long as we note that an asset's rate of return may depend on transaction costs and the holding period of the asset.

We say that an asset is **liquid** if it is exchanged easily, quickly, and at little cost. Fiat money is obviously a more liquid asset than a house, but why? What properties of houses make them so costly to exchange? Houses are useful as an extreme example of transaction costs because just about everything about them makes them difficult to exchange. To start with, they cannot be transported, and they come in units far too large for most transactions. One might get around these difficulties by issuing portable paper titles to a fraction of a house (entitling the owner to a fraction of the rent), but even these house-backed assets are unlikely to circulate.

There remains the problem of ascertaining the value of the title. A store manager will not accept a fractional house title in exchange for goods because it is not possible to verify that it is worth what the seller claims without checking for termites and the quality of the local schools. Such costs are transaction costs because they are incurred only if the house changes ownership. Other assets, such as personal IOUs or stocks, without land's problems of portability or divisibility, still have values that are costly for buyers to learn. In contrast, the value of fiat money is easy to learn. If counterfeiting is not a major problem, the value of fiat money is learned instantly or after a few seconds of counting.

A Model of Illiquidity

Let us now try to capture the essential distinctions between liquid and illiquid assets in an expanded version of our model.[1] In particular, we will seek to describe a model economy consistent with the following observations about real economies:

1. Fiat money and capital are both valued.
2. The rate of return of capital exceeds that of fiat money.
3. Fiat money is exchanged more often than capital (fiat money is held for the short term, and capital is held for the long term).

---

[1] This model is taken from Freeman (1985).

Consider an economy of overlapping generations in which people live for three periods. People are endowed with y units of the consumption good when young and with nothing in the other two periods of life. We will extend our usual assumptions about preferences to a three-period case. As before, let N_t represent the number of people in the generation born at t, with $N_t = nN_{t-1}$. We will also assume that there is a constant supply of fiat money M in the economy. The initial old possess this stock of money in the first period. Extending our previous notation, $c_{1,t}, c_{2,t+1}, c_{3,t+2}$ will denote a member of generation t's consumption in the first, second, and third periods of life, respectively.

There is a single physical asset, capital, in this economy.[2] A unit of capital, k_t, may be created from a unit of the consumption good in any period t. Capital may be created in any amount. Two periods after it is created, a unit of capital produces X units of the consumption good and then disintegrates. Let $X > n^2$.

Two assumptions about information will be key to the liquidity of capital in this economy. First, assume that it is expensive to observe the capital created by others; indeed, to avoid any ambiguity, let us assume that it is impossible for others to observe it. Second, let us assume (for now) that it is impossible to enforce the repayment of IOUs because people can costlessly hide from anyone looking for them and in this way avoid repaying their IOUs. As a result, no one is willing to lend. Later in the chapter we will examine this economy when the repayment of IOUs can be enforced.

We can easily characterize the individual's holdings of capital and money. Given the pattern of endowments, individuals must find a means of providing for consumption in the second and third periods of their lives. To provide for consumption in the third period of life, an individual can create capital in the first period of life. Capital, however, produces nothing in the second period of life. Moreover, an individual cannot trade the capital for second-period consumption because it is impossible for others to observe the holdings of capital and ascertain its value.

So how does an individual provide for second-period consumption? An individual born in period t can sell some of the endowment in the first period of life for fiat money. These holdings of fiat money will then be used in the second period of life to buy some of the consumption good from the young born in that period.

Individuals can also provide for third-period consumption by holding fiat money, but they will not choose to do so. To see this, we need to compare the rate of return on capital and the rate of return on fiat money. Given our assumptions of a changing population and a constant fiat money supply, the one-period rate of return on fiat

---

[2] As we saw in Chapter 6, alternatives to capital will offer the same rate of return, adjusted for risk. For this reason, we lose little by looking only at a single asset. We chose capital to be that asset for most of this book because its rate of return is easily described and, more importantly, because the capital stock affects output.

money in a stationary equilibrium is n. However, in providing for third-period consumption (two periods in the future for a young person), it is the two-period rate of return on fiat money that is relevant (v_{t+2}/v_t).

Following our earlier derivations, it is easy to show that the rate of return on fiat money over two periods is n^2. To see this, recall that the one-period rate of return on fiat money, given a constant fiat money stock, is n. Furthermore, this is true in every period. This implies that the two-period rate of return on fiat money is

$$\frac{v_{t+2}}{v_t} = \frac{v_{t+2}}{v_{t+1}} \frac{v_{t+1}}{v_t} = nn = n^2. \tag{7.1}$$

Given our assumption that $X > n^2$, the rate of return on capital exceeds the rate of return on fiat money over a two-period horizon. Hence, individuals will choose to provide for third-period consumption by holding capital.

We can summarize these observations by writing down the budget constraints faced by an individual born in period t:

$$c_{1,t} + v_t m_t + k_t \leq y, \tag{7.2}$$

$$c_{2,t+1} \leq v_{t+1} m_t, \tag{7.3}$$

$$c_{3,t+2} \leq X k_t. \tag{7.4}$$

If we combine these three equations, we can write the lifetime budget constraint for an individual born in period t as

$$c_{1,t} + \left[\frac{v_t}{v_{t+1}}\right] c_{2,t+1} + \left[\frac{1}{X}\right] c_{3,t+2} \leq y. \tag{7.5}$$

This is a linear equation in $c_{1,t}, c_{2,t+1}$, and $c_{3,t+2}$. Unfortunately, our usual method of graphing budget constraints becomes cumbersome in this three-dimensional problem; the frontier of the budget set would be a plane in three-dimensional space. The optimal ($c^*_{1,t}, c^*_{2,t+1}, c^*_{3,t+2}$) combination would be located where an indifference curve is tangent to this plane.

Let us make some observations about our results. The two-period rate of return on capital is X, whereas that on fiat money is n^2. Because $X > n^2$, we see that the two-period rate of return on capital exceeds that of fiat money. Furthermore, the one-period rate of return on capital is zero and that on fiat money is n, establishing that the one-period rate of return on fiat money exceeds that of capital. A casual interpretation of our analysis in Chapter 6 suggested that, if individuals are willing to hold two types of assets simultaneously, then their rates of return must be equal. However, that clearly is not the case here. It appears that the general rule of rate-of-return equality is violated in this economy. Why?

To understand this, it is important to reiterate some of our earlier observations. For the rule of rate-of-return equality to hold, the assets involved must be perceived as perfect substitutes. In this model, fiat money and capital are not perfect substitutes. In particular, the assumption that individuals cannot observe another individual's holdings of capital means that it is impossible for this economy to develop a market where a middle-aged individual's holding of capital is traded. In other words, capital is illiquid. An individual can never sell capital for a medium of exchange in the second period of life, nor can capital itself be used as a medium of exchange.

Given these fundamental differences between fiat money and capital, it should seem reasonable that the two do not pay the same rate of return. The principle of rate-of-return equality still applies to this economy, although in modified form. Individuals hold capital over two periods because it offers the best two-period rate of return; they hold money over one period because it offers the best one-period rate of return.

Also note the frequency of trade of the two assets in this model. The **velocity** of an asset may be defined as the amount of the asset that is exchanged in a given period of time divided by the total stock of that asset. In any period t, the total stock of fiat money exchanges hands. This implies that the velocity of fiat money is 1. What is the velocity of capital?

Suppose we view a young person's creation of capital as an exchange. In each period t, the current young create a total of $N_t k_t$ units of capital. What is the total capital stock in period t? It consists of the capital held by the current young ($N_t k_t$) and by the middle-aged who purchased capital in period $t - 1$. The latter amount is $N_{t-1} k_{t-1}$. Hence, the total capital stock in period t is $N_t k_t + N_{t-1} k_{t-1}$. Viewing the young people's creation of capital as capital being exchanged, we then have that

$$(\text{velocity of capital})_t = \frac{N_t k_t}{N_t k_t + N_{t-1} k_{t-1}} < 1. \tag{7.6}$$

Consider, for example, the simple case in which the total capital stock does not change in size over time; then the velocity of capital is $1/2$. More generally, we see from Equation 7.6 that the velocity of capital is less than the velocity of fiat money (which is 1).[3] Because it is difficult to exchange, capital is an asset that people hold for the long run (two periods), and fiat money is held for the short run (one period).

---

[3] If we do not view a young individual's original creation of capital as an exchange, then the velocity of capital is 0.

The Business of Banking

Let us return to the economy of three-period-lived individuals, with one change. Assume now that at least some people cannot hide from their creditors, so the enforcement of their IOUs is possible. This will allow the emergence of banking and a new form of liquid asset – **inside money** – money issued by private intermediaries.

Suppose you are the only person in this economy who can issue IOUs. How might you use your ability to borrow to make large profits? Recall the difference in the rates of return on long- and short-term assets (capital and money, respectively) in the previous economy. Making profits through rate-of-return differences is called **arbitrage**. Is there a way to borrow at the low rate and invest at the high rate?

A Sample Arbitrage Plan

Given your monopoly on issuing private IOUs, it is easy to conceive of such an arbitrage plan. In period t, you could borrow one good and invest it in the creation of capital. This good could be borrowed from a young individual who was born in that period. This young person, in the previous case in which there were no IOUs, would use fiat money to finance second-period consumption. We know that fiat money pays a one-period rate of return of n. If you offered to pay at least the rate of return on fiat money (n), this person would be willing to make a one-period loan to you.

Given that you borrowed 1 unit of the consumption good in period t, you owe n goods to your lender in period $t + 1$ but you have no payoff from capital yet. To pay off your lender, you then borrow n goods from the next generation of young people.

At $t + 2$ you owe the rate of return n on the n goods you borrowed at time $t + 1$, for a total of n^2 goods. Your return from the unit of capital you created is X, which exceeds n^2. This leaves you with a clear profit of $X - n^2 > 0$.

This act of arbitrage represents financial intermediation, the job of banking. The intermediary issues a string of one-period IOUs (accepts deposits) and uses the proceeds to invest in capital with a two-period maturity. The opportunity to make arbitrage profits induced the intermediary to correct the mismatch of the maturities of the liquid fiat money and the illiquid capital.

The Effect of Arbitrage on Equilibrium

Let us now assume that you are not the only one able to issue IOUs. If a large number of competitive people can costlessly issue IOUs and invest in capital, what will be the one-period rate of return (call it r^*) paid on these IOUs in a competitive equilibrium?

To answer this question, let us consider a numerical example. Suppose the two-period rate of return on capital X is 1.21 and the rate of population growth n is 1.05. Let's suppose that the intermediary agrees to pay a one-period rate of return of 1.05 on deposits. Call this rate of return on deposits r. By the previous argument, this is the minimum rate of return that the intermediary must offer to attract depositors. Suppose an intermediary accepts deposits at time t equal to 100 units of the consumption good and invests the deposits in capital. In period $t + 1$, the intermediary must repay 105 units of the good to depositors. To do so, the intermediary accepts deposits of 105 units of the good from the young born in that period, again offering the same 1.05 rate of return. The intermediary will owe 110.25 $[= (100)(1.05)(105) = 100r^2]$ goods in period $t + 2$ to these depositors. In period $t + 2$, the intermediary's capital matures, yielding a gross amount of 121 $[= (100)(1.21) = 100X]$ goods. This intermediary makes a profit of 10.75 $(= 121 - 110.25)$ goods. Note that the profit made is equal to $100(X - r^2)$.

However, by similar reasoning, a bank down the street could also make profits and attract all the depositors of the previous bank by offering a rate of return of $r = 1.06$ on deposits. This bank will make profits equal to $100(1.21 - 1.06^2) = 8.64$ goods.

If we continue this analysis, we see that for $r < 1.1$, an intermediary makes profits. As long as $r < 1.1$, new intermediaries will enter the industry and offer higher rates of return on deposits. To stay in business, the existing intermediaries will have to follow suit. We see that a competitive intermediation industry will force the rate of return on deposits to be equal to $r^* = 1.1$. Note that 1.1 is equal to $\sqrt{1.21} = \sqrt{X}$. When $r^* = \sqrt{X}$, the intermediary's profits are equal to $100(X - \sqrt{X}\sqrt{X}) = 0$. There will be no incentive to offer higher interest rates on deposits; doing so would lead to negative profits. This argument should sound familiar. It is much the same as the argument that perfectly competitive firms will force the price of their output down to marginal cost, so that zero profits are displayed.

Intermediation will also affect capital and output in this economy. In the absence of intermediation, capital was held only to acquire consumption in the third period of life; fiat money was held to acquire consumption in the second period of life. With intermediation, inside money replaces fiat money in the acquisition of consumption in the second period of life. People not only invest in capital directly to acquire consumption in the third period of life but also indirectly through intermediaries to acquire consumption in the second period of life. In this way, intermediation serves to mobilize all the saving of the economy for investment in capital, including saving in the form of liquid assets, money balances. The greater investment in capital due to intermediation implies greater output.

The welfare effects of replacing fiat money with inside money are mixed. Future generations will benefit from inside money's greater rate of return. On the other hand, those holding fiat money balances in the initial period (the initial middle-aged) lose the value of those money balances if fiat money is abandoned.

Summary

Chapter 6 concluded that if money and other assets are considered as perfect substitutes for one another, then money will be valued only if its rate of return is at least as large as those of the other assets. However, we can point to many real-world assets whose rates of return are greater than that of money while at the same time money is valued. Why does the principle of rate-of-return equality appear to be violated? To answer this question, this chapter has focused on the possibility that money and other assets are not perfect substitutes. In particular, the first model of this chapter concentrated on the observation that money may be more liquid than other assets. By looking at a model with illiquid capital and money, we found that capital can indeed pay a higher rate of return than valued fiat money.

We have also discovered that rate-of-return differences provide a natural incentive for the development of financial intermediaries. These intermediaries provide a service by correcting the mismatch of maturities between liquid money and illiquid capital. By funneling saving to investment in capital, the presence of intermediaries leads to higher output in an economy.

The appendix of this chapter proposes another role for banks. Banks may serve as monitors of risky ventures. Banks offer lower risk through diversification and lower monitoring costs than people could find by lending on their own.

Exercises

7.1 Consider our model of three-period-lived individuals of this chapter. Suppose the two-period real rate of return on capital is $X = 1.44$, the rate of population growth is $n = 1.1$, and the rate of fiat money creation is $z = 1.2$. Find the following net rates for both one and two periods:
   a. nominal rate of interest,
   b. real rate of interest,
   c. rate of inflation, and
   d. real rate of return on money.

7.2 Suppose the intermediation of capital costs ϕ units of the consumption good for each unit of capital intermediated ($\phi < \sqrt{X}$). Assume these transaction costs occur when agents withdraw from banks (when they are middle-aged). What will be the equilibrium rate of return offered by intermediaries if they are the ones who bear the transaction costs? For what values of ϕ, X, z, and n will fiat money be valued in this economy?

7.3 Consider an economy in which people live two-period lives in overlapping generations but are endowed only in the first period of life. Capital has a minimum size, k^*, which is greater than the endowment of any single individual but less than the total endowment of a single generation. Capital pays a one-period gross real rate of return equal to x. The population grows 10 percent in each period. There exists a constant nominal stock of fiat money owned by the initial old.

a. In what sense is capital illiquid in this economy? Is fiat money subject to this same liquidity problem?

b. Describe an intermediary that might overcome the illiquidity of capital so that intermediated capital may be used to acquire consumption in the second period of life.

c. Suppose there is only one person in each generation who is able to run an intermediary. What is the minimum rate of return that person must offer in order to attract depositors? For what values of x can this individual make a profit?

d. What rate of return will be offered on deposits if there are many people in each generation able to run an intermediary?

Appendix

Banks as Monitors

In the previous model, financial intermediation emerged to reconcile a mismatch of asset maturities; capital produced a return only in the long run but individuals needed an asset that paid a return in the short run. This is only one of many possible services that intermediation may provide.[4]

Other services offered by banks include monitoring the repayment of loans. Banks also offer depositors a (nearly) risk-free way to invest in risky assets. Therefore, let us examine why banks may emerge as a way to reduce the cost of monitoring the repayment of loans and the risks to which depositors are exposed.[5] The model we build will display four features of banks that we observe in actual modern economies:

1. Each bank deals with large numbers of both depositors and entrepreneurs.
2. Loans that must be monitored are made by banks (or other financial intermediaries) rather than individuals.
3. Banks offer depositors a risk-free return while holding risky assets.
4. Depositors do not monitor the banks' performance.

---

[4] It may also be that through financial intermediation people can insure each other (Diamond and Dybvig, 1983), reduce the cost of evaluating loans (Boyd and Prescott, 1986), or enjoy other economies of scale (Greenwood and Jovanovic, 1990). Recent work on financial intermediation is surveyed by Bhattachrya and Thakor (1991). We study additional models of intermediation in Exercise 7.3 and in Chapter 12.

[5] The model of banks as monitors that we will present is adapted from that of Diamond (1984). The initial study of optimal contracts with monitoring is Townsend's (1979). The simplified version here owes much to Williamson (1987), who also presents some simple extensions.

Consider an economy with a large number of potential restaurateurs (males) who lack the funds to start their restaurants and an equal number of potential investors (females) who have funds to invest but have no desire to run a restaurant. For simplicity, assume that it takes no effort to run a restaurant. Each investor has k goods to invest, and each restaurant requires an investment of μk goods (μ is an integer greater than 1). (Note that there are not enough goods to fund all potential restaurants. There must be μ investors for each funded restaurant.)

Restaurants are a risky business. We will assume that each restaurant has a 2/3 chance of being successful, with a return equal to $x\mu$ and a 1/3 chance of failure, with a return equal to 0. Only after investment has occurred does the restaurateur learn whether or not he is successful. The success or failure of a restaurant is not costlessly observable to others. Only by an investigation costing θ goods can someone other than the restaurateur learn of the success or failure of a restaurant. (Assume also that the consumption by the restaurateur and his payments to others are unobservable, so that an investor cannot infer success or failure indirectly.)

Note that when a restaurant fails, the restaurateur has no resources with which to pay anything to his investors. Therefore, whatever contract is written between the restaurateur and his investors, it cannot require the restaurateur to make payments when his restaurant fails.

Can there be a contract without monitoring? In the absence of monitoring, a successful restaurateur has an incentive to declare his restaurant a failure and therefore that he is unable to repay what he owes. Knowing that the restaurateur will otherwise want to lie, investors will want to investigate claims of failure by the restaurateur. We assume they will investigate every claim of failure.[6]

Unintermediated Investment

Because there are more potential restaurants than can be funded, and because it takes no effort to run a restaurant, competition among potential restaurants will ensure that investors receive the entire output of the restaurants, x goods for each good invested.[7]

Suppose each investor splits the k goods she invests among J restaurants (i.e., she invests k/J goods with each of J restaurants). Then the average return to an investor from each restaurant is

$$\frac{2}{3}x\frac{k}{J} + \frac{1}{3}(-\theta). \tag{7.7}$$

---

[6] In general, it is optimal to engage in random monitoring, but to keep things simple we ignore that strategy here.
[7] If it takes effort to run a restaurant (as it surely does), competition will ensure that investors receive all of output that remains after the restaurateurs are compensated for their effort.

Note that the cost of investigating does not depend on the size of an investor's investment. The total return to J such investments is therefore

$$\frac{2}{3}xk + \frac{1}{3}(-\theta)J. \tag{7.8}$$

The costs of monitoring hurt investors without intermediaries in two ways. First, because it costs an investor θ goods to investigate each failure, regardless of the size of her investment, an investor who splits her goods among many different restaurants will spend more on average for investigations. To minimize investigations, she must therefore minimize the number of restaurants in which she invests by investing in only one. This lack of diversification, however, puts all her eggs in one basket, exposing her to the risk that this single restaurant will fail, lowering the expected utility of risk-averse investors.

Second, without intermediation, there is a great deal of duplication in monitoring restaurants. Each investor who monitors a restaurant spends resources to learn only what others are also learning. Might there not be some way to conduct only a single investigation of each restaurant?

Suppose a single investor is designated to be the sole monitor of a restaurant. A successful restaurateur could then lie and announce a failure, offering to split with the monitor the amount owed to others if she will back up his lie. In other words, who monitors the monitor?

Intermediated Investment

There is, however, a way to avoid both the costly duplication of monitoring and the risk from not diversifying. Consider an intermediary that promises a fixed return, r^*, on all goods entrusted to it. It invests these goods with a large number of restaurateurs but guarantees depositors r^* whatever happens to its investments. The intermediary monitors restaurateurs who claim to have failed.

How can the intermediary guarantee a fixed return when restaurants are risky investments? The answer is that, although each individual restaurant is a risky enterprise, diversifying investments among a large number of restaurants is not very risky, because 2/3 of them will succeed. An intermediary investing in a large number of restaurants will take in approximately the average rate of return for each restaurant in which it invests

$$\frac{2}{3}x\mu + \frac{1}{3}(-\theta). \tag{7.9}$$

Because there are μ depositors (of k goods each), it can offer a depositor of k goods the return

$$\frac{2}{3}x + \frac{1}{3}\left(\frac{-\theta}{\mu}\right). \tag{7.10}$$

If there is free entry into the business of intermediation, this is the return that will be offered in (a competitive) equilibrium. Note that, because of its lower monitoring costs, this return exceeds the return that could be earned without intermediation [from Equation 7.8, $(2/3)x + (1/3)(-\theta)J$].[8]

This financial arrangement achieves this greater return by minimizing monitoring without inducing anyone to lie. Each restaurant that declares itself a failure is monitored only once. Moreover, depositors do not have to monitor the intermediary because their return is not contingent on anything. The arrangement also reduces risk. Through the intermediary, each depositor diversifies her investment over a large number of projects, which is why the intermediary can offer depositors a riskless return.

---

[8] Recall that the minimum for J is 1 and that $\mu > 1$.

Chapter 8

Central Banking and the Money Supply

ONCE FIAT MONEY is not the only form of money, the monetary authority may wish to regulate money-creating institutions in order to control the total stock of money or to enhance revenue from seigniorage. To meet these ends, the monetary authority, which now may also be called a central bank, generally has two tools at its disposal – reserve requirements and loans to banks – in addition to its ability to print fiat money. In this chapter we will study the effects of each. We will also ask, in this chapter and the next, whether control of the total money stock is always a worthwhile objective of the monetary authority.

Legal Restrictions on Financial Intermediation

Financial intermediation allows privately created assets to serve as money. One consequence of permitting unfettered intermediation is that, if intermediation is not too costly to use and operate, people may choose to use inside money instead of fiat money. This will occur if the rate of return of inside money, net of transaction costs, exceeds that of government-created fiat money.

If people prefer inside money to fiat money for every use of money, fiat money will lose its value. This would have two effects. First, prices would have to be expressed in some other unit of account. Second, the government would be unable to raise any revenue from seigniorage. If the government still wishes to maintain fiat money as a unit of account or a means of revenue, it must force people to hold fiat money.

There are many ways for the government to shore up the demand for fiat money. Most directly, it can simply require people to hold a certain amount of fiat money. An example is a **reserve requirement** – a requirement that a bank must hold fiat money balances equal to a legally prescribed fraction of its deposits. Less directly, the government may simply outlaw certain forms of intermediation or certain alternatives to fiat money. For example, banks are often prohibited from issuing their own currency (notes payable to the bearer, or bank notes).

Because of the prevalence of these interventions into the monetary system, in this chapter we examine the effects and desirability of these interventions and related government policies.[1]

Reserve Requirements

Let us start by introducing into our model of intermediation a common form of legal restriction on financial intermediaries, a reserve requirement. A **reserve requirement** obliges financial intermediaries to hold in the form of fiat money a legally specified fraction of their deposits. Before introducing reserve requirements into our model, let us briefly discuss their implementation under U.S. and Canadian law. Depository institutions in both countries are required by law to hold reserves in relation to their levels of deposits.

In the United States, these reserves must be held in the form of vault cash or deposits with the Federal Reserve Banks.[2] Reserve requirements are imposed on what the Federal Reserve (the Fed) calls net transactions accounts – basically checkable deposits. As of December 1999, these accounts were subject to the following reserve requirements: On the first $46.5 million of deposits, the reserve requirement is 3 percent; for amounts in excess of $46.5 million it is 10 percent.

Reserve requirements on Canadian chartered banks were completely phased out as of the summer of 1994. We will have more to say about the implications of this policy change later in the chapter.

Banks with Reserve Requirements

Let us continue our analysis using Chapter 7's model of people with three-period lives and illiquid capital.[3] Capital pays a rate of return of X two periods after its creation. Let $X > (n/z)^2$. Let $M_t = zM_{t-1}$ with $z \geq 1$. Because money will be used to consume in the second period of life, we will assume that the initial middle-aged begin with the stock of fiat money.

As we saw in Chapter 7, the difference in the rates of return of capital and fiat money will induce people to try to make arbitrage profits through intermediation. We assume that the intermediation of capital is costless and competitive.

The following reserve requirement is imposed on banks or anyone else intermediating capital. For each good deposited at a bank, the bank is required to acquire and hold a reserve of fiat money worth γ goods. The rest, $1 - \gamma$, can be invested in capital.

---

[1] See Fama (1980) for a discussion of banking with and without interventions.
[2] Institutions that are not members of the Federal Reserve System may hold reserve balances with institutions approved by the Federal Reserve.
[3] This analysis builds on the work of Romer (1985) and Freeman (1987).

Assets		**Liabilities**	
Reserves	γH	Deposits	H
Interest-bearing assets	$(1-\gamma)H$	Net worth	0
Total assets	H	Total liabilities	H

Figure 8.1. A bank's balance sheet. A balance sheet shows the relationship between assets and liabilities. For a bank, its deposits represent a liability. Deposits (H) are subject to a reserve requirement of γ, so that the bank must hold total reserves equal to γH. After satisfying these requirements, the bank uses the funds raised from deposits to purchase interest-bearing assets to the amount of $H - \gamma H = (1 - \gamma)H$.

The operation of a bank may be summarized in its balance sheet. A balance sheet lists side by side a bank's assets and its liabilities. The assets of a bank may be divided into two parts – reserves and interest-bearing assets. The liabilities of a bank are the deposits at the bank (what is owed to the depositors at the bank) and the bank's net worth (what is owed to the shareholders of the bank). The total assets of a solvent bank equal its liabilities (the lists of assets and liabilities must balance). For simplicity, we have assumed that the banks of our model have zero net worth. The balance sheet of such a bank with deposits equal to H is presented in Figure 8.1.

Let us now examine the determinants of key variables in the model.

Prices

The price level, which we call p_t, is the value of a good in dollars, the inverse of the value of a unit of fiat money, v_t. Define h_t as the goods deposited in banks by an individual. As always, v_t is determined by the equality of the supply and demand for fiat money

$$v_t M_t = \gamma N_t h_t. \tag{8.1}$$

Equation 8.1 requires some explanation. In period t each individual makes h_t deposits in banks (in real terms). In the aggregate, $N_t h_t$ deposits are placed in banks. Against those deposits, banks are required to hold the fraction γ in fiat currency as reserves. This implies that the total amount of required reserves in real terms is $\gamma N_t h_t$. Given that individuals in this model do not hold currency, the banks' demand for fiat money as reserves represents the total demand for fiat money. Note that increases in the reserve requirement increase the value of fiat money by increasing the demand for fiat money. From Equation 8.1 we can find the price level, the inverse of v_t:

$$p_t = \frac{M_t}{\gamma N_t h_t}. \tag{8.2}$$

At this point, a note is in order about the zero reserve requirement policy now in effect in Canada. Equation 8.2 tells us that if $\gamma = 0$, the price level is infinite ($v_t = 0$). The intuition is that in this model, if $\gamma = 0$, there is no demand for fiat money, making it valueless. So why don't we observe an infinite price level in Canada? The answer must be that our model is missing an important source of demand for fiat money. There must be another source of demand for fiat money other than by banks as reserves. In Chapter 9, we present a model in which fiat money is desired to serve as individually held currency.

Seigniorage

Another variable that might be of interest is seigniorage, the revenue from fiat money creation. Recall from Equations 3.16 and 3.17 that seigniorage equals

$$(\text{seigniorage})_t = v_t[M_t - M_{t-1}] = v_t M_t \left[1 - \frac{1}{z}\right] \tag{8.3}$$

when $M_t = z M_{t-1}$. Using the expression for $v_t M_t$ that we found in Equation 8.1, we can write seigniorage as

$$(\text{seigniorage})_t = \gamma N_t h_t \left[1 - \frac{1}{z}\right]. \tag{8.4}$$

From this equation we can determine the factors that can increase seigniorage:

- an increase in the reserve requirement γ;
- an increase in $N_t h_t$, the real stock of bank deposits; and
- an increase in z, the rate of fiat money creation.

Capital and Real Output

Real output is the sum of the production of labor (the endowment) and of capital. In this economy, capital comes from both direct investment k_t and investment through intermediaries $(1 - \gamma)h_t$. Recall that capital produces output with a lag of two periods. Hence, output in period t will be affected by capital created in period $t - 2$, whether from direct investment or through intermediaries. Therefore

$$\text{GDP}_t = N_t y + N_{t-2} X k_{t-2} + N_{t-2} X (1 - \gamma) h_{t-2}. \tag{8.5}$$

Note that an increase in the reserve requirement γ reduces GDP (gross domestic product) because, for any given level of deposits (h_{t-2}), less capital is intermediated through banks. An increase in the monetary base M_t has no such direct effect on real output.

Equation 8.5 tells us that a reduction in reserve requirements would lead to an increase in real GDP caused by an increase in intermediated capital. How large might this effect be? At the end of 1997, the total net private capital stock in the United States was \$17,316 billion. At this time, total reserves held by U.S. commercial banks amounted to \$47 billion.[4] If reserve requirements were completely eliminated and commercial banks chose to replace all reserves with loans to new capital, the capital stock would rise by less than 0.3%.

Deposits

In examining the effects of reserve requirements and the monetary base on prices, seigniorage, and output, we took the amount deposited at banks, $N_t h_t$, as given. The willingness of people to make deposits at banks, however, is likely to depend on the rate of return offered on deposits. Let's find this rate of return.

Given that the two-period rate of return on capital is X, the one-period rate of return on intermediated capital is $\sqrt{X}$, which we call x. If the intermediation of capital is costless, competition will force banks to offer depositors the rate of return they earn on the assets held by the banks. Therefore, the total one-period return from the deposit of one good, the gross real rate of return on deposits, must equal the amount held in reserves of fiat money times the rate of return on fiat money plus the amount held in capital times the rate of return on capital:

$$r^* = \gamma \left(\frac{n}{z}\right) + (1 - \gamma)x \qquad (8.6)$$

$$= x - \gamma \left[x - \left(\frac{n}{z}\right)\right]. \qquad (8.7)$$

By assumption, fiat money pays a lower rate of return than capital ($x > n/z$), implying from Equation 8.7 that r^* is a diminishing function of γ. Therefore, an increase in the reserve requirement lowers the rate of return on deposits. Although the current monetary base M_t has no direct effect on the rate of return of deposits,

---

[4] The capital stock data is from the *Survey of Current Business* (August 1999, Table B.12, p. D-35). The capital stock is measured as the amount of fixed private capital (nonresidential and residential). The measure of reserves is total reserves held by commercial banks, adjusted for changes in reserve requirements (from the Federal Reserve Bank of St. Louis FRED database, http://www.stls.frb.org/fred/index.html, series trarr).

the expected rate of money creation z reduces the rate of return on fiat money reserves and thus on deposits partially backed by fiat money reserves.

The effect of a lower rate of return on deposits is ambiguous. On the one hand, a lower rate of return may discourage people from using deposits. On the other hand, the low return on deposits reduces c_2 for any given level of deposits. Therefore, individuals may increase their deposits in order to reduce the drop in c_2.[5]

Welfare

Finally, and most importantly, let us ask about the effects of the reserve requirement on the welfare of the members of this economy. As always, we wish to distinguish between future generations and initial generations.

The initial moneyholders (the middle-aged) begin with the initial stock of fiat money. What effect would a larger reserve requirement have on the real value of this stock? Setting t equal to 1 in Equation 8.1, we see that an increase in γ will cause an increase in the value of money in period 1. Because this will increase the total amount of goods that can be purchased with a given holding of fiat money, the initial moneyholders can attain a higher level of utility with an increase in the reserve requirement.

An increase in the fiat money stock will reduce the value of each initial unit of fiat money. Therefore, the initial moneyholders are made worse off if the initial fiat money stock is increased unless the increase in the fiat money stock is given to them. The initial moneyholders will also be made worse off by anything that reduces the demand for deposits and thus the demand for fiat money.

An increase in the reserve requirement or the rate of money creation would affect the utility of future generations through its effect on the rate of return paid on deposits. We have already found that an increase in either γ or z lowers the rate of return to deposits, thus reducing the utility of future generations. The higher reserve requirement lowers the utility of future generations by forcing them to hold more of the asset (fiat money) with the lower rate of return. The greater seigniorage revenue taxes members of the future generations, reducing what they can consume over their lifetimes. However, if the seigniorage revenue is returned to future generations, the lower rate of return on deposits artificially discourages the use of deposits (consumption in the second period of life). The utility of future generations is reduced in much the same way that a lower return on fiat money reduces the welfare of future generations when it discourages the holding of fiat money, as we learned in Chapter 3.

---

[5] If the revenue from seigniorage were not spent by the government but were returned to people as a lump-sum subsidy to the middle-aged, c_2 for any given level of deposits would not be reduced. In this case, therefore, only the first effect would occur and the lower rate of return on deposits would discourage deposits.

Central Bank Definitions of Money

Economists often try to measure the total nominal value of everything that may serve as money in an economy. In economies with no alternative to fiat money, this measurement is easy; the total nominal money stock is simply the stock of fiat money. In economies in which inside money serves as money, it is less trivial to measure the total nominal money stock.

Central banks around the world have defined several measures of money, which are often called **monetary aggregates**. It is important to realize that there is no universally accepted method of defining these measures. The definitions of monetary aggregates vary from country to country. Furthermore, the measures used in a particular country have often been redefined, and it would be naive to believe that they will not change in the future.

We will present the monetary aggregates as defined by the central banks of the United States and Canada. These central banks are called the Federal Reserve and the Bank of Canada, respectively. There are some common features in the measures of the two countries. The narrowest measure of money in both countries is called **M1** and includes only highly liquid assets that typically can be used to make transactions. Other measures of money build on one another with each successive monetary aggregate including assets which are somewhat less liquid than the previous measure. For example, **M2** includes all the components of M1 plus assets that can be easily converted into a medium of exchange.

Table 8.1 details the components of the various monetary aggregates as defined by the Federal Reserve and the Bank of Canada, along with their magnitudes. In viewing this table, be sure to note that, although there are some similarities between the two countries' definitions, there are many important differences. The components of these measures are discussed in more detail later.

The monetary aggregates in both countries include only amounts held by the nonbank public. Quantities of the above assets held by banks, the governments, and the central banks are not included in these measures.

Some of the components of the monetary aggregates may deserve some discussion to clarify exactly what they include. Let's begin with the narrowest measure of money, M1.

- **M1** – In the United States, M1 includes currency, travelers checks of nonbank issuers, demand deposits at commercial banks, and other checkable deposits in the hands of the nonbank public. Currency, of course, is composed of paper currency and coins. The quantity of demand deposits at commercial banks is adjusted for checks in the process of being collected and for the effect of float. Other checkable deposits include negotiable orders of withdrawal (NOW accounts) and automatic transfer services (ATS) at depository institutions, credit union share draft accounts, and demand deposits at thrift institutions.

Table 8.1. *Monetary aggregates as defined by the Federal Reserve and the Bank of Canada*

U.S. monetary aggregates	Amount	Canadian monetary aggregates	Amount
M1		*M1*	
Currency	499.0	Currency	32.9
+ Demand deposits[a]	354.0	+ Demand deposits less float	53.6
+ Travelers checks	8.4	+ Adjustments[b]	−1.3
+ Other checkable deposits	234.9	= *M1*	90.2
= *M1*	1,096.4		
M2		*M2*	
M1	1,096.4	*M1*	90.2
+ Savings deposits, including money market deposit accounts[d]	1,733.1	+ Personal notice deposits[c]	92.3
		+ Personal term deposits	200.8
+ Small-denomination time deposits	940.7	+ Nonpersonal notice deposits[e]	38.5
+ Retail money market mutual fund balances	820.7	+ Adjustments	−0.0
= *M2*	4,590.9	= *M2*	421.7
M3		*M3*	
M2	4,590.9	*M2*	421.7
+ Large-denomination time deposits	658.0	+ Nonpersonal term deposits	110.0
+ Repurchase agreements[f]	305.9	+ Foreign currency deposits	56.2
+ Eurodollars[g]	158.1	+ Adjustments	−4.0
+ Money market mutual funds (institution-only)	566.7	= *M3*	583.9
= *M3*	6,279.7		

Figures are daily averages for the month of October 1999, in billions of dollars, not seasonally adjusted.

[a] U.S. demand deposits are less cash items in the process of collection and Federal Reserve float.

[b] The adjustments in the Canadian monetary aggregates are rather complicated. For further information, see the *Bank of Canada Review*, Summer 1995, p. S109.

[c] Includes checkable and noncheckable personal notice deposits.

[d] Also includes small-denomination repurchase agreements.

[e] Includes checkable and noncheckable nonpersonal notice deposits.

[f] Includes overnight and term repurchase agreements.

[g] Includes overnight and term Eurodollars.

Sources: The U.S. monetary aggregates are from the Federal Reserve Board of Governors web site, http://www.bog.frb.fed.us/, Table H.6 of the historical series. The Canadian measures are from the *Bank of Canada Review*, Table E1, December 1999, and the data for foreign currency deposits, personal term deposits, and nonpersonal term deposits are from Table C2.

The Canadian definition of M1 is narrower than its U.S. counterpart. Only demand deposits created by Canadian chartered banks are included in M1. Checkable deposits created by other depository institutions (trust and mortgage loan companies, credit unions, and *caisses populaires*) are not counted in M1.[6] This is an illustration of the arbitrary nature of these measures.

In general, M1 in both countries consists of currency and various types of checkable deposits – those on which checks can be drawn. As mentioned previously, all the components are typically accepted in making transactions.

- **M2** – M2 builds on M1 by also including certain assets that are readily converted into a medium of exchange. For the most part, the assets that are added to M1 to obtain M2 are savings and time deposits at depository institutions (commercial banks and thrift institutions).

More precisely, M2 in the United States includes the components of M1 as well as savings deposits, money market deposit accounts, small-denomination (less than $100,000) time deposits, small-denomination retail repurchase agreements,[7] and balances in retail money market mutual funds.

In Canada, M2 adds to M1 personal notice and term deposits[8] as well as nonpersonal notice deposits. As in the United States, these types of deposits are essentially various types of savings deposits. However, a portion of the notice deposits included in Canadian M2 are checkable, whereas in the United States all checkable deposits are included in its measure of M1. This points out another discrepancy between the U.S. and Canadian measures.

- **M3** – The broadest monetary aggregate, M3, adds to M2 assets that are typically held by large asset holders.

Specifically, M3 in the United States includes M2, large-denomination time deposits issued by all depository institutions, balances in institution-only money market mutual funds, repurchase agreement liabilities (overnight and term) issued by all depository institutions, and Eurodollars (overnight and term).[9]

The Canadian version of M3 adds foreign currency deposits and nonpersonal term deposits to M2.

---

[6] These other checkable deposits, among other items, are included in a Canadian measure called M2+. This measure is not presented in Table 8.1.

[7] A repurchase agreement is a short-term loan (often overnight) by an institution with temporarily idle funds to another institution. The borrower puts up collateral in the form of U.S. government securities and agrees to "repurchase" the securities on the agreed date.

[8] Notice deposits are deposits that technically (although not in practice) require that the holder give "notice" to the bank before withdrawal. Term deposits, analogous to U.S. time deposits, have a specific maturity date.

[9] Eurodollars are deposits, denominated in U.S. dollars, in foreign banks or U.S. bank branches located in foreign countries. The amounts included in M3 are those held by U.S. residents at foreign branches of U.S. banks worldwide and at all banking offices in the United Kingdom and Canada.

The Total Money Supply in Our Model

Define $(M1)_t$ as a measure of what is often called the **money supply**, the total nominal stock of deposits at banks in period t. [Note that, because at this point in our analysis there is no money held outside of banks (no money held as currency), deposits are the only form of money in this economy. We will change this assumption in Chapter 9. Hence, for now, our definition of $(M1)_t$ roughly corresponds to the Federal Reserve's and Bank of Canada's M1 measures in the absence of currency.] Recall that a fraction γ of $(M1)_t$ must be held in fiat money. The stock of fiat money M_t in a reserve requirement economy is called the **monetary base**. We can express the relation between the money supply and the monetary base in a reserve requirement economy through either of the following equations

$$M_t = \gamma (M1)_t \tag{8.8}$$

$$\Rightarrow (M1)_t = \frac{M_t}{\gamma}. \tag{8.9}$$

Equation 8.9 tells us how we can find the total money supply from two things known by the central bank: the reserve requirement and the monetary base. Because $\gamma < 1$, we know that $(1/\gamma) > 1$. An increase in the monetary base will result in an increase in the total money stock of $1/\gamma$ times the increase in the monetary base. The total money stock is $1/\gamma$ times the monetary base. For this reason, the ratio of $(M1)_t$ to M_t, which in this economy equals $1/\gamma$, is often called the **money multiplier** and the monetary base is often called the stock of **high-powered money**.[10]

Example 8.1

a. Suppose the reserve requirement is 20 percent. By how much would $(M1)_t$ change if the monetary base were increased by 100?
b. What would happen to the total money supply $(M1)_t$ if the reserve requirement were doubled?

Is the total money stock a useful measure? If so, it should help us to predict important economic variables. Let us look first at the relation between the total money stock and the price level.

$$p_t = \frac{M_t}{\gamma N_t h_t}. \tag{8.10}$$

Recalling that $(M_t/\gamma) = (M1)_t$, we can rewrite our expression for the price level as

$$p_t = \frac{(M1)_t}{N_t h_t}. \tag{8.11}$$

---

[10] As we will learn in the Chapter 9, the money multiplier will not always equal $1/\gamma$.

As in previous chapters, the behavior of prices in this economy is consistent with the quantity theory of money; any increase in the total nominal money stock causes a proportionate increase in the price level (assuming a constant demand for money, $N_t h_t$). In this economy, the total nominal stock of money (*M1*) is more useful than the monetary base alone in predicting the behavior of prices. Prices change in proportion to *M1*, regardless of whether the change in *M1* is caused by a change in γ or in the stock of fiat money. The stock of fiat money is not as tightly linked to prices because prices change with no change in the fiat money stock if there is a change in the reserve requirement.

If, however, the demand for deposits $N_t h_t$ is affected by the rate of return on deposits, the change in the price level will depend on the tool used to change *M1*. We have seen that an increase in *M1* from a decrease in the reserve requirement will increase the rate of return on deposits, but an increase in *M1* from an increase in the monetary base will lower the rate of return on deposits (if the increase comes from a permanently higher rate of fiat money expansion, z) or will have no effect on the rate of return on deposits (if the increase comes from a one-time increase in the monetary base). Because the tool through which the money stock is changed affects the rate of return on deposits, the demand for deposits and thus the price level will depend on the tool used.

We will now check whether *M1* is a useful measure for predicting the behavior of other economic variables. That is, do the relations between *M1* and other variables depend only on *M1*, or do they depend on the way in which *M1* is changed?

We have already found that the two ways of increasing the total money stock, an increase in the monetary base M_t and a decrease in the reserve requirement, have opposite effects on seigniorage; an increase in M_t (i.e., $z > 1$) increases seigniorage, but a decrease in the reserve requirement γ lowers seigniorage. We have found similar differences in their effects on output. An increase in the total money stock resulting from a decrease in the reserve requirement would increase capital and real output. In contrast, an increase in the monetary base M_t has no such direct effect on real output. In this economy, the effects on seigniorage and output of a change in *M1* depend on the means by which *M1* is changed. For these reasons, we may not wish to look only at *M1* when we ask about monetary policy.

Example 8.2

a. Suppose that each of the economy's 600 young agents has deposits worth 100 goods with a bank no matter what the rate of return. Assume that the reserve requirement is 10 percent and the monetary base is $3,000. Let $x > n$.

   i. What is the total nominal money stock?
   ii. What is the value of a unit of fiat money?
   iii. What is the price of a good in units of fiat money?

iv. How many goods would the government acquire if it increased the monetary base by 50 percent?

v. What is the real value of investment by banks?

b. How would your answer to each question in part a change if the reserve requirement doubled to 20 percent? Explain each of these changes in your own words.

c. Suppose the reserve requirement stays at 10 percent but banks voluntarily hold an extra 10 percent of deposits as fiat money reserves. Would your answers to part b change?

Central Bank Lending

Banks are required to demonstrate regularly[11] that they meet the level of reserves required for their level of deposits. If they fall short, they are faced with one of three options: (1) they can sell interest-bearing assets for fiat money; (2) they may borrow from other banks;[12] or (3) they may borrow from the monetary authority.[13]

The generally stated purpose of central bank lending is to permit banks to meet their reserve requirements when they find themselves unexpectedly short without being forced to sell off precipitously their interest-bearing assets. If the central bank approves, banks with reserves below the level required may borrow from the central bank to make up the difference. The reserves borrowed must be paid back with interest. This role of central bank lending in meeting temporary reserve shortages is described in Chapter 11.

Central bank lending may also be used to affect capital, output, the price level, and seigniorage even in stationary equilibria. It does so essentially by acting as an alteration of the effective reserve requirement faced by banks. In this section, we examine this role of central bank lending.

With its control over the stock of fiat money, a central bank has no trouble lending to a private bank: it simply prints whatever amount it wishes to lend and gives it to the private bank in return for the bank's promise to repay the loan, possibly with interest, at a later date. As long as the rate of interest owed to the central bank does not exceed the rate of return that can be earned on the bank's interest-bearing assets, the private bank will want to borrow from the central bank.

Limited Central Bank Lending

Let's now carefully work through the effects of central bank lending. A central bank's lending policy consists of the amount it is willing to lend and the rate of

---

[11] For example, biweekly in the United States.

[12] In the United States the market for loans between banks is called the **federal funds market**.

[13] Banks in the United States borrow at the Federal Reserve's **discount window**.

Assets		Liabilities	
Reserves	γH	Deposits	H
Interest-bearing assets $\delta\gamma H + (1-\gamma)H$		Loans from the central bank	$\delta\gamma H$
		Net worth	0
Total assets	$\delta\gamma H + H$	Total liabilities	$\delta\gamma H + H$

Figure 8.2. A bank's balance sheet.

return it charges. Let δ represent the fraction of a bank's reserves financed by loans from the central bank. A bank with deposits of H and reserves of δH is entitled to borrow $\delta\gamma H$ from the central bank. Let Γ_t^B represent the total nominal amount of borrowed reserves. We will continue to let M_t denote the stock of fiat money that has not been borrowed from the central bank (*nonborrowed reserves*).[14] It follows that borrowed reserves as a fraction of all reserves are given by

$$\delta = \frac{\Gamma_t^B}{\Gamma_t^B + M_t}. \tag{8.12}$$

implying that, as Γ_t^B goes to infinity, δ goes to 1.

A profit maximizing bank will use central bank loans to acquire additional interest-bearing assets. As a result of a central bank loan, the balance sheet of a private bank is altered as shown in Figure 8.2.

We can find the effects of central bank lending on key variables by following the same steps we used to find the effects of reserve requirements.

The value of a unit of fiat money is found as always from the equality of fiat money's supply and demand. The demand for fiat money comes from the reserve requirement, which may now be satisfied from a combination of borrowed ($\delta\gamma H_t = \delta\gamma N_t h_t$) and nonborrowed ($v_t M_t$) reserves

$$\delta\gamma N_t h_t + v_t M_t = \gamma N_t h_t. \tag{8.13}$$

From Equation 8.13 we can find the price level, the inverse of v_t:

$$v_t M_t = \gamma N_t h_t - \delta\gamma N_t h_t$$

$$v_t M_t = \gamma(1-\delta)N_t h_t$$

$$v_t = \frac{\gamma(1-\delta)N_t h_t}{M_t}$$

$$p_t = \frac{1}{v_t} = \frac{M_t}{\gamma(1-\delta)N_t h_t}. \tag{8.14}$$

---

[14] Because deposits are the only form of money, fiat money is held only as reserves. This changes in Chapter 9, when fiat money is also used as currency.

Note from Equation 8.14 that the presence of central bank lending ($\delta > 0$) results in a higher price level than when it is absent ($\delta = 0$). Note from Equation 8.14 that, if all reserves are provided by the central bank ($\delta = 1$), the effect is the same as having no reserve requirement – fiat money will have no value (the price level will be infinite).

Lending by the central bank functions as a reduction in the reserve requirement. By supplying some of the reserves needed to meet the reserve requirement, central bank lending essentially lowers the reserve requirement from γ to $\gamma(1 - \delta)$. By lowering the demand for the nonborrowed reserves in public hands (M_t), it lowers the value of fiat money, increasing the price level.

Central bank lending also expands intermediated investment. Note from the bank's balance sheet in Figure 8.2 that central bank lending allows private banks to increase their holdings of interest-bearing assets to

$$(1 - \gamma)N_t h_t + \delta \gamma N_t h_t = [1 - \gamma(1 - \delta)]N_t h_t. \tag{8.15}$$

Central bank lending has the same effect on intermediated investment as a reserve requirement lowered to $\gamma(1 - \delta)$. Note that the size of the change in intermediated investment depends on the size of the central bank loan (δ) but not on the rate of interest charged by the central bank. Although the nominal amount of central bank lending is unlimited, in real terms the most that central bank lending can add to intermediated investment is $\gamma N_t h_t$, the real value of reserves.

Central bank lending also affects the total nominal money stock. Required reserves must now equal the sum of borrowed and nonborrowed reserves,

$$\gamma (M1)_t = \delta \gamma (M1)_t + M_t, \tag{8.16}$$

which yields a new form for the equation defining the money multiplier:

$$(M1)_t = \frac{M_t}{\gamma(1 - \delta)}. \tag{8.17}$$

Central bank lending expands the total nominal stock of money by allowing greater nominal deposits for each dollar of nonborrowed reserves. Once again, central bank lending works exactly like lowering the reserve requirement to $\gamma(1 - \delta)$.

The effects of central bank lending on government revenue and the rate of return to depositors depend on the rate of return that must be paid to the central bank for its loans. Let ψ denote the real gross rate of return paid on central bank loans.

Let us now derive the rate of return paid by banks on deposits. Against each unit of deposits, the fraction γ is held as reserves, which pay the real rate of return n/z. When the central bank lends a fraction δ of the required reserves, the fraction $[1 - \gamma(1 - \delta)]$ of deposits is held in capital, which pays the real rate of return

x. Hence, the total real rate of return that the bank receives on its assets is equal to $\gamma(n/z) + [1 - \gamma(1 - \delta)]x$. To find the real rate of return on deposits we must subtract from this amount the return that must be paid to the central bank for its loan of $\delta\gamma$:

$$r^* = \gamma\left(\frac{n}{z}\right) + [1 - \gamma(1 - \delta)]x - \psi\delta\gamma. \tag{8.18}$$

Note that, in the absence of central bank lending ($\delta = 0$), Equation 8.18 is equivalent to our earlier expression for r^*, Equation 8.6.

Suppose the real interest rate of central bank loans ψ is equal to the market interest rate x. In this special case, Equation 8.18 simplifies to

$$r^* = \gamma\left(\frac{n}{z}\right) + [1 - \gamma(1 - \delta)]x - x\delta\gamma$$

$$= \gamma\left(\frac{n}{z}\right) + x - \gamma x + \gamma\delta x - \gamma\delta x$$

$$= \gamma\left(\frac{n}{z}\right) + (1 - \gamma)x \qquad \text{[given } \psi = x\text{]}. \tag{8.19}$$

In this case, the rate of return on deposits is unaffected by central bank lending [δ does not appear in the expression determining r^* (Equation 8.19)]. Although central bank loans enable banks to invest more in capital, the return from these investments is paid back to the central bank, leaving depositors no better off. If the central bank offers loans at interest rates below the market return (i.e., if $\psi < x$), the rate of return on deposits will increase as a result of central bank lending.

As another special case, suppose the central bank charges no nominal interest on its loans ($\psi = n/z$). Then we see from Equation 8.18 that

$$r^* = \gamma\left(\frac{n}{z}\right) + [1 - \gamma(1 - \delta)]x - \left(\frac{n}{z}\right)\delta\gamma$$

$$= [1 - \gamma(1 - \delta)]x + \gamma(1 - \delta)\left(\frac{n}{z}\right) \qquad \text{[given } \psi = n/z\text{]}. \tag{8.20}$$

In this case, the return on deposits increases to the same rate as it would for a decrease in the reserve requirement to $\gamma(1 - \delta)$.

Unlimited Central Bank Lending

We have assumed until now that the central bank sets a limit, δ, on the fraction of reserves that may be borrowed. An alternative policy is for the central bank to

Figure 8.3. The effect of lowering the central bank's interest rate on loans to banks. If a central bank lowers its interest rate on loans to banks from ψ^* to $\tilde{\psi}$, the total capital stock rises from K^* to $\tilde{K}$. The total capital stock is limited by the amount of the total endowment that is not consumed, $N(y - c_1^*)$.

set only the interest it will charge, ψ, and permit banks to borrow as much as they desire.

When the market rate of return is determined by a fixed rate of return to capital, x, a policy of unlimited central bank lending results in a degenerate set of possible equilibria. If $\psi > x$, no bank will borrow from the central bank. If $\psi < x$, banks will borrow unlimited amounts, driving δ to 1 and the price level to infinity. If $\psi = x$, any amount of borrowed reserves may be an equilibrium.

It is easier to envisage a policy of unlimited central bank lending when the marginal product of capital, $f'(K)$, is a diminishing function of the total capital stock. As always, banks wish to borrow from the central bank as long as the rate of return they earn, $f'(K)$, exceeds the rate of return they must pay, ψ. As borrowing from the central bank expands, bank investment in capital also expands, lowering the marginal product of capital and thus the market rate of return. Borrowing from the central bank and capital expand until the marginal product of capital just equals the rate of return charged by the central bank. By lowering the rate of return it charges, the central bank in this way can expand lending by private banks and thus the capital stock. Examine in Figure 8.3 the effect on capital of lowering the central bank's interest rate from ψ^* to $\tilde{\psi}$.

Before advocating ever lower interest rates on central bank loans as a way to greatly expand the economy, we must remember to consider other factors. First, expanded central bank lending raises the price level (which hurts the current holders of fiat money). Second, the real effect on capital of lowering the rate charged by the central bank is limited to the real value of reserves $\gamma N h_t$. This is but a small fraction of the total capital stock.

Example 8.3 Assume the demand for deposits equals 100,000 goods and the nonborrowed part of the monetary base is $20,000. Let the reserve requirement be 12 percent.

a. Find the price level, the total money stock, and the real value of investment by banks in the absence of central bank lending.
b. Now assume that the central bank allows banks to meet one-third of their reserve requirement by borrowing from the central bank and that banks take full advantage of this privilege. Answer part a given this new assumption.

Central Bank Lending Policies in Canada and the United States

The extent of borrowing from the central bank depends on the difference between the rate charged by the central bank (the **discount rate** in the United States, the **Bank rate** in Canada) and the rate private banks charge each other (called the **federal funds rate** in the United States). The rate banks charge each other is determined by the market and therefore is tied to the rate of return banks can get through loans or the purchase of securities. If the central bank rate is below the market interbank rate, banks have an arbitrage incentive to borrow as much as possible from the central bank in order to lend at the higher market rate.

To prevent banks from exploiting their borrowing privilege at the central bank, the central bank may choose to limit bank borrowing to cases of special need. Alternatively, it could choose to set the central bank rate equal to or greater than the market rate to eliminate the arbitrage incentive to borrow from the central bank.

As examples of the actual implementation of central bank lending policies, it is interesting to compare and contrast those of the Bank of Canada and the Federal Reserve. From 1980 through 1995, the Bank of Canada pursued a policy whereby its Bank rate was set equal to the Government of Canada's 91-day Treasury bill rate plus one-fourth of 1 percent. Such a policy could be called a floating penalty rate, because the rate adjusts to market conditions and is above market rates. In this way, the incentive for banks to take out loans from the central bank for profit motives is reduced. During this period, the Bank of Canada could affect the Bank rate only indirectly by policies that impacted the Treasury bill rate. Because the arbitrage incentive is reduced with such a policy, the Bank of Canada did not discourage loans to the chartered banks during this period.

In contrast, the discount rate in the United States is an administered rate. It is set by the Federal Reserve and changes relatively infrequently. Consequently, there are times when the discount rate is lower than market interest rates. When this occurs,

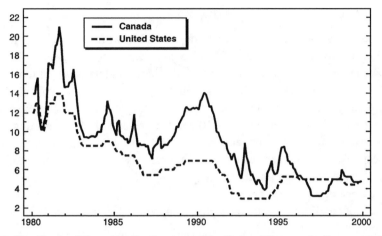

Figure 8.4. The Bank of Canada's Bank rate and the Federal Reserve's discount rate. Before 1996, the Bank of Canada followed a policy whereby its lending rate to chartered banks (the Bank rate) was set slightly above the interest rate on Government of Canada Treasury bills. By contrast, the Federal Reserve's discount rate is an administered rate that remains constant for periods of time. *Sources:* The Bank rate is from various issues of the Bank of Canada *Review*. The discount rate is from the Federal Reserve *Bulletin* (various issues). Both series consist of monthly observations.

banks have an incentive to borrow from the Federal Reserve. Since 1995, the Bank of Canada also has followed a policy of an administered rate.

To illustrate the differences between administered rate and penalty rate policies, Figure 8.4 displays a graph of the Bank of Canada's Bank rate and the Federal Reserve's discount rate over the past two decades.

Summary

This chapter has focused on two tools typically used by central banks – reserve requirements and loans to banks.

Reserve requirements give rise to a simple money multiplier whereby the total money supply is a multiple of the monetary base. This money multiplier is inversely related to the size of the reserve requirement. Reserve requirements increase the value of fiat money by increasing the demand for it. However, they also allow less intermediation of capital by banks, which in turn causes lower output. Higher reserve requirements also induce a lower level of utility for future generations by lowering the rate of return that banks can pay on deposits.

Banks that find themselves short of the amount of reserves required by law may turn to the central bank as a source of loans. In its effect, central bank lending is generally equivalent to a decrease in the reserve requirement.

Exercises

8.1 Consider an economy with a constant population in which people wish to hold bank checking deposits worth a total of 5,000 goods in every period. The economy has a total endowment of 10,000 goods in each period. There is a total stock of unintermediated capital of 1,000 goods in each period. Bank deposits are the only form of money in the economy. Deposits at banks are subject to a reserve requirement of 20 percent. The net real rate of return on capital is 10 percent per period. After meeting the reserve requirement, banks invest the remainder of all deposits into capital. Individuals do not hold capital. The fiat money stock (monetary base) is $2,000 in every period. Calculate values for the following variables.

   a. The price of a good (in dollars).

   b. The gross real rate of return on deposits that will be offered by banks in a competitive economy.

   c. The total nominal money stock *M1*.

   d. The money multiplier.

   e. The total capital stock.

   f. Real GDP.

8.2 Answer each part of Exercise 8.1 assuming that the central bank allows banks to borrow up to one-half of required reserves at a net interest rate of 8 percent.

Chapter 9

Money Stock Fluctuations

WE OBSERVE IN real-world data a great deal of fluctuation in our measures of the money stock. Why is this so? Are central banks playing with the money stock, capriciously increasing or decreasing it? To this point in our studies, the government has determined the nominal stock of money through its complete control over the monetary base and reserve requirements. We observe, however, that central banks often miss their announced targets for the money stock. Are the people in charge hopelessly incompetent, or have our models overlooked some important source of fluctuation in the money stock?

By definition, the total money stock is the product of the monetary base and the money multiplier. When we observe (as we do) changes in the money stock that do not come from changes in the monetary base, they must result from changes in the money multiplier. If the money multiplier is random, a central bank cannot exactly predict the total money supply even though it knows how much money it has printed (the monetary base). In Chapter 8 the money multiplier was found to be simply the inverse of the reserve requirement. Because reserve requirements rarely change (and would be well known to the central bank), they cannot be the source of the observed fluctuations in the money multiplier. Something else must be responsible.

Figure 9.1 plots quarterly money multiplier data for the U.S economy. Note the patterns in the money multiplier in relation to recession years (shaded regions of the graph).

Fluctuations in the money multiplier are of special interest because they appear to be linked with real output. Several studies have found that innovations (fluctuations unpredictable from past behavior) in the money multiplier are positively correlated with innovations in real output. If we can find a source of fluctuations in the money multiplier, we may also be able to explain one of the most puzzling monetary phenomena: the observed correlation between the nominal money stock and real output. That is the goal of this chapter.

Figure 9.1. The money multiplier for the U.S. economy. Shaded regions of the graph represent periods when the U.S. economy was in recession (two or more consecutive quarters of falling real gross national product). Note that, among many other fluctuations, the money multiplier declines in the recession years of 1961, 1970, 1974, 1980, and 1991. (The trend decline in the multiplier comes from an increased use of forms of money not measured in M1 and from the dramatic rise in foreign demand for currency with the break-up of the Soviet Union.) *Sources:* The money multiplier is calculated as the ratio of M1 to the monetary base. Both series are from various issues of the *Federal Reserve Bulletin*.

The Correlation Between Money and Output

One of the most puzzling phenomena in monetary economics is an observed positive correlation between the nominal money stock and real output. Although it is easy to understand a link between the number of dollars and nominal output (the dollar value of production), why should there be any link between the number of dollars and real output (the goods value of production)? Can these nearly fictitious units of account have any influence on the productivity of workers and machines?

This is potentially the most important question in monetary economics. The monetary authority has the power to change the money stock at will. Therefore, if the money stock influences real output, the monetary authority can influence real output. At a minimum, this implies that reducing fluctuations in the money stock will reduce fluctuations in real output; at best, this implies that the monetary authority can stimulate real output at will.

Before we get carried away with visions of ending the business cycle through the creative manipulation of the money stock, we should acknowledge some other possibilities. Perhaps the changes in output cause the changes in the money stock. It is also possible that an observed correlation between two variables does not imply that one of the variables causes the other to change. Instead it may be that changes in some third, unobserved, variable cause the changes in both observed variables, generating the observed correlation.

Let us be more explicit about the patterns observed in the data concerning money and output. An **innovation** in some variable may be defined as the difference between a variable's actual value and the value predicted by the variable's recent behavior; loosely speaking, an innovation represents the unpredicted change, or surprise, in a variable. The following patterns in the data have been observed:

1. Innovations in real output are positively correlated with innovations in the total nominal money stock.[1]
2. The innovations in the total nominal money stock occur before the innovations in real output.[2] An innovation in money thus helps to predict a subsequent innovation in output.
3. When observations of the interest rate are studied together with observations of money and output, innovations in the interest rate help to predict innovations in money and output, and innovations in the money stock do not provide additional help in predicting innovations in output.[3]
4. The money innovations linked to output innovations primarily take the form of changes in the deposit-to-currency ratio (and the money multiplier).[4]

The observed precedence of money innovations to output innovations (pattern 2) led many to suspect that the innovations in the money stock cause the innovations in output. The loose reasoning was that if instead the output innovations caused the money innovations, the output innovations would have occurred first.[5]

The other evidence, however, casts doubts on the idea that the monetary authority can use its control of the money stock to effect changes in output. An economist who looks only at money and output, omitting interest rates, will observe only the correlation between money and output. Pattern 3 suggests that this correlation may be spurious. Both money and output may be reacting to interest rates or some other variable related to interest rates.

Pattern 4 links output to the deposit-to-currency ratio, which is precisely that part of the money stock the government does not control. The existence of a money/output correlation therefore may not imply that output can be influenced by the parts of the money stock that are under the control of the monetary authority – for example, the monetary base.

We need an explanation consistent with all the observed patterns. Because one of these observations is that the money multiplier fluctuates with output (pattern 4), let us start by building a model of the money multiplier.

---

[1] See Friedman and Schwartz (1963b).
[2] See Sims (1972, 1980).
[3] See Sims (1980) and Litterman and Weiss (1985).
[4] See Cagan (1965) and King and Plosser (1984).
[5] Output innovations still might be the cause of the money innovations if the monetary authority anticipates the output changes and acts even before the output innovations occur. This was suggested by Tobin (1970).

A Model of Currency and Deposits

In the model of Chapter 8, the money supply was exactly determined by the fiat money stock and reserve requirements. The special assumptions in that model – that bank deposits are the only form of money and that these deposits are subject to a binding reserve requirement – led to the model's simple prediction of a fixed money multiplier equal to the inverse of the reserve ratio.

In the model of Chapter 8, we discovered that changes in reserve requirements could lead to changes in the total money stock and output. However, because reserve requirements rarely change, they cannot be important determinants of the observed fluctuations in money and output. Because the link between money and output appears to be primarily a link between the money multiplier and output,[6] we will adapt our model to permit a money multiplier that can fluctuate even when the reserve requirement is fixed. We will do so by allowing the people in our model to choose between currency (made up of fiat money) and bank deposits (inside money backed by bank assets invested in capital). For simplicity, we assume that there are no reserve requirements. (The appendix presents a version of this chapter's model with reserve requirements imposed.)

A Model of Inside and Outside Money

Consider an economy of overlapping generations of two-period-lived people.[7] There exists a constant stock of fiat money. In each generation there are three types of people – workers, entrepreneurs, and bankers. All three types are risk neutral. A constant number of people of each type are born in each period.

Workers have an endowment of (they produce) the nonstorable consumption good when young but not when old. Workers are unable to create capital but want to acquire money in order to consume when old. Every worker has an endowment of a different size and thus wishes to hold a different amount of money balances. We will say that worker i desires money balances worth s_i units of the consumption good.

Workers all look alike. They are impossible to tell apart unless a worker chooses to reveal his identity. If he chooses, a worker may reveal his identity at a cost of ϕ goods.

Entrepreneurs have the endowments and preferences of workers but are also able to create capital that produces x goods ($x > 1$) in the next period for each good invested in the current period. The goods invested may be from their own endowment or from the endowment of others. The greater the rate of return on capital, the more entrepreneurs will invest from their own endowments. Entrepreneurs cannot be located by workers.

---

[6] See, for example, the evidence cited by Cagan (1965) or by King and Plosser (1984).

[7] This model is adapted from Freeman and Huffman (1991), which draws on Sargent and Wallace (1982) and Prescott (1987). See also Lacker (1988) and Schreft (1992).

Bankers represent the third type of person. Bankers have no endowment and no ability to create to capital but they have two advantages over other types: (1) they are able to locate entrepreneurs; and (2) their identity is costlessly known to all.

If workers in this economy try to acquire money on their own, their only option is fiat money with the rate of return 1. Bankers, however, are able to locate entrepreneurs who may invest in capital with the rate of return x, which is greater than 1. This difference in rates of return should encourage enterprising bankers to seek to profit through arbitrage. They can profit if they borrow from workers at a low rate of return and lend to entrepreneurs at a higher rate of return.

Let us describe an intermediation arrangement that may spring up as a result of this rate-of-return difference. The arguments for the development of such an arrangement are similar to those developed in Chapter 7. In a competitive market, bankers will be able to receive the rate of return x on anything lent to entrepreneurs. Any lower rate of return implies excess profits to the entrepreneurs. In this case, any banker could demand a higher rate of return, r, knowing that some entrepreneur will accept the loan because he could still make profits of $x - r$ on each good he accepts from the banker. In this way, the interest rate paid to bankers will rise until $r = x$, where entrepreneurs are no longer interested in accepting any more loans. In the same way competition among bankers will also increase the rate of return on workers' deposits to x.

A note is also in order regarding the transaction cost ϕ of this model. We can view this cost as one that a person incurs when withdrawing deposits from a bank. It could represent the costs of going to the bank, waiting in line, and identifying oneself in order to make a withdrawal. Alternatively, it could be the cost associated with identifying oneself when writing a check or the fee the bank charges to cover the cost of clearing the check. This identification cost is not inherent in all transactions. If banks were allowed to issue private bank notes (tradable notes payable to the bearer but issued by private banks), no identification cost would be incurred when these notes were exchanged (ϕ would be zero).

We assume instead that privately issued bank notes are outlawed, leaving fiat money as the only available form of currency. The prohibition on private bank notes is a nearly universal restriction in modern economies, perhaps to enable the collection of seigniorage.

The gross rate of return of an asset is the amount received from the asset divided by the amount put into the asset. From the earlier discussion, we know that banks will pay a rate of return of x on deposits (before transaction costs).[8] If we now include transaction costs, the return from depositing s_i with a banker is $xs_i - \phi$. Then the

---

[8] As we found in Chapter 8, banks subject to a requirement to hold fraction γ of deposits in reserves of fiat money would pay the rate of return $(1 - \gamma)x + \gamma n/z$. To keep things simple, we assume here that banks are not subject to a reserve requirement.

average rate of return from deposits after transaction costs is $(xs_i - \phi)/s_i = x - (\phi/s_i)$. This average rate of return is negatively related to the size of the transaction cost and positively related to the size of the deposit (s_i). With a small deposit, the transaction cost will be large relative to the size of the deposit and therefore will have a large adverse effect on the average rate of return.

Currency does not have a transaction cost (because there is no need to identify oneself when using fiat money). Its rate of return is the same, v_{t+1}/v_t, whatever the size of the individual's currency balances. If the stock of fiat money and the demand for currency do not change from time t to time $t + 1$, the rate of return on currency is simply 1.

In Figure 9.2 we graph the rates of return of deposits and currency as functions of the size of the transaction. Note from the graph that fiat money provides a better rate of return than deposits for small transactions but not for large ones. Ask yourself if you behave in the same way when making purchases.

Let's define H_t as the real value of total inside money balances in any period t and Q_t as the real value of total fiat money balances at t. The **deposit-to-currency ratio** in this economy can therefore be written as H_t/Q_t. Ask yourself what happens to the deposit-to-currency ratio as s^* increases or decreases.

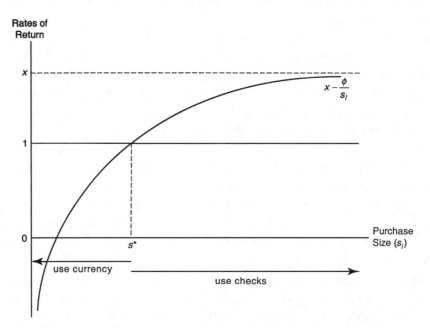

Figure 9.2. The choice of using currency versus checks. In determining whether to use currency or checks (deposits in banks) for making purchases, individuals will compare the rates of return on the two alternative assets. For small purchases (less than s^*), the rate of return on currency exceeds that on deposits, so that individuals will use currency. For large purchases, the rate of return on deposits dominates and, therefore, deposits will be used.

Let us now take a closer look at three key macroeconomic aggregates in this economy in any period t – the price level, p_t (the price of a good in units of fiat money, say dollars); the total nominal money stock, $(M1)_t$; and total real output, GDP_t (gross domestic product). Note first that, if the price of a good in dollars is p_t, then

$$p_t Q_t = M_t \quad \text{or} \quad p_t = \frac{M_t}{Q_t}. \tag{9.1}$$

Now recall that the total nominal money stock $(M1)_t$ is the sum of currency and bank deposits, measured in dollars. The nominal stock of currency equals M_t because fiat money is used entirely for currency, given that banks in this version of the model hold no reserves. The nominal stock of deposits can be written as real deposits multiplied by price of goods, or $p_t H_t$. Therefore, we have that

$$(M1)_t = M_t + p_t H_t. \tag{9.2}$$

Because $p_t = M_t / Q_t$ from Equation 9.1, we can also write

$$(M1)_t = M_t + \left[\frac{M_t}{Q_t} \right] H_t \tag{9.3}$$

$$= \left[1 + \frac{H_t}{Q_t} \right] M_t. \tag{9.4}$$

We see that $[1 + (H_t/Q_t)]$ is the **money multiplier** – the number by which we multiply the monetary base to find the total money stock. Unlike an economy where deposits (subject to a reserve requirement) are the only form of money, this economy has a money multiplier that depends on the public's relative preference for deposits and currency (the deposit-to-currency ratio, H_t/Q_t). As a result the money multiplier can no longer be reduced to the simple $1/\gamma$.

To see the mechanics of the money multiplier, suppose that in period t individuals display an increased desire to hold deposits at banks and less currency. In such a circumstance, H_t rises and Q_t falls. From Equation 9.4, the money multiplier clearly increases. For a fixed fiat money stock, the money supply as measured by $(M1)_t$ rises.

What might cause fluctuations in the money multiplier? We see from Figure 9.2 that anything affecting the rates of return of currency or deposits will changes s^*, altering the deposit-to-currency ratio and so the money multiplier. We suggest one possible source of fluctuations in the next section, a source that also accounts for the observed correlation between the money multiplier and real output.

Linking Output and the Money Multiplier

Suppose that in period t there is an unanticipated permanent increase in the productivity of capital as represented by x. More precisely, suppose that x increases to x'. Such a change is captured by an upward shift in the rate of return on deposits, as shown below in Figure 9.3.

Clearly from the diagram, the increase in x causes a decrease in s^* to $s^{*\prime}$. This implies that there is a decrease in the minimum purchase size for which deposits offer a higher rate of return than fiat money. In the aggregate, more individuals will use deposits (H_t, inside money, increases) as a form of money and fewer will use fiat money (Q_t, outside money, decreases). Hence, the deposit-to-currency ratio H_t / Q_t will increase. This, in turn, implies an increase in the money multiplier $[1 + (H_t / Q_t)]$. For a given monetary base (M_t), the increase in the money multiplier will cause an increase in $(M1)_t$.

The decreased demand for currency (fiat money) causes a decrease in its value – that is, an increase in the price level p_t (see Equation 9.1). Note that the price

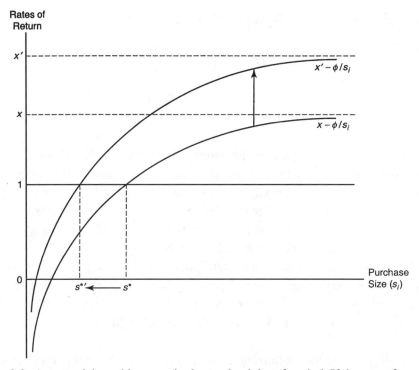

Figure 9.3. An unanticipated increase in the productivity of capital. If the rate of return on capital unexpectedly increases from x to x', banks can increase the rate of return paid on deposits. The curve representing this rate of return shifts up in the diagram. This causes a decrease in the minimum purchase size for which deposits offer a higher rate of return, causing an increase in the use of deposits and a decrease in the use of fiat money.

An unanticipated rise in productivity, $x \uparrow$

The Real Sector	The Monetary Sector
Capital rises	Money multiplier rises, $\left[1 + \dfrac{H_t}{Q_t}\right] \uparrow$
Direct investment rises, $K_t \uparrow$	Deposits rise, $H_t \uparrow$
Intermediated investment rises, $H_t \uparrow$	Currency demand falls, $Q_t \downarrow$
(Bank loans rise)	
	The price level rises, $p_t \uparrow$
Output rises, $\text{GDP}_{t+1} \uparrow$	The total money stock rises, $(M1)_t \uparrow$

Figure 9.4. Effect of a productivity change on real and monetary sectors.

level moves in the same direction as the total money stock even if there has been no change in the monetary base. Because the shock is permanent, it decreases the demand for currency in both periods t and $t + 1$, leaving currency's rate of return unaffected.[9]

What are the effects of the productivity change on the real sector of the economy? The rise in the productivity of capital means that, for any given stock of capital, more output will be produced. In addition, capital's greater rate of return will encourage more investment in capital from entrepreneurs, who invest directly, and from workers, who invest indirectly, when they make deposits at banks. Capital produces in the period after it is created, so output in period $t + 1$ will be

$$\text{GDP}_{t+1} = Y_{t+1} + x' H_t + x' K_t, \tag{9.5}$$

where Y_{t+1} is the sum of the endowments of the young workers and entrepreneurs born in period $t + 1$, $x' H_t$ is the output created in period $t + 1$ by capital that was created by intermediaries in period t, and $x' K_t$ is the output from capital created through direct investment. The increase in output in period $t + 1$ is caused by the combined effect of increases in x, H_t, and K_t.

The effects of the productivity change on the real and monetary sectors of the economy are summarized in Figure 9.4.

Note that our model displays the features described at the beginning of this chapter. First, the total money stock $(M1)_t$ is positively correlated with real output (here, they both increase). Second, the increase in the money stock precedes the increase in output by one period. Finally, changes take place in the form of changes in the deposit-to-currency ratio and the money multiplier.

---

[9] If the shock is temporary, the rate of return of currency is affected but the model's implications are not. See Freeman and Huffman (1991).

Correlation or Causality?

A casual observer looking at monetary aggregates and measures of real output may come to the conclusion that because the increase in $(M1)_t$ preceded the change in output, it caused the change in output. This is an unwarranted conclusion. The original source of the change in output was the increase in the productivity of capital as measured by x. This change in x also induced an increase in the rate of return on deposits, which, in turn, caused an increase in deposits and thus in the total money stock. However, the initial cause of the increase in output was the change in x and not the change in $(M1)_t$. The changes in the money stock preceded the output changes because people were able to adjust the composition of their money balances more rapidly than they could adjust production.

This is an important lesson to remember. We have noted that the total money stock is positively correlated with real output. This merely states that, as the money stock increases, so does real output. It is not a statement of causality. Even though the change in the total money stock preceded the change in real output, we cannot infer that it caused the change. The example demonstrates that correlation, or even precedence, does not imply causality.[10]

A Once-and-for-All Change in the Fiat Money Stock

Now let us consider another experiment. Suppose there is a once-and-for-all increase in the stock of fiat money owned by the initial old (M_0 increases). For example, suppose we double the stock of fiat money owned by the initial old. However, as before, the fiat money stock will remain fixed at this new higher level in subsequent periods ($M_t = M_0$ for all t). What will be the effect of such a change in our model?

Clearly, because the fiat money stock remains fixed over time, the rate of return on fiat money is still equal to 1 (recall that the population is fixed). Figure 9.2 indicates that nothing has been altered by this change. Only changes in the rate of return on fiat money or the rate of return on deposits affect s^*. Because s^* is unaltered, there is no effect on H_t or Q_t. Given that there is no change in the deposit-to-currency ratio, the money multiplier will remain fixed. Furthermore, the absence of any change in H_t or x implies that output (as measured in Equation 9.5) will remain the same.

Are there any effects from this change? Yes. From Equation 9.1, the price level in all periods increases because of the increase in M_t. In the case of a doubling of M_t, the price level is twice as high in every period. Furthermore, Equation 9.4 indicates that the total money stock $(M1)_t$ increases (doubles). Here we note an increase in the total money stock with no increase in output.

---

[10] See Leamer (1985) and Cooley and LeRoy (1985).

Suppose now that an economy experiences shocks to both the productivity of capital (x) and the monetary base (M_t).[11] Both shocks affect the total money stock. Real output, however, changes only in response to changes in the productivity of capital. An economist who looks only at the total money stock $[(M1)_t]$ and real output will still find a correlation between the two because both are affected by changes in the productivity of capital. An economist who looks at the real interest rate (x) along with money and output, however, will find that it is the real interest rate, not money, that is correlated with output. In this economy, output changes if and only if the real interest rate changes but only some of the time that money changes. Therefore, money has no remaining correlation with output once interest rate changes have been accounted for. This is consistent with pattern 3 in the data. It is also a good illustration of how the omission of important variables can mislead empirical work. Two variables (here, money and output) that are directly unrelated but are affected by a third variable (the productivity of capital) can appear to be linked to one another. An economist who looked only at money and output would be overlooking the variable that is the true source of all the changes.

A Monetary Stabilization Policy?

Many economists argue that active monetary policies can help to alleviate fluctuations in output. Our model can help to give some insights into this claim. By an active monetary policy, we mean one that changes in response to the state of the economy. The nature of such an active policy will become clear in the following example.

Suppose economists have been studying an economy where shocks to x have occurred over a long period of time. They note and statistically verify that the total nominal money stock is positively correlated with output. They are convinced that, because the shocks to money occur before the shocks to output, the money shocks must cause the output shocks. They go on to argue that, if the stock of fiat money is increased enough to offset a decline in the stock of inside money, the fluctuations in output will not occur because the total money stock will no longer fluctuate.

Let us examine these arguments in the context of our model. Suppose there is a decline in the productivity of capital as measured by x. This is the opposite of the case studied previously. This is represented by a downward shift in the curve depicting the rate of return on deposits that appeared in Figure 9.2. By reasoning similar to that pursued earlier, such a development would cause an increase in outside money (Q_t), decrease in inside money (H_t), a decline in the deposit-to-currency ratio (H_t/Q_t), and a decline in the money multiplier $[1 + (H_t/Q_t)]$. In the absence of any offsetting monetary policy, it would also cause a decline in the total money stock $(M1)_t$. We also know that it would cause a decline in intermediated capital,

---

[11] Repeated shocks make currency a risky asset and thus less desirable to risk-averse people. This does not affect the behavior of the risk-neutral people we have chosen to study here.

resulting in a decline in output in the following period. Can we void the decline in output by printing more fiat money, as suggested by the economists?

An unchanged total money stock can be maintained by offsetting the decline in inside money with an increase in the fiat money stock. To see how this might be accomplished, recall Equation 9.4:

$$(M1)_t = \left[1 + \frac{H_t}{Q_t}\right]M_t.$$

The decline in $[1 + (H_t/Q_t)]$ could be perfectly offset by increasing M_t by an appropriate amount. For example, if the money multiplier fell by half, the total money stock $(M1)_t$ could be held constant by doubling the monetary base.

Would such a policy succeed in its goal of avoiding the decline in output in the following period? The answer is no. The decline in the productivity and stock of capital would still cause a decline in output in the following period. The total money stock is statistically linked to real output only because the stock of inside money is linked to real output. If we offset the decline in inside money with an increase in outside money, there will still be a decline in total real output in the following period. The stabilization of the monetary aggregate (M1) does nothing to stabilize real output, despite the previously observed correlation.

Example 9.1 Suppose there is an unanticipated permanent decrease in transaction costs as represented by ϕ. Find its effect on s^*, the price level, the deposit-to-currency ratio, the money multiplier, the total nominal money stock, capital, and output. Explain each of these effects. Verify that the model economy displays a correlation between the nominal money stock and real output. Will a one-time increase in the monetary base cause an increase in real output?

Another Look at Monetary Aggregates

Much attention is paid to monetary aggregates, measures of the total quantity of money that include both inside and outside money. Because these aggregates do not distinguish between inside and outside money, we should pay attention to them only if the total stock of money is important but its composition is not.

In the model economy that we have just studied, the total money stock is a good indicator of the price level. We see that, whenever there is an increase in the money stock, whether from an increase in the monetary base or an increase in the money multiplier, there is also an increase in the price level.

The total money stock is not a useful measure when looking at real output in this model. Inside and outside money have very different statistical links to real output. It is not surprising that inside money has links to real output, and outside money does not. Inside money is deposits invested through banks in productive capital. In contrast, outside money is merely unbacked pieces of paper with no direct links to production.

If we look only at aggregates of the total money stock and ignore the composition of these aggregates, we can easily be misled. A correlation of inside money with real output appears to be a correlation of total money with real output when economists do not distinguish between changes in inside or outside money. This tempts the observer to believe incorrectly that changes in outside money, which is controlled by the central bank, may exhibit the same correlation. This error can be avoided if economists distinguish between changes in inside and outside money in their observations.

Anticipated Inflation and Output Revisited

Although current increases in the monetary base are not linked to current or future real output, in this economy anticipated future increases in the monetary base will affect the money multiplier and so capital and output. If the fiat money stock grows at the rate z, then the rate of return on fiat money with a constant population is $1/z$. Suppose there is an increase in the (anticipated) rate of money creation. An increase in z lowers the rate of return on fiat money, causing s^* to fall as shown in Figure 9.5. The lower rate of return on fiat money makes currency less desirable relative to bank deposits. As people substitute toward bank deposits, there is an

Figure 9.5. The effect of an increase in the rate of fiat money creation on the use of currency and bank deposits. When the anticipated rate of fiat money creation rises from z to z', the rate of return on fiat money falls. As the figure shows, this causes a decline in s^* to $s^{*'}$, resulting in an increase in the use of bank deposits and a decline in the use of currency.

increase in (intermediated) capital and subsequent output. This is the Tobin effect that we discussed in Chapter 6.

Does this mean that inflation is desirable in this economy? No. The shift away from currency implies that transaction costs have also increased. It should be reiterated that the total stock of currency is a small fraction of the size of the nation's capital stock, so that even if deposits replaced the entire stock of currency, the effect on output might be rather small. (See the section "The Tobin Effect" in Chapter 6.)

Summary

In this chapter we introduced a model of both currency and deposits. The model explains possible sources of observed fluctuations in the money stock that cannot be accounted for by changes in reserves requirements or the monetary base. We found that the money multiplier is determined by the deposit-to-currency ratio, which is outside the central bank's control. Factors that change the public's desired mix of currency relative to deposits lead to changes in the money multiplier and, hence, in the total money supply. These factors consist of anything that might cause the rates of return of deposits or currency to change.

Because deposits – inside money – are used by banks to invest in capital, deposits and the money multiplier are linked to events in the real economy. Such events, like an anticipated productivity of capital, may therefore affect both output and the money stock, through the money multiplier, and real output. Therefore, the observation of a money/output correlation does not imply that changes in the money supply cause the changes in output.

Appendix: The Money Supply with Reserves and Currency

In Example 8.1 we determined the money supply assuming that there were bank deposits with reserve requirements but no currency. In the actual U.S. economy, there are both currency and bank deposits with reserve requirements. To study this case and for further practice in distinguishing between inside and outside money, do Appendix Exercise 9.1.

To do the exercise, you may want to remind yourself of the following definitions. The total nominal money stock $(M1)_t$ is defined as the sum of currency and bank deposits held by the nonbank public, measured in dollars.

$$(M1)_t = \text{nominal currency held by the nonbank public at } t \\ + \text{ nominal bank deposits at } t. \tag{9.6}$$

Part of the fiat money stock is held as currency by the nonbank public and part is held by banks as reserves:

$$M_t = \text{nominal currency at } t + \text{nominal reserves at } t. \tag{9.7}$$

This implies that

$$
\begin{aligned}
(M1)_t &= M_t + \text{nominal bank deposits at } t - \text{nominal reserves at } t \\
&= M_t + p_t H_t - \gamma p_t H_t \\
&= M_t + p_t(1 - \gamma) H_t \\
&= M_t + \text{nominal intermediated capital at } t.
\end{aligned} \tag{9.8}
$$

Note that real inside money $(1 - \gamma)H_t$, which represented all deposits when there was no reserve requirement ($\gamma = 0$), now represents only that part of deposits backed by capital. The total real demand for fiat (outside) money includes currency held by the nonbank public (Q_t) and bank holdings of reserves, which are a fraction of the demand for deposits (γH_t).

By following the steps taken in Equations 9.1 to 9.4, we can derive the money multiplier in the presence of a reserve requirement. The money market-clearing condition becomes

$$M_t = p_t Q_t + \gamma p_t H_t \implies p_t = \frac{M_t}{Q_t + \gamma H_t}. \tag{9.9}$$

From Equation 9.8, the total nominal money stock is

$$
\begin{aligned}
(M1)_t &= M_t + \left[\frac{M_t}{Q_t + \gamma H_t} \right] (1 - \gamma) H_t \\
&= \left[1 + \frac{H_t(1 - \gamma)}{Q_t + \gamma H_t} \right] M_t.
\end{aligned} \tag{9.10}
$$

The term in brackets is the money multiplier in the presence of both currency and deposits subject to reserve requirements. As we found in Chapter 8, a decrease in the reserve requirement causes an increase in the total money stock $(M1)_t$.

Note that the expression for the money multiplier in Equation 9.10 includes the two special cases we have already studied. When no currency balances are held ($Q_t = 0$), the money multiplier from Equation 9.10 reduces to $1/\gamma$. When no reserves are held ($\gamma = 0$), it reduces to $[1 + (H_t/Q_t)]$.

Appendix Exercise

9.1 Consider an economy in which people wish to hold bank checking deposits worth a total of 5 million goods and currency worth 2 million goods in every period. In addition there is a stock of unintermediated capital worth 10 million goods. Fiat money is the only asset used as currency. Deposits at banks are subject to a reserve requirement of 20 percent. After meeting the reserve requirement, banks invest the remainder of all deposits into capital. The monetary base is $1 million. *Hint*: The key to this exercise is understanding the difference between inside and outside money.

   a. Find the value (in goods) of a dollar.

   b. Find the total nominal money stock as measured by the Federal Reserve's definition of M1.

   c. Find the money multiplier.

   d. Find the total capital stock.

   e. Find the revenue (in goods) from seigniorage if the monetary base triples every period.

   f. Suppose people want to keep more of their money balances in the form of cash, although their total demand for money does not change. What will happen to each of your answers to parts a to e?

Chapter 10

Fully Backed Central Bank Money

A RECURRING MESSAGE throughout Part II of this book is that, in the presence of productive capital (i.e., when $x > n$), the holding of fiat money may be inefficient in two possible ways. First, fiat money offers a lower rate of return, which discourages people from holding and using this liquid form of money. Second, as people hold more real balances of fiat money, they hold less of productive capital, which reduces real output. In Chapter 9, for example, we saw that people were forced to choose between fiat money – with no transaction costs but unbacked by capital – and deposits – backed by capital but more costly to use.

Isn't there a way to have both minimal transaction costs and money backed by capital? We have speculated that, if we freed private intermediation from all restrictions, inside money might replace fiat money entirely, giving us a money fully backed by capital and paying the same rate of return as capital. Some, having observed the long pattern of government involvement in monetary affairs, might be reluctant to abandon all government involvement. They may doubt the ability of private banking to provide a single money acceptable to all or they may wonder how the economy would function without nominal prices. Without passing judgment on these claims, let us ask in this chapter whether there is a way to organize the central bank to use capital to pay the market rate of return on its money.

To be specific, in this chapter we consider a plan to back the money of the government or central bank with productive capital. We will find that the effects of monetary policy differ greatly when the central bank pays interest on the money it issues. We will see that, by paying interest on money, the central bank acts as a zero-profit financial intermediary rather than as a revenue agent for the government.[1] This chapter is not a description of the current monetary institutions of most countries

---

[1] For an empirical look at these issues, see Smith (1988).

Assets	Liabilities
Interest-bearing assets (including loans to banks)	Notes of the central bank (to be held as currency or reserves)

Figure 10.1. A central bank's balance sheet.

but is offered as a description of how we might want our monetary institutions to operate.[2]

Paying Interest on Money

An obvious way to increase the rate of return on government money is to pay interest to those who hold that money. How can this interest be paid?

To this point, we have studied only economies in which the government in the initial and subsequent periods issues unbacked money, which it can give away or use to purchase goods. An alternative monetary arrangement would use the issuance of money to back government-issued money with productive assets. A monetary arrangement with backed money requires that any issuance of government money, including the initial stock of money, must be used to purchase a real asset paying interest at the prevailing market rate. A purchase (or sale) of an interest-paying asset by the monetary authority is called an **open market operation**.[3] In this way, the monetary authority itself becomes an intermediary with assets and liabilities, just like a privately owned financial intermediary. Its liabilities are the notes it issues as money, whether held as currency or deposited with the central bank as bank reserves. The balance sheet of a central bank may be represented as shown in Figure 10.1.

From the return on the assets it owns, the central bank can pay interest on the money it issues.[4] The monetary authority is now no longer a revenue agent for the government but truly a central *bank*.

The model of three-period-lived people in which capital pays a return after two periods will prove a bit cumbersome at this point. The reason people turn to financial intermediaries is not essential to the point we wish to study – the backing of money. Therefore, let us return to the simpler model of intermediation described in Exercise 7.3. People live for two periods. Capital pays a one-period gross real rate of return equal to $x > 1$. We assume that capital has a minimum size, k^*, which is greater than the endowment of most individuals.

---

[2] Among others, the payment of interest on reserves has been advocated by Tolley (1957), Friedman (1960), and the U.S. Federal Reserve itself [see Feinman (1993)]. This particular model of paying interest on government money is adapted from the work of Smith (1991) and of Freeman and Haslag (1995).

[3] The distinction between open market operations and monetary expansions to fund subsidies or government spending is proposed by Metzler (1951).

[4] If the central bank receives interest from its assets but does not pay interest on its liabilities (money), the central bank earns profits, which can be turned over to the government. We take up this case in Chapter 13.

Capital is illiquid in this economy because of its lack of divisibility into small units. It is easy to see how an intermediary can overcome this illiquidity. Simply pool the savings of many individuals to an amount greater than k^*. Assuming that this intermediation is costless and competitive, private intermediaries will offer the rate of return x on deposits. (If it were costly, the competitive return would be x minus the cost.) There may be some individuals who have an endowment large enough to invest in capital without the aid of an intermediary, but we will focus our attention on those who must use intermediaries. For the rest of the model, let us return to the simplest overlapping generations model, with a constant population of two-period-lived people endowed with y when young and nothing when old.

Consider specifically a central bank conducting the following open market operation in the initial period: it sells the initial stock of money for goods that are invested in capital owned by the central bank.[5] Thereafter, the nominal stock of money will be held constant at M dollars and the stock of central bank capital will be held constant at K^g goods. Then, in the initial period,

$$v_1 M = K^g. \tag{10.1}$$

Proceeds from the central bank's holdings of capital will be used to pay net interest of ρ dollars in every period for each dollar held by the public. We assume that the central bank will pay the same interest in every period and will use all its net earnings from capital to pay this interest.

What will be the real rate of return on this backed central bank money for a given interest rate ρ? The cost of a dollar at t is v_t, and at $t+1$ the dollar returns $1+\rho$ dollars at its value, v_{t+1}. Thus the dollar's real (gross) rate of return is

$$\frac{v_{t+1}(1+\rho)}{v_t}. \tag{10.2}$$

The value of a unit of central bank money is determined by its supply and demand,

$$v_t M = N(y - c_{1,t} - h_t), \tag{10.3}$$

where h_t is the individual's holdings of deposits at banks, so that $y - c_{1,t} - h_t$ represents the individual's demand for real balances of central bank money.

Let us look at a stationary equilibrium. In a stationary equilibrium with values of $c_{1,t}$ and h_t that are constant over time, the value of a unit of central bank money is also constant over time ($v_1 = v_t = v$). Then the rate of return of a unit of central

---

[5] If the bank does not want to actually operate the capital, it may lend to the operators of capital by buying bonds they issue. In either arrangement, the bank owns an interest-bearing asset backed, directly or indirectly, by capital.

bank money in a stationary equilibrium is

$$\frac{v_{t+1}(1+\rho)}{v_t} = 1+\rho. \tag{10.4}$$

In the absence of legal restrictions on private banking, the central bank must compete with private intermediaries – its money must offer a real rate of return at least as great as that offered by the private banks, which is x in a competitive economy:

$$1+\rho \geq x \quad \text{or} \quad \rho \geq x-1. \tag{10.5}$$

Can the central bank afford to pay this rate of return? The total return from the central bank's investment is $x K^g$. To maintain a fixed stock of capital, K^g of this return must be used to replenish the bank's stock of capital (recall that capital is assumed to last only a single period). What remains is the net return

$$x K^g - K^g = (x-1)K^g. \tag{10.6}$$

In each period of a stationary equilibrium, the real money stock is Mv. The central bank promises to pay net nominal interest of ρ dollars on each dollar held, implying that total real interest payments by the central bank are ρMv. Note that because the stock of money is held constant the interest on money will be paid with dollars earned from the production of the bank's stock of capital and not from freshly printed dollars. This can be written as the central bank's budget constraint:

$$(x-1)K^g = \rho Mv. \tag{10.7}$$

Because ρ must equal $x-1$ if the rate of return on central bank money is to meet the competition from private bank money, the central bank's budget constraint is met only when

$$K^g = vM. \tag{10.8}$$

In summary, if the central bank uses all the net return from its assets to pay interest on its money, it must be that $K^g = vM$. This constraint is met when all money issued is used to purchase real capital. Essentially, the central bank has become a zero-profit, zero-cost intermediary offering the same rate of return on its liabilities (money) that it receives from its assets.[6] The central bank's balance sheet in real terms is displayed in Figure 10.2.

---

[6] If there are costs to private intermediation, the same costs can be expected to apply to intermediation by the central bank.

Assets		Liabilities	
Capital	K^g	Money in circulation	vM

Figure 10.2. The central bank's real balance sheet when paying interest on money.

Another Look at the Quantity Theory

What happens to the price level if the central bank increases the nominal stock of its money? Will the price level rise as it did when money was unbacked (in Chapter 3, for example), or will it be unchanged? The answer depends on what is done with the increased stock of money.

First, suppose the central bank uses the increase in the stock of money to purchase an even larger stock of capital. Suppose, in particular, that we double the central bank nominal money stock and use it to double the stock of capital. Is there still an equilibrium at the same price level as before? To answer, recall that to pay the market rate of return ($\rho = x - 1$), the central bank's budget constraint requires that the stock of central bank's capital K^g equal the real value of the central bank's liabilities (the money it issues) vM or

$$v = \frac{K^g}{M} \Rightarrow p = \frac{1}{v} = \frac{M}{K^g}. \tag{10.9}$$

Obviously, if we double both the nominal stock of central bank money and the stock of central bank capital, this equality still holds. When the central bank doubles its real capital, it doubles the amount it can pay in real interest. It can then afford to pay the market rate of interest on twice as much central bank money with no change in the value of that money (no change in the price level). How can the economy absorb twice as much central bank money without lowering its value? Look again at the supply and demand for central bank money in a stationary equilibrium (where real money holdings and real balances of deposits are constant over time):

$$vM = N(y - c_1 - h). \tag{10.10}$$

To determine what happens to c_1 and h when $K^g = vM$, let us examine the budget constraints of our usual two-period-lived individuals (endowed when young but not when old) who must choose their real balances of central bank money ($v_t m_t = vm$) and their real balances of deposits ($h_t = h$). The first-period budget constraint is

$$c_1 + vm + h = y. \tag{10.11}$$

Second-period consumption is financed by the returns from an individual's holdings of money and deposits at banks. With the central bank paying the net interest rate ρ for each dollar held, the real return from an individual's fiat money holdings when old are $(1 + \rho)vm$. Adding to that the real return from holding deposits (xh), we obtain the individual's second-period budget constraint:

$$c_2 = (1 + \rho)vm + xh. \tag{10.12}$$

Because both assets offer the same rate of return $(1 + \rho = x)$, Equation 10.12 can be written as

$$c_2 = xvm + xh = x(vm + h). \tag{10.13}$$

The sum $vm + h$ represents an individual's total real money balances (real balances of central bank money plus real balances of money in the form of deposits at private banks). Note that, because both forms of money offer the same return, an individual is indifferent between them. If we solve Equation 10.13 for this sum and substitute the result into the first-period budget constraint (Equation 10.11), we find the lifetime budget constraint:

$$c_1 + \frac{c_2}{x} = y. \tag{10.14}$$

An individual will pick the c_1^* and c_2^* that maximizes his utility subject to this budget constraint (Equation 10.14). Note from Equation 10.14 that an individual's budget constraint does not depend on the relative size of his balances of private bank and central bank money (h and vm). Therefore, he will choose the same c_1^* and c_2^*, whatever his balances of central bank money. If he holds more central bank money, by choice or by government requirement, he will simply hold that much less private bank money so that c_1^* and c_2^* remain at the levels that maximize his utility. In this way, the size of the open market operation in the initial period is irrelevant to the welfare of individuals and the total capital stock.[7]

Suppose, for example, that $y = 10$ and $x = 1.1$ and that facing this budget constraint, an individual chooses $c_1^* = 4$ and $c_2^* = 6.6$. [Check that this choice satisfies the lifetime budget constraint (Equation 10.14).] His budget Equations 10.11 and 10.13 reveal that he can achieve his choice of consumption with any combination of h and vm so that $h + vm = y - c_1^* = 6$. The individual is indifferent between $h = 4$ with $vm = 2$ and $h = 1$ with $vm = 5$, for example, because in both cases his real money balances total 6. Moreover, because both types of money are now backed by capital, the capital stock of a young person is the same (6 in this example) whatever the real value of central bank money.

Let us now return to the question of how the economy adjusts to an increase in central bank money when money is fully backed ($K^g = vM$). We have just learned that the consumption choice of the individual does not depend on the amount of

---

[7] For a related case and fuller exposition of the irrelevance of open market operations, see Wallace (1981).

central bank money. We can therefore write the equality of supply and demand for central bank money (Equation 10.10) as

$$vM = N(y - c_1^* - h), \tag{10.15}$$

or

$$Nh + K^g = N(y - c_1^*). \tag{10.16}$$

If the real stock of central bank money $vM = K^g$ increases and consumption stays the same, private bank money Nh must decrease by the same amount as the increase in central bank money. Note that the total real money stock, the total stock of intermediated capital, is $K^g + Nh$, which must equal $N(y - c_1^*)$, which is unaffected by the size of the central bank money stock. In earlier chapters we saw that an increase in real balances of fiat money may lead to a reduction in the economy's capital stock. This is no longer the case when the central bank backs its money with capital. An increase in real balances of unbacked, fiat money (for example, through an increase in the reserve requirement) implied that people held more balances consisting of unproductive pieces of paper and less balances of deposits backed by capital at private banks. However, when the money of both the central bank and private banks is backed by capital, a switch from private bank money to central bank money does not change the total holding of capital.[8]

The only limit to the expansion of central bank money is that it cannot exceed $N(y - c_1^*)$ if we assume that private banks cannot have negative deposits ($Nh \geq 0$). Up to this limit, however, one can increase the stock of backed central bank money without affecting the value of a unit of that money. An increase in the quantity of central bank money does not raise the price level – it lowers the quantity of private bank money. The equality of money supply and demand ensures that quantity equation is satisfied (nominal total money equals the price level times a constant),

$$M + pNh = pN(y - c_1^*), \tag{10.17}$$

but it is satisfied by the adjustment of nominal private bank money and not by the adjustment of the price level.

Why doesn't an expansion of backed central bank money have the same effect on the price level as an expansion of fiat money, as studied in Chapter 3? The key is the difference in the backing of the two types of money. To see this, suppose that our central bank decides to double the initial stock of its money but, instead of using the increase to purchase capital, it uses it to purchase consumption goods for the pleasure of government officials. As before, the central bank commits to using its

---

[8] Whether we want private or public intermediation of capital therefore depends on which is more likely to choose the wisest investments and operate at the lowest costs, two factors we have omitted from our simple model.

entire net revenue from capital to pay interest [the central bank's budget constraint (Equation 10.7)]. The real value of the interest payment ρv must therefore equal net revenue $[(x - 1)K^g]$ divided by the number of dollars (M) on which it must pay interest:

$$\rho v = \frac{(x - 1)K^g}{M}. \tag{10.18}$$

Recall that to meet the competition from private banks, the central bank must offer a rate of interest, $\rho = x - 1$, which implies that

$$v = \frac{K^g}{M} \Rightarrow p = \frac{1}{v} = \frac{M}{K^g}. \tag{10.19}$$

In this case the nominal stock of money M has doubled but not the capital stock backing it, K^g. The central bank has twice as many dollars on which to pay interest but the same real capital stock from which to pay this interest. For this reason, the central bank's budget constraint (Equation 10.19) reveals that the value of a unit of the central bank's money must fall by 50 percent (the price level doubles). However, the ability of the bank to pay interest is limited by the stock of capital in its portfolio. It cannot increase the real value of its interest payments without increasing its real stock of capital. Therefore, the real value of the stock of central bank money vM must always equal the real value of its stock of capital K^g.

We can explain the difference in price level effects of these two types of expansions of central bank money if we think of a unit of central bank money as a share in the assets of a firm called the central bank.[9] If a firm doubles the number of its shares without doubling its investment in capital, each new share is worth half the value of an old share. If, instead, a firm doubles the number of shares while doubling its capital stock and resulting profits, there is no change in the value of the firm's shares. The same must hold for a central bank that pays interest on money out of its return from capital. The analysis does not change when we change the labels from "firm" to "central bank" and from "shares" to "money."

Deflation

How can a central bank pay interest on money? It shouldn't be much of a problem to pay interest on the reserves deposited at the central bank, but how can one pay interest on currency in circulation? The advantage of currency in transactions is that one can exchange it for goods without the costly record-keeping involved in registering the transaction at a bank. This advantage would be lost if one had to take one's currency to the central bank from time to time to receive interest. Isn't there

---

[9] A further exposition of this analogy is offered by Smith (1985).

some way to increase the real rate of return on currency without directly paying interest?

Suppose the central bank uses the return from its assets not to pay interest but to purchase and destroy a fraction of the stock of central bank money in public hands. In particular, let the stock of central bank money, M_t, shrink over time according to the rule $M_t = z M_{t-1}$ with $z < 1$. The number of goods spent to reduce the stock of central bank money each period equals

$$v_t(M_{t-1} - M_t) \quad \text{or} \quad v_t M_t \left[\frac{1}{z} - 1 \right]. \tag{10.20}$$

We have already found that the net return from central bank assets (after renewing the capital stock) is $(x - 1)K^g$. If the net return is used only to purchase central bank money, the central bank's budget constraint is

$$v_t M_t \left[\frac{1}{z} - 1 \right] = (x - 1)K^g. \tag{10.21}$$

If the value of central bank money is equal to the stock of capital behind it $(v_t M_t = K^g)$, the central bank's budget constraint (Equation 10.21) becomes

$$K^g \left[\frac{1}{z} - 1 \right] = (x - 1)K^g, \tag{10.22}$$

which reveals that the central bank can afford to deflate at the rate z so that

$$\frac{1}{z} = x \quad \text{or} \quad z = \frac{1}{x}. \tag{10.23}$$

To find the rate of return of fiat money, we will proceed as always from the equality of money supply and demand. The demand for central bank money is again $y - c_{1,t} - h_t$ per young person. Therefore, the equality of supply and demand in a stationary equilibrium with a constant population requires that

$$v_t M_t = N(y - c_1 - h), \tag{10.24}$$

implying that

$$\frac{v_{t+1}}{v_t} = \frac{\frac{N(y - c_1 - h)}{M_{t+1}}}{\frac{N(y - c_1 - h)}{M_t}} = \frac{1}{z}. \tag{10.25}$$

Therefore, if the central bank deflates setting $z = 1/x$, it can give central bank money the rate of return of capital x. At this rate of return, people can receive the

same rate of return from central bank money that they receive from private intermediaries. Therefore, they do not care how much of the money stock is intermediated
through the central bank.

Our analogy to shares in a firm continues to apply. A firm is not limited to
dividends if it wishes to distribute business profits to its shareholders. Shareholders
are also paid if the firm buys up a fraction of its own shares. The reduction in
the number of shares increases the value of the remaining shares, distributing the
business profits to the shareholders. A central bank with backed money that reduces
the number of its outstanding dollars (shares) similarly makes the remaining dollars
more valuable.

Currency Boards[10]

Backing the stock of central bank money with interest-bearing assets can also be
used to ward off speculative attacks that occur in international currency markets.
When we studied speculative attacks in Chapter 4, we noted that a country can
prevent a speculative attack if it has enough funds to buy up all its currency in the
hands of speculators at the announced exchange rate. We assumed in Chapter 4
that these funds came from a government's ability to tax its citizens. This raised
the question of whether a government would actually go through with a plan to tax
its own citizens to pay off foreign exchange speculators.

A country that fully backs its money with interest-bearing assets has made a commitment that it can use to ward off speculative attacks against its currency. With a
fully backed currency, a central bank has the resources to redeem any amount of its
money that is turned in, whether by its own citizens or by foreign speculators. For
example, suppose a central bank has a nominal money stock of M^*, a value of that
money of v^*, and a capital stock of K^{g*}. If the money is fully backed, it must be
that these three satisfy the central bank's budget constraint (Equation 10.1), here
written as

$$v^* M^* = K^{g*}. \qquad (10.26)$$

If redemptions cause the nominal stock of central bank money to fall in half, from
M^* to $M^*/2$, the central bank can simply sell off half its capital stock to buy up
the money turned in, reducing it from K^{g*} to $K^{g*}/2$. The central bank's budget
constraint after these redemptions,

$$v^* \left[\frac{M^*}{2} \right] = \frac{K^{g*}}{2}, \qquad (10.27)$$

is met without affecting the value v^* of the money.

---

[10] This section presumes a familiarity with the material of Chapter 4.

A currency board works in almost exactly the same way. Consider a currency board along the rough lines of that introduced by Argentina in 1991. Argentina wants to fix the exchange rate of its currency, the peso, relative to the currency of a major trading partner, the U.S. dollar. Suppose the target exchange rate is e^*. To this end, Argentina issues M units of currency (pesos), using it to buy interest-bearing bonds, giving Argentina's currency board $\$A$ of assets, worth $\$e^*M$:

$$e^*M = A. \tag{10.28}$$

The currency board's budget constraint (Equation 10.28) is the same as the central bank's budget constraint (Equation 10.1), with e^* replacing v and A replacing K^g. The response of a backed currency to redemptions is unchanged by these changes in units from goods to dollars. If the current holders of Argentina's money come to the currency board to exchange one-third of their holdings for $e^*M/3$ dollars, the currency board can sell one-third of its dollar assets to meet this demand without triggering a devaluation of its currency. In this way, a country with the will to fully back its currency can unilaterally fix its exchange rate.

Should a country running a currency board back its money with the currency of the other country or with assets denominated in that currency? Obviously, holding assets that pay interest earns a superior return for the currency board, which can be passed along to moneyholders. A currency board that simply purchases the (non-interest-bearing) currency of the other country increases the seigniorage base of that currency, which enriches the other government.

There are two caveats, however. If the currency board earns interest but does not pay interest to its moneyholders, it earns a profit. If this profit is important to government revenue, people may believe there is a limit to the government's willingness to allow individuals to trade their currency for the reserve currency. In this case, a speculative attack (see Chapter 4) again becomes possible. To avoid this, the government must convince the public that revenue from the currency board is not essential. One obvious way to do so is to pay interest on money balances wherever possible (on reserves, for example).

As shown in Figure 10.3, the Argentine peso depreciated dramatically throughout the 1980s and into the early 1990s, with the exchange rate reaching nearly 10,000 pesos per U.S. dollar and with the Argentine inflation rate approaching 1,000 percent per year. In April 1991, Argentina adopted a currency board. Under this plan, the Argentine central bank agrees to exchange pesos for the U.S. dollar at a fixed ratio, in this case one-to-one. Such a policy disciplines the central bank in that the Argentine monetary base can expand only if dollars are exchanged for pesos at the central bank. After this plan was adopted by the currency board, Argentina's inflation rate dropped to single-digit levels.

Figure 10.3. The exchange rate between the Argentine peso and the U.S. dollar. After a substantial depreciation of the Argentine peso during the 1980s and early 1990s, a currency board was adopted in Argentina in April 1991. The currency board led to a dramatic stabilization of the exchange rate between the Argentine peso and the U.S. dollar.

Summary

In this chapter, we considered a plan in which money issued by a central bank is backed by productive capital. Under a system of fully backed money, the central bank issues money only by purchasing interest-bearing real assets. All interest the central bank receives from its holdings of real assets is used to pay interest on the money it issues. This backing of money effectively turns the central bank into a zero-profit financial intermediary, unlike the arrangements studied in earlier chapters, where a central bank issuing unbacked money was a revenue-generating device for the government.

This policy of backing government-issued money has dramatic implications on how the economy responds to increases in the quantity of central bank money. In previous chapters, where money was unbacked, increasing the supply of central bank money led to commensurate increases in the price level, transferring wealth from moneyholders to the government. However, if the central bank increases the stock of central bank money by purchasing productive assets and by paying interest from the returns on those assets, the increase in central bank money merely displaces individual holdings of private bank money. This displacement of private bank money leaves government revenue and the price level unchanged. Wealth is not transferred from moneyholders to the government.

From a practical point of view, paying interest on currency in circulation would be cumbersome. To avoid this difficulty, the central bank could implicitly pay a rate of return on its money by following a deflationary policy.

Another possible role for fully backed central bank money comes in the form of currency boards. With currency fully backed with interest-bearing assets, a central bank can ward off speculative attacks against its currency.

Exercises

10.1 Consider an economy in which people wish to hold money balances worth a total of 5,000,000 goods. They are indifferent between money issued by the central bank and money issued by private banks (so long as both offer the same rate of return). In the initial period the central bank issues $1,000,000 and uses the proceeds to purchase capital. The central bank owns a stock of capital equal to its stock of money and uses the return to pay interest on its money. Assume that $x = 1.2$ and a dollar always buys 2 goods. Intermediation, including the payment of interest on money, is costless.

    a. What rate of interest ρ must the central bank offer to induce people to accept its money? Does this satisfy the central bank's budget constraint?

    b. What is the real value of the total amount of money issued by private banks?

    c. Is there an equilibrium in which a dollar always purchases 3 goods? In this case, what is the real value of money issued by private banks?

    d. Argue that the people are indifferent between the equilibrium in which a dollar is worth 3 goods and the equilibrium in which a dollar is worth 2 goods.

    e. Suppose the central bank pays no interest on its money but maintains a constant stock of capital, using the net return from the capital it owns to buy up and burn a fraction of its money. Find z, the rate of change of the nominal central bank money stock. Check that the government budget constraint is met. (You should no longer assume that $v_t = 2$ in all periods.)

10.2 Consider an economy in which people wish to hold money balances worth a total of 4,000 goods. They are indifferent between money issued by the central bank and money issued by private banks (so long as both offer the same rate of return). The central bank owns a constant stock of capital equal to its stock of money and uses the net return to pay interest on its money. Assume that $x = 1.15$ and a dollar always buys 2 goods. Intermediation, including the payment of interest on money, is costless.

    a. What net rate of interest must the central bank offer to induce people to accept its money? What is the total net return from the assets owned by the central bank? Prove that this satisfies the central bank's budget constraint.

    b. What is the range of dollars that may be issued by the central bank so that a dollar always buys 2 goods? If the central bank issues $500, what is the total nominal value of money that will be issued by private banks?

    c. Assume again that the central bank has issued $500. If the central bank doubles the nominal stock of central bank money, for what central bank policy will a dollar still buy 2 goods? For what central bank policy will the value of a dollar fall to 1 good? Explain why your answer depends on what the central bank does with the new money.

Appendix: Price Level Indeterminacy

A consequence of the public's indifference between the money of private banks and of the central bank is that the price level may be undetermined – a wide range of price levels may be an equilibrium. Look again at the market-clearing condition for money balances (from Equation 10.15):

$$Nh + vM = N(y - c_1^*). \tag{10.29}$$

This equation can be satisfied by a range of possible combinations of v and h. If people should decide to hold exclusively central bank money, we find an equilibrium in which $h = 0$ and $v = N(y - c_1^*)/M$. If instead they decide to accept none of the central bank's money, we find an equilibrium in which $h = (y - c_1^*)$ and $v = 0$. Any values of h and v that satisfy Equation 10.29 and lie between these two extremes can also be an equilibrium.

Because people are indifferent between the two forms of money, given that each offers the same rate of return, it is impossible to guess which of the many equilibria will occur.

The central bank has a number of options to pin down the value of a unit of its money. It could set v equal to any number between 0 and $N(y - c_1^*)/M$. With the public indifferent among the various possible equilibria, there would be no difficulty in enforcing any particular value of v within this range. Almost as straightforwardly, the central bank could pick the real value of central bank investments K^g. Because $K^g = vM$ when money is fully backed, by picking K^g and M, the government can determine v.

Another way to determine the value of central bank money involves setting reserve requirements as we studied in Chapter 8. The central bank can require that each private bank hold reserves of central bank money equal to a fraction (γ) of the value of the private bank's deposits and bank notes. To ensure that banks or the public will not hold central bank money in excess of the required reserves, the central bank can promise to pay interest only on required reserves. Under this monetary regime, the market-clearing condition for money balances becomes

$$Nh = N(y - c_1^*), \tag{10.30}$$

with the reserve requirement specified as

$$\gamma N h = v M. \tag{10.31}$$

Combining Equations 10.30 and 10.31, we obtain the result

$$v M = \gamma N (y - c_1^*)$$

$$\Rightarrow v = \frac{\gamma N (y - c_1^*)}{M}. \tag{10.32}$$

It is easy to see from Equation 10.32 that, by choosing γ, the central bank may fix the price level.

Chapter 11

The Payments System

WE EXAMINE IN this chapter the role of banks in clearing private debt and the ways central bank policy may help or hinder banks in their role as clearinghouses. We have seen in earlier chapters how fiat money may be used to help people purchase goods. In reality, goods are not only purchased via a cash payment at the time of the transaction but also with a promise to pay at a more convenient time in the future. A purchase by check is an example. A merchant accepting a check receives final payment only when the shopper's bank honors the check. It may honor the check by sending fiat money in the form of reserves to the merchant's bank, which then credits the merchant's account. Alternatively, if the shopper's bank also possesses a positive balance of checks from accounts at the merchant's bank, it may simply subtract the amount of the check from this balance.

In the United States, an average of $2.6 trillion is cleared each day by the combination of Fedwire and CHIPS, the payments clearinghouses run, respectively, by the Federal Reserve and the New York Clearinghouse Association (Bank for International Settlements, Statistics on Payments Systems in the Group of Ten Countries, Basle, 1998.) Obviously, clearing the checks of shoppers is only a small part of the need to settle debt. Settlements of debt from trading in securities and foreign exchange markets account for much of this volume.

If the exchange of fiat money for the clearing of debts always worked seamlessly, there would be little interest in studying it. There are signs, however, that impediments to the smooth clearing of debt may exist. The settlers of British North America complained constantly that, although they had sufficient wealth, they lacked the currency to pay their debts and taxes.[1] It is not only in the distant past that economists have stressed the importance of supplying sufficient nominal money stocks in times of particular need. Ben Bernanke (1990) suggests that the Federal Reserve's rapid temporary increase in fiat money was the action needed to handle the enormous

---

[1] See Hammond (1957, Chapter I).

volume of transactions without financial disruption during the stock market crash of 1987.

Can a lack of nominal quantities of outside money actually cause financial disruptions? Why won't the price level simply adjust to the nominal stock of money in a way that ensures adequate real money balances? What tells us that current money balances are inadequate? Can open market purchases or other central bank policies "relieve the stringency" of financial disruptions? If so, what is the proper central bank response to a financial disruption? Must this response be one by a government authority?

We address these questions in this chapter. We find a role for institutions, public or private, that aid in clearing debt. We also find that the efficiency of the clearing of debt greatly depends on the policies of the central bank. We find in particular a need for short-run flexibility in the size of the nominal money stock.

A Model of the Clearing of Debt

To model a bank's role as a clearinghouse of private debts our model must feature demands for both currency and private nonbank debt. There must also be an impediment to the bilateral settlement of debt, to explain why debt is cleared through third parties. Our model displays these features in a model of spatially separated people who trade using credit and currency. Debt is redeemed as each person travels through a common area in which clearinghouses emerge in response to the needs of trading parties. Moreover, in equilibrium, people choose to use currency both as a medium of exchange (to make purchases of goods) and as a means for the repayment of debts.

The model is essentially our standard overlapping generations model with two new features: a market for debt and the spatial separation of people, which impedes the repayment of that debt.[2]

There exist I (a large number) pairs of outer islands arranged around a central island. Each pair of islands consists of one creditor island and one debtor island. On each island, N two-period-lived people are born in each period. In the first period, each island also has N people (the initial old) who live only in the first period.

Each person born on a debtor island (each debtor) is endowed at birth with y units of a nonstorable good specific to his island and with nothing when old. He wishes to consume the goods of creditor islands when young and nothing when old.

---

[2] The model is based on work by Freeman (1996a,b), which are extensions of a model of nominal debt by Freeman and Tabellini (1998).

Each person born on a creditor island (each creditor) is endowed at birth with y units of a nonstorable good specific to her island and with nothing when old. She wishes to consume the good of debtor islands when old and nothing when young. The initial old creditors own a fixed stock of fiat money, totaling M dollars per creditor island.

Each young creditor is paired with a young debtor with whom she may trade. When old, everyone travels to the central island. Creditors then continue to trade with young debtors. The old creditors arrive at their final destination after all trades among the young have been completed.

On the central island live a large number of bankers. They have no endowment of goods themselves. They are endowed only with costless technologies of record keeping and contract enforcement. They wish to consume the goods of debtor islands (though they may lack the means to make the purchases). An institution with the authority to print fiat money also exists on the central island.

Trading

To consume when old, creditors must bring something of value to the young debtors. Fiat money is accepted by young debtors if it helps them to acquire the goods they desire.

The young debtors wish to consume goods from creditor islands but own no goods valued by the young creditors that can be offered in immediate direct exchange. (Recall that the creditors desire to consume the debtor good when only old, not when young.) Nor do the debtors have any money at the time of this visit. They will be able to sell some of their endowment later for the money of the old, but this money is not yet in the hands of a young debtor when he visits his neighbor. The only thing a debtor can offer creditors is a promise to pay a sum of money in the next period on the central island. The young debtor will acquire this money by selling some of his endowment to old creditors or to others who bring money to the island.

In this monetary equilibrium both fiat money and privately issued debt are valued. Money serves both to purchase goods and to repay debts. Money is essential in this model for clearing debts and for the existence of a credit market: without valued money, there is no debt. As we will see, there may be another form of money in addition to fiat money.

To aid your understanding of the sequence of trades that occurs in this economy, see Figure 11.1. A visual image of the island economy and its trading patterns appears in Figure 11.2.

The price level is determined as always by the money market-clearing condition. In this case, the demand for currency must equal the stock of money arriving at

Figure 11.1. The sequence of trades within a period. At the beginning of each period, young individuals are born and endowed with goods specific to their type of island. In the middle of each period, young debtors travel to neighboring islands and purchase goods from creditors using IOUs, which will be repaid later. Simultaneous to this trade, old individuals visit the central island where IOUs are cleared using fiat money. At the end of each period, young debtors sell their goods to old creditors for fiat money.

Figure 11.2. The creditor-debtor island economy. The island economy consists of pairs of creditor and debtor islands. Also present is a central island where previously arranged debts are settled.

each debtor island. Valuing only the consumption of the neighboring credit island goods, each debtor will choose to sell his entire endowment (y) for currency. He will then use that currency in the following period to repay the debts he incurred when young from the acquisition of goods at the neighboring credit island. The market-clearing condition for currency is therefore

$$Ny = Mv_t = \frac{M}{p_t} \quad \text{or} \quad p_t = \frac{M}{Ny}. \tag{11.1}$$

Institutions for the Clearing of Debt

The description of the equilibrium is not yet complete. It takes as given some not-yet-specified arrangement for the clearing of debt, a *payments system*. If debt markets operate, creditors arrive at the central island with the IOUs of the debtors, and debtors arrive with currency to repay the IOUs. The nature of the transactions at the central island depends on the timing of the visits to the central island. Direct repayment of debt, repayment through a clearinghouse, and the issuance of clearinghouse debt can each represent the equilibrium institutional structure through which debts can be settled. Let us now examine some possible arrival patterns and payments systems.

If all agents arrive simultaneously at the central island, debtors can repay their debts, directly or indirectly, using their currency balances. If it is costless to seek out the issuer of an IOU, the settlement of debts may be accomplished through a direct meeting of a debtor and his particular creditor.

The settlement of debts may also take place through a clearinghouse operated by agents of the central island. At a clearinghouse, creditors present the IOUs they possess in exchange for currency, and debtors present enough currency to clear their debts. At the conclusion of all transactions, the clearinghouse posseses neither IOUs nor fiat money. The intermediary in this case offers simply a check-clearing service (perhaps because of some cost advantage) but never actually purchases private debt because all debts are cleared simultaneously, before anyone leaves the central island.

If agents do not visit the central island simultaneously, the direct repayment of IOUs is not possible, and thus a clearinghouse plays a much more useful role. Suppose, for example, that people visit the central island in pairs of a creditor and a debtor drawn from nonadjacent islands. Because the two members are drawn from each of the two different types of islands, the net debt of the two sums to zero. However, because they come from nonadjacent islands, neither holds the personal debt of the other. In this case, the clearinghouse can purchase the IOUs brought to it and accept fiat money in payment of the IOUs issued by the pair. The clearinghouse records these transactions and uses the fiat money payment of the debtor to pay the creditor what she is owed. At any given point in this sequence the clearinghouse holds positive balances of IOUs payable and receivable but has no net position in debt.[3]

The role of the clearinghouse becomes even more important if the arrival of debtors and creditors is not perfectly synchronized. Suppose there is no overlap in the visits of debtors and creditors to the central island; one group arrives and departs before the other arrives. If the first to arrive are debtors, they will deposit fiat money to repay what they owe. As a result, the clearinghouse will at first accumulate

---

[3] Kahn and Roberds (1999) take a closer look at some of the institutional features and problems of clearing offsetting debts.

positive balances of fiat money, which it will then use to pay off the creditors upon their arrival.

If creditors arrive first, the clearing of debt is more problematic. Creditors wish to redeem their debt for currency to take to their destinations. In the other cases we have studied, creditors could be paid their due with the currency balances brought by the debtors. In this case, however, debtors arrive too late for their currency to be used in payments to creditors. In this way the model displays a currency shortage to which private banks or the central bank may wish to respond.

How creditors can be paid when they arrive first is the central topic of this chapter and an important component of central bank policy. We examine several institutional monetary arrangements for the functioning of a clearinghouse when creditors desire payment from the clearinghouse before debtors arrive.

Providing Liquidity

Equilibrium with an Inelastic Money Supply

Suppose fiat money is restricted to be the only monetary asset – the only asset that may be carried by the old from the central island to their destinations around the circle of islands – and that the stock of fiat money is fixed.

Under this strict monetary regime the clearinghouse has no means of paying creditors if they arrive before debtors. Any agent arriving at the clearinghouse as a creditor receives nothing in exchange for any debt she presents to the clearinghouse. Anticipating that she won't be repaid, a young creditor will refuse to make a loan. In such an autarkic equilibrium, utility is low for both creditors and debtors, because neither has the means to acquire the goods they desire. Monetary arrangements that remove this constraint will be welfare improving.

To remove the constraint, the clearinghouse must have some means of paying creditors if they arrive before debtors. Additions to the fiat money stock or bank notes issued by the clearinghouse could be used for this purpose. Let us examine these in turn.

An Elastic Fiat Money Supply

Suppose the monetary authority agrees to print temporarily enough new fiat money to allow creditors to be paid. One institutional arrangement effecting such a policy is a **discount window** (Figure 11.3). At a discount window the monetary authority (central bank) stands ready to lend at some announced interest rate (discount rate) to clearinghouse bankers who can demonstrate that they are using the loan to purchase "real bills," in this model the debt of late-arriving borrowers. Later, once the debtors

The Clearinghouse's Balance Sheet
after the Exchanges with Creditors and the Discount Window

Assets	Liabilities
IOUs issued by debtors	Discount window loans

The Clearinghouse's Balance Sheet
after the Exchanges with Debtors

Assets	Liabilities
Fiat money reserves	Discount window loans

Figure 11.3. The clearinghouse's balance sheet with discount window loans. Creditors arrive at the clearinghouse before debtors, with the creditors carrying debtor IOUs. The monetary authority makes discount window loans in the form of currency to the clearing-house bankers. This currency is exchanged by the clearinghouse for the IOUs of the debtors. When the debtors later arrive at the clearinghouse, they redeem their debt with currency holdings. The clearinghouse then pays off its discount loans with these currency holdings.

have arrived at the clearinghouse to redeem their debts with fiat money balances, the clearinghouse bankers in turn use these fiat money balances to redeem the IOUs left with the central bank. The central bank keeps this money out of circulation.

Equivalently, the central bank may print extra money and use it simply to buy the debt held by creditors, an open market operation. Later, the debtors bring money to the central bank to pay off their debt, which the central bank keeps out of circulation. By this temporary printing of fiat money, the liquidity problem has been circumvented.

This increase in the supply of fiat money is not inflationary if it is only temporary – that is, if the fiat money brought by debtors to pay off their debts is removed from circulation once it reaches the central bank. Recall that the price level is determined by the equality of the demand for currency with the stock of money arriving at each debtor island: $Ny = M/p_t$, implying $p_t = M/Ny$. Because the stock of newly printed money is no larger than last period's stock of fiat money (it is now out of circulation in the vaults or furnaces of the central bank), the price level does not rise as a result of this printing of money.

An Elastic Supply of Inside Money

Consider now an alternative monetary regime, in which clearinghouses are permit-ted to print their own bank notes entitling the bearer of the note to $1, payable on the demand of the bearer. A clearinghouse may now pay off old creditors with its own money, which they may exchange for the endowment of the young debtors. The young debtors will accept clearinghouse notes as perfect substitutes for fiat money because they know they will travel to the central island in the next period,

**The Clearinghouse's Balance Sheet
after the Exchanges with Creditors**

Assets	Liabilities
IOUs issued by debtors	Bank notes

**The Clearinghouse's Balance Sheet
after the Exchanges with Debtors**

Assets	Liabilities
Fiat money reserves	Bank notes

Figure 11.4. The clearinghouse balance sheet with note issue permitted. In this scenario, the clearinghouse is permitted to issue its own notes. Creditors arrive at the clearinghouse carrying IOUs of the debtors. The clearinghouse pays off the creditors with its own notes. Later, when debtors arrive, the debtors pay off their IOUs with currency.

where they may redeem the notes for fiat money if they choose. Figure 11.4 presents the balance sheet of the clearinghouse after the creditors arrive and again after the debtors arrive.

It is clear that the use of private bank notes overcomes the liquidity problem as simply as a discount window with an elastic fiat money supply. The remaining question is its effect on inflation. Will the issuance of private bank notes cause inflation?

To answer this question, we must examine the link between the total money stock and the price level. The quantity theory defines the total money stock as the sum of all assets in public hands that may be readily used to make purchases. In this economy the total money stock on each debtor island at t is the sum of publicly held balances of fiat money (denote this as M_t^P) and privately issued bank notes (M_t^B). Publicly held fiat money balances do not include the amounts held by the clearinghouse.

As we found earlier, prices will be determined by the clearing of the currency market on each island:

$$p_t = \frac{M_t^P + M_t^B}{Ny}.$$ (11.2)

Note that, in accordance with the quantity theory, the price level is strictly proportional to the total money stock, including privately issued bank notes, in public hands.

Fully Backed Bank Notes

The effects of this regime depend on the backing of the clearinghouse notes. If the notes are always redeemed for fiat money in the period after their issue, the clearinghouse must hold as reserves all the fiat money it receives from debtors in order to meet the anticipated redemptions. What does this imply for the total stock of currency used on each island? Publicly held currency is made up of publicly held fiat money plus bank notes. By definition, public balances of fiat money (M_t^P) equal the total fiat money stock minus bank reserves Γ_t:

$$M_t^P = M - \Gamma_t, \tag{11.3}$$

Bank reserves must be equal to the stock of bank notes in anticipation of their redemption:

$$\Gamma_t = M_t^B. \tag{11.4}$$

Therefore, public currency holdings,

$$M_t^P + M_t^B = (M - \Gamma_t) + M_t^B = M, \tag{11.5}$$

are equal in size to the fiat money stock. Total currency in public hands has not been changed by the issuance of bank notes because the bank notes in public hands simply replace an equal stock of fiat money now held out of circulation in the vault of the clearinghouse. Because the currency stock is unaffected by the extent of private bank note issue, the price level is also unaffected:

$$p_t = \frac{M_t^P + M_t^B}{Ny} = \frac{M}{Ny}. \tag{11.6}$$

Therefore, the equilibrium under this regime is identical to that of the discount window regime – a full provision of liquidity with no inflationary consequence.[4]

A Potential for an Inflationary Overissue of Bank Notes

If the bank notes of the clearinghouse have no expiration date and are perceived as perfect substitutes for fiat money, there is no reason for people to redeem them for fiat money. If bank notes are never redeemed, however, the reserves of the clearinghouse are never needed to meet the obligations of the clearinghouse. There is an opportunity for profit taking here; a clearinghouse could use its fiat money reserves to purchase goods for its own consumption without ever going into default.[5] In this case, an issue of bank notes represents an expansion of the total stock of unbacked money: the privately created money is added to the total stock of currency

---

[4] For an interesting study of the Suffolk system, a privately run clearing arrangement for privately issued bank notes in nineteenth century New England, see Rolnick, Smith, and Weber (1998).

[5] If an interest-bearing investment opportunity were available on the central island, a clearinghouse could also lend its reserves and take the interest as profits.

in public hands without an offsetting subtraction of fiat money from circulation. In essence, clearinghouses are given (limited) permission to print fiat money and thus enjoy the profits from creating valued money at no cost. This of course is inflationary. To see this, note that when banks hold no reserves of fiat money, Γ_t equals zero and public holdings of fiat money M_t^P are equal to M. The market-clearing condition for money in this case is

$$p_t = \frac{M_t^P + M_t^B}{Ny} = \frac{M + M_t^B}{Ny} > \frac{M}{Ny}. \tag{11.7}$$

Prices rise with the increase in bank notes because an offsetting amount of fiat money has not been withdrawn from circulation, leaving the total money supply larger than before.

We see here that the mere option of exchanging bank notes for fiat money on demand is not sufficient to prevent an inflationary bank note issue, for nothing induces or forces people to turn in their bank notes if people view them as perfect substitutes for fiat money. The absence of bank note redemption is plausible. Because bank notes are a perfect substitute for fiat currency, even a small cost or bother of redemption may discourage all redemption. Even if such a cost did not exist for natural reasons, banks, whose seigniorage profits depend on less than full redemption, can be expected to actively discourage bank note redemption.[6]

Even though the clearinghouses are restricted to issuing notes only when presented with evidence of private debt that needs to be redeemed, we see the possibility for inflationary bank note creation.[7]

Example 11.1 Graph the path of the total currency supply and prices over time

a. if bank notes are never redeemed,
b. if half the outstanding stock of bank notes are redeemed in each period.

To prevent the overissue of bank notes, one must ensure that they are fully backed by reserves of fiat money by the end of every period. An obvious way to do this is to require that clearinghouses hold reserves of fiat money equal to 100 percent of the notes issued. In this way, any increase in the issuing of private currency is matched one-for-one by a decrease in the public holding of fiat money, just as it was when notes were always redeemed after a single period (Equation 11.6). Then the total stock of currency in public hands remains the same, leaving prices unaffected by the amount of privately issued bank notes.

---

[6] Although the overissue of bank notes and the inflationary pressures that this implies has received much attention, there is evidence suggesting that overissue need not be a feature of privately issued bank notes. For example, it appears that bank notes issued by Canadian banks during the late 1800s and early 1900s were promptly presented for redemption. See Johnson (1910, p. 23).
[7] See Laidler (1984).

The Short-Term Interest Rate

Until now for simplicity we have considered an extreme version of the model: the private banking sector has complete credibility when it issues notes and initially has absolutely no fiat money available for creditors. Suppose instead that the initial old bankers living on the central island cannot credibly issue their own bank notes but own a stock of M^* units of fiat money. When young, bankers receive an endowment of nonstorable central island goods. The old bankers use their stock of money to purchase and consume goods from the young of the central island or any debtor island.

In this case, the old bankers own something, fiat money, of value to the creditors who arrive at the central island holding the debt of debtors arriving later. This opens up the possibility of a market in which the bankers use their fiat money to purchase this debt from the creditors. The creditors take this money to make purchases at their final destinations and the bankers take the debt, wait for it to be redeemed with fiat money by the arriving debtors, and then use the fiat money to make their purchases.

Although the fiat money balances of the bankers offer a way for creditors to exchange their debt holdings for the fiat money they need, the liquidity problem of the creditors is not completely overcome if the fiat money balances of the bankers M^* are less than the nominal value of the debt brought in for redemption. By the model's construction, all money balances in the hands of debtors are used to redeem debt. Because there are I islands, each of which has a stock of fiat money equal to M, the total money balances in the hands of debtors is IM. Therefore, if $M^* < IM$, the bankers cannot possibly redeem the entire debt at **par** (its full promised value). Creditors instead are forced to sell their debt to bankers at a discount. Let ξ represent the discounted value of a debt promising to pay \$1. If $M^* < IM$ then, because there are only M^* dollars of fiat money available to purchase IM dollars of debt, the discount in a competitive banking market must be the ratio of the two:

$$\xi = \frac{M^*}{IM} < 1. \tag{11.8}$$

The sale of debt below par hurts creditors by lowering the rate of return actually received by them – for each dollar in debt they now receive only ξ dollars (with $\xi < 1$). (Even if there were only a chance that they must sell their debt below par, the average return to lending would still fall.) Clearinghouse bankers obviously benefit from the chance to buy up debt for less than the value at which it will be repaid.[8] If lower rates of return induce lenders to lend less, borrowers will also be made worse off. (Lenders receive a lower rate of return because the owners of

---

[8] This was the experience in the panic of 1907, when the profits of New York reserve banks rose (returning later to their prepanic level). See Tallman and Moen (1990).

reserves pay less than par value for debt and not because the rate of return paid by borrowers has been reduced.)

Example 11.2 Suppose the old bankers on the central island own $1,000,000 of fiat money and creditors are owed $1,200,000. At what price will creditors be able to sell the debt they own? How much interest would a banker be willing to pay once the debtors have arrived in order to have one more dollar of fiat money before the debtors have arrived?

Policy Options

What can be done to lower the short-term interest rate? Suppose the central bank is authorized to issue and lend fiat money equal to the nominal amount of debt presented by any of the bankers.[9] This central bank loan is required to be repaid with fiat money upon the arrival on the central island of the late-arriving borrowers. Let Ψ denote the gross nominal interest rate charged on this central bank loan. The fiat money with which the central bank loan is repaid is removed from circulation.

To determine the effects of this policy we must first examine the return earned by bankers buying up debt. Each unit of debt costs a banker ξ_t and pays him $1 for a gross rate of return of $1/\$\xi_t$ or $1/\xi_t$. Therefore bankers can make a nonnegative profit by borrowing from the central bank as long as the rate of interest charged by the central bank does not exceed $1/\xi_t$. Recall that the price of debt ξ_t is determined by the ratio of currency owned by bankers to the size of the debt (Equation 11.8). As bankers borrow and supply more currency to creditors, the price at which creditors can sell their debt ξ_t rises. In this way arbitrage induces bankers to borrow from the central bank until $1/\xi_t = \Psi_t$. By choosing Ψ_t, the central bank can determine ξ_t, the extent to which bankers temporarily lack the fiat money balances needed to purchase the debt of others. The lower the rate of interest at the discount window ($\Psi \geq 1$), the more currency clearinghouse bankers will borrow and supply to the creditors. This simple discount window policy of setting $\Psi = 1$ allows bankers as much fiat money as they need to purchase the debt of the early-leaving creditors at par ($\xi = 1$).

There is a limit to the power of the central bank to affect the short-term interest rate. Because the price of debt ξ_t cannot rise above par, the short-term interest rate Ψ cannot be pushed below 1. Note also that the central bank intervention directly affects only the short-term (within period) interest rate. It has no direct effect on the long-run (period to period) interest rate paid by the debtors.

The temporary issue of fiat money is not inflationary because the total stock of fiat money is the same at the end of the period as it was at the beginning. In this way there is no conflict between the provision of liquidity by the central bank and any price level or inflation targets it may have.

---

[9] An obvious requirement for the workability of this policy is that the central bank is able to identify the bankers, or the debt they present, as creditworthy.

Figure 11.5. Short-term loan rates. Before the founding of the Federal Reserve in 1913, short-term interest rates in the United States were characterized by strong seasonal movements, with peaks in these interest rates often occurring during the fall crop-moving season. Note that after the founding of the Federal Reserve, these short-term loan rate fluctuations appear to diminish. *Source:* Federal Reserve *Banking and Monetary Statistics.*

Example 11.3 Suppose the old bankers on the central island own $16,000,000 of fiat money and creditors are owed $20,000,000. What is the short-term rate of interest if the central bank does not intervene? How much will the bankers borrow if the central bank offers loans with a gross short-term interest rate of 1? How much will the bankers borrow if the central bank offers loans with a gross short-term interest rate of 1.1?

Can central bank policies actually affect the pattern of nominal interest rate fluctuations? Look at Figure 11.5. There appears to be an immediate reduction in the variability of the short-term interest rates upon establishment of the Federal Reserve System at the end of 1913. Because establishment of the Federal Reserve involved a number of major changes in the financial system, a look at a time-series graph cannot establish which reform actually led to the reduced volatility of the short-term interest rate.[10] However, given that the variability of the money stock also rose with the creation of the Federal Reserve System, the time series is at least consistent with the goal of furnishing an elastic currency as announced in the title of the Act creating the Federal Reserve:

An Act to provide for the establishment of Federal Reserve Banks, to furnish an elastic currency, to afford means of rediscounting commercial paper, to establish a more effective supervision of banking in the United States, and for other purposes.

---

[10] The pattern of interest rates before and after the founding of the Federal Reserve is investigated by Miron (1986). Alternative models of the inelastic stock of money in the years preceding the Federal Reserve System are offered by Champ, Smith, and Williamson (1996) and by Champ, Freeman, and Weber (1999).

Summary

We have now seen two ways a central bank can provide the liquidity needed for redemption of debt. It may permit private banks to issue their own currency substitutes or it may itself run a discount window where banks are permitted to borrow at a low interest rate currency that may be paid to creditors until debtors arrive to redeem their debts. In both cases the central bank allows an elastic stock of currency to satisfy temporary changes in the need for currency. As long as the stock of currency does not expand from period to period, the provision of an elastic money stock within a period is not inflationary.

Chapter 12

Bank Risk

THE BANKS WE have studied so far have been very simple. They face no risk and are always solvent. In contrast, we observe in the world many instances of failures of banks, savings and loans, and other similar financial intermediaries to meet their obligations to depositors. Failure is an unfortunate but integral part of life. Why should the government care more about bank failures than about the much more common business failures of restaurants? Bank failures seem to attract more attention. Banks are seen by many as fragile institutions that depend for their survival on the public trust, a trust that may require support from government guarantees. As the U.S. public has discovered with the recent bailout of savings and loans, these guarantees can be costly to taxpayers, leading the government to regulate the behavior of the financial institutions guaranteed. Ironically, some forms of government regulation may be blamed for the failures they seek to prevent. These questions are addressed in this chapter.

In this chapter, we investigate two possible reasons for bank failures. A bank may fail because the assets it owns or the loans it has made may realize such unexpectedly low returns that the bank no longer has the resources to pay depositors what it owes them. It may also fail if a sudden rush of withdrawals forces it to sell off assets at a loss. We look at the second possibility first.

Demand Deposit Banking

Actual banks are different from the banks we have modeled thus far in an important way. They have liabilities payable on demand but assets that are not. This mismatch of bank assets and liabilities raises the possibility of a **bank panic** or **run**. If depositors all withdraw at once, a bank must borrow or sell its assets to pay them off. If it is unable to borrow or sell quickly without losses, it may not have enough resources to meet its promises even if it has the resources to pay off depositors if they withdraw gradually. If all depositors fear that the rush of others

214

to withdraw will leave them with nothing, all will rationally join the rush. This is called a *bank run*. When a number of banks experience bank runs it is called a *bank panic*.

To understand bank runs, we must therefore first understand why banks might offer demand deposits even though the assets the bank holds cannot be costlessly liquidated quickly. In so doing, we illustrate another way banks offer liquidity unavailable to an individual holding assets on his own.

A Model of Demand Deposit Banking

Assume that N (a constant) three-period-lived people are born each period (in overlapping generations), each endowed with y goods, only when young.[1]

No one consumes when young. Each person wants to consume in one of the next two periods of life, depending on his type. Each young person has an equal chance of being either of the following types:

- Type 1 consumes in the first period after birth.
- Type 2 consumes in the second period after birth.

No person knows his own type when young. In the first period after birth, a person learns his type; that is, he then knows when he wants to consume. An individual's need for liquidity is thus represented by his uncertainty over when he will want to consume.

An individual's type is never directly observable by anyone else (it is impossible to tell by looking at a person when he wants to consume). Exactly half of each generation belongs to each type.

People have access to two assets, storage and capital. Storage, the act of hiding goods in the basement, pays the gross rate of return 1 over one period. Storage can be done secretly. Capital produces X goods for each good invested ($X > 1$) but only after two periods have elapsed. Capital that has not yet produced can be sold within or between generations. Let v^k denote the price of capital in the period before it produces. It is possible to issue fake capital or fake titles to capital, which are distinguishable from real capital only through costly effort. Verifying that capital is not a fake costs θ goods per unit of capital. Assume that $\theta > X - 1$.

IOUs and other contracts promising future payments are possible among members of the same generation but not between generations. (People know the members of their own generation better than members of other generations.)

The preceding assumptions about assets lead us to find the rates of return for storage and capital presented in Table 12.1. Notice that, because of the transaction

---

[1] This model is taken from Freeman (1988), which builds on the ideas and framework of Bryant (1980) and of Diamond and Dybvig (1983).

Table 12.1. *Rates of return for storage and capital*

Effective rates of return on:	One period	Two periods
Storage	1	1
Capital	$v^k - \theta$	X

Note: In the model, storage always pays a gross rate of return of 1, regardless of how long goods are stored. Capital produces after two periods and if held for that period of time pays the gross rate of return X. If a unit of capital is sold after only one period, the seller receives the price v^k. Furthermore, a verification cost of θ is incurred at the point of sale, making the effective one-period gross rate of return on capital $v^k - \theta$.

cost θ, the rate of return on capital sold before it produces, $v^k - \theta$, is different from its rate of return when held until it produces, X.

What will people pay for capital producing X goods one period later? They should be willing to pay the present value of X goods. The present value of X is X divided by the one-period gross rate of return. Because storage offers the one-period gross rate of return 1, the one-period gross rate of return must be at least 1. Therefore, people will pay at most $X/1 = X$ goods today for capital worth X goods tomorrow. Therefore, $v^k \le X$. Because $\theta > X - 1$ by assumption, we now know that $\theta > v^k - 1$ or $1 > v^k - \theta$. This ensures that the one-period rate of return on storage exceeds the rate of return on capital sold after a single period.

Like the people we have studied in earlier models, these people wish to save goods so that they may consume later. In this model economy, however, no individual knows when he will want to consume. This need for liquidity makes an individual's selection of assets difficult. If he holds capital but it turns out that he wants to consume after only one period, he will receive the low rate of return $v^k - \theta$ instead of the better one-period rate of return offered by storage. On the other hand, if he holds storage but it turns out that he doesn't want to consume until two periods have passed, he receives only the rate of return 1 instead of the greater two-period rate of return X offered by capital. Because a person does not know his type at the time he must choose his assets, he cannot be sure of getting the best rate of return by holding his own portfolio of assets.[2]

There is, however, a way for people to join together so that each person receives the best rate of return whatever his type. Note that, although no single person knows his type, each generation knows that half of its people will be of each type. Imagine

---

[2] If it were not true that $1 > v^k - \theta$, capital would offer the better rate of return in both the long and short run, leaving the individual a trivial choice of a portfolio and no role for intermediation. This explains the importance of our assumption that $\theta > X - 1$.

therefore an intermediary that offers each person the rate of return 1 after one period if it turns out that he is type 1 and the rate of return X after two periods if it turns out that he is type 2. If each person in a generation deposits his entire endowment, the intermediary can finance these returns by investing half of its deposits [$(Ny/2)$ goods] in storage and half in capital. Because it will turn out that half the depositors will be of each type, the intermediary can pay off the type 1 people with the returns from its storage [$(Ny/2)$ goods] and the type 2 people with the returns from its capital [$(XNy/2)$ goods].[3]

One of the assumptions of our model is that no one can observe when another person wants to consume. How then can the intermediary determine who receives the type 1 and who receives the type 2 return? The intermediary must rely on the word of the depositor and make the type 1 returns available to any depositor who asks for them after only one period. Deposits that are returned to the depositor whenever requested are called **demand deposits**.

Reliance on the truthfulness of depositors works only if depositors are better off when they tell the truth than when they lie. Is this the case? No type 1 person will pretend to be a type 2 person because to do so means consuming in the second period after birth instead of the first, when he wants to consume. If a single type 2 person claimed to be a type 1 person, he could withdraw his deposit after only one period and then secretly store it until he was ready to consume. This behavior, however, would make him worse off. It would get him only one good in the second period after birth for each good deposited, while he could have received X goods if he had not withdrawn early from the intermediary.

In this model we see another way through which intermediaries, in particular banks, provide liquidity. Banks create liquid liabilities (demand deposits) from illiquid assets. They allow people flexibility in the timing of their spending even when assets are not flexible in their returns. They do so by taking advantage of the fact that there is more randomness for an individual than for the aggregate economy. An individual does not know when he wants to consume and thus cannot select the asset with the best return for his situation. By pooling the resources of many individuals, however, a bank can be confident that it knows the fraction of its depositors who will withdraw after one period, and thus it can hold the correct fraction of good long-run assets (here, capital) and good short-run assets (storage).[4]

Bank Runs

Suppose you are a type 2 person who hears a rumor that every other type 2 person is going to pretend to be a type 1 person in order to withdraw his deposits from the

---

[3] If one type has a lower level of utility than another, the bank may arrange to insure people against that risk by offering that type more than the return from deposits of y goods. We ignore here this form of insurance, which is studied by Diamond and Dybvig (1983).

[4] For a formal model of bank runs in which fiat money serves as the short-run asset, see Loewy (1991).

bank. (Recall that people are free to retrieve their deposits from the bank at any time because banks cannot tell a lying type 2 person, who is withdrawing earlier than necessary, from an honest type 1 person, who needs to withdraw early.) Should you rush to the bank and also try to withdraw early, or should you wait another period until you truly want to consume?

To answer this question, let us examine the solvency of the bank when a large number of type 2 people withdraw early. The bank has enough in storage to pay the promised return of y goods to only $N/2$ people, the number of truly type 1 people. If, however, type 2 people are also withdrawing early, the bank must sell some of its capital to meet its promise to pay the rate of return 1 to anyone who asks after one period. When the bank sells a unit of capital, it receives only $v^k - \theta$ goods, which is less than 1. Therefore, for each lying type 2 person withdrawing y goods, the bank must sell more than y units of capital to meet its promise to pay y goods on demand. This implies that the bank is selling the capital that normally would finance the return to the honest type 2 people who wait. After the bank has made its payments to the type 1 people and the lying type 2 people, there may be no capital left to pay anything to type 2 people who wait.

An honest type 2 person may get nothing if all others withdraw early and he does not. If, therefore, each type 2 person believes that all others will rush to the bank and withdraw early, he will also rush to the bank to get what he can before the assets of the bank are exhausted. All are worse off if such a panic occurs, because by withdrawing early, each gets at best a rate of return of 1 instead of X. Nevertheless, each individual is rational in withdrawing early, given that the others are also withdrawing early. In this way, a bank that would have met all its obligations if the type 2 people had not withdrawn early is unable to meet its obligations during a panic.

Example 12.1 Consider the model of demand deposits described above. Suppose $N = 900$, $y = 10$, $v^k - \theta = 0.9$, and $X = 1.2$. Let each person have a 2/3 chance of being type 1 and a 1/3 chance of being type 2.

a. What bank portfolio can guarantee the rate of return 1 to all type 1 people and the rate of return 1.2 to all type 2 people? How many goods are placed in storage? In capital?
b. Now suppose the type 2 people pretend to be type 1 people and withdraw early. How many people can be paid before the bank runs out of assets?
c. Suppose that in the period after you made your deposit at the bank you turn out to be a type 2 person and you learn that all the other type 2 people are about to pretend to be type 1 people so that they can withdraw early. Is it in your self-interest to also try to withdraw early?
d. Are type 2 people better off than they would be if no type 2 person tried to withdraw early? Reconcile your answer with your answer to part c.

Preventing Panics

The possibility of runs in this model resulted from a few key assumptions. Among these are the assumptions that banks cannot borrow from others and that no one can learn an individual's type. If these assumptions are altered, banks may not be subject to runs.

Interbank Lending

A run on a bank makes that bank insolvent by forcing it to sell off its assets at a loss to meet the rush of depositors. If a bank faced with a run can borrow enough to meet all withdrawals, it can avoid the losses that would result from the sale of its capital. These loans could then be repaid in the following period when the bank's capital matures. In this way, the bank would maintain enough capital to meet its obligation to every type 2 person who does not withdraw early. With the capital backing his deposits protected from loss, no type 2 person would have any incentive to misrepresent himself in order to withdraw early.[5]

From whom might a bank borrow? If a bank is threatened by a run, it must borrow from banks or from people who are not experiencing runs. In our model, the young of the next generation would be willing to lend for one period goods they would otherwise store for a period. If these intergenerational loans are possible, panics may not occur. Indeed, if intergenerational loans were costless, banks would never need to hold reserves of the liquid but low-return storage. As we saw in Chapter 7, a bank could afford to place all its assets in high-return capital, despite its two-period maturity, and borrow (accept deposits) from the next generation in order to meet withdrawals that occur after one period.

Identifying Unnecessary Withdrawals

If banks could learn an individual's type, they would be able to stop runs by simply refusing to allow type 2 people to withdraw early. In times of runs, banks often have refused to allow large withdrawals without verifying that the withdrawal genuinely was needed. Bank officers would release funds only to those who showed them a bill or payroll that had to be paid.

Even if banks cannot borrow or determine an individual's true need to withdraw, there are several ways banks can structure themselves to prevent panics. In each case, the key is for the bank to ensure that individuals who panic and withdraw early are worse off than those who do not panic, no matter how many others withdraw early.

---

[5] Interbank lending in the United States takes place in the federal funds market.

Suspensions of Withdrawals

One way a bank might structure itself to prevent panics is by temporarily closing its doors once its reserves of the liquid short-term asset (storage) have been used up. The bank can then reopen in the next period when its long-term capital pays its return. If a bank follows such a policy, it will never be required to sell its capital hastily and at a loss. In this way, a type 2 depositor will know that if he waits to withdraw, the bank will still be able to pay him his promised return. Because this return, X, is greater than the return he could get by withdrawing early, 1, the depositor will not rush to the bank.

Note that if a bank has the right to suspend withdrawals, it may never actually need to do so because depositors no longer panic. Ironically, bank charters and laws have often forced banks to remain open and pay all the depositors who want to be paid. Such a restriction may make panics possible by taking away a means by which a bank can protect its assets from the losses that would result from a hasty sale. The suspension of withdrawals by banks has historical precedence. During the banking panics of 1893 and 1907, banks in the United States restricted the convertibility of deposits into currency or specie.[6]

The suspension of withdrawals will not work as perfectly if the number of type 1 people, who truly need to withdraw early, is random. Suspending the rights of depositors to make withdrawals may then stop a truly type 1 person late in the line at the bank from consuming when he wants. In this case, a bank would better serve its depositors by reducing the payments to early withdrawers when there are a large number of them. In this way, the bank can protect the capital behind the deposits of the type 2 people without leaving an unlucky type 1 person with nothing to consume.

Government Deposit Insurance

The government can also help prevent bank runs by guaranteeing type 2 people that they will receive their promised return even if the bank becomes insolvent. If credible, such a guarantee would leave type 2 people with no reason to panic.

How can the government back up its guarantee? The government can promise to tax the endowment of the currently young generation if it needs revenue to pay off the depositors of a failed bank. Note that this power of taxation is available only to the government; a private bank cannot tax people. Nor could the bank have arranged this guarantee privately. The current young were not born when the bank was formed.

---

[6] For excellent discussions of bank panics in the United States during the late 1800s and early 1900s, see Sprague (1910) and Friedman and Schwartz (1963b).

If the government guarantee is believable and believed, no type 2 person will want to withdraw early from a bank, so there will be no panics. If no runs occur, the government will never have to use its power of taxation to bail out a bank that fails because of a run. In this way, the government guarantee prevents panics costlessly. The power to bail out depositors effectively eliminates the need to bail them out.

The costless nature of government deposit insurance disappears, however, when the number of type 1 depositors is random. In this case, a government that has guaranteed the returns promised by the banks will actually have to make some payments to depositors when banks have been forced to sell capital because the number of type 1 people is unusually large.

The government may also have to bail out insured banks if bank assets are risky. When bank assets pay an unusually low rate of return, the banks are unable to make their promised payments. In this case, the government is forced to collect taxes to pay depositors their promised return. U.S. taxpayers have been painfully reminded of this fact. The Federal Deposit Insurance Corporation (FDIC) gives the resolution costs of the FDIC and Resolution Trust Corporation as $197.68 billion for all resolutions during the period 1980–1994 [Federal Deposit Insurance Corporation (1998), Chart C.18].

This case of bank failures due to the riskiness of bank assets is the subject of the next section.

Bank Failures

The United States has a troubled history of bank failures. The worst experience occurred during the period from 1930 to 1933, when bank failures averaged over 2,000 per year.[7] After the tumultuous 1930s, the number of bank failures dropped significantly. From 1941 through 1981, the number of bank failures averaged 5 per year. However, beginning in 1982, bank failures rose dramatically, peaking at over 200 failures in 1988. This significant increase in bank failures during the 1980s is shown in Figure 12.1, which plots total failures expressed as a percentage of the number of banks in operation.

In the preceding sections we looked at the way the structure of bank liabilities may make banks insolvent. Now let us look at how bank assets may contribute to bank insolvency.

All investments contain an element of risk. Assets pay off in the future, which is never known with total certainty. Banks, like any other investment opportunity, therefore may suffer low returns on the assets they hold. Relative to other investments, however, banks are seen as fairly safe repositories of wealth.

---

[7] See Friedman and Schwartz (1963b, Chapter 7) for a detailed account of problems in the banking system during the Great Depression.

Figure 12.1. Failure rate of FDIC-insured commercial banks and trusts. The figure shows the percentage of beginning-of-year institutions that failed during each year from 1934 to 1998. Failure rates during the 1980s rose to more than 10 times the levels experienced in the period from 1941 to 1979. *Source:* The web site of the Federal Deposit Insurance Corporation, http://www.fdic.gov/ bank/index.html.

There are a couple of plausible explanations for the relative safety of banks. Because bank deposits are used to make payments, it is helpful if people know the exact value of their deposits. If the value of deposits fluctuated greatly, a depositor would have to verify constantly that there was enough in his account to cover his checks.[8]

In addition, a safe portfolio is necessary to prevent runs. Should depositors learn that a bank's assets are insufficient to meet its liabilities, they will rush to the bank to get back their deposits before the other depositors. As we saw in the last section, this may force the bank to sell off its long-term assets precipitously, causing a further fall in the value of the bank's portfolio.

Banks can protect themselves from risk in a number of ways. Most obviously, they can choose to hold a large fraction of their portfolios in safe assets.

Depositors can be protected from losses even when bank assets are risky if the bank attracts investors as shareholders in the bank in addition to depositors. Banks organized this way have a positive net worth, W, as illustrated by the balance sheet in Figure 12.2.

Deposits are protected from changes in the value of bank assets by the positive net worth of a bank. The equity holders of a bank put up W dollars in return for a

---

[8] An alternative is to maintain a large enough balance in the account so that there are sufficient funds to cover all checks even with substantial fluctuation in the value of the account (due to fluctuations in the bank's portfolio value). Money market mutual funds, whose value fluctuates with the value of the fund's portfolio, require large minimum balances.

Assets		Liabilities	
Reserves	γH	Deposits	H
Interest-bearing assets	$(1 - \gamma)H + W$	Net worth	W
Total assets	$H + W$	Total liabilities	$H + W$

Figure 12.2. A bank's balance sheet.

Assets		Liabilities	
Reserves	$ 2M	Deposits	$20M
Interest-bearing assets	22M	Net worth	4M
Total assets	$24M	Total liabilities	$24M

Figure 12.3. A bank's balance sheet.

Assets		Liabilities	
Reserves	$ 2.0M	Deposits	$20.0M
Interest-bearing assets	20.9M	Net worth	2.9M
Total assets	$22.9M	Total liabilities	$22.9M

Figure 12.4. A bank's balance sheet.

share of the bank's value after depositors have been paid. Depositors have the first claim on the assets of a bank and must be paid before any shareholders. The priority of depositors' claims implies that any changes in the value of bank assets affect net worth first. If a bank should suffer a sudden loss, this is subtracted from the bank's net worth and not from deposits. Only after net worth falls to zero will depositors lose anything. Of course, if the bank's assets rise in value, the net worth of the bank will rise by that amount. The depositors are entitled only to their deposits and the interest promised on those deposits.

The shareholders of the bank are therefore heavily exposed to risk. Consider, as an example, the bank described in Figure 12.3 with $20 million (or $20M) of deposits, a reserve requirement of 10 percent, and an initial net worth of $4M. Suppose this bank loses 5 percent of its interest-bearing assets ($1.1M) because of a unexpected surge in loan defaults. The financial position of the bank is now described in Figure 12.4. Although the bank lost only 5 percent of its interest-bearing assets, the shareholders lost 27.5 percent of their investment in the bank, because the entire loss is subtracted from net worth. If shareholders are risk averse, the possibility of these magnified losses will induce the bank to avoid investing in risky assets.

The Moral Hazard of Deposit Insurance

If a bank is not insured, it must choose its assets carefully, weighing the risks and average returns of assets, in order to attract shareholders and depositors. A bank that takes on too much risk will be unable to attract shareholders or depositors (who bear the risk once net worth has fallen to zero). The careful consideration of risk and return is distorted, however, if a bank is fully or partially insured against losses.[9]

If the government insures depositors against all losses, depositors will no longer care about their bank's exposure to risk. A high rate of return is then the only thing they care about.[10] Banks seeking depositors must therefore offer the highest rates of return they can find.

Where can they find high rates of return? The rates of return on risky assets must be high (on average) in order to induce risk-averse people to hold them. Banks can therefore increase the average rate of return of their portfolios by holding risky assets. This pleases depositors, who like the high rates of return and don't care about the risk because their deposits are insured. In this way, deposit insurance will induce banks to take greater risks than they would if all the risks were borne by the shareholders and depositors of the bank. This is the **moral hazard** problem of insurance: insuring people against losses removes the incentives for the insured to act to reduce the risk of these losses.

How can the government limit the risk taking that deposit insurance encourages? The most direct approach is to limit banks legally to safe assets.[11] There are many projects worth funding, however, that are risky. A way to allow more risk taking without actually subsidizing risk is to charge insurance premiums that depend on the bank's exposure to risk so that the bank, and not the taxpayer, bears the cost of the risk. The difficulty with such a policy is in establishing a proper method to evaluate the riskiness of a bank's portfolio. An alternative to basing insurance premiums on the riskiness of bank assets is to allow banks to choose between being insured but regulated in the assets they may hold and being unregulated but uninsured.

The Importance of Capital Requirements

The imposition of capital requirements on banks is another way to reduce risk-taking behavior by banks. A **capital requirement** forces banks to maintain a net worth no less than some fraction of their assets. This provides a larger cushion to

---

[9] See Kareken (1983) for a clear warning about the dangers of deregulating insured financial intermediaries, written before the recent wave of savings and loan failures. For a detailed study of the problems associated with deposit insurance in Canada, see Carr, Matthewson, and Quigley (1994).

[10] A high rate of return may be paid to depositors in the form of either a high interest rate on their deposits or as a high level of convenience and service. Both are expensive for the bank.

[11] To some extent, regulation of the types of assets that a bank can hold currently exists. For example, banks in the United States are prohibited from holding shares of stock. The establishment of this regulation was clearly an attempt to reduce the exposure of banks to risk.

absorb asset losses before depositors or the insurer of the deposits suffer any losses. Shareholders will exercise more care in their selection of assets the greater their exposure to risk.

Consider some examples. Look again at the bank in Figure 12.3. Would the bank shareholders have any interest in a $4 million bet on a coin flip? No (if they are risk averse). Although they would double their net worth if they won, they would lose their entire net worth of $4 million if they lost. Now suppose the bank's original net worth was only $1 million. Would the bank's shareholders now be more interested in the coin flip? If they won, they would get $4 million as before. If they lost, however, they would lose only $1 million because shareholder liability is limited to the net worth of the bank. Their potential gain is four times their potential loss. Certainly, the shareholders will be more inclined to take this risky proposition.

Capital Requirements for Insured Banks

If shareholders can lose only their $1 million net worth, who stands to lose the other $3 million? If depositors are uninsured, they do. As a result of their greater exposure to risk, depositors will be reluctant to make deposits at a bank with a small net worth.

If deposits are insured, depositors will no longer care about the net worth of the bank and its propensity to take risks. It is the insurer (the government) that stands to lose when banks take risks and lose. In this case, it is the government that will be interested in requiring banks to have a net worth large enough to discourage shareholders from taking large risks.

Reacting to the United States' experience with intermediary failures in the 1980s, recent U.S. legislation has taken steps toward addressing these issues. The Financial Institutions Reform, Recovery, and Enforcement Act of 1989 increased core capital requirements of savings and loans from 3 percent of total assets to 8 percent. The Federal Deposit Insurance Corporation Improvement Act of 1991 instituted deposit insurance premiums based on capital-asset ratios and recommended the establishment of capital requirements based on the riskiness of a bank's portfolio. Risk-based capital requirements on commercial banks were fully phased in as of December 1992. The Financial Institutions Reform, Recovery, and Enforcement Act stipulated that savings and loans must eventually be subject to the same risk-based capital requirements as those imposed on banks.

Closing Insolvent Banks

Similar reasoning explains why the government is interested in uncovering and shutting down insolvent banks (banks with a negative net worth or deposits that exceed their assets). Think of the reactions of the depositors and shareholders of an insured bank if they see that it is insolvent. Depositors do not care because they are insured. The shareholders of the insolvent bank will lose everything if they close down. Investing in safe assets will just slowly reduce their already negative net worth, because they have fewer assets paying interest than they have deposits on which interest must be paid. What is the alternative? The shareholders' only chance to regain a positive net worth is to gamble big. If they win enough to make their net worth positive, their shares again have value. If they lose, the bank's net worth falls even further – but the shareholders do not suffer any further losses. Shareholders' liability is limited to the amount invested in the bank, the bank's original net worth. Once this has been lost, shareholders can lose no more. With nothing to lose and everything to gain by making risky loans and investments, insolvent banks will gamble more and more desperately until they either win enough to regain a positive net worth or they are forced to shut down.

This scenario sounds all too familiar in light of the crisis involving savings and loans (S&Ls) in the United States. The Depository Institutions Deregulation and Monetary Control Act of 1980 and the Garn–St. Germain Act of 1982 made it possible for these intermediaries to hold riskier assets than previously.[12] When many of the loans made by savings and loans went sour, savings and loans experienced losses of $4.6 billion in 1981 and a large number of them became insolvent. This, as we have noted, increased the incentive for these insolvent intermediaries to assume even riskier assets.

Figure 12.5 illustrates the growing number of insolvent savings and loans during the early 1980s. The decline in the net worth of savings and loans is also apparent in Figure 12.6, which shows the ratio of net worth to assets for the thrift industry.

The Federal Deposit Insurance Corporation Improvement Act of 1991 took steps toward dealing with financial institutions that hold inadequate capital. This act stipulated that the FDIC must take action to close banks that have capital-asset ratios of less than 2 percent. This act also introduced provisions that require the FDIC to intervene more quickly in the case of a troubled institution. Furthermore, the act severely limits the FDIC's ability to impose its "too big to fail" policy. Under this policy, which was adopted during the 1980s, the FDIC automatically excluded the largest banks in the country from being closed in the event of inadequate capital. This policy will be invoked only under special circumstances in the future.[13]

---

[12] Reversing this deregulatory trend, the Financial Institutions Reform, Recovery, and Enforcement Act of 1989 reinstituted stricter regulations on the types of assets that S&Ls could hold.

[13] Invocation of the "too big to fail" policy by the FDIC requires approval of a two-thirds majority of the Federal Reserve's Board of Governors and the directors of the FDIC as well as of the Secretary of the Treasury.

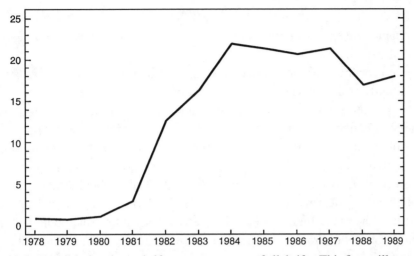

Figure 12.5. Tangible-insolvent thrifts as a percentage of all thrifts. This figure illustrates the increase in the percentage of thrifts that became tangible insolvent during the early 1980s. Thrifts include S&L associations and mutual savings banks, with S&Ls being the main component. A thrift is tangible insolvent if its net worth, excluding goodwill, is negative. *Source:* Federal Home Loan Bank Board and Office of Thrift Supervision data cited by White (1991, Table 2-6, p. 20).

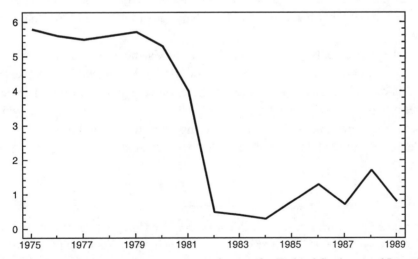

Figure 12.6. Tangible net worth as a percent of assets for Federal Savings and Loan Insurance Corporation (FSLIC)-insured thrifts. Declining net worth for S&Ls is reflected in the ratio of net worth to assets. During the early 1980s tangible net worth as a percentage of total assets fell below 1 percent. FSLIC-insured thrifts are those thrifts whose deposits were insured by FSLIC. The Financial Institutions Reform, Recovery, and Enforcement Act of 1989 replaced FSLIC with a new insurance fund. *Source:* Federal Home Loan Bank Board and Office of Thrift Supervision data cited in White (1991, Table 2-5, p. 19). The observation for 1989 is for thrifts insured by the newly founded Savings Association Insurance Fund.

Summary

In this chapter we examined two sources of bank failures – runs on banks and bank holding of risky assets.

A reason for the existence of banks is that, through banks, people can invest in illiquid long-term assets, yet be able to withdraw funds when needed. This service – that a bank's liabilities are payable on demand, whereas its assets are not – is also the source of bank instability. If a bank is forced to liquidate its assets prematurely because of unexpected withdrawals of deposits, it may be forced to sell those assets at a loss. Realizing that their deposits may be at risk, depositors may attempt to withdraw their deposits before the resources of the bank are exhausted.

Realizing the problems associated with these bank runs, we analyzed a variety of actions that may aid in their prevention. These include interbank lending, identifying unnecessary withdrawals, suspension of withdrawals, and government deposit insurance.

If banks can invest in risky assets, government deposit insurance gives rise to a situation of moral hazard. With deposit insurance, customers no longer monitor the riskiness of bank asset holdings. Banks, in order to attract depositors, have the incentive to take on risky assets that pay higher average rates of return than safe assets. To deal with this moral hazard problem, governments must either regulate the types of assets that banks can hold or charge insurance premiums that are risk related.

Capital requirements may also reduce a bank's incentive to take on risk by providing shareholders a reason to monitor the bank's selection of assets. The larger this capital requirement, the more shareholders stand to lose in the event of poor returns on a bank's asset holdings. We have seen that, when the net worth of a bank falls to zero, shareholders have nothing more to lose and may be willing to gamble heavily in the bank's acquisition of risky assets.

Exercises

12.1 Suppose you are the sole shareholder of a savings and loan with deposits of $1,200,000 and assets of $1,000,000. There is no reserve requirement. Your liability in the S&L is limited by law to your investment (if it fails, you needn't make up losses to depositors). You are risk neutral.

　　a. What is the net worth of the S&L?

　　b. Suppose you may reinvest your assets into one but only one of the following projects before the examiners audit your books.

　　Project *A*: pays a certain return of 7 percent.

　　Project *B*: has a 50 percent chance of a 21 percent net return and a 50 percent chance of a net return of −21 percent.

Project C: has a 10 percent chance of doubling your assets and a 90 percent chance of losing everything.

Rank the three projects according to which will benefit you personally.

c. How would your ranking change if the assets of the S&L were $1,200,000?

d. How would your ranking change if the assets of the S&L were $2,000,000?

e. If you have the chance to abscond with $100,000 at the cost of losing ownership in the S&L, would you do it (setting aside questions of morality)? How does your answer depend on the net worth of the S&L?

f. If S&Ls are covered by government deposit insurance, why should the government take an active role in closing down failed S&Ls as soon as they can be discovered? Answer with references to the examples in this exercise.

Part III

Government Debt

IN PARTS I and II we concentrated on money itself, whether fiat, commodity, or inside money. But money's effect on the economy is not limited to the direct effects we have studied so far. In Part III we look at the indirect effects of monetary policy, in particular its effect on the national debt. We will see that the national debt may have important effects on aggregate saving and investment. We will therefore examine the effect of monetary policy on the national debt and, through this, its effect on saving and investment.

Chapter 13 begins by presenting a model in which individuals willingly hold both fiat money and interest-bearing government debt. With this model in hand, we can begin to answer crucial questions such as the feasibility of continual debt financing. We also explore more thoroughly the government budget constraint to determine how the presence of government debt affects the options available to governments over time and the interaction of fiscal and monetary policy.

Chapter 14 provides a detailed look at individual decisions about saving and consumption. We unravel the important determinants of these variables. In particular, we study the effect of taxes on an individual's choices of saving and consumption over time.

Chapter 15 applies the lessons of the previous chapter to study the effect of the national debt on consumption, saving, investment, and output. Appendix A of Chapter 15 studies the effect of fiat money balances on wealth and the formation of private capital. This appendix also shows how the issuance of government debt can be used to transfer wealth between generations as a means to offset the redistributional effects of changes in the demand for money. In Appendix B of Chapter 15, we examine models of infinitely lived agents, comparing and contrasting the results of such models with those of finitely lived agents.

Chapter 16 continues our study of government debt by examining the effect of monetary surprises on the national debt, capital, and output. The appendix to Chapter 16 shows how monetary policy, through its impact on the real rate of return on government debt, can be used to offset the effects of real shocks to an economy.

Chapter 13

Deficits and the National Debt

THE MODELS THAT we have presented up to this point have had a government creating fiat money and taxing or providing transfers to individuals in the economy. Although these are important aspects of government finance in today's world, we have neglected one important factor. Governments frequently finance current deficits by borrowing. In this chapter we analyze the effects of the national debt on government revenue and some effects of monetary policy on the national debt.

High-Denomination Government Debt

We observe in most of today's economies that governments often issue two forms of debt – assets held by the public – one called money (for example, currency) and one called government bonds (for example, Treasury bills). Although they seem equally safe and negotiable, they have different rates of return. The net nominal rate of return on currency is zero, whereas that on Treasury bills held to maturity is positive. Clearly, Treasury bills dominate currency in rate of return. Why would anyone hold currency if an equally safe asset offers a higher rate of return? What difference in the nature of these two assets can explain the observed disparity in rates of return?

One difference in the two assets is the denominations in which they are offered. Currency is issued in small denominations easily usable in exchange, whereas Treasury bills are supplied only in large denominations. Imagine the expression on the face of the checkout clerk if you presented a $10,000 Treasury bill in payment for your $50 grocery bill!

There is a great gap today in the rate of return of currency and that of interest-bearing $10,000 Treasury bills. As always, a gap in rates of return leads one to wonder if there might not be some way for a financial intermediary to make a profit through arbitrage. This intermediary could purchase the large-denomination bonds and issue small-denomination notes. If the return from the bonds exceeded the cost of issuing the notes, then the intermediary would profit from the enterprise.

Suppose it costs a negligible amount to engage in such intermediation. What will then happen to the two rates of return? Let us attempt to answer that question by asking a few more. Suppose you could buy bonds that currently display a 20 percent rate of return. As the manager of an intermediary, you attempt to raise funds to purchase these bonds by attracting depositors. You begin by offering a zero rate of return on deposits. Given that many potential depositors also can purchase the same bonds and receive a much higher rate of return than you are offering on deposits, you have few customers. As an incentive to attract more deposits, you begin to offer higher and higher interest rates on deposits. As your intermediary (and presumably other intermediaries) enters bond markets, bond prices are bid up and rates of return on bonds begin to fall. Note that the spread between the rates of return on bonds and deposits begins to narrow. As long as there is a difference, profits can be made by engaging in this process. Hence, over time, rates of return on bonds fall as prices are bid up and rates of return on deposits rise as intermediaries attempt to attract depositors. If this intermediation is costless (or inexpensive), we expect this process to continue until there is no (or little) difference between the rates of return on bonds and deposits.

Can intermediation costs plausibly explain the rate-of-return difference? If so, we would have to believe that nominal interest rates soared in the inflationary 1970s because the wages of tellers or some other cost of operating a bank dramatically increased, only to fall again in recent years.

If the cost of intermediation is not a plausible explanation for high interest rates on government debt relative to that on currency, then what are other possible explanations? One possibility is that legal restrictions on governing intermediation have led to this difference. The prohibition on privately issued bank notes is an example of such a regulation.[1]

But why might the government wish to issue this high-denomination asset that requires it to pay interest and, at the same time, to regulate intermediation? The awkward denomination on this asset and the limits on its intermediation indicate that the asset is not being issued in order to provide a convenient medium of exchange.

A Model of Separated Asset Markets

Let us now consider a simple model in which the government may wish to issue high-denomination bonds in addition to fiat money in order to finance a deficit.[2] Imagine an economy in which there are two types of people – rich people who are endowed with Y when young and poor people who are endowed with y when

---

[1] Wallace (1983) presents a discussion of related issues that is accessible by undergraduates.
[2] This model is adapted from one presented by Bryant and Wallace (1984).

young. Let Y be much larger than y. No one is endowed when old. The populations of rich and poor both grow over time at the rate n.

We assume the following linear capital technology: if k units of the consumption good are invested in capital in period t, $x \cdot k$ units will be produced by capital in period $t + 1$. However, to utilize this technology, an individual must invest more than k^* units. We assume that the amount k^* is so much less than Y that the rich are effectively unconstrained in investing in capital. On the other hand, k^* is greater than y, so that no individual poor person is able to invest personally. Investment in capital cannot be observed by the government if the investment is done by an individual.

There is a supply of fiat money that increases in each period according to the rule $M_t = z M_{t-1}$ where $z > 1$.

First, suppose we allow the formation of an intermediation industry that pools the endowments of the poor so that they can invest in capital. This intermediation process also operates costlessly. Through intermediation all individuals in the economy have access to capital that yields a rate of return of x.

Consider the case of a monetary equilibrium. Individuals have a choice of two assets – capital and fiat money. Recall that if the rate of money creation is z and the growth rate of money demand (from population growth) is n, then the rate of return on fiat money will be n/z. For people to be willing to hold money voluntarily, the rate of return on fiat money must be at least as large as the rate of return on the alternative, capital. In other words, for a monetary equilibrium, we must have that

$$\frac{n}{z} \geq x.$$

If this were not true, then fiat money would be an inferior asset. Individuals would do better if they invested in capital. Note that the previous equation implies that

$$z \leq \frac{n}{x}.$$

This places an upper bound on the rate of fiat money creation in the absence of legal restrictions. If fiat money is created at a rate that exceeds n/x, then individuals will refuse to hold fiat money. We see that a monetary equilibrium will not exist if z is greater than n/x. Of course, if z is strictly less than n/x, then holding fiat money will provide a greater rate of return than holding capital. In that case, individuals will not invest in capital.

Now let us consider the imposition of a set of laws that effectively ban any intermediation that would enable people to pool their endowments to invest in capital. Recall that this implies that the poor will not have access to the capital technology. In such a case, the poor will have only one asset available to them – fiat money. In this case, fiat money can be created at a greater rate than n/x. Regardless of the rate of return on fiat money, the poor will still hold it, because it is the only means of providing for second-period consumption.

The rich, however, will invest in capital if $z > n/x$, because it yields a higher rate of return. Because the rich do not hold fiat money, the government obtains no seigniorage revenue from them. Note that the rich have an alternative unavailable to the poor – they can invest in capital individually, unobserved by the government. If the government could observe all investments, it could eliminate this option of the rich and force them, too, to hold only fiat money.

Introducing Government Bonds

We see that, by pushing the rate of fiat money creation beyond n/x, the government may have increased the seigniorage it takes in from the poor, but it has lost all seigniorage from the rich. Is there some means by which the government might take in revenue from both rich and poor?

Suppose the government issues bonds intended to substitute for capital in the portfolios of the rich. We will assume that these government bonds have a one-period maturity. In other words, a given issue of bonds is retired with interest after one period. At that point in time, the government may issue additional bonds.

In order for the rich to be willing to hold government bonds, the bonds must pay a rate of return at least as large as that of capital. Hence, x is a lower bound for the rate of return on government bonds intended as substitutes for capital.

But if bonds pay the rate of return of capital, won't the poor, who are otherwise stuck with low-return fiat money, use bonds rather than fiat money to consume in the second period of life? If so, the government will lose all revenue from seigniorage. How can the government use the bonds to raise revenue from the rich without forgoing the seigniorage raised from the poor? A revenue-hungry government must find a way to make the bonds available to the rich but not the poor.

Suppose then that the government issues bonds with a minimum price of k^* goods while banning all intermediation. The minimum price effectively prevents any individual poor person from buying these bonds because a poor person's endowment y is less than k^*, and the ban on intermediation prevents anyone from pooling the funds of the poor to buy bonds. Now perhaps we can see why the government may take actions that reduce the liquidity of its debt. The bonds are designed to be a substitute for capital but not for fiat money, so the government can raise revenue from the bonds without losing revenue from seigniorage on fiat money holdings.

Continual Debt Issue

It is apparent that the government can induce the rich to lend to the government, adding to the government's revenue in that period. Unlike fiat money, however,

Table 13.1. *Government Bond Issuance and Revenue with x* = 0.9 *and n* = 1

Period	Real bond issue	Real bond repayment	Real net revenue
1	1,000		1,000
2	1,000	900	100
3	1,000	900	100
4	1,000	900	100
⋮	⋮	⋮	⋮

these bonds must be repaid with interest in a future period. In this way, government debt may defer rather than permanently answer the need to raise revenue.

Is it possible that the government can defer the payment of the debt forever? To do so in every period, the government must borrow enough to pay off its debt from the previous period. If this is possible, government bonds can be used to raise revenue permanently – that is, without ever using future taxes to pay off the debt or the interest on the debt.

Let us first address this question with a numerical example of government debt issuance and repayment. Suppose there are 10 young rich people in each generation and the government issues bonds worth 100 goods per young rich person in each period. This implies that in every period the government issues bonds worth a total of 1,000 goods. As reasoned previously, the government must pay the real rate of return x on these bonds. This means that the government must pay back $100x$ units of goods to each young person, for a total of $1,000x$ goods. The government again issues bonds worth a total of 1,000 goods. Clearly, if $x < 1$, the government's new issuance of bonds will enable it to retire the old bonds and generate real revenue of $1,000(1 - x)$ goods. For example, if $x = 0.9$, the government repays the 900 goods $(= 1,000x)$ and obtains real revenue equal to 100 goods $[= 1,000(1 - x)]$. Table 13.1 details the government's bond issuance and revenue for these parameter values.

Clearly, the government can sustain this level of debt issue forever and obtain 100 units of real revenue in each period. Hence, bond issue can provide a source of revenue for a government.

We can also see why a revenue-maximizing government would want to issue bonds with a minimum denomination of k^*. This enables a government to generate revenue from bond issue and money creation. Given the high denomination of government debt, the poor have no alternative but to use fiat money. This enables the government to obtain revenue by taxing their money holdings. If, contrary to our setup, government bonds were issued in small denominations and paid the rate of return x, the poor would choose to hold the government bonds instead of fiat money (if $z > 1/x$). The government would be severely constrained as to its rate of fiat money creation and, hence, its amount of seigniorage revenue.

Table 13.2. *Government Bond Issuance and Revenue with $x = 1.1$ and $n = 1.2$*

Period	Real bond issue	Real bond repayment	Real net revenue
1	1,000		1,000
2	1,200	1,100	100
3	1,440	1,320	120
4	1,728	1,584	144
⋮	⋮	⋮	⋮

However, it is clear from the numerical example that revenue is raised from bonds because we have assumed a low rate of return on capital; indeed, the net rate of return, $x - 1$, is negative. Is it possible for the government to permanently generate revenue by repeatedly issuing bonds in the more realistic case in which the real net rate of return is positive (i.e., $x > 1$)? In this case, the government would have to issue an increasing amount of bonds in each period just to repay the old debt.

It is still possible to raise revenue permanently by continually issuing government debt but only if the population is growing at a sufficiently high rate. To return to our numerical example, suppose that now $x = 1.1$ and $n = 1.2$. As before, the number of young rich people in period 1 is 10. The government still issues bonds worth 100 goods per young rich person in each period. Now, however, total bond issue will grow in each period, because the population is growing. In this case, the government will issue a total amount of bonds equal to 1,200 [$= (10)(1.2)(100)$] goods in period 2. It will have to repay a total real amount of 1,100 [$= (10)(100)(1.1)$] goods. This implies the generation of 100 units of goods in real revenue. Table 13.2 details the results for these parameter values. Note that from period 3 on, the government's real revenue from the bond issue grows at the rate n, the rate of population growth. Clearly, total government borrowing and real debt repayment grow at the same rate.

It is important to note that the preceding examples always assumed that if $x < n$. We will see that if $x > n$, the government cannot permanently obtain revenue from the issuance of bonds.

Rolling Over the Debt

To see the limitation on the government's ability to raise revenue permanently, let us look at one more numeric example. Suppose that instead of generating revenue by a bond issue, the government merely issues enough bonds in each period to make the repayments (including interest) on the previous period's bond issue. We'll call this practice **rolling over the debt**. Using the same parameter values as in the previous example, we obtain Table 13.3.

Table 13.3. *Government Bond Issuance and Revenue with x = 1.1 and Zero Bond Revenue*

Period	Real bond issue	Real bond repayment	Real net revenue
1	1,000		1,000
2	1,100	1,100	0
3	1,210	1,210	0
4	1,331	1,331	0
$\vdots$	$\vdots$	$\vdots$	$\vdots$

In the case where the government obtains zero revenue from a bond issue, the total amount of government bonds issued grows at the rate x. This chapter took a detailed look at how the presence of government debt alters the government budget constraint. We found that issuing government debt today changes the options that the government has available tomorrow. If perpetual debt financing is infeasible, an increase in the government's debt forces an eventual decrease in government expenditures or increase in future taxation.

One of the taxation options is to monetize the debt. When the central bank does not pay interest to the holders of its money, it earns profits that are handed back to the fiscal authority (Treasury). In this case, the net effect of the two steps of printing bonds to cover government expenditures and then monetizing the bonds is exactly the same as having the government simply print money to pay for the expenditures without bothering to issue bonds.

Let us compare this time path of government debt to the government's ability to borrow. The most the government could ever borrow would be the entire endowment of the rich. Let us now determine the time path of this upper limit on bonds. Note that, if the population is growing at the rate n, the total endowment of the young rich people obeys (we will denote the total number of young rich people in period t as N_t for simplicity) the following rules:

$$N_1 Y = n N_0 Y$$
$$N_2 Y = n N_1 Y = n^2 N_0 Y$$
$$N_3 Y = n N_2 Y = n^3 N_0 Y$$
$$\vdots$$
$$N_t Y = n^t N_0 Y. \tag{13.1}$$

If we take the natural logarithm of both sides of this equation, we obtain

$$\ln(N_t Y) = t \ln(n) + \ln(N_0 Y). \tag{13.2}$$

Let us denote the total real amount of the government bond issue in period t as B_t. We know that, when the government obtains no revenue from bond issue, B_t

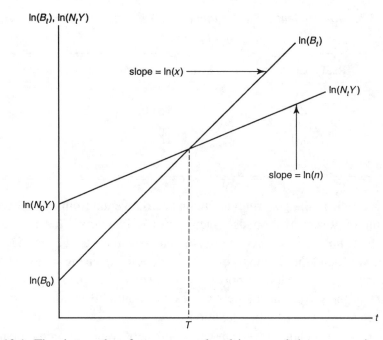

Figure 13.1. The time paths of government bond issue and the economy's endowment ($x > n$). When a government rolls over its debt, the total amount of debt outstanding grows at the rate x, the interest rate it must pay on its debt. When expressed in logarithms, this translates into a straight-line time path, $\ln(B_t)$, with a slope of $\ln(x)$. On the other hand, the economy's total endowment grows at the rate of population growth n and is represented by the line $\ln(N_t Y)$. Beyond time T, the real value of the government debt exceeds the total endowment of the economy. This is infeasible, demonstrating the eventual impossibility of rolling over the debt if $x > n$.

grows at rate x. Following the techniques used to derive Equations 13.1 and 13.2, we find that

$$B_t = x^t B_0 \tag{13.3}$$
$$\Rightarrow \ln(B_t) = t \ln(x) + \ln(B_0). \tag{13.4}$$

The reason we took natural logarithms of Equations 13.1 and 13.3 is that the resulting Equations 13.2 and 13.4 are linear equations in t that are easy to graph. Figure 13.1 illustrates the time paths of $\ln(B_t)$ and $\ln(N_t Y)$. The graph is drawn for the case where $x > n$. What is the importance of this graph? After time T the total amount of the real government bond issue exceeds the total real endowment of the young rich people in the economy. This is infeasible.[3] If the growth rate of the

---

[3] This result was emphasized by Sargent and Wallace (1981).

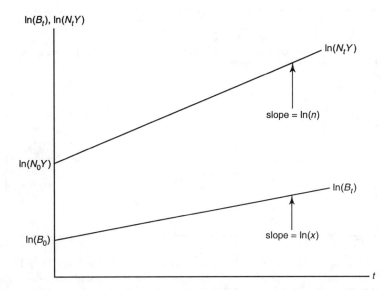

Figure 13.2. The time paths of government bond issue and the economy's endowment ($x \leq n$). When the real interest rate x is less than the growth rate of the economy n the total stock of government debt grows at a slower rate than that of the economy. Under these conditions, perpetual bond financing is possible because the growing economy has sufficient resources to absorb the growing quantity of bonds.

population (n) is less than the growth rate of the government bond issue (x), then eventually the government will be unable to find holders for its bonds. The supply of government bonds will outstrip the demand for them. In the case where $x > n$, perpetual government debt issue will become impossible. Eventually the government will have to issue more bonds than people are willing to hold. Note that this will actually occur before time T, because the young rich will not be willing to save their entire endowment. More generally, we obtain the important conclusion that if the real interest rate on government bonds exceeds the growth rate of the economy, perpetual debt financing becomes impossible.

It is equally important to note that if $x \leq n$, then perpetual government bond financing will be possible. In Figure 13.2, the line representing the total endowment of young rich people has a greater slope than the line representing the total bond issue, so that no period of reckoning T is ever reached. Indeed, the rolled-over debt shrinks as a fraction of the endowment.

Example 13.1 Suppose that in addition to population growth, there is growth in the endowment of each young rich person so that $Y_t = \alpha Y_{t-1}$ where $\alpha > 1$. Graph the time path of the log of the total endowment of the rich. For which values of x, n, and α can the government roll over its debt?

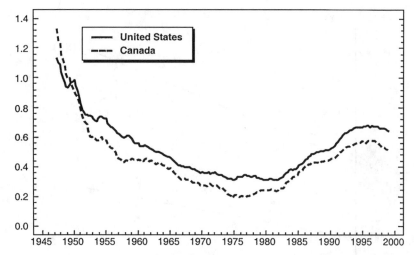

Figure 13.3. The ratio of government debt outstanding to GNP for Canada and the United States. *Sources:* The U.S. data are from the Federal Reserve Bank of St. Louis FRED database (http://www.stls.frb.org/fred/index.html). The Canadian data are from various issues of the *Bank of Canada Review*. The data are quarterly observations for each country. For the United States, FRED series gnp was divided into FRED series gfdebt. For Canada, series D20056 (GNP) was divided into Cansim series B2400 (Government of Canada bonds outstanding).

From this discussion, we recognize two important facts about the feasibility of rolling over the government debt. First, we realize that the ability of a government to place its debt is related to the economy's ability to absorb it. In the first case considered, where $x > n$, we note that the amount of government debt relative to the total endowment [total gross national product (GNP)] of the economy rises over time. In fact, if we were to measure a debt-GNP ratio for this economy, it would go to infinity. However, in a case where $x < n$, the debt-GNP ratio would fall over time. We may then view the debt-GNP ratio as an important determinant of how large a burden that debt is for the economy. An economy with a high debt-GNP ratio would find it much more difficult to retire its debt than an economy with a low debt-GNP ratio. In light of this, we may wish to look at some data.

Figure 13.3 plots the ratio of government debt outstanding to GNP for the Canadian and U.S. economies. The debt-GNP ratios for the two economies look quite similar. Immediately after World War II, both countries had debt-GNP ratios in excess of 1 because of the large issuance of government debt to finance wartime expenditures. Although both countries display falling debt-GNP ratios in the postwar period, this trend reversed during the 1980s.

We have also seen that the feasibility of rolling over the government debt depends on the relative magnitudes of an economy's real interest rate and its growth rate.

Figure 13.4. The real interest rate and growth rate of the U.S. economy. Examination of quarterly U.S. data on real interest rates (x) and the growth rate of the economy (n) indicates a changing relationship between these two variables over time. *Sources:* All series are from the FRED database of the Federal Reserve Bank of St. Louis (http://www.stls.frb.org/fred/index.html). The 3-month Treasury bill nominal interest rate (FRED series tb3ms) is converted to an estimate of the real interest rate by using the GNP deflator price index (series gnpdef). See Equation 6.7 for the method of calculation. The growth rate of the economy is measured by the growth rate of real GNP (series gnp92).

Figure 13.4 illustrates U.S. data representing these two variables.[4] Figure 13.4 shows that the relative magnitudes of x and n have shifted over time. According to these data, the growth rate of the U.S. economy has often exceeded the real interest rate in recent decades. However, there are clearly time periods (for example, the early 1980s) when the opposite is true. As we show in Chapter 15, a government that chooses to run larger deficits may cause real interest rates to rise, a situation that tends to move the policy of perpetual deficit financing toward the realm of infeasibility.[5]

Example 13.2 Recall the model of three-period-lived people described in Chapter 7. In this model, capital paid the rate of return X but only after two periods. All people had the same endowments – y goods when young but nothing when middle-aged and old. In every period the population grows at the gross rate n. Assume that intermediation (or IOU issue)

---

[4] How to calculate a real interest rate for an economy is a difficult question, one that we are sidestepping here. Such a calculation requires the choice of a nominal interest rate and a price index from which to calculate an inflation rate. Choices of alternative interest rates or price indices would change the appearance of Figure 13.4 but would not alter the basic conclusions in the text.

[5] For interesting discussions of this issue, see those of Sargent and Wallace (1981), Darby (1984), and Miller and Sargent (1984). These papers present both sides of the issue regarding the feasibility of perpetual deficit financing.

is costless but observable by the government and that capital creation is not observable by the government.

a. Describe how the government can earn revenue from both seigniorage and bonds in this economy. Describe in particular the form of the bonds and any legal restrictions on financial markets.

b. For what values of X can the government roll over the debt?

The Burden of the National Debt

When discussing government spending, it is useful to introduce the **government budget constraint**. Like an individual's budget constraint, the government budget constraint simply states that a government cannot use up more goods than it acquires. In Chapter 3, we derived a simple form of a government budget constraint. This constraint stated that government expenditures cannot exceed revenue obtained from seigniorage. However, in this chapter, we have introduced another source of government revenue – the issue of government bonds. Because of this new source of revenue, Chapter 3's government budget constraint must be revised. The new government budget constraint will not only generalize the results from our numerical examples but will also help to set down carefully the choices facing the government.

The Government Budget Constraint

Bonds affect a government's budget constraint in two ways. When issued, they provide a source of revenue to the government. However, when they are retired with interest, bonds represent expenditures for the government. To keep the form of the bonds simple, we assume that each government bond will be worth 1 unit of the consumption good and have a one-period maturity; a government bond issued in period t will mature and be retired in period $t + 1$. At that time, the government will repay the principal of the loan plus interest.

As an example, let us find the government budget constraint for an economy in which all the individuals are alike (unlike the rich/poor economy discussed earlier in this chapter). Furthermore, in this economy, both bonds and money are held; bonds are a substitute for capital but not for money (for example, the case of reserve requirements that can be satisfied only by fiat money holdings). We denote the number of bonds issued in period t per young person as b_t and the gross real rate of return (principal plus interest) on bonds as r. The government also collects taxes from each young person. This tax per young person is denoted as τ_t. In addition, in each period, the government purchases g units of the consumption good per young person.

Revenue for the government has three possible sources – bond issue, seigniorage from printing new money, and tax collections. In the aggregate, total tax revenue in period t is $N_t \tau_t$, seigniorage revenue amounts to $v_t[M_t - M_{t-1}]$, and the amount of revenue generated by bond issue is $N_t b_t$. This implies that total government revenue from these three sources is $N_t \tau_t + v_t[M_t - M_{t-1}] + N_t b_t$.

On the expenditure side, the government purchases $N_t g$ units of the consumption good in period t. In the previous period, period $t-1$, the government issued $N_{t-1} b_{t-1}$ bonds. These bonds mature in period t and represent an additional source of expenditures for the government. They must pay back the principal plus interest on these bonds. Hence, expenditures to retire the bonds from the previous period amount to $r N_{t-1} b_{t-1}$.

We are now ready to state the government's budget constraint. This is merely that total government expenditures equal total government revenues. In terms of our notation, the government budget constraint is

$$N_t g + r N_{t-1} b_{t-1} = N_t \tau_t + v_t[M_t - M_{t-1}] + + N_t b_t. \qquad (13.5)$$

If we divide through both sides of this equation by N_t, we obtain

$$g + r\left[\frac{N_{t-1}}{N_t}\right] b_{t-1} = \tau_t + \frac{v_t[M_t - M_{t-1}]}{N_t} + b_t. \qquad (13.6)$$

Let z_t denote the rate of expansion of the fiat money stock at time t ($M_t = z_t M_{t-1}$). Noting that $(N_{t-1}/N_t) = (1/n)$ and that $M_{t-1} = (1/z_t)M_t$, we can rewrite Equation 13.6 as

$$g + \left[\frac{r}{n}\right] b_{t-1} = \tau_t + \left[\frac{v_t M_t}{N_t}\right]\left[1 - \frac{1}{z_t}\right] + b_t, \qquad (13.7)$$

or

$$g + \left[\frac{r}{n}\right] b_{t-1} = \tau_t + q_t\left[1 - \frac{1}{z_t}\right] + b_t. \qquad (13.8)$$

where $q_t = (v_t M_t / N_t)$ is the real value of money balances per young person in period t.

The Government's Intertemporal Choice

Let us look at the government's position at the beginning of the economy. In period 1, the government's budget constraint is

$$g + \left[\frac{r}{n}\right] b_0 = \tau_1 + q_1\left[1 - \frac{1}{z_1}\right] + b_1. \qquad (13.9)$$

The term $[r/n]b_0$ represents the initial debt of the government and b_1 represents the debt to be passed on to future generations. To simplify our analysis, suppose the government in future periods $(t > 1)$ maintains the debt per young person at this level $(b = b_1)$. Furthermore, the government will pursue a constant tax (τ) and seigniorage policy (with $q_t = q$ and $z_t = z$). Future taxes and seigniorage may differ from their present levels but will not change after the first period. This will let us represent the future as a stationary equilibrium that can easily be compared with the present. Then for $t > 1$ the government's budget constraint simplifies to

$$g + \left[\frac{r}{n}\right]b = \tau + q\left[1 - \frac{1}{z}\right] + b$$

$$g = \tau + q\left[1 - \frac{1}{z}\right] + b\left[1 - \frac{r}{n}\right] \quad (t > 1). \tag{13.10}$$

Note that the two government budget constraints (Equations 13.9 and 13.10) are linked in that the b_1 of Equation 13.9 is the b of Equation 13.10. In other words, the bonds that are issued in period 1 are the bonds on which interest must be paid in the future.

By looking at Equations 13.9 and 13.10, we can analyze the effects of changes in government spending decisions. Suppose the government wishes to increase government spending g in period 1 without increasing taxes or the rate of money creation in period 1. How can this be accomplished? Reference to Equation 13.9 quickly reveals the answer. Recall that the value of b_0 was determined in period 0 and is outside the government's control in period 1. In this scenario, the government chooses not to increase τ_1 or z_1. The only choice left is to increase b_1 – issue bonds in period 1 to pay for the increased government expenditures.

Recall that the b_1 of Equation 13.9 is the b of Equation 13.10. In other words, the increase in bond issuance in period 1 affects the options available to the government in subsequent periods. If $r > n$, the increase in b causes the right-hand side of Equation 13.10 to fall [because $(1 - r/n)$ is negative in this case]. For equality to be maintained, something must "give" in Equation 13.10. Either τ or z or both must increase. Alternatively stated, if the government is to pursue this policy, either taxes or inflation must increase in the future.

During the 1980s, the United States experienced large budgetary deficits, financed by the issuance of government debt. This increase in debt issue led to corresponding increases in interest payments to service this debt, as illustrated in Figure 13.5. By the beginning of the 1990s, total interest payments on the debt amounted to over 14 percent of total government expenditures.

Figure 13.5. Net interest payments as a percent of total U.S. government expenditures. We see here the effect of the U.S. deficits of the 1980s on the fraction of government spending that must be devoted to paying interest on the national debt. *Sources:* All series are from the FRED database of the Federal Reserve Bank of St. Louis (http://www.stls.frb.org/fred/index.html). U.S. federal government net interest payment (FRED series afceneti) is expressed as a percentage of total U.S. federal government expenditures (series fgexpnd).

This represents an important lesson. Government decisions made today about spending, taxation, borrowing, and money creation affect the options available for the government in the future. In this case, the decision to spend more in period 1 implies higher taxes and/or inflation in the future. If the government decides to spend more currently, it cannot expect to lower both taxes and inflation in the future. The option simply does not exist if $r > n$.

The government may have sensible reasons not explicitly modeled here to defer taxes temporarily by running a deficit even if $r > n$. It may wish to run a deficit to help out an unlucky generation burdened with a war or a recession. It may wish to make future generations pay for durable government projects like schools and dams that benefit more than one generation. It may also wish to spread over time the distortions that result from non-lump-sum taxes, such as income taxes.[6] The government budget constraint does not say that the government should never run a deficit; it says that (if $r > n$) lower taxes or seigniorage today imply higher taxes or seigniorage in the future. The government may rationally choose to run deficits in wartime and recessions, but then the government budget constraint requires surpluses in peacetime and prosperous times. The government cannot always run deficits.

---

[6] See Barro (1989) for a survey on deficit policy.

A Central Bank's Balance Sheet

Assets	Liabilities
Interest-bearing assets (government debt)	Central bank money (as currency or reserves)

Figure 13.6. The balance sheet of a central bank issuing money backed by government debt.

Another important lesson is that there are strong links between fiscal and monetary policy – links that cannot be ignored. Decisions about taxation (τ), spending (g), and borrowing (b) are linked through the government budget to monetary policy (z). This provides a strong argument for coordination of fiscal and monetary policy.[7]

Example 13.3 Use the government budget constraints (Equations 13.9 and 13.10) to answer the following questions. In answering these questions, assume that $r > n$.

a. Suppose that every year the government runs the same deficit, $g - \tau$. If the central bank tries to reduce inflation today, what must happen to inflation in the future?

b. Suppose the central bank is very independent and has vowed never to increase the rate of monetary expansion. If the government reduces taxes today, what must happen to taxes in the future?

c. Suppose the government vows to reduce taxes forever, and at the same time the central bank vows to reduce forever the rate of expansion of the money supply. Can both promises be kept without reducing government expenditures?

Open Market Operations

The institutional arrangements defining the seigniorage power of most monetary authorities in economically advanced countries are not quite as straightforward as just presented. The fiscal authority is generally not allowed to print money at will to make government purchases. The authority to print money is generally given to a central bank, which is allowed to issue money only for **open market purchases** of government debt.

The balance sheet of such a central bank is that shown in Figure 10.1 in the chapter on fully backed money, but with government debt serving as the interest-bearing asset, depicted here as Figure 13.6.

What will be the effects of an expansion of the money stock by this type of central bank? Will it be an inflationary tax on moneyholders, as it was when we assumed that the fiscal authority could itself print money to purchase the goods it

---

[7] The costs of uncoordinated fiscal and monetary policy are described by Sargent and Wallace (1981) and Sargent (1986b).

desires (Chapter 3)? Will it be completely neutral in its effects as it was when the government printed money to purchase productive assets (Chapter 10)? To answer, we must first specify what happens to the interest earned from the assets of the central bank.

If the central bank receives interest from its assets but does not pay interest on its liabilities (money), it earns profits. In the United States and elsewhere, these profits are turned over to the government. Under this arrangement, when the central bank prints money to buy up government bonds, it has reduced the burden of the government's debt. It has **monetized** the government's debt. Any interest paid on government debt in the hands of the central bank represents a profit and so is returned to the government's treasury. An increase in the money stock remains a tax on those holding money (seigniorage): wealth is transferred from moneyholders to the government.

The only difference is that seigniorage from open market operations provides government revenue in the future instead of the present because the government uses the expansion of the money stock to buy up assets (reducing the debt on which it must pay interest) rather than to buy current goods. Therefore, if the government does not pay interest on money, we may think of an open market purchase as the combination of two policy actions – the taxation of money balances and the purchase of assets by the government. Remember that, although the central bank carries these assets on its books, the assets are effectively owned by the government because the interest from these assets is turned over to the government (after central bank expenses). Recalling the government budget constraints for $t = 1$ and $t > 1$,

$$g + \left[\frac{r}{n}\right]b_0 = \tau_1 + q_1\left[1 - \frac{1}{z_1}\right] + b_1, \tag{13.11}$$

$$g + \left(\frac{r}{n} - 1\right)b = \tau + q\left[1 - \frac{1}{z}\right] \quad (t > 1), \tag{13.12}$$

we see from Equation 13.11 that for a given demand for money, q, an increase in the fiat money stock in the first period (an increase in z_1 above) is used to reduce the real debt that must be financed in the future, $b_1 = b$. If $r > n$, this reduction in b reduces the interest that must be paid to finance the debt $[(r/n) - 1]b$ in all future periods of a stationary equilibrium. As a result, in the future, government expenditures may be increased or taxes may be decreased.

Seigniorage that is used to buy goods directly (as we studied in Chapter 3) allows the government to increase government expenditures or reduce taxes in the current period. Therefore, open market operations change only the timing of these effects. Moreover, if a government can count on the central bank to monetize its debt, it can issue debt to increase expenditures or reduce taxes, knowing that the central bank will monetize this debt. The net effect of this combination of issuing debt and monetizing it is exactly that of simply printing money to buy goods for the government: the government acquires goods in the current period at the expense of those holding money balances. While a veneer of respectability may be added by restricting the central bank to open market operations, if the central bank earns profits from its portfolio of government debt and returns them to the government's treasury, the revenue effects of open market operations are essentially the same as expanding the money stock to buy goods.

(In Chapter 10 we worked out the implications of monetary expansions if the central bank takes the interest it earns and uses it in turn to pay interest to those who hold its money. In this case, central bank money is a perfect substitute for inside money in the portfolios of moneyholders. Increases in central bank money then simply cause people to reduce their holdings of inside money to keep their total money balances the same. Specifying that government debt is the interest-bearing asset backing central bank money does nothing to change this analysis.)

Political Strategy and the National Debt

We have seen that the decisions a government makes today with regard to fiscal and monetary policies affect the options available for these policies in the future. Could a politician exploit this fact to detrimentally alter the options available for a political party that may come into power in the future?[8]

To answer this question, let's consider an example. For simplicity, assume that the population is constant. Suppose a government faces the following constraints on its ability to raise revenue. In each period, the most the government can raise through all taxes, including seigniorage, is 1,000,000 goods. Also assume that the maximum real government debt that the fixed population can willingly hold, given the limitations of their endowments, is 950,000 goods. Government debt pays a real rate of return of 1.2. In period 1, government expenditures are equal to 900,000 goods. Finally, suppose no debt was issued in the previous period ($B_0 = b_0 = 0$).

The current leaders of the government detest government expenditures but know they will not be in power next period. Let's see how they can use their power over current taxes and government debt to force their successors to reduce government expenditures.

---

[8] See Persson and Svensson (1989) for a more complete discussion of this topic.

The government budget constraint facing the current leaders in period 1 is

$$Ng_1 + rNb_0 = N\tau_1 + v_1[M_1 - M_0] + Nb_1,$$

or

$$Ng_1 = N\tau_1 + v_1[M_1 - M_0] + Nb_1 \quad \text{(since } b_0 = 0\text{)}. \tag{13.13}$$

With our assumptions, current government expenditures are $Ng_1 = 900,000$. To severely limit the next government's options, the current leaders choose to raise no revenue from taxes or seigniorage. In other words, they choose to finance the entire amount of government expenditures through issuing debt. From Equation 13.13, with $N\tau_1 + v_1[M_1 - M_0] = 0$, we see that the total amount of debt that must be issued is

$$900,000 = Nb_1, \tag{13.14}$$

which is feasible because it is less than the maximum the public is willing to hold. The current leaders have forced the next leaders to inherit government debt, which must be repaid with interest.

Now let us see the options that this implies for the new leaders who take power in period 2. We know that if these leaders do nothing about the outstanding government debt, it will grow at the rate r. We also know that if $r > n = 1$, which is the case in this example, the government cannot permanently roll over the debt.

The government budget constraint in period 2 is

$$Ng_2 + rNb_1 = N\tau_2 + v_2[M_2 - M_1] + Nb_2. \tag{13.15}$$

Substituting $r = 1.2$ and $Nb_1 = 900,000$ into Equation 13.15, we obtain

$$Ng_2 + (1.2)(900,000) = N\tau_2 + v_2[M_2 - M_1] + Nb_2$$
$$Ng_2 + 1,080,000 = N\tau_2 + v_2[M_2 - M_1] + Nb_2. \tag{13.16}$$

If leaders in period 2 choose to raise revenue from seigniorage and taxes up to the maximum, Equation 13.16 becomes

$$Ng_2 + 1,080,000 = 1,000,000 + Nb_2. \tag{13.17}$$

We also assumed that the maximum amount of government debt the public desires to hold is 950,000 goods. If these leaders choose to issue debt equal to that amount, we see from Equation 13.17 that

$$Ng_2 + 1,080,000 = 1,000,000 + 950,000$$
$$Ng_2 = 870,000. \tag{13.18}$$

We see that the old leaders have forced the new leaders to reduce government expenditures from their period 1 level of 900,000 to 870,000. If the leaders had not chosen to raise taxes or issue debt up to the maximum amounts, government expenditures would have to be reduced even further.

The political ramifications of this example are clear. The expense of the interest payments on government debt forced the new leaders to lower government expenditures, whatever they would normally have wanted to do. In this way the old leaders were able to force the new leaders to choose a lower level of government expenditures as the old leaders desired. Of course, future leaders will inherit the debt that the leaders in period 2 issue. This will limit the choices that are available to them in a similar manner.

Summary

We began this chapter by noting that there are significant rate of return differences between government bonds and fiat money. Chapter 7 investigated one possible explanation for rate of return differentials – the liquidity advantage of fiat money over other assets. The model of this chapter focused on the large denominations of government bonds as the source of their illiquidity. We found the government may wish to issue illiquid bonds as a substitute for capital but not fiat money. In this way the government is able to raise revenue from both seigniorage and the issuance of debt.

Another important topic of this chapter was the feasibility of perpetual debt financing, often referred to as rolling over the debt. We found that, if the real interest rate paid on government debt exceeds the growth rate of the economy, perpetual debt financing is infeasible. In such a case, the ever-expanding volume of government bonds would outstrip the economy's limited ability to absorb them. On the other hand, we found that perpetual debt financing is possible when the real interest rate is less than the growth rate of the economy.

This chapter took a detailed look at how the presence of government debt alters the government budget constraint. We found that issuing government debt today changes the options that the government has available tomorrow. If perpetual debt financing is infeasible, an increase in the government's debt forces an eventual decrease in government expenditures or increase in future taxation.

One of the taxation options is to monetize the debt. When the central bank does not pay interest to the holders of its money, it earns profits that are handed back to the fiscal authority (Treasury). In this case, the net effect of the two steps of printing bonds to cover government expenditures and then monetizing the bonds is exactly the same as having the government simply print money to pay for the expenditures without bothering to issue bonds.

Exercises

13.1 Assume that the maximum revenue that can be collected from all taxes, including seigniorage, is 5,000 goods and that the maximum debt is 6,000 goods. The real gross market rate of return is 1.2. Government expenditures currently equal 4,500 goods. The current leaders of the country detest government expenditures but know they will not be in power next period. How can these leaders use their control over current taxes, subsidies, and the government debt to force their successors to reduce steady-state government expenditures below 4,500 goods? Use the government budget constraint in giving your answer.

13.2 Consider an overlapping generations economy in which capital pays a 25 percent net rate of return. The population of a generation grows by 10 percent each period. In the initial period (period 1) there are 100 young people and a preexisting fiat money stock of $M_0 = \$1$ million. Because of a political impasse, government expenditures exceed (nonseigniorage) tax revenues by 50 goods per young person in every period. Each young person wishes to hold real money balances worth 200 goods regardless of the rate of inflation.[9]

    a. Use the government budget constraint to find the rate of fiat money creation that is required to finance the excess of government expenditures over taxes. Find also the fiat money stock and the price level in periods 1 and 2.

    b. Suppose that in the initial period the monetary authority hesitates to print new money, forcing the government to issue debt at the market rate of interest. In the second period the monetary authority relents, printing enough new money to pay off the debt as well as to pay for the second period's excess of government expenditures over taxes. Find the fiat money stock in period 2 and compare it with your answers in part a. Explain the difference.

    c. Suppose that in the initial period you anticipate the actions of the monetary authority described in part b. What rate of inflation do you expect? If (contrary to our assumption) anticipated inflation discourages the use of fiat money, why will the price level rise in period 1 even though no fiat money is printed?

13.3 Suppose there are 100 young rich people born in every period. Government debt and capital both pay real net rates of return equal to 25 percent. The fiat money stock is fixed. Each young rich person wishes to save 50 goods in each period. In period 0, the

---

[9] This exercise illustrates an idea presented by Sargent and Wallace (1981).

government issues a total amount of real government debt equal to 2,000 goods. The government attempts to roll over this initial debt in subsequent periods.

a. What are the real holdings of capital and bonds of each young rich person in period 0 and in period 1?

b. In what period does it become impossible for the government to continue to roll over its debt?

c. Now suppose the number of young rich people born in each period grows at the net rate of 10 percent. There are 100 young rich people born in period 0. Recalculate your answer to part b. Explain the difference in your answer.

Chapter 14

Savings and Investment

IN EARLIER CHAPTERS we used the overlapping generations model as a model of money. People needed money, whether fiat, commodity, or inside money, to acquire a market good for which they must pay with a form of money. We did not interpret this good literally as consumption in old age because money balances are a trivial source of savings for retirement. We used the overlapping generations structure as a simple way to model exchange without taking the age of the model's people very seriously.

Now we will take the age structure of the overlapping generations model more seriously as we turn to the subject of the determinants of aggregate saving and investment. Our attitude changes because government bonds and capital, the focuses of our inquiry, are important parts of people's lifetime savings.

The Savings Decisions

Let us now look at how individuals choose their level of savings. We will do this in the context of the overlapping generations model of two-period-lived people who must choose how much to consume when young and when old. Let us generalize the model by assuming that people have endowments of y_1 goods when young and y_2 goods when old. We may think of the endowments as labor income. We will assume that young people face a gross real interest rate, r, and choose accordingly the number of goods they wish to save, s_t.

We can now describe the budget of someone born at t. When young, this person has y_1 goods from her labor, which she can either consume or save. We express the individual's budget constraint when young as

$$c_{1,t} + s_t \leq y_1. \tag{14.1}$$

When old, she can consume both her old-age endowment/labor income and the

Figure 14.1. The savings choice. An individual endowed when young and old, able to save at the real interest rate r, faces the lifetime budget line portrayed above. The level of savings s^* is determined by the difference between the individual's first-period endowment and the utility-maximizing choice of first-period consumption.

return (interest and principal) from her saving, implying the following old-age budget constraint:

$$c_{2,t+1} \le y_2 + rs_t. \tag{14.2}$$

Solving Equation 14.2 for s_t and substituting into Equation 14.1 we find the lifetime budget set:

$$c_{1,t} + \frac{c_{2,t+1}}{r} \le y_1 + \frac{y_2}{r}. \tag{14.3}$$

This budget set is graphed in Figure 14.1. Note that the budget line goes through the point (y_1, y_2), because individuals could always choose merely to consume their endowment in each period and have zero savings.

For a given budget, the savings s^* that allows the highest utility (reaches the highest possible indifference curve) is found where the line defining the budget set is just tangent to an indifference curve. As shown in the diagram, the utility-maximizing choice of savings satisfies $s^* = y_1 - c_1^*$. It should be noted that the relative positions of c_1^* and y_1 depend on individual preferences. As drawn, $s^* = y_1 - c_1^*$ is positive. With a different set of preferences, the indifference curve could be tangent to the budget line so that c_1^* would lie to the right of y_1, implying a negative value for savings. Try drawing such a diagram on your own. We interpret a situation of negative savings later in the chapter.

Wealth

Note from Equations 14.1 and 14.2 that without saving ($s_t = 0$), an individual's consumption in each period would be completely determined by her current **income** (her endowment). Saving allows a person to choose a combination of consumption constrained only by her **wealth**, a measure of her income over her entire lifetime $y_1 + y_2/r$.

Note that an individual's wealth is not simply the sum of income in both periods of life. Income in the second period of life is divided by the interest rate. To explain why income in the second period of life is treated differently from income in the first period of life in the determination of wealth, we must understand the concept of present value.

Present Value

Is the value of goods independent of time? Would you rather own 10 goods today or 10 goods in the future? To answer this question, suppose you have 10 goods today. You can transform these current goods into future goods by saving them. If saving pays a positive net real interest rate (gross rate r greater than 1), 10 goods saved today will yield more than 10 goods in the future. In this way, 10 goods today are more valuable than 10 goods in the future.

The analysis applies also to the problem of a borrower. If the individual borrows 100 units of the good and r equals 1.10, $(1.10)(100) = 110$ units of the goods will be repaid in the following period. In other words, given this interest rate and our scheme of borrowing, 100 units of the goods today are worth 110 units of the good tomorrow.

Now reverse the direction of this analysis. If an individual is to repay 110 units of the good in the next period, what must be the amount that is borrowed? The answer, of course, is 100. The answer is obvious in this simple example, but it is useful to realize how it is derived. The answer of 100 is obtained by taking 110 and dividing it by the gross real interest rate to obtain $110/r = 110/1.10 = 100$.

The 100 units of the good that is obtained today via the loan is often termed the **present value** of the loan. Correspondingly, the 110 units representing the loan repayment in the *next* period is called the **future value** of the loan. The two concepts of value in this simple example of a one-period loan are related by

$$\text{present value} = \frac{\text{future value}}{r}. \tag{14.4}$$

Alternatively, we could write the relationship as

$$\text{future value} = r(\text{present value}). \qquad (14.5)$$

In many of our models, individuals live only two periods, so the simple version of the concept of present value just presented is adequate. Here loans are made only over a one-period horizon.

However, what if a loan is made for a larger number of periods? Assume that an individual who lives three periods borrows 100 units of the consumption good at a one-period gross interest rate of $r = 1.10$. In the following period, the loan must be repaid and the total repayment, as before, is 110 units of the good. Suppose the individual borrows 110 units at the same interest rate to repay the first loan. What is the total loan repayment in the following (third) period? It is, of course, $(1.10)(110) = 121$. Note that this amount is $(r)(r)(100) = (r^2)(100)$. Alternatively stated, the present value of the loan (100) is the future value (121) divided by r raised to the number of periods over which the loan extends. In general, we can write that

$$\text{present value} = \frac{\text{future value}}{r^T} \qquad (14.6)$$

or

$$\text{future value} = r^T(\text{present value}), \qquad (14.7)$$

where T represents the number of periods that transpire before the loan is repaid or matures (often called the **duration** of the loan). In general, to convert a future value to a present value, we say that we **discount** the future value by a discount factor (r^T). Note that Equations 14.6 and 14.7 are consistent with Equations 14.4 and 14.5 because, in those equations, T was equal to 1.

Armed with our knowledge of the concept of present value, we can now understand the presence of r in the lifetime budget constraint. Look again at the lifetime budget constraint (Equation 14.3)

$$c_{1,t} + \frac{c_{2,t+1}}{r} \leq y_1 + \frac{y_2}{r}. \qquad (14.8)$$

The terms divided by r are y_2 and $c_{2,t+1}$. Because the old-age consumption and endowment occur one period in the future, we must discount by $r^1 = r$ to convert them into a present value. Because $c_{1,t}$ and y_1 occur in the first period of life, they are already present values and there is no need to discount them.[1]

---

[1] The astute student may very well ask: Why have we waited until this chapter to worry about the discounting of quantities that occur in the future? In fact, we have been appropriately discounting all along. For example, in Chapter 1, the only asset available was fiat money and people were endowed only when young. In that chapter, the lifetime budget constraint was $c_{1,t} + [v_t/v_{t+1}]c_{2,t+1} = y$. There we discounted the future value $c_{2,t+1}$ by the rate of return of fiat money v_{t+1}/v_t.

Because all variables are now expressed in present value terms, we call the left-hand side of Equation 14.8 the present value of an individual's lifetime consumption. The right-hand side of Equation 14.8 is the present value of her lifetime endowments. We refer to the present value of lifetime endowments as an individual's measured wealth or simply her **wealth**.[2] We denote the wealth of an individual born at t as w_t.

$$w_t = y_1 + \frac{y_2}{r}. \tag{14.9}$$

Example 14.1 Suppose a three-period-lived person is constrained to receive an endowment in only one period of her life. She may choose between receiving 90 goods when young, 100 goods when middle-aged, or 115 when old. Which will she pick if the net real interest rate is 10 percent? ... if the net real interest rate is 20 percent? *Hint:* Generalize the definition of wealth in Equation 14.9 to three periods.

Wealth and Consumption

If we apply our definition of wealth to the lifetime budget constraint graphed in Figure 14.1, we find that an individual's consumption bundle will be entirely determined by her wealth w_t and the interest rate r. Let us now ask how her consumption bundle will respond to an increase in her wealth. An increase in a person's wealth enables her to consume more over her lifetime. The breakdown of this extra consumption depends on her relative preferences for consumption when young and old.

If an individual responds to an increase in wealth by consuming less of a certain good, we say that the good is an **inferior good**. Hamburger and bus transportation may be examples of inferior goods. When our wealth rises we buy fewer of these items and replace them with steak and sports cars.

Consumption when young and consumption when old do not seem likely to be inferior goods. We expect a person faced with an increase in wealth to consume more when young and when old. Goods whose consumption rises with wealth are called **normal goods**. We assume that consumption when young and consumption when old are both normal goods. An increase in wealth induces an individual to increase both c_1 and c_2, as illustrated in Figure 14.2. We see from Figure 14.2 that when people may freely choose their level of saving, the consumption pattern they choose depends uniquely on their wealth and the interest rate. Note in particular that for a given level of wealth the consumption pattern chosen does not depend on when that wealth is received. Suppose, for example, that an individual's wealth is 100 goods and the real (gross) interest rate is 1.1. Many different combinations of

---

[2] The true measure of an individual's wealth is utility she can afford, but we need a measure of wealth denominated in goods.

Table 14.1. *Endowment combinations for which wealth is 100 (when $r = 1$)*

Combination	y_1	y_2	Wealth $= y_1 + y_2/r$
A	50	55	100
B	100	0	100
C	70	33	100
D	0	110	100

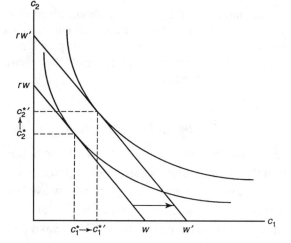

Figure 14.2. The effect of an increase in wealth on lifetime consumption. When an individual's wealth increases from w to w', the lifetime budget constraint shifts to the right. Assuming that c_1 and c_2 are normal goods, consumption increases in both periods of life.

the endowments y_1 and y_2 are consistent with this wealth of 100 goods. Four such combinations are given in Table 14.1.

In all four combinations listed in Table 14.1, wealth is the same and thus people will choose the same consumption bundle, (c_1^*, c_2^*), regardless of the timing of their endowment combination that gives them that wealth. In each of the four cases, the lifetime budget set would be the same. It is important therefore to distinguish between income and wealth. **Income** represents the goods an individual produces or receives in any single period. In contrast, wealth is the present value of an individual's lifetime income stream. It is wealth, not income, that determines consumption.

Example 14.2 Suppose a three-period-lived person is constrained to receive an endowment in only one period of her life. She may receive 95 goods when young, 100 goods when middle-aged, or 105 when old. Assume that the net real interest rate is 10 percent and that all goods are normal goods. For which endowment will she consume the most in middle age?

Income and Saving

What happens if a person's income in some period is not sufficient to support her desired consumption in that period? She can adjust her savings to allow her consumption to exceed her income in that period.

Suppose, for example, that when the net real interest rate is 10 percent ($r = 1.1$) and an individual's wealth equals 100 goods (in present value terms), she receives the highest utility by consuming 50 goods when young and 55 goods when old. [Check that this consumption bundle satisfies the individual's lifetime budget constraint (Equation 14.8)]. Note that all four endowment patterns of Table 14.1, despite their very different timing, represent wealth of 100 goods. It follows that an individual with any of the four endowment patterns will wish to consume 50 goods when young and 55 goods when old. How can the individual arrange this consumption pattern?

If an individual has the endowment pattern A in Table 14.1, she can simply consume her endowments as they arrive. What if, however, she has endowment pattern B, where y_1 is 100 and y_2 is 0? Her endowment income exceeds her desired consumption when young and is less than her desired consumption when old. How does she reconcile her income with her consumption? She simply saves 50 goods when young, which, when she is old, will yield the 55 goods he wishes to consume. (Recall that an individual's budget when young is $s_t = y_1 - c_1$, which in this case equals $100 - 50$.) An individual with endowment pattern C ($y_1 = 70$, $y_2 = 33$) will save only 20 goods to arrive at the desired consumption pattern ($s_t = 70 - 50$). Note that the level of saving adjusts to the level of income when young in order to achieve the desired consumption bundle. Consumption does not adjust to income; it is determined by wealth (and the interest rate).

Consider finally the endowment pattern D ($y_1 = 0$, $y_2 = 110$), in which the individual has an endowment only when old. In this case, using the young person's budget constraint, $s_t = y_1 - c_1$, suggests that saving must be equal to -50 in order to arrive at the desired consumption bundle. Can an individual save a negative number of goods? Yes, if she borrows.[3] Borrowing 50 goods is the same as saving -50 goods (sometimes referred to as **dissaving**). Table 14.2 summarizes the behavior of saving for the endowment patterns listed in Table 14.1.

At this point, let us summarize what we have learned about the determination of consumption and saving:

1. Consumption is determined by wealth. In particular, an increase in wealth brings about an increase in consumption in each period of life (assuming normal goods).

---

[3] While an individual can save a negative amount by borrowing, the economy as a whole cannot do so because an individual can borrow (save a negative amount) only from another individual willing to lend (save a positive amount).

Table 14.2. *Consumption and saving when wealth is 100 and $r = 1$*

Combination	y_1	c_2	s	$c_2 = rs + y_2$
A	50	50	0	55
B	100	50	50	55
C	70	50	20	55
D	0	50	−50	55

2. Saving adjusts to income. The saving of the young will equal the difference between their current income and their desired consumption.

The Effect of Taxes on Consumption and Savings

Let us now apply these lessons to study the effects of some tax policies on consumption and savings. To focus on the effects of taxes on savings, we will look only at two lump-sum taxes – a tax of τ_1 goods on each young person and a tax of τ_2 goods on each old person.

To see how these taxes affect an individual's wealth, let us incorporate them into her budget constraints:

$$c_{1,t} + s_t \leq y_1 - \tau_1, \qquad (14.10)$$

$$c_{2,t+1} \leq y_2 - \tau_2 + rs_t. \qquad (14.11)$$

Solving Equation 14.11 for s_t and substituting into Equation 14.10, we find the lifetime budget set (Equation 13.11), graphed in Figure 14.3:

$$c_{1,t} + \frac{c_{2,t+1}}{r} \leq y_1 - \tau_1 + \frac{y_2 - \tau_2}{r} \equiv w_t. \qquad (14.12)$$

The right-hand side of Equation 14.12 represents the present value of a taxpayer's *after-tax* endowments. This is the limit on the present value of the taxpayer's (private) consumption (the left-hand side of Equation 14.12) and thus the true measure of the taxpayer's (private) wealth.[4] Note that taxes paid when old are future values and are therefore discounted by the gross interest rate (r).

Wealth-Neutral Tax Changes

We would like to analyze the effect of taxes on individual decisions about consumption and saving. Consider first changes in taxes that do not affect an individual

---

[4] We insert the adjective *private* here to emphasize that we are ignoring any benefits the individual may receive from government expenditures paid from tax revenues.

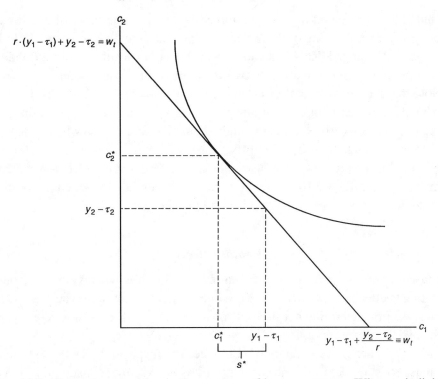

Figure 14.3. The savings decision in the presence of lump-sum taxes. When an individual is subject to lump-sum taxes in both periods of life, the lifetime budget constraint is as shown in the diagram. The lifetime consumption pattern is determined by preferences, the real interest rate, and the present value of the after-tax income stream.

taxpayer's wealth. Let τ_1^* and τ_2^* represent the initial taxes on the young and old, respectively. Now suppose that we increase the taxes of the young by 10 (to $\tau_1^* + 10$) but decrease the taxes on the old by $10r$ (to $\tau_2^* - 10r$).

Has this change in taxes affected the taxpayer's wealth? To find out let us substitute the new levels of taxes into the measure of wealth defined in Equation 14.12:

$$y_1 - \tau_1 + \frac{y_2 - \tau_2}{r} = y_1 - (\tau_1^* + 10) + \frac{y_2 - (\tau_2^* - 10r)}{r}$$
$$= y_1 - \tau_1^* - 10 + \frac{y_2 - \tau_2^*}{r} + \frac{10r}{r}$$
$$= y_1 - \tau_1^* + \frac{y_2 - \tau_2^*}{r}. \tag{14.13}$$

We see from Equation 14.13 that the taxpayer's wealth has not changed. In present value terms, the decrease in taxes paid when old exactly offsets the increase in taxes paid when young. Because this tax change did not affect the taxpayer's wealth, her desired consumption combination will also be unaffected by the change.

An individual's consumption is determined by the present value of her lifetime taxes but not by the timing of those taxes. In this case, the present value of lifetime taxes has not changed. This is analogous to the earlier result that an individual's consumption pattern is not affected by the timing of the endowments.

Note that the taxpayer's after-tax income when young has fallen by 10. What then happens to the savings of a young person? Look at the budget constraint of the young (Equation 14.10). She can maintain the same consumption when young only if she reduces her savings by 10 to offset the tax increase. How will this affect her when old? Look at the budget constraint of the old (Equation 14.11): her income from savings will fall by $10r$, but that is exactly the amount by which her taxes are reduced, leaving her consumption when old unchanged.

Wealth Effects

Suppose that our taxpayer now faces an increase in taxes when young without an offsetting tax decrease when old. How will this affect consumption and saving? As always, we first determine her desired consumption then look at how she can save to achieve this consumption.

The rise in her lifetime tax burden reduces the taxpayer's wealth. As a result, she must consume less over her lifetime. If, as we assume, consumption in each period of life is a normal good, she will spread the reduction in consumption over her entire life; that is, she will consume less in each period of life.

How must her saving adapt to these changes? The taxpayer wishes to reduce consumption in both periods of life, but her income has fallen only in the first period of life. To reduce her consumption when old, she must reduce her savings. In this way, young people split their reduction in income between consumption and savings.

Summary

In this chapter, we have taken the age structure of the overlapping generations model more literally in order to study economic decisions related to saving and investment. Our goal was to understand the factors that influence those variables.

We found that wealth – the present value of the lifetime income stream – is the important determinant of consumption. An increase in wealth generates higher levels of consumption in both periods of life. On the other hand, savings responds to income. A shift of income from one period to another that does not affect wealth does not alter consumption but does alter savings.

We also explored the effect of taxes on consumption and savings. A change in the timing of taxes that leaves wealth unaltered has no impact on the lifetime consumption pattern. Savings adjusts in order to maintain consumption. However, tax changes that cause changes in wealth generate changes in savings and consumption. These results will prove to have important implications with respect to the economic effects of government debt issue, a topic we take up in Chapter 15.

Exercises

14.1 Consider an increase in the lump-sum taxes paid by old people. Find its effect on wealth, consumption when young and old, and saving by the young. Assume that capital is the only asset in the economy. What effect does the tax increase have on output?

14.2 Suppose people live three-period lives. If the government cuts taxes on the middle-aged, what will happen to the consumption and saving of the young? ... to the consumption and saving of the middle-aged?

Appendix: Social Security

With its generational structure, this model of saving and investment is well equipped to address one of the more important issues of the day: the effects of government-run pension plans, such as the U.S. social security system or the social insurance program of Canada.

There are two basic ways to finance government social security payments to the old. In a **fully funded** pension plan, the government taxes young workers and uses these contributions to purchase interest-bearing assets that will finance the pension payments to that same cohort of workers when they are old. In a **pay-as-you-go** plan, the payments to the old are funded by taxes on those who are young in that period. Although government pension systems often involve a mix of these two, most government pensions can be broken down into these two elements.

Fully Funded Government Pensions

A **fully funded** pension plan pays a pension to old people financed by the forced contributions they paid when young. We represent this plan in our model as a tax of τ goods on each young person to pay a pension of σ goods to each of these people when they are old. The plan is considered fully funded because payments of the young are saved at the market rate of return r and then used to finance the pensions of the same people who made the payments. For simplicity, we assume there are no other sources of government revenue or other government expenditures. This is represented by the following government budget constraint:

$$N_t \tau r = N_t \sigma \Rightarrow \tau r = \sigma. \tag{14.14}$$

The budget constraints of the individual when young and old, respectively, are

$$c_{1,t} + s_t \leq y_1 - \tau \tag{14.15}$$

$$c_{2,t+1} \leq y_2 + rs_t + \sigma. \tag{14.16}$$

If s_t is free to take any value, positive or negative (negative savings representing borrowing), we can solve Equation 14.16 for s_t and substitute into Equation 14.15 to find the lifetime budget set:

$$c_{1,t} + \frac{c_{2,t+1}}{r} \leq y_1 + \frac{y_2}{r} - \tau + \frac{\sigma}{r}. \tag{14.17}$$

The right-hand side of Equation 14.17 is the individual's wealth in the presence of the fully funded social security plan.

From the government budget constraint (Equation 14.14) we know that $\sigma = r\tau$, implying that wealth

$$y_1 + \frac{y_2}{r} - \tau + \frac{\sigma}{r} = y_1 + \frac{y_2}{r} - \tau + \frac{r\tau}{r} = y_1 + \frac{y_2}{r} \tag{14.18}$$

is unchanged by the government pension plan. Because wealth is unchanged, people are free to choose the same consumption combination they would have chosen without the government's pension plan. The government's pension has no effect on people's consumption and welfare.

What is the reaction of saving to this fully funded pension plan? If the government increases the tax contributions of the young from 0 to some positive number τ, how can the individual still reach her desired consumption pattern? Look at the budget constraints (Equations 14.14 and 14.15). To keep consumption when young unchanged, savings must fall by τ, reducing the returns from saving by $r\tau$ when old. But this reduction of the returns from saving exactly matches the increased income when old from the government pension, leaving consumption when old also unchanged. The effect of the government's pension plan is illustrated in Figure 14.4. The government here is acting like a private pension. Therefore, when the government tells people to increase their contributions to the government plan, the people can still arrive at their desired consumption pattern by reducing their voluntary contributions to their private pension plans (in our notation, by reducing s). In this way a fully funded pension plan merely causes a shift from one pension plan to another, this one run by the government. If both offer the same rate of return, people really don't care which plan manages their pension funds; only the total matters.

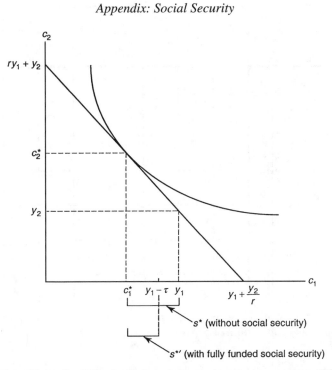

Figure 14.4. The effect of a fully funded social security plan on saving. Without a social security plan, the individual's choice of saving is determined by the gap between the first-period endowment y_1 and the individual's first-period consumption choice c_1^*. This level of saving is represented by s^* in the diagram. As we have seen, individual wealth and choice of consumption are identical under a fully funded social security plan. However, from the individual's first-period budget constraint (Equation 14.15), saving under the social security plan is the difference between the after-tax endowment and first-period consumption. This lower level of saving is denoted by $s^{*\prime}$ in the diagram.

Pay-as-You-Go

An alternative way to finance government pensions to those who are old in any period t is to tax those who are young in that period, a **pay-as-you-go** system. The government undertakes no investment on behalf of the old, relying instead on intergenerational transfers, as depicted in Figure 14.5.

The government budget constraint under a pay-as-you-go system requires that the total subsidies paid to the old in each period t equal the total taxes paid by the young at t:

$$N_{t-1}\sigma = N_t\tau \qquad (14.19)$$

or

$$\sigma = \frac{N_t}{N_{t-1}}\tau = \frac{nN_{t-1}}{N_{t-1}}\tau = n\tau. \qquad (14.20)$$

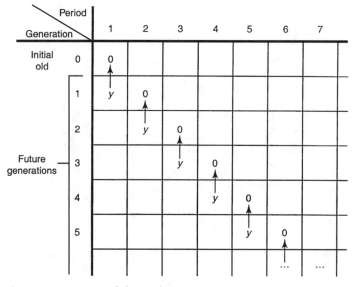

Figure 14.5. A pay-as-you-go social security system. Arrows depict intergenerational transfers in a pay-as-you-go government pension plan.

Note from the government budget constraint (Equation 14.20) that a growing population ($n > 1$) implies that there are more young people than old so that each of the old can receive more for any given tax paid by each young person. The total tax paid by the young is spread over a smaller number of old individuals.

Substituting this new government budget constraint (Equation 14.20) into the individual's wealth as found in the lifetime budget constraint (Equation 14.17), we find

$$y_1 + \frac{y_2}{r} - \tau + \frac{\sigma}{r} = y_1 + \frac{y_2}{r} - \tau + \frac{n\tau}{r} = y_1 + \frac{y_2}{r} + \left[\frac{n}{r} - 1\right]\tau. \quad (14.21)$$

Do future generations like a pay-as-you-go system? From Equation 14.21, we see that a pay-as-you-go system increases the wealth of future generations only if $n > r$; in that case the last term in Equation 14.21 is positive and, hence, adds to individual wealth. If $n < r$, why don't the future generations like pay-as-you-go government pensions? To understand, suppose the young were allowed to opt out of the plan, eliminating both their tax contributions and their benefits. If a young person then invested what she would have contributed in taxes (τ), she would receive a return of $r\tau$ from her investment, while losing $n\tau$ in benefits. Clearly, she is better off investing on her own if $r > n$, and she is worse off if $n > r$.

So who would object if the government were to allow young people to opt out of a pay-as-you-go government pension system? The current old, those who are old when the pay-as-you-go system is dropped. Whether or not these people made payments when they were young themselves, they favor the largest possible pay-as-you-go transfers from this point forward because the days of their contributions (if any) are in the past.

Appendix Exercises

14.1 Suppose we introduce the following fully funded government pension system in an overlapping generations economy where capital pays the fixed gross rate of return x. The government taxes each young person τ goods and invests the tax payments in capital (and only in capital). When old each person receives the full return from her tax payments.

    a. Find the budget constraints and first-order conditions for a person endowed with y when young and nothing when old. Argue that, for small values of τ, the value of τ has no effect on the equilibrium consumption path.

    b. Use the budget constraints of the individual and the government to show that the sum of private and government capital does not change if consumption does not change.

    c. Describe the values of τ for which the consumption path is affected.

14.2 Consider a pay-as-you-go social security plan that would collect 10 goods from each young person and distribute these goods evenly to old people. Find the effect of this plan on the wealth of future generations, consumption when young and old, private saving by the young, and investment by the young in each of the following cases. Specify as much as possible about the magnitudes of the changes.

    a. Population is constant and $r = 1$.

    b. Population is constant and $r > 1$.

    c. Population grows at the rate $n > r$.

Chapter 15

The Effect of the National Debt
on Capital and Savings

DURING THE LAST decade, the economic impact of the issuance of government debt is a topic that has received a great deal of attention from the media, politicians, and economists. As governments have significantly relied on government debt issue, the topic is worthy of that attention. The public has often been confused by what appears to be a wide variety of opinions regarding this subject. In this chapter, we hope to clarify the relevant issues. To do so, we will apply what we learned about wealth, consumption, and saving in the previous chapter to study the effects of the national debt.

The National Debt and the Crowding Out of Capital

Government bonds and capital are both assets through which people save. If the government increases the stock of bonds, does this mean that people will invest in less capital? We will address this question by examining two cases: one in which government deficits cause a reduction in capital investment and one in which the deficits have no effect on capital. The two cases differ only in a single assumption. This assumption will therefore prove to be the key to understanding when the size of the national debt is important to the size of the capital stock.

In both cases, we examine the overlapping generations economy developed in Chapter 14, of two-period-lived agents, each endowed with y_1 goods when young and y_2 when old. For simplicity, assume a constant population. Capital in this economy will pay the one-period rate of return x, a constant. There will be no money, but if the government chooses, it may issue bonds paying the same rate of return as capital. At time t, each young person pays a lump-sum tax of $\tau_{1,t}$ goods and each old person pays a lump-sum tax of $\tau_{2,t}$ goods. The lifetime budget constraint is

$$c_{1,t} + \frac{c_{2,t+1}}{r} \leq y_1 - \tau_{1,t} + \frac{y_2 - \tau_{2,t+1}}{r} \equiv w_t. \tag{15.1}$$

Note also the government budget constraint for this economy:

$$g_t + rb_{t-1} = \tau_{1,t} + \tau_{2,t} + b_t. \tag{15.2}$$

Consider now the effect of a cut in taxes of 100 units per young person in period t with no change in government expenditures. From the government budget constraint, we see that this can be accomplished only with an increase of 100 goods in government debt per young person. We assume that the debt will be paid off at some future date by some other generation. This will prove to be a critical assumption.

How will people change their lifetime consumption plan, $c_{1,t}$ and $c_{2,t+1}$, in response to this tax cut? People who receive a tax cut with no later increase in taxes experience an increase in their (after-tax) wealth. If, as we assume, $c_{1,t}$ and $c_{2,t+1}$ are normal goods, the consumption of each will rise with the increase in wealth.

How does this affect the savings of a member of this generation? To provide more consumption when old, her savings must rise. However, to consume more when young, her savings will rise only by a number less than 100. In other words, for first-period consumption to rise, the individual cannot save the entire tax cut.

Now that we know what happens to savings, we can determine what happens to capital. There are two assets with which one can save in this economy – capital and government bonds. Therefore

$$s_t = k_t + b_t. \tag{15.3}$$

Let us use the symbol Δ to represent changes in a variable that result from the policy change. Then it follows from Equation 15.3 that

$$\Delta s_t = \Delta k_t + \Delta b_t. \tag{15.4}$$

To finance the tax cut, government bonds have risen by 100 ($\Delta b_t = 100$) but saving has risen by some number less than 100 ($\Delta s_t = 100 - \Delta c_{1,t} < 100$, because $\Delta c_{1,t} > 0$). From Equation 15.4, capital must have fallen:

$$\Delta s_t = 100 - \Delta c_{1,t} = \Delta k_t + 100$$
$$\Rightarrow \Delta k_t = -\Delta c_{1,t} < 0. \tag{15.5}$$

We see that capital would fall by the increase in consumption when young. Although the stock of assets increased by the number of bonds issued – that is, by the size of the tax cut – people did not wish to increase their savings by the full amount of the tax cut. Therefore, the bonds could be held only if people reduced their holdings of capital. The reduction of capital because of the increase in government debt is often called the **crowding-out of capital** because bonds are substituting for capital in personal saving.[1]

Example 15.1 Consider an economy of two-period-lived people in overlapping generations. Let there be capital paying the rate of return x. Assume for simplicity that there is no fiat money.

What will be the effects on a young person's wealth, saving, consumption, and capital investment of a tax cut of 100 goods per young person in period t financed by an equal increase in the government debt? Assume that in the following period ($t + 1$) the debt will be paid off with a tax on the young of the next generation. Use the lifetime budget sets in your answer.

Deficits and Interest Rates

By rate-of-return equality, the (real) interest rate equals the marginal product of capital, which for simplicity was assumed to be fixed. If we assume instead that capital has a diminishing marginal product, we can determine the effects of government debt on the interest rate. As we discussed in Chapter 6, rate-of-return equality and a diminishing marginal product of capital imply an inverse relation between the capital stock and the interest rate. It follows directly that if an increase in government debt reduces the capital stock, it will increase capital's marginal product and thus the interest rate.

A second interpretation of the model may help us understand the relation between the debt and interest rates. In the previous example, an increase in the national debt increases desired savings by less than the increase in bonds. In other words, for any given interest rate, the supply of savings has risen by less than the demand for those savings by capitalists and the government. In a free market, supply cannot exceed demand, so how can the government (or any other a "demander" of savings) induce people to hold its bonds? It can offer a higher interest rate. The higher interest rate on government bonds will entice savers away from capital with a marginal product lower than the interest rate, thus crowding out capital.

Neutral Government Debt

With one key change in this policy, we can find an example of a deficit that does not crowd out capital. Assume now that the debt created at t will be repaid not by taxing generations in the future but by taxing the old at $t + 1$. Under this assumption, the tax to repay the debt falls on the generation that enjoys the tax reduction. We will analyze this case by comparing the lifetime budget constraints under two fiscal

---

[1] Any reduction of capital will also reduce wages if the marginal product of labor is an increasing function of the capital stock. See Diamond (1965).

Table 15.1. *Comparison of government financing alternatives*

Plan *A*	Plan *B*
$\tau_1 = g_t$	$\tau_1 = 0$
$b_t = 0$	$b_t = g_t$
$\tau_2 = 0$	$\tau_2 = r b_t$

Table 15.2. *Comparison of individual's budgets under alternative government financing*

Plan *A*	Plan *B*
$c_{1,t} + \dfrac{c_{2,t+1}}{r} \leq y_1 - g_t + \dfrac{y_2}{r}$	$c_{1,t} + \dfrac{c_{2,t+1}}{r} \leq y_1 + \dfrac{y_2 - r g_t}{r}$

plans that provide the same level of government expenditure per young person, g_t. In plan *A* each member of generation t simply pays a tax equal to g_t goods when young. No government debt is issued because government expenditures are completely financed by taxes. In plan *B* the generation pays no taxes when young; instead the government spending is covered by an issue of government debt worth g_t goods per young person so that b_t is equal to g_t. This debt is then retired with interest by a tax on the old at $t + 1$. Because government bonds pay the gross rate of return r, each old person has to pay a tax equal to the amount $r b_t$.

Recall that the lifetime budget constraint in general is

$$c_{1,t} + \frac{c_{2,t+1}}{r} \leq y_1 - \tau_{1,t} + \frac{y_2 - \tau_{2,t+1}}{r}.$$

By substituting the particulars of each plan listed in Table 15.1 into this constraint, we can compare the budgets of individuals under the alternative plans (see Table 15.2).

Table 15.2 reveals that the lifetime budget set is the same under the two plans. The deficit-funded tax cut does not change the wealth of the generation because the increase in income from the tax cut when young is exactly offset in present value by the decrease in income from the tax to retire the debt. Generation t pays for the entire government expenditure in both plans. It doesn't affect their wealth when they are taxed to pay for it.

Because wealth is the same with or without the deficit, people will choose the same consumption in both periods of life. People do not consume any part of their tax cut when young; they save the entire tax cut in anticipation of the forthcoming tax hike that will be required to pay off the deficit. By saving the entire tax cut, they will have just the right amount of funds to pay the higher taxes when they are old.

What is the effect of this deficit on the stock of capital? Again, saving equals capital plus bonds, so that changes in savings must equal the sum of changes in capital and government bonds:

$$s_t = k_t + b_t \quad \Rightarrow \quad \Delta s_t = \Delta k_t + \Delta b_t. \tag{15.6}$$

Although bonds rise by the size of the tax cut, so does saving, because the entire tax cut is saved ($\Delta s_t = \Delta b_t$). This implies that there is no change in capital as a result of this deficit ($\Delta k_t = 0$). There is no crowding out of capital. There is therefore no effect on the marginal product of capital or the interest rate. The desire to save rose by exactly the amount of the government's issue of bonds, so that the government did not need to offer a higher interest rate in order to induce people to hold its bonds.

We see that a deficit-financed tax cut has no effect on real variables such as consumption or capital in this case. This result is often referred to as the **Ricardian Equivalence Theorem** after David Ricardo (1792–1823), a well-known philosopher and classical economist, who was the first to consider this case.

We have looked at two cases that have led to two quite different results. In the first case, the deficit-financed tax cut leads to altered consumption, savings, and capital holdings. In the case just considered, no such effects are found. What is the crucial difference between these two cases?

In the first case, the tax cut alters real variables because the individuals who benefit from the tax cut do not have to pay the tax increase that retires the debt. Because of this, these individuals experience an increase in their wealth, which leads them to higher consumption. In the second case, individuals pay a higher tax in the second period of life in order to retire the debt. These individuals experience no change in their wealth and thus do not alter their consumption. Clearly, the effects of bond-financed tax cuts depend on whether the people who receive the tax cut will live to pay the increase in taxes that will retire the resulting debt.

Example 15.2 Answer the question in Example 15.1 assuming that the debt is paid off with a tax on the old in the period immediately after the tax cut. Explain the difference in your answers to the two exercises.

Summary

This chapter has examined how the presence of government debt affects decisions about consumption, saving, and investment. The results crucially depend on the timing of debt issuance and retirement. To illustrate this, we considered two distinct cases – one where government debt issue had real effects and one where it did not.

We first analyzed a case where the presence of government debt does have an important impact on economic variables. In this case, we gave individuals a debt-financed tax cut where the resulting debt was retired by a tax on some other generation. This caused an increase in wealth for the individuals receiving the tax cut, with all the effects that we encountered in Chapter 14. Here, consumption in both periods of life increased and individuals reduced their holdings of capital. With a diminishing marginal product of capital, the fall in the capital stock would imply an increase in the real interest rate.

The second case was similar to the first in that we gave individuals a debt-financed tax cut. However, this case differed in that the debt was retired by a tax increase imposed on those individuals who enjoyed the tax cut. We found that if individuals saved all their tax cut, they would have just enough to pay the tax increase. The policy had no impact on individual wealth, implying that the lifetime consumption pattern was unaltered. Because savings completely absorbed the tax cut, there was no crowding out of capital. Here, government debt issue was neutral.

Exercise

15.1 Suppose the government debt of 100 goods in period t financed not the tax cut of Example 15.1 but a government capital project that will pay off $100x^g$ goods in the following period $(t + 1)$. At that time, the government retires the debt. Assume that the returns from the capital project are used to reduce the taxes of the old in period $t + 1$.

    a. How large must x^g be so that the next generation need not pay extra taxes to retire the debt?

    b. What will be the effect of the debt-financed capital project on the consumption, saving, and privately owned capital of the people born in period t if $x^g = x$?

    c. What will be the effect of the debt-financed capital project on the consumption, saving, and privately owned capital of the people born in period t if $x^g > x$?

15.2 Consider an overlapping generations economy in which people are endowed with 100 goods when young and with nothing when old. Population grows at the rate n. Capital pays the gross rate of return x. Utility is given by $\ln(c_{1,t}) + \ln(c_{2,t+1})$. If people have no income when old, this implies that young people want to save half their after-tax income when young.

    a. Suppose there is no government expenditure, taxation, or government debt. What is the budget constraint of a young person born in period 1? ... of an old person in period 2? Combine these to find the lifetime budget constraint of a young person born in period 1.

    b. Using the assumption on the utility function, find an individual's choice of first-period consumption, second-period consumption, savings, and capital holdings.

    c. Find an expression for gross national product (GNP) in period 2.

d. Now suppose that, in period 1, the government decides to issue bonds of a one-period maturity worth 10 goods per young person, the proceeds of which will be offered as a gift to the king of a distant country. In period 2 government expenditure reverts to 0, and the outstanding debt (both principal and interest) is rolled over into a new debt issue. What is the budget constraint of a young person born in period 1? ... of an old person in period 2? Combine these to find the lifetime budget constraint of a young person born in period 1.

e. Compare the consumption pattern of this generation to that found in part b. Compare the savings of this generation to that found in part b. Compare the capital of this generation to that found in part b.

f. Find an expression for GNP in period 2. Why does GNP differ from that found in part c? What will be the real value of debt per young person issued in period 2?

g. Can the policy to introduce the one-time government expenditure be financed in such a way that the consumption of no future generation is affected? For what parameter values is this possible?

h. As an alternative to the bond finance of part d, suppose the one-time expenditure is financed with taxes of 10 goods per young person in period 1. What is the budget constraint of a young person born in period 1? ... of an old person in period 2? Combine these to find the lifetime budget constraint of a young person born in period 1.

i. Compare the consumption pattern of this generation to that found in part b. Compare the savings of this generation to that found in part b. Compare the capital of this generation to that found in part b. Compare the capital of this generation to that found in part b.

j. (**advanced**) Use calculus and the budget constraints found in part a to verify the assertion that, if people have no income when old, young people want to save half their after-tax income when young.

Appendix A: Fiat Money and the Crowding Out of Capital

Fiat money, like interest-bearing government bonds, is a form of government debt. Does it crowd out capital?

To answer this question, let us reintroduce fiat money into our model. Fiat money is held to satisfy a government requirement that each young person must hold fiat money worth φ goods. This is essentially a lump-sum reserve requirement in that each individual must hold these reserves, regardless of her total savings or bank balances. In this way, the requirement does not affect the rate of return on savings or bank balances, as did the fractional reserve requirement of Chapter 8. We assume that fiat money is held by requirement rather than to reduce transaction costs or for some other motive so that we can isolate money's effect on wealth from its effect on transactions.

Let there be a constant stock of fiat money. In the initial period, the stock of fiat money is divided equally among the initial old ($m_0 = M/N_0$). Assume, as before, that there is capital paying the gross one-period rate of return $x > n$. Capital and fiat money are the only assets available in the economy.

The budget of a member of the future generations is given by the two equations

$$c_{1,t} + v_t m_t + k_1 = y, \tag{15.7}$$

$$c_{2,t+1} = v_{t+1} m_t + x k_t, \tag{15.8}$$

which, if k_t is positive, yields the lifetime budget constraint

$$c_{1,t} + \frac{c_{2,t+1}}{x} = y - v_t m_t + \frac{v_{t+1} m_t}{x}$$

$$= y + v_t m_t \left[\frac{v_{t+1}}{v_t x} - 1 \right]. \tag{15.9}$$

The condition for the clearing of supply and demand for money when fiat money is held only to satisfy the legal requirement is

$$v_t M = N \varphi. \tag{15.10}$$

In a stationary equilibrium (as we have seen many times) the constant money stock implies a value of money that grows at the population growth rate n. Therefore, when $v_t m_t = \varphi$, we have that $v_{t+1} m_t = n\varphi$. The budget constraints (Equations 15.7 to 15.9) can then be written as

$$c_1 + \varphi + k = y, \tag{15.11}$$

$$c_2 = n\varphi + xk, \tag{15.12}$$

$$c_1 + \frac{c_2}{x} \le y + \varphi \left[\frac{n}{x} - 1 \right]. \tag{15.13}$$

We find easily the effect of real money balances on the wealth of future generations, the right-hand side of Equation 15.13. If, as assumed, $x > n$, the greater are real money balances φ and the lower is the wealth of the future generations. People forced to hold fiat money in place of capital receive a lower rate of return on their savings, which reduces their wealth.

The reason relates back to the concept of present value. Fiat money is both an expense and an income for future generations: it is an expense of φ goods when young because future generations must give up goods to acquire the money but it is income of $n\varphi$ goods when old because fiat money is used to purchase goods when old. Because the income from fiat money is received one period after the expense is incurred, however, it must be discounted by the gross interest rate x. For $x > n$, the present value of the benefits is less than the present value of the expense. For this reason the net benefit of holding fiat money, $\varphi[(n/x) - 1]$, is negative when $x > n$.

Where does this wealth go? If, as assumed, the initial stock of fiat money is owned equally by each of the initial old, the consumption of a member of the initial old is

$$c_{2,1} = xk_0 + v\left[\frac{M}{N_0}\right] = xk_0 + n\varphi, \tag{15.14}$$

where k_0 is some given nonnegative number representing the stock of capital held by a member of the initial old. An increase in the value of a unit of fiat money, v, from an increase in the demand for money φ, increases the wealth of the initial generation by increasing the value of its initial stock of fiat money.

What is the effect of real money balances on capital and output? Recall that the budget when old for future generations in a stationary equilibrium is $c_2 = n\varphi + xk$ (Equation 15.12).

For any given level of desired c_2, a rise in real fiat money balances φ, by providing more income when old, reduces the need to save through capital. In this way, fiat money balances crowd out capital. Moreover, if c_2 is a normal good, it will fall with the drop in wealth, further decreasing desired saving through capital. Lower steady-state capital implies lower real output.

Offsetting Wealth Transfers

Policy changes studied in this book have often affected the demand for money and thus the value of any fiat money balances owned by the initial old. A decrease in the reserve requirement, for example, increases the rate of return on deposits, helping future generations, but also lowers the value of initial fiat money balances, hurting the initial old. If a policy change involves a transfer of wealth between generations, it is difficult to recommend such a policy from an objective standpoint – the desirability of the policy change depends on which generation's welfare is valued more by the one who must make the decision.

We have seen in this chapter that government debt may be used to transfer wealth between generations by altering the incidence of taxes. This suggests that we might be able to use government debt to offset the wealth transfers that occur when a policy changes the value of initial balances of fiat money. Let us consider in particular the suggestion of Auernheimer (1974) that, if any policy decreases the value of initial fiat money balances through a decrease in the demand for fiat money, the government can reduce the supply of fiat money by exactly enough to leave the value of fiat money (and hence also the price level) unchanged, thus offsetting any transfer of wealth from the initial old.

Such a decrease in the fiat money stock must of course be financed in some way. An increase in the taxes of the initial old would defeat the purpose of helping the initial old, so consider instead financing the decrease of the fiat money stock through an issuance of government debt. The debt per person is to be held constant and interest on the debt is to be paid from taxes collected on future generations. The wealth transfer from the initial old to the future generations that was caused by the drop in the demand for fiat money has now been offset by an increase in the national debt, which transfers wealth back from the future generations (who must pay taxes to fund interest payments) to the initial old (who benefit from the reduction in the fiat money stock).

The issuance of debt to reduce the stock of fiat money represents an open market sale of government debt for fiat money. In a similar fashion, an open market purchase of government debt by an expansion of the fiat money stock may be used to keep the value of fiat money unchanged in the face of any policy-induced increase in the demand for fiat money. The purchase of debt by the government reduces the tax revenue needed to pay interest on the government debt. With the wealth of the initial old maintained at its initial level by these open market operations, we are free to judge the effects of monetary policies solely by their effects on future generations.[2]

Appendix B: Infinitely Lived Agents

At the beginning of this book, we asked what assumptions would be necessary to build a model of money. We noted that intrinsically useless fiat money can have value only in economies with no known terminal date. Looking for model economies that go on forever, we came to a choice between two frameworks – models with people (or families) who live forever or models with an infinite number of overlapping generations of finitely lived people. We chose to work within the overlapping generations framework. For completeness, it is now time to examine the other framework to learn where our choice has made a difference in the results we have found.

For most of the topics we have studied, whether or not the decision maker lives forever does not matter. The assumption does matter, however, for the effects of the national debt and money balances on wealth and capital, a subject we take up in this appendix.

A Model of Infinitely Lived People

Consider an economy with a single generation of N identical, infinitely lived people, each of whom owns an endowment of y goods in each period of life. We write the

---

[2] Auernheimer studied open market operations in a model with only a single generation. For applications of his open market operations to models of overlapping generations see Bacchetta and Caminal (1994) and Freeman and Haslag (1995, 1996).

lifetime utility of an infinitely lived person as a weighted sum of the instantaneous utility enjoyed from consumption (c_t) at each of an infinite series of periods:

$$u(c_1) + \beta u(c_2) + \beta^2 u(c_3) + \cdots = \sum_{t=0}^{\infty} \beta^t u(c_{t+1}). \qquad (15.15)$$

Here β represents the **discount factor** applied to utility obtained in the future. We assume that $\beta < 1$. This assumption implies that future instantaneous utility does not receive as much "weight" in the measure of lifetime utility as does instantaneous utility derived in the present. For example, an additional unit of instantaneous utility in period 1 also causes lifetime utility to increase by 1 unit. However, an additional unit of utility in period 3 causes lifetime utility to increase by only β^2 units, which is less than 1 unit.[3] Notice that because there are no additions to the population in this model, there is only a single type of person. Models in which everyone is alike are called **representative agent models**.

Assume that there are capital and government bonds, both paying the gross one-period rate of return $r > 1$.[4]

Wealth, Capital, and Interest-Bearing Government Debt

Recall that a reduction in (lump-sum) taxes financed by an increase in government bonds will have no effect on individual wealth if the people who pay the future taxes to retire the bonds are those who benefit from the tax cut. If an individual's wealth does not change, she will not alter her consumption or investment. In models of a single generation of identical infinitely lived people, those who pay the tax increase are always those who receive the tax cut, regardless of when future taxes are increased. Therefore, deficit-financed tax cuts are always neutral in their effects.

A look at the lifetime budget constraint of an infinitely lived person will confirm this. We build the lifetime budget constraint from the individual's period t budget constraint. In any period t, her expenditures to acquire consumption and assets (here, government bonds and capital) cannot exceed her after-tax income, including the return from assets previously acquired:

$$c_t + s_t \leq y - \tau_t + r s_{t-1}, \qquad (15.16)$$

---

[3] Without this discounting of the future (i.e., for $\beta \geq 1$), utility would be infinite for any constant level of consumption simply because the person lives an infinite number of periods.

[4] For utility to be finite (which is of course necessary to allow a discussion of maximizing utility), r cannot be too large. Exactly what is meant by "too large" is explained by Jones and Manuelli (1990).

where $s_t = k_t + b_t$. For the first three periods, we have

$$c_1 + s_1 \leq y - \tau_1 + rs_0, \tag{15.17}$$
$$c_2 + s_2 \leq y - \tau_2 + rs_1, \tag{15.18}$$
$$c_3 + s_3 \leq y - \tau_3 + rs_2. \tag{15.19}$$

To construct the lifetime budget of this individual, we solve Equation 15.18 for s_1 and then substitute this expression into Equation 15.17 to get

$$c_1 + \frac{c_2 + s_2 - y + \tau_2}{r} \leq y - \tau_1 + rs_0,$$

or

$$c_1 + \frac{c_2}{r} + \frac{s_2}{r} \leq y - \tau_1 + \frac{y - \tau_2}{r} + rs_0. \tag{15.20}$$

Now repeat these steps by solving Equation 15.19 for s_2 and substitute this expression into Equation 15.20:

$$c_1 + \frac{c_2}{r} + \frac{1}{r}\left[\frac{c_3 + s_3 - y + \tau_3}{r}\right] \leq y - \tau_1 + \frac{y - \tau_2}{r} + rs_0. \tag{15.21}$$

Repeating these steps indefinitely gives us the lifetime budget constraint of the infinitely lived person:

$$c_1 + \frac{c_2}{r} + \frac{c_3}{r^2} + \frac{c_4}{r^3} + \cdots \leq y - \tau_1 + \frac{y - \tau_2}{r} + \frac{y - \tau_3}{r^2} + \frac{y - \tau_4}{r^3} + \cdots + rs_0. \tag{15.22}$$

The lifetime budget constraint for an infinitely lived person is essentially the same (although longer) as for anyone else; the present value of lifetime consumption cannot exceed the present value of lifetime after-tax income (wealth). Also note that Equation 15.22 appropriately discounts values that occur in the future. For example, fourth-period consumption, which occurs three periods in the future, is discounted by r^3. Because s_0 occurred one period in the *past*, it must be multiplied by $r^1 = r$.

Consider now a tax cut of 10 goods in period 1 financed by an increase in government debt. This debt is paid off with interest after T periods (in period $T + 1$) by an increase in taxes of $10r^T$. In present value terms, the tax increase is worth $10r^T/r^T = 10$ goods, exactly the present value of the tax cut. Wealth has not been changed, so consumption will also remain unchanged.

What will be the effect on capital? By definition, $s_t = k_t + b_t$ so that $\Delta s_t = \Delta k_t + \Delta b_t$. Because their wealth has not changed, people save the entire proceeds of the tax cut in anticipation of the future tax increase. This increase in saving equals the increase in government bonds ($\Delta s_t = \Delta b_t$), so that capital is not crowded out [$\Delta k_t = 0$].

Example 15.3 Consider an economy of identical infinitely lived people. Suppose that in period 3 taxes are cut by 50 goods per person. The tax cut is financed by an increase in the national debt, which will be repaid with an increase in taxes in period 7. By how much will taxes rise in period 7? How much of the tax cut will be saved and how much consumed in period 3? Explain.

Wealth, Capital, and Real Money Balances

Models with infinitely lived people also differ from overlapping generations models in the effects of money balances on wealth and capital. To see this, let us examine the effect of a lump-sum reserve requirement on wealth and capital in models of people with infinite lives.

Let there be a constant stock of fiat money. In the initial period, the stock of fiat money is divided equally among all individuals ($m_0 = M/N$). Fiat money is held to satisfy a government requirement that each person must hold fiat money worth φ goods ($v_t m_t = \varphi$). Therefore

$$v_t m_t = \varphi. \tag{15.23}$$

For simplicity, we assume there are no government bonds. The budget set of an individual in any period t can then be written at equality as

$$c_t + v_t m_t + k_t = y + v_t m_{t-1} + x k_{t-1}. \tag{15.24}$$

The right-hand side of Equation 15.24 tells us that the total sources of funds available to an individual at time t consist of the person's endowment, the real value of money held by the individual from the previous period, and the return from last period's savings in the form of capital. These sources of funds are used to consume and acquire assets (money and capital). These assets will, in turn, be sources of funds in the following period $t + 1$.

As always, equilibrium requires that the nominal supply of fiat money equal the nominal demand in any period t,

$$M = Nm_t,$$

or

$$m_t = \frac{M}{N} = m_{t-1}. \tag{15.25}$$

This simplifies the budget constraint (Equation 15.24) through the cancelation of the two terms that involve money:

$$c_t + v_t \left[\frac{M}{N} \right] + k_t = y + v_t \left[\frac{M}{N} \right] + x k_{t-1}, \qquad (15.26)$$

$$\Rightarrow c_t + k_t = y + x k_{t-1}. \qquad (15.27)$$

Following the same steps of repeated substitution used to find Equation 15.22, you can verify that Equation 15.27 implies a lifetime budget constraint of

$$c_1 + \frac{c_2}{r} + \frac{c_3}{r^2} + \frac{c_4}{r^3} + \cdots \leq y + \frac{y}{x} + \frac{y}{x^2} + \frac{y}{x^3} + \cdots + x k_0. \qquad (15.28)$$

Note that the value of a unit of fiat money, v_t, does not affect the budget of an average individual. An increase in the value of fiat money equally increases the value of the money balances she already owns (m_{t-1}) and of the money balances she acquires for the next period (m_t). Because in every period individuals must acquire new money balances to replace any money balances they spend, an increased value of money does not lead to increased wealth, consumption, or investment. Because a change in the demand for fiat money (from a change in φ) does not affect their constraints on consumption and capital (Equation 15.27 or Equation 15.28), it will not affect their choices of consumption or capital.

For the same reason, there is no Tobin effect in a representative agent model. An increase in the rate of inflation may discourage the use of fiat money, just as it does in the overlapping generations model. In a representative agent model, however, a decreased use of fiat money, whatever distortions it may cause, does not transfer wealth. The constraints on consumption and capital (Equation 15.27 or Equation 15.28) are therefore unchanged and thus will not lead to an increased use of capital. Be aware, however, that increases in the rate of inflation discourage the use of fiat money, reducing utility, whether people are assumed to live finite or infinite lives.[5] Inflation in both cases also discourages intermediation by institutions required to hold reserves in proportion to deposits.

In the overlapping generations models, anything increasing the value of fiat money transfers wealth from the future generations to the initial generation, who own the initial stock. This transfer does not take place in models of infinitely lived people because such models have only one type of person. If people have infinite lives, an increase in the value of money increases income from old money balances by as much as it increases purchases of new money balances, leaving the individual's budget unchanged. If there is no change in an individual's budget or preferences, there will be no change in her actions, implying that an infinitely lived individual's

---

[5] In models with infinitely lived people, deflation is the optimal monetary policy, in contrast to the overlapping generations model's golden rule of a fixed stock of fiat money. The difference is examined by Freeman (1993).

choice of consumption and investment are not affected by changes in the size of real money balances.

Example 15.4 Let the stock of fiat money change according to the rule $M_{t+1} = zM_t$ with $z > 1$. Assume that the increases in the money stock are given to the infinitely lived people as lump-sum subsidies. Show that an individual's budget in period t is unaffected by φ. *Hint:* You will need to use the government budget constraint.

Parents, Bequests, and Infinite Lives

People don't live forever, so one might well ask why we should bother to consider models that assume infinite lives. The exercise is useful if finitely lived people might behave as if they lived forever. Might not people, in a sense, live forever though their children and their children's children? Barro (1974) proposed that if parents care about the utility of their offspring and provide for them by leaving them bequests, these parents behave as if they live forever through their children. The decision-making unit is the family, which goes on forever, even though every individual family member lives a finite life.

   In this section, we construct an example of an economy in which mortal people behave as if they will live forever because they value the utility of their offspring. We will do so by specifying a model of infinitely lived people and then construct a model of finitely lived people who have the same preferences and budgets as the infinitely lived people and thus the same behavior. The example is adapted from Barro's (1974) well-known model.[6]

A Simple Model of Parents

Are there preferences of finitely lived people that would induce them to behave as if they lived infinite lives? Consider an economy of two-period-lived people, each of whom has a single child when old. Each person born in period t cares only about her own consumption when old (c_{t+1}) and about the utility of her child (U_{t+1}).[7] Although each parent is concerned about her child's welfare, we assume that she values the utility from her own consumption at least slightly more than she values the utility of her child. This notion is captured, as discussed previously, by multiplying the child's utility by the **discount factor** β where $0 < \beta < 1$. We can express this person's total utility U_t as the sum of utility derived from the individual's own consumption $u(c_{t+1})$ and the discounted value of the child's total utility βU_{t+1}:

$$U_t = u(c_{t+1}) + \beta U_{t+1}. \tag{15.29}$$

---

[6] A fuller but still accessible treatment of this model can be found in Aiyagari (1987).

[7] We ignore here consumption when young. This ensures that only one generation is consuming in any given period. This simplifies the analysis but does not alter any important conclusions.

The utility of a member of the initial generation is therefore

$$U_0 = u(c_1) + \beta U_1. \tag{15.30}$$

Her child's utility can similarly be written as

$$U_1 = u(c_2) + \beta U_2, \tag{15.31}$$

and her grandchild's utility can be written as

$$U_2 = u(c_3) + \beta U_3. \tag{15.32}$$

If we substitute the expression in Equation 15.32 into the utility of a member of the initial generation, we find

$$U_0 = u(c_1) + \beta[u(c_2) + \beta U_2]. \tag{15.33}$$

If we now substitute the expression in Equation 15.32 for U_2 into Equation 15.31, we find

$$\begin{aligned} U_0 &= u(c_1) + \beta\{u(c_2) + \beta[u(c_3) + \beta U_3]\} \\ &= u(c_1) + \beta u(c_2) + \beta^2 u(c_3) + \beta^3 U_3. \end{aligned} \tag{15.34}$$

Note that, because the parent cares for the utility of her child, she also cares for the utility of her grandchild because her child does. Substitution continued infinitely along these lines reveals that the preferences of a member of the initial generation may be expressed as an infinite weighted sum of the utilities from the consumption of her offspring:

$$U_0 = u(c_1) + \beta u(c_2) + \beta^2 u(c_3) + \beta^3 u(c_4) + \cdots = \sum_{t=0}^{\infty} \beta^t u(c_{t+1}). \tag{15.35}$$

We find in Equation 15.35 that the member of the initial generation indeed has preferences like those of an infinitely lived person, even though she will not live forever.

A finitely lived person will behave like an infinitely lived person only if she has both the same preferences and the same constraints. Having found that her preferences may be like those of an infinitely lived person, let us now examine her constraints. As previously, we will consider people endowed when young with y goods who choose nominal money balances m_t and capital k_t paying the rate of return x. In addition, each old person in period t chooses her personal consumption and a bequest worth ψ_t goods to her child. The budget sets of the young and old alive in period t are, respectively,

$$k_t + v_t m_t = y + \psi_t, \tag{15.36}$$

$$c_t + \psi_t = x k_{t-1} + v_t m_{t-1}. \tag{15.37}$$

Recall that individuals do not consume when young. This explains the absence of a consumption term in the young person's budget set (Equation 15.36). Note that, in these budget constraints, the bequest ψ_t is a source of income for the young and is an expenditure for the old.

The old are the ones who decide on the size of the bequest. In so doing, they will weigh the utility they derive from their own consumption against the utility they derive from their children's consumption. If they decide to leave a positive bequest, the budget constraint they face can be found by solving Equation 15.36 for ψ_t and substituting that expression into Equation 15.37. The resulting constraint is the same as the budget constraint for an infinitely lived person (Equation 15.24):

$$c_t + k_t + v_t m_t - y = x k_{t-1} + v_t m_{t-1}. \tag{15.38}$$

Given that altruistic parents face the same constraint and preferences as infinitely lived persons, they will behave exactly the same way. Note, for example, that because $m_t = M/N = m_{t-1}$, the budget constraint simplifies to

$$c_t + k_t = x k_{t-1} + y, \tag{15.39}$$

in which money balances do not affect a person's budget, just as it did not affect the budget of the infinitely lived person described in Equation 15.24.

Parents Leaving No Bequest

There is an important exception to the notion that an altruistic parent will behave like an infinitely lived person. Suppose that when weighing her own consumption against the utility she derives from her child's consumption, a parent decides her child is so well off (or so unlovable) that on the margin she would like to take resources from the child in order to increase her own consumption – in essence, she would like the bequest to be negative.[8] Unless the child can be coerced into giving resources to the parent, the negative bequest desired by the parent will not occur. The best that the parent can do for herself in this situation is to simply leave no bequest. In this case, $\psi_t = 0 = \psi_{t+1}$ and the budget constraints for a person born at t are

$$k_t + v_t m_t = y, \tag{15.40}$$

$$c_{t+1} = x k_t + v_{t+1} m_t. \tag{15.41}$$

---

[8] In a stationary equilibrium, negative bequests are desired by the parent if $r < 1/\beta$, which may result from low rates of return or from low degrees of altruism (β).

Each generation saves only for its own old-age consumption, leaving nothing for its descendants. In this case, the lifetime budget constraint simplifies to that of a finitely lived person,

$$\frac{c}{x} = y + v\left[\frac{M}{N}\right]\left[\frac{1}{x} - 1\right],\tag{15.42}$$

in which money balances are a drain on the wealth of an individual, as we found earlier in Equation 15.13.

Appendix Exercises

15.3 Consider an economy of altruistic two-period-lived people who care about the utility of their children. Children do not care about the utility of their parents. Parents currently leave a bequest worth 50 goods. For each of the following policies, find the size of the bequest in period 1 and the effect of this policy on the capital stock.

  a. The government decreases taxes paid by each old person in period 1 by 40 goods, running a deficit that will be paid off with taxes imposed on those old in period 3.

  b. The government increases taxes paid by each old person in period 1 by 40 goods, running a deficit that will be paid off with taxes imposed on those old in period 3.

  c. The government increases taxes paid by each old person in period 1 by 70 goods, reducing a national debt that will be paid off in full with taxes imposed on those old in period 3.

15.4 Consider an economy of identical infinitely lived people. Suppose there is a tax cut in period 1 of d goods per person financed by long-term government debt that is never retired but pays the net real interest rate $i = r - 1$ in every period. Interest payments are financed by lump-sum taxes in each period.

  a. Write the government budget constraints for period 1 and for periods $t \geq 2$.

  b. Demonstrate that this tax cut and bond issue will not alter the wealth of an infinitely lived person. *Hint:* You need to make use of the fact that

$$\sum_{t=0}^{\infty} i^t = \frac{1}{1-i}$$

or

$$\sum_{t=1}^{\infty} i^t = \frac{i}{1-i}$$

for any constant i so that $0 < i < 1$.

Chapter 16

The Temptation of Inflation

AN INFLATION unanticipated by the owners of nominal debt reduces the real value of that debt. Might a government therefore be tempted to rid itself of a burdensome national debt by inflating it away? If so, why would a potential bondholder ever trust the government not to inflate? To address these questions, this chapter examines the consequences of a default on the national debt and the temptation of the government to default. Then the chapter shows the equivalence of a surprise inflation to a default. Finally, it examines ways the monetary authority can convince the public that it will not give in to the temptation of inflation.

Defaulting on the Debt

If government debt crowds out capital and obliges the government to raise revenue just to pay the interest on the old debt, why put up with it? Why not simply default on the debt, refusing to pay it off? Certainly this is a tempting idea to any government that wants to lower taxes.

Suppose the government unexpectedly enacted a one-time default on the debt owed in period t. A look at the government budget constraint (Equation 13.8) reveals that this would enable the government to increase its expenditures, reduce taxes or seigniorage, or reduce the debt passed along to future generations. What would be the consequences of this default?

The most obvious consequence is that the default would redistribute resources from the generation that owned the initial debt to the generations that follow, who no longer need be taxed to pay the interest on the debt. In effect, therefore, the default functions like a tax on bondholders.

If the default at t is truly unexpected, it will have the same effect as a lump-sum tax on the generation born at $t-1$; that is, the default effectively taxes generation $t-1$ without affecting its behavior. Generation $t-1$ chose to acquire the bonds in period $t-1$, before it knew of the default. (If it had known of the default in advance, the generation would have refused to buy the bonds, forcing the government to raise taxes or lower expenditures.) When the default unexpectedly occurs at t, the generation is unable to go back in time to refuse to buy the bonds. In this way, the government induced generation $t - 1$ to contribute revenue by buying bonds at $t - 1$ but does not have to repay that contribution at t.

An income tax on generation $t - 1$ also would have raised revenue. The income tax, however, would have reduced the incentives of the generation to work or invest, because the private return to these income-generating activities is reduced by the tax. A government that must rely on taxes like the income tax that are not lump-sum taxes therefore may be tempted by the idea of raising revenue by issuing bonds and failing to pay them off. Note that the temptation to default exists *even if the government benevolently acts in the best interests of the public*. Because a surprise default works like a lump-sum tax, collecting revenue without distorting incentives, even the public will prefer it to an income tax that raises the same revenue from the same people.

The Inconsistency of Default

A default works as a lump-sum tax only if it takes people by surprise. Could the government make default a permanent means of raising revenue by defaulting on the bonds in every period? Only if people are very stupid or indifferent to their own welfare. Rational people who care about their own welfare would certainly catch on to the idea that the government does not intend to pay off on any bonds it issues. They will refuse to buy the bonds. For this reason, default is not a permanent solution to the revenue needs of the government.

What if the government defaults once and promises never to do so again? Will people believe the government? Suppose the government defaults at t and then issues some new debt. Would you buy this debt? If you know the government was willing to default in the past, you may well believe that it will break its promise and default once again. Once you have purchased its debt, the government's temptation to default will be as strong as it was when the government defaulted before.

The incentive of the government to behave in one way today (e.g., to default) but promise not to behave that way in the future is referred to as the **time consistency** problem of government policy.[1] When there is a time consistency problem, the best policy in the short run is not the best long-run policy. The time consistency problem is that, as time passes, the future becomes the present and the government is tempted to break its promise and follow the best short-run policy. If the government's policy is to default today but not in the future, the government will always default because it is always today.

---

[1] The expression *time consistency* and recognition of the problems it poses for macroeconomic policy making come from Kydland and Prescott (1977).

If people know the government will always give in to an incentive to default, they will never buy government debt. To induce people to buy its debt, the government must therefore convince people that it will not default.

Commitment

The most effective means of convincing people about one's future actions is to bind oneself in advance to these actions. For example, an individual taking a loan can offer the creditor something of value as collateral, to be seized by the creditor if the debtor fails to repay the loan. A contract that makes this arrangement formal can be enforced by the legal system. The debtor now has an incentive not to default on the loan. By making the repayment of the loan in her best interest, the debtor becomes committed to the future action, repayment. The creditor now believes that the debtor will repay the loan not because the debtor is particularly honest by nature, but because the creditor knows the debtor will want to repay the loan in order to avoid the seizure of the collateral.

Commitment is not as easy for the government because the government is both the debtor and the enforcer of contracts. As such, the government may be able to arrange that it not be punished if it fails to repay its debt. As a result, the government may be unable to commit itself to promised future actions and thus may be unable to secure loans. As an analogy, imagine the consequences of a law that prohibited penalizing debtors who default. Anticipating that debtors will never wish to repay their debts, whatever their promises, creditors will be unwilling to lend. As a result, both creditors and debtors will be worse off under such a law.

To commit itself to its promised future actions, the government must surrender some of its freedom to act in the future. One way to do this is to establish an independent judiciary that can oblige the government to keep its promises. A related way for the government to commit itself in the future is to write the promise into the constitution. If the government is later tempted to break its promise, it will be difficult to do so because changing the constitution is a lengthy process.[2] Consider a constitutional amendment that prohibited default on the national debt. To repeal the amendment would take so long that much of the government debt would have already been repaid.

Reputation

The government may also try to convince people that it will always repay the debt simply by always repaying whatever it borrows in order to maintain its reputation.

---

[2] Commitment through constitutional guarantees are more effective in nations with long, stable democratic traditions. Politically unstable nations may find it much more difficult to borrow, either internally or externally, because even their constitutional guarantees mean little.

The government demonstrates that it won't give in to the short-run incentives by always following the best long-run policy. If the government is aware that people are watching its current behavior as a signal of its future behavior, it may rationally decide that the gains from defaulting on today's debt may be outweighed by the costs of the government's inability to borrow in the future because of the public's lack of trust.

A reputation for repayment, however, still requires people to trust that the government will not change its mind and that the government believes the long-run costs of default exceed its short-run benefits. Because of its dependence on the public's trust, a reputation is less certain than commitment as a means of changing people's expectations.

The Rate of Return on Risky Debt

Suppose you think that there is only a chance of default. You may then buy this debt if it offers a sufficiently high rate of return. How high? Suppose a perfectly safe asset pays the rate of return x with certainty. If the government promised the same rate of return, would you buy the government debt? No. Because there is a chance that the government will default, the average rate of return on government debt is lower than that of the safe asset. Because of the chance of default, the risky government debt must promise a rate of return greater than x in order to yield the same average rate of return. For example, if there is a 50 percent chance the government will default on its debt, the government must promise to pay $2x$ in order to give its debt the same average rate of return as the safe asset.

Will people willingly hold the risky government debt if its average rate of return equals that of the safe asset? Risk-averse people won't, because the debt is riskier than the safe asset. Only if the government debt offers a return that is on average greater than that of the safe asset will risk-averse people accept the debt. Therefore, a government that randomly defaults on its obligations will have to pay a greater average rate of return than a government that never defaults. In this way, random defaults on the national debt do not offer a government a long-run solution to the problem of financing government expenditures.

Inflation and the Nominal National Debt

The Treasury bills that comprise the national debt are pledges to pay a specific number of dollars at some future date. Because the Federal Reserve can print dollars at will, one might believe that we need never fear the insolvency of the federal government. At any time, the Federal Reserve can print enough dollars to buy up the entire national debt through open market operations. Let us now evaluate this claim with a look at the effects of unanticipated and anticipated inflation on the real value of the national debt.

Unanticipated Inflation and the Real National Debt

We start by examining the government's budget constraint at t, measured in dollars, for the case of a total national debt worth D_t dollars issued at t paying the gross nominal interest rate R_t:

$$p_t N_t g_t + R_{t-1} D_{t-1} = p_t N_t \tau_t + [M_t - M_{t-1}] + D_t. \qquad (16.1)$$

Dividing both sides by p_t, we find the government budget constraint in real terms:

$$N_t g_t + \frac{R_{t-1} D_{t-1}}{p_t} = N_t \tau_t + \frac{M_t - M_{t-1}}{p_t} + \frac{D_t}{p_t}. \qquad (16.2)$$

The second term in Equation 16.2 represents the current real value of last period's government debt.

Suppose now that in period t the government prints fiat money at a rate unanticipated in the previous period. If this inflation was not anticipated, it cannot have affected variables determined at $t-1$, in particular, the initial nominal debt D_{t-1} and the nominal interest rate R_{t-1}. For given values of these variables, an increase in the current price level reduces the real value of the principal and interest on last period's national debt. A lower real value of the old national debt on the left-hand side of Equation 16.2 means the government can reduce the terms on the right-hand side of Equation 16.2 by an equal amount, implying a reduction of taxes, seigniorage, or new government debt. In other words, we now *seem* to have an extra tool with which to manage the government's budget. By increasing the fiat money stock we can raise the price level, which lowers the real value of what the government owes to others (in addition to its usual effect of raising revenue through seigniorage, which itself represents a lowering of the real value of another government issued asset, fiat money).

Some claim that the power to print money implies that the government need never default on its debt because it can always print enough money to buy up all the debt, since the debt is denominated in dollars. In fact, an unanticipated inflation is exactly equivalent to a default. Look at who loses with unanticipated inflation. Bondholders purchased the bonds to provide for the consumption of real goods in the future. If unanticipated inflation occurs, nominally denominated bonds will purchase fewer goods than the bondholders expected when they bought the bonds. Aren't the bondholders being cheated? Even if bondholders are paid the explicitly promised number of dollars during unanticipated inflation, they haven't been paid what they really care about – the goods they were implicitly promised. The real effect of unanticipated inflation is exactly that of a default: the government reduces or eliminates its obligations at the expense of the bondholders.

What will be the effect of unanticipated inflation on output? The resulting reduction of the real value of the national debt will reduce the crowding out of capital.[3] This increase in capital, in turn, will increase output in the following period. If capital displays a diminishing marginal product, the increase in capital also results in a reduction of that marginal product and thus (by rate-of-return equality) in the interest rate as well. This analysis suggests that, if the nominal fiat money stock stimulates real output, it may be an indirect effect. Surprise increases in fiat money reduce the real value of the national debt, which increases capital and thus real output.[4]

Anticipated Inflation and the Real National Debt

Let us now look at the effect of a rise in the price level on the real value of the old national debt if the rise is anticipated. As we found previously, the real value of the old national debt can be written as the second term in Equation 16.2, $(R_{t-1}D_{t-1})/p_t$. Let us write this in terms of the real national debt issued in the previous period, $B_{t-1} = D_{t-1}/p_{t-1}$, or $D_{t-1} = B_{t-1}p_{t-1}$, to get

$$\frac{R_{t-1}D_{t-1}}{p_t} = R_{t-1}\left[\frac{p_{t-1}}{p_t}\right]B_{t-1}. \tag{16.3}$$

The term $R_{t-1}[(p_{t-1})/p_t]$ can be interpreted as the actual real rate of return on bonds (i.e., the current real value of the old national debt must equal its initial real value times its actual real rate of return).

Consider individuals contemplating the purchase of government bonds at time $t - 1$. At that point in time, individuals do not know the price level that will exist one period in the future (p_t). Let p_t^e denote the individuals' expectation (anticipation) of the price level at time t. Keep in mind that this expectation is formed on the information available to individuals at time $t - 1$.

To attract savers to bonds, the government must offer an *anticipated* or *expected* rate of return equal to the rate they can get from alternative assets. Therefore if capital with the rate of return x is the alternative asset, it must be that

$$R_{t-1}\left[\frac{p_{t-1}}{p_t^e}\right] = x,$$

---

[3] See Appendix B in Chapter 15 on "infinitely lived people" for an exception to the crowding out of capital.
[4] See Champ and Freeman (1990) for a formal model of this money/output link.

or

$$R_{t-1} = x\left[\frac{p_t^e}{p_{t-1}}\right]. \tag{16.4}$$

Equation 16.4 tells us that the nominal interest rate will rise with whatever rate of inflation p_t^e/p_{t-1} is anticipated at $t-1$. This means that the current real value of the old debt issued at $t-1$ must equal $xN_{t-1}b_{t-1}$. In other words, the value of the old debt is unaffected by anticipated inflation because the nominal interest rate charged on debt will include any anticipated inflation.

Is inflation a solution to the problem of the national debt? Can the government issue debt in every period and count on being able to inflate away this debt in the next period? To answer this question, state what will happen to the nominal interest rate if the government always tries to inflate away the debt.

We can use Equation 16.4 to find an expression for the net nominal interest rate, $R_{t-1}-1$, as we did in back in Chapter 6 (Equation 6.7). Here we replace p_t with individuals' expectation of the price level p_t^e:

$$R_{t-1} - 1 = (x-1) + \left(\frac{p_t^e}{p_{t-1}} - 1\right) + (x-1)\left(\frac{p_t^e}{p_{t-1}} - 1\right). \tag{16.5}$$

The net nominal rate of interest equals the net real rate plus the anticipated net rate of inflation (plus a term generally small enough to be safely ignored). If individuals know the growth rate of the economy (n), then the anticipated net inflation rate p_t^e/p_{t-1} is equal to z^e/n, where z^e is the expected rate of fiat money creation.

Example 16.1 Suppose in period 1 the government must borrow 10,000 goods. Let the gross real marginal product of capital equal 1.05. Assume that people always want to hold fiat money balances worth a total of 500 goods and that the fiat money stock in period 1 is $1,000. Suppose people expect the government to increase the fiat money stock by 10 percent and that the population is constant.

a. What will be the nominal net interest rate?
b. What will be the real value of the debt in period 2 if the fiat money stock rises by 10 percent?
c. What will it be if there is no change in the fiat money stock?
d. What will it be if the fiat money stock rises by 20 percent?
e. What will it be if the fiat money stock rises by 20 percent but this rise is expected?

Rational Expectations

Is inflation a long-run solution to the problem of the national debt? Can the government issue debt in every period and count on being able to inflate away this debt in the next period? Not if people are rational. Consider some examples. If the real net rate of return from capital is 3 percent, what net nominal interest rate is required to induce rational people to hold nominal bonds in each of the following cases?

1. The government inflates at a net rate of 10 percent in every year.
2. An election is coming next year, and the government inflates at a net rate of 20 percent in every election year.
3. The government tries to stay ahead of the public by increasing the rate of inflation by 5 percent each period. The current net rate of inflation is 20 percent.
4. The government flips a fair coin, inflating at a 10 percent net rate if the coin comes up heads but doesn't inflate at all if the coin comes up tails. Assume that people are risk neutral.

If you answered 13 percent to case 1, 23 percent to case 2, 28 percent to case 3, and 8 percent to case 4, you have used the concept of **rational expectations**. Rational expectations (first introduced in Chapter 5) may be defined as the most accurate expectations possible, given the information currently available. This is not simply an assumption that people expect future inflation to equal past inflation, as in case 1. Under rational expectations, people try to anticipate the government's actions, even if they fit a more complicated pattern as in cases 2 and 3. A government policy based on surprising or fooling the public in any systematic way will not work if people have rational expectations. Rational expectations assume that people will catch on to any pattern of behavior the government follows, because failure to catch on will leave each of these people worse off.

Only if the government behavior is random will rational people fail to infer correctly the government's next move. People with rational expectations can make forecasts of the future that differ from what actually occurs, but this difference can result only from some unforeseeable surprise, some information that was not available in the previous period, like the way the coin lands in case 4. Rational expectations assume only that individuals will not make preventable mistakes when forming their expectations of the future. But even if policy is unpredictable, the public will set their expectations so that they are correct on average (so that on average they receive the same real rate of return from bonds as from capital).

Example 16.2 If the real net rate of return from capital is 4 percent, what net nominal interest rate is required to induce rational people to hold nominal bonds in each of the following cases?

a. The government inflates at a net rate of 7 percent in every year.
b. This is an election year, and the government inflates at a net rate of 20 percent in every election year.
c. The government tries to stay ahead of the public by doubling the net rate of inflation by each period. The current net rate of inflation is 4 percent.

d. The government rolls a fair die, inflating at a 30 percent net rate if a 6 is rolled but not inflating at all for any other roll. Assume that people are risk neutral.

e. The government rolls a fair die, inflating at a 30 percent net rate if a 6 is rolled but not inflating at all for any other roll. Assume that people are risk averse.

The Lucas Critique Revisited

We have previously examined the negative correlation between nominal wages and the unemployment rate commonly called the Phillips curve (Chapter 5) as well as the related positive correlation between money and output (Chapter 9). We noted in both cases the disappearance of that relation at the time governments sought to systematically exploit it.

This chapter's model of nominal government debt suggests another possible link between monetary surprises and output increases. Suppose that for a century a monetary authority keeps the stock of fiat money and the price level rather fixed. The fluctuations that do occur are unpredictable accidents. As we have seen in our model if the national debt is nominally denominated, an unanticipated increase in the price level reduces the real value of the national debt, thereby reducing the crowding out of capital and increasing real output.

Suppose these correlations are studied by economists who do not know anything about the structure of the economy that gave rise to these patterns in the data. They would be tempted to speculate that there is a trade-off between price increases and real output. With a leap of faith, they might even suggest to the monetary authority and the public that one can systematically raise output through inflation.

Suppose the monetary authority adopts this suggestion and proceeds on an announced policy of inflating at a variety of rates. What would happen to the correlation of inflation with output? Recall that anticipated inflation does nothing to change the real value of the national debt because the government must pay a higher nominal rate of interest to attract people to the debt; therefore, it has no effect on output.

The monetary authority generates inflation but not the intended increase in output. The trade-off proves illusory.

If the monetary authority adopts this policy secretly, it may succeed in stimulating output for a time. In this period people may dismiss observed inflation as an aberration, just one of those rare random bursts of inflation they had observed for a century. If the monetary authority continues to inflate in any systematic way, however, rational people will catch on to the policy and adjust their expectations (and the nominal interest rate) accordingly.

Why did the suggestion of our fictional economists fail? The correlations they observed were generated by unanticipated inflation when the government was following a policy of monetary and price stability. These correlations disappeared when the government followed a policy of inflation designed to systematically stimulate output. Obviously the data generated when the economy was subjected to inflation under one type of policy regime (price stability) did not help to predict its reaction to inflation under another policy regime (systematic inflation).[5]

What does our example and recent experience tell us about designing monetary policy? It warns us about drawing policy inferences from simple correlations in the data if we do not understand the working of the economy that generated those data. If our fictional economists understood our model economy, they would have known that only unanticipated inflation would have an effect on real output; any systematic inflation would be anticipated and thus would have no effect. Looking at the data alone, they could not learn this because systematic inflation had not been tried during the period for which they had data. Only if they had reason to believe the effects of inflation would be the same whether inflation is anticipated or unanticipated should they have confidently advised the monetary authority to deliberately inflate. To give reasonable policy advice it is not enough to observe patterns in the data; one must understand how those patterns were caused so that one can be confident about the reaction of the economy to a change in policy.[6]

Example 16.3 Consider the overlapping generations economy with a constant population of two-period-lived people endowed only when young. Suppose the real net rate of return from capital is always 4 percent and young people always save a total of 5,000 goods, including fiat money, worth 1,000 goods. Last period the price of a good was $1, people expected a 10 percent net rate of inflation, the fiat money stock was worth $1,000, and the national debt (of one-period bonds) was worth $2,000. In this period the government will issue bonds equal to the principal and interest on the old debt. Find the current real values of the old debt (principal plus interest), the capital stock, and next period's output from capital for the following three cases:

a. The government inflates at a net rate of 10 percent, as expected.
b. The government unexpectedly inflates at a net rate of 20 percent.
c. The government unexpectedly refuses to inflate.

Self-Fulfilling Inflationary Expectations

Rational expectations imply that the public will try to anticipate the policy the government will want to follow even before the government begins to implement it.

---

[5] As we learned in Chapter 5, the suggestion that correlations observed under one type of macroeconomic policy regime may not be found under another policy regime is commonly called the Lucas critique. For further reading, see Lucas (1976, 1981).

[6] Of course, if an economist's understanding (model) of the economy is wrong, so may be that economist's advice. Nevertheless, policy advice is more likely to succeed if it is based on some carefully worked out understanding/model of the economy than if it is based on correlations observed but unexplained.

In this section, we will examine the danger that the public's rational expectation of inflation may itself cause or contribute to the inflation it expects.[7]

In every period the government is tempted to inflate away some of the real value of the national debt. Rational, forward-looking people may therefore anticipate inflation and demand a nominal interest rate, $R_{t-1} = x(p_t^e/p_{t-1})$, high enough to yield at least the real rate of return offered by capital.

Now suppose the government in place truly does not wish to use inflation to default on its debt and announces its intentions. Will people be able to distinguish this government from one that wishes to default on its debt through unanticipated inflation? No. The government that plans unanticipated inflation will also announce that it will not inflate. Therefore, if the people cannot distinguish between truthful and deceitful promises to end inflation, they may anticipate inflation and thus require a high nominal interest rate.

Suppose the government refuses to inflate even though people expect inflation. In this case, the government pays a high real interest rate and the real burden of the national debt will increase. Consider as an example an economy with a real debt of 1 million goods in which $n = 1$, $x = 1.1$, and $p_t = \$1$. Suppose the people expect the government to double the fiat money stock ($z^e = 2$). To induce people to hold their bonds, the government must offer a nominal interest rate of $x(z^e/n) = 2.2$. This means the government at $t + 1$ will owe $2.2 million. If the government does not actually inflate, this nominal rate is also the real rate and the government finds itself with a real national debt of 2.2 million goods. If the government inflates as expected, the nominal debt of $2.2 million is worth only 1.1 million goods because the doubling of the fiat money stock will cause the price level to double to $p_{t+1} = 2$. In this way, the honest government that meant what it said about ending inflation finds itself with a real debt twice the size of the real debt it would have found if it had inflated as expected.

From this example, we see that a government faced with inflationary expectations will have a hard time refusing to inflate. If it does not inflate when expected, it will find itself with a large real debt that eventually must be covered through taxes or government expenditure cuts (assuming $x > n$). It is easy to understand why a government with no deceitful intentions, but faced with the alternative of a large real debt, may choose to inflate as expected.

In such a case, inflationary expectations are self-fulfilling. The inflation occurs because people expect it and thus require a high nominal interest rate, which forces the government to inflate in order to avoid a large real national debt.

---

[7] See Calvo (1978) and Barro and Gordon (1983).

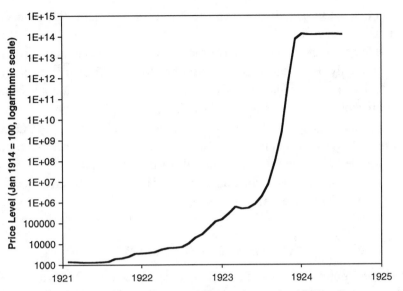

Figure 16.1. The German hyperinflation. During the early 1920s, Germany, Austria, Hungary, and Poland each experienced hyperinflations. The German case is illustrated here. By the end of the German hyperinflation the price level stood at over one trillion time ، its pre-World War I level. *Source:* Data from Young (1925) as published by Sargent (1986a, Table 3.18 pp. 80–81).

Hyperinflation

Although most countries have net inflation rates of 5, 10, or 20 percent a year, a few experience hyperinflation, inflation rates that rapidly accelerate to annual rates of a thousand or million percent. What may lead to the dramatic episodes of hyperinflation that we have observed recently in Latin America and even more dramatically in Germany and other central European nations after World War I?

Figure 16.1 presents price level data from the German hyperinflation of the 1920s. The German case is similar to that of Austria, Hungary, and Poland during the same time period. During the most dramatic part of the German hyperinflation, the inflation rate peaked at almost 15,000 percent per month.

One feature common to countries experiencing hyperinflation is fiscal difficulty. To see why, suppose the government has run up an enormous national debt, one so large that the interest payments cannot possibly be financed through taxes or government expenditure cuts. Even if the government has never before inflated, it is easy to anticipate that it must now turn to inflation as its only hope of reducing the real value of its debt. The public will therefore demand high rates of nominal interest before it will agree to hold any bonds of the government. The resulting large nominal interest obligations of the government require the government to print money at yet a faster rate.

We see from Figure 16.1 that the German hyperinflation was stopped and indeed stopped suddenly. How can hyperinflation be stopped when it is fueled by self-fulfilling inflationary expectations? Certainly, the government cannot just announce that it will stop inflating. Who would believe the announcement, knowing the government has a huge debt that it cannot finance any other way? Only if the government solves its fiscal problems, and thus eliminates the need to inflate, can rational people believe the government will stop printing money. For this reason, the end of hyperinflation is accompanied by fiscal reforms that reduce government spending or increase government revenue.[8]

Commitment in Monetary Policy

A binding commitment to avoid inflation is the surest way to convince the public that it will not try to inflate away the national debt. How might the government convince the public that it will be unable or unwilling to inflate in the future?

One way is to index government debt to changes in the price level so that the real value of the national debt does not change when there is inflation. Such indexed government debt removes the government's incentive to inflate as a means to reduce the real value of its debt.

Another approach is to keep the central bank independent of the government and free from political pressure. If an independent central bank is directed by opponents of inflation, such as those who might have much to lose from an inflation (e.g., owners of government debt), the government can convince the public that the central bank will be unwilling to inflate, however much inflation is desired by other branches of government.

Alesina and Summers (1993) investigated the relationship between central bank independence and macroeconomic performance across several countries. Devising a measure of central bank independence is a difficult task and any proposed measure certainly will be subject to debate. That said, Alesina and Summers build their index using as a starting point other indices of central bank performance presented by Bade and Parkin (1982), Alesina (1988), and Grilli, Masciandaro, and Tabellini (1991). The index focuses on two main areas – political independence and economic independence. Political independence measures the degree of separation of the central bank from political influences stemming from the executive and legislative branches of government. Economic independence is an indication

---

[8] The causes and ends of the hyperinflations of central Europe are carefully analyzed by Sargent (1986a). He identifies in particular the policies implemented to help the central banks commit themselves to noninflationary policies.

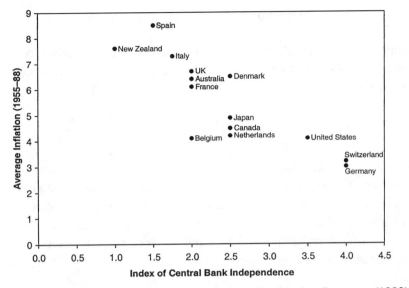

Figure 16.2. Central bank independence and inflation. The Alesina-Summers (1993) index of central bank independence ranks central banks on a scale of 1 (least independent) to 5 (most independent). As shown in this figure, countries with more independent central banks tend to have lower inflation rates. *Source:* Alesina and Summers (1993, Table A1, p. 160).

of how unrestricted the central bank is in its use of monetary policy tools. (A key component of this is to what degree the central bank is relied upon to facilitate the financing of government deficits.) Utilizing this constructed index of central bank independence, Figure 16.2 illustrates the tendency of inflation rates to be lower in countries with more independent central banks.

A more direct way to convince the public that the central bank will not inflate is a constitutional amendment prohibiting expansion of the money stock.[9] Once the amendment has been adopted, a government that wished to inflate away the national debt would have to go through the long task of repealing the amendment, signaling the government's intention to inflate. By the time the amendment was repealed, inflation would catch no one by surprise.

The Temptation of Seigniorage

Nominally denominated interest-bearing debt is not the only source of the government's temptation to inflate away its budgetary problems. Fiat money is also nominally denominated, which allows the government to tax away some of the

---

[9] If there are contingencies under which inflation is desirable, the amendment might specify narrowly defined exceptions for which more money can be printed. Of course, such an amendment eliminates the ability of the central bank to respond to contingencies that cannot be anticipated or defined.

value of the public's fiat money balances by printing new money, as we learned in Chapter 3.

Seigniorage, like default on the debt, exhibits a time consistency problem because the optimal short-run rate of inflation differs from the optimal long-run rate. Seigniorage in the initial period equals

$$v_1[M_1 - M_0] = v_1 M_1 \left[1 - \frac{1}{z_1}\right] = N_1 q_1 \left[1 - \frac{1}{z_1}\right], \qquad (16.6)$$

the product of the seigniorage tax rate $[1 - (1/z_1)]$ and the seigniorage tax base $v_1 M_1 = N_1 q_1$. For any given value of fiat money, the government acquires revenue by printing additional units of fiat money ($z_1 > 1$). This expansion of the fiat money stock taxes those already holding fiat money balances. Because these people have already acquired their balances, they cannot change these balances to avoid the tax. The inflation tax is a lump-sum tax on current moneyholders, the initial old in period 1.

The real value of the seigniorage tax base $v_1 M_1 = N_1 q_1$ depends on the demand for fiat money, which depends on the expected future rate of fiat money creation (z_2). The government would like people to expect a low rate of inflation in the future so that their demand for fiat money (and thus the seigniorage tax base) is strong. Ideally, then, the government wants to print fiat money today (period 1) while convincing people that it will not inflate in the future (period 2). However, when period 2 arrives, the government will want to inflate, despite any previous promise, while trying to convince the people that it will not inflate in period 3. The incentive to inflate today but to promise no future inflation is again the time consistency problem.[10]

Inflation and Private Debt

Private debt, when nominally denominated, also may tempt a government to inflate if the government wishes to help borrowers at the expense of lenders. If, for example, the government favoring a more equal distribution of wealth sees the poor as borrowers, it may wish to inflate away the real value of the borrowers' debt. As with government debt, the government will be unable to use inflation to help borrowers in any systematic way if lenders anticipate the government's desires. Lenders will expect the government to inflate and thus will lend at only nominal interest rates that take into account the expected inflation.

If a country borrows a great deal from abroad (as a developing nation might well do) or acquires foreign debt to back money issued by a currency board,

---

[10] See Auernheimer (1974) and Calvo (1978).

the government's temptation to inflate is even greater. A surprise inflation would then help the domestic citizens, the borrowers, at the expense of foreigners, the lenders. Lenders, of course, are aware of this inflationary temptation and will be reluctant to sign contracts denominated in the money of the borrowers' country.

Loans denominated in the money of the lender country introduce their own incentive problems. A nation that is a net lender to other nations will wish to have a surprise deflation (price decreases) in order to increase the real value of loans denominated in the lender country's money.[11] Only debt indexed to the price level or denominated in the currency of disinterested third nations is free from the temptations of inflation or deflation.

Summary

We began this chapter with a discussion of defaulting on the government debt. Here we encountered the time consistency problem of government policy wherein the best short-run policy (here, default) may not always be the best long-run policy. A government that defaults on its debt may find it difficult to convince people that it will not default again in the future.

This chapter also investigated the effects of inflation on the real value of the government debt. At first glance, it appears that, by inflating, a government can lower the real burden of its debt. However, we discovered that, if inflation is anticipated, nominal interest rates on government debt will rise sufficiently to offset the effect that inflation has on the real value of the debt.

Only if inflation is unanticipated will the inflationary policy succeed in lowering the debt's real value. In this case, the inflation acts as a default on the government debt. The reduction in the real value of the debt lessens crowding out of capital and, subsequently, increases output. However, a government policy that continues to inflate in the hope of further reducing the burden of its debt will eventually fail. Rational individuals will come to expect inflation and demand higher nominal interest rates on government bonds. The government will be frustrated in its attempt to lower the burden of its debt.

We also found that, if individuals have come to expect inflation, the government will find it difficult not to fulfill those expectations. Because inflationary expectations are already built into the nominal interest rate, a government that does not inflate will find itself with a larger debt burden than if it refuses to inflate.

---

[11] The rapid reduction of U.S. inflation from 20 percent in 1979 to 6 percent in 1982 may well have caught heavily borrowing developing nations by surprise, greatly increasing the real value of the outstanding debt denominated in U.S. dollars, whether or not this effect was intended.

Exercises

16.1 Explain why a government that must run up a large national debt to finance extraordinary spending over the next several years might choose to surrender the power of money creation to a central bank beyond the government's control.

16.2 What will happen to the demand for fiat money, the nominal interest rate, and the real interest rate if the government tries to use inflation to default on the national debt every other year? ... in randomly selected years? Explain each of your answers.

Appendix: An Activist Monetary Policy

(Calculus and simple statistics – the concepts of expected value and covariance – are used in this appendix. The material in the appendix to Chapter 1 is also a prerequisite to this appendix.)

If it is impossible to fool people in any predictable way, can there be any role for an activist monetary policy, one that occasionally surprises the public with inflation that reduces the real value of the national debt? In a world of certainty, such a policy would seem foolish. It would increase the risk faced by bondholders and thus would also increase the average rate of return (because of the risk premium) the government must offer on its bonds.

To see this consider an overlapping generations economy in which capital and one-period government bonds are the only two assets. Capital pays the sure real rate of return x, and bonds pay the risky real rate of return r_{t+1}. Let the preferences of each of the model's risk-averse people born at t be described by the utility function $U(c_{1,t}) + V(c_{2,t+1})$, where $U(\cdot)$ and $V(\cdot)$ are continuous, differentiable, increasing, and strictly concave. Each person is endowed with y_1 goods when young and y_2 when old.

The budget constraints of the individual may be written as

$$c_{1,t} + k_t + b_t = y_1, \qquad (16.7)$$
$$c_{2,t+1} = y_2 + xk_t + r_{t+1}b_t. \qquad (16.8)$$

Substituting these constraints into the utility function, we can express the individual's problem as the choice of k_t and b_t to maximize

$$U(y_1 - k_t - b_t) + E_t V(y_2 + xk_t + r_{t+1}b_t), \qquad (16.9)$$

where $E_t V(\cdot)$ refers to the expected value of $V(\cdot)$, given the information known in period t (the period in which the individual must choose her asset portfolio). Following the same steps outlined in the appendix to Chapter 1, we differentiate Equation 16.9 with respect to k_t and b_t to find the first-order conditions that identify the maximum expected utility of someone born at t:

$$-U'(c_{1,t}) + x E_t V'(c_{2,t+1}) = 0, \tag{16.10}$$

$$-U'(c_{1,t}) + E_t[r_{t+1} V'(c_{2,t+1})] = 0. \tag{16.11}$$

Together these imply that

$$
\begin{aligned}
x &= \frac{E_t[r_{t+1} V'(c_{2,t+1})]}{E_t V'(c_{2,t+1})} \\
&= \frac{E_t r_{t+1} E_t V'(c_{2,t+1}) + Cov[r_{t+1}, V'(c_{2,t+1})]}{E_t V'(c_{2,t+1})},
\end{aligned}
\tag{16.12}
$$

by the definition of a covariance.[12]

After canceling terms and rearranging, Equation 16.12 becomes

$$E_t r_{t+1} = x - \frac{Cov[r_{t+1}, V'(c_{2,t+1})]}{E_t V'(c_{2,t+1})}. \tag{16.13}$$

The covariance between two random variables is a measure of how those two variables move together. Consider an increase in one of the two random variables. If the covariance is positive, then the other variable also tends to increase. If the covariance is negative, then the other variable tends to decrease.

If the random return on government debt is the only source of randomness in the economy, high values of r_{t+1} cause high values of $c_{2,t+1}$ and low values of $V'(c_{2,t+1})$ because of diminishing marginal utility. In this case $Cov[r_{t+1}, V'(c_{2,t+1})]$ is negative.

Equation 16.13 therefore tells us that, to induce people to hold a risky bond, its expected rate of return must be greater than that of the safe asset. If the government randomizes the rate of return on its bonds, it will wind up paying higher rates of return. This is called the risk premium:

$$\text{risk premium} = \frac{-Cov[r_{t+1}, V'(C_{2,t+1})]}{E_t V'(c_{2,t+1})} > 0. \tag{16.14}$$

Note that, if the covariance of r_{t+1} and $V'(c_{2,t+1})$ were positive, this risk premium would be negative, implying that the rate of return that must be offered

---

[12] Equation 16.12 follows from the definition of a covariance of two random variables. Suppose two random variables X and Y have expected values $E(X)$ and $E(Y)$, respectively. Their covariance (Cov) is defined to be

$$
\begin{aligned}
Cov(X, Y) &= E\{[X - E(X)][Y - E(Y)]\} \\
&= E[XY - E(X)Y - E(Y)X + E(X)E(Y)] \\
&= E(XY) - E(X)E(Y) - E(X)E(Y) + E(X)E(Y) \\
&= E(XY) - E(X)E(Y).
\end{aligned}
$$

From this, it follows that $E(XY) = E(X)E(Y) + Cov(X, Y)$. Equation 16.12 is an application of this result, where r_{t+1} plays the role of X and $V'(c_{2,t+1})$ plays the role of Y.

by government bonds is less than that of the safe asset. Can we imagine such a case?

Suppose there is a second source of randomness in the economy – for example, randomness in the endowment y_2 received by all the old people in a generation. Every old person in a given generation receives the same endowment, but this endowment varies randomly from generation to generation.[13] A below-average endowment when old implies low consumption when old and thus a high marginal utility when old, other things equal.

Suppose the government sets bond returns to be slightly higher than average when people receive a below-average endowment when old (and lower when the endowment is above average). Then high rates of return will occur when consumption is low and thus when the marginal utility of consumption is high. This implies a positive covariance between rates of return and marginal utility and thus, from Equation 16.14, a negative risk premium. People will be willing to hold the risky bonds even if their average rate of return is lower than that of a safe asset. Although in this way the return on the bonds is made random, by paying more when consumption is low, the consumption of bondholders is made less risky. As a result, the average rate of return the government must offer to get people to hold these bonds will actually be less than it would offer if the bonds themselves paid a fixed real rate of return (i.e., the risk premium that must be paid on these bonds will be negative).[14] In this way the bonds may serve as a form of insurance for bondholders. This is essentially a way in which the government may insure generations against low consumption by paying more to unlucky generations, financed by paying less to lucky generations.

Monetary policy in this case is merely a device through which government bonds can be made to pay real rates of return contingent on shocks. When bondholders receive a good shock, the government inflates to lower the real return on nominal bonds; similarly, it deflates when the shock is bad. With nominal bonds there still remains, of course, the temptation for the government to announce whatever will justify an inflation with which it can default on its real obligations.

---

[13] If there were randomness in the old age endowments within a generation, members of that generation could protect themselves against risk through insurance contracts with the other members of their generation. Private insurance contracts will not eliminate risk across generations, given that a generation already knows whether it has won or lost by the time the next generation comes along.

[14] See Lucas and Stokey (1983) for another justification of government bonds paying rates of return contingent on shocks.

References

Readings marked by "*" are written at a level suitable for undergraduates. Many of the cited publications of Federal Reserve banks are now freely available from Bank web sites.

Abel, A. 1987. "Optimal Monetary Growth." *Journal of Monetary Economics* 19:437–50.

*Aiyagari, S. R. 1987. "Intergenerational Linkages and Government Budget Policies." Federal Reserve Bank of Minneapolis *Quarterly Review* 11(Spring):14–23.

*Aiyagari, S. R. 1990. "Deflating the Case for Zero Inflation." Federal Reserve Bank of Minneapolis *Quarterly Review* 14(Summer):2–11.

Alesina, A. 1988. "Macroeconomics and Politics." In *NBER Macroeconomics Annual*, S. Fischer, ed. Cambridge, MA: MIT Press: 17–52.

*Alesina, A. and L. Summers. 1993. "Central Bank Independence and Macroeconomic Performance." *Journal of Money, Credit, and Banking* 25(2)(May):151–62.

Auernheimer, L. 1974. "The Honest Government's Guide to the Revenue from the Creation of Money." *Journal of Political Economy* 82(May/June):598–606.

*Avery, R. B., G. G. Elliehausen, A. B. Kennickell, and P. A. Spindt. 1987. "Changes in the Use of Transactions Accounts and Cash from 1984 to 1986." *Federal Reserve Bulletin* 73(March):179–96.

Azariadas, C. 1981. "Self-Fulfilling Prophesies." *Journal of Economic Theory* 25(December):380–96.

Bacchetta, P., and R. Caminal. 1994. "A Note on Reserve Requirements and Public Finance." *International Review of Economics and Finance* 3(1):108–18.

Bade, R., and M. Parkin. 1982. "Central Bank Laws and Monetary Policy." Unpublished manuscript.

Bailey, M. J. 1956. "The Welfare Cost of Inflationary Finance." *Journal of Political Economy* 64(April):93–110.

Barro, R. J. 1974. "Are Government Bonds Net Wealth?" *Journal of Political Economy* 91(November/December):1095–1117.

Barro, R. J. 1982. "Measuring the Fed's Revenue from Money Creation." *Economics Letters* 10:327–32.

Barro, R. J. 1989. "The Neoclassical Approach to Fiscal Policy." In *Modern Business Cycle Theory*, R. J. Barro, ed. Cambridge: Harvard University Press.

Barro, R. J., and D. B. Gordon. 1983. "A Positive Theory of Monetary Policy in a Natural Rate Model." *Journal of Political Economy* 4(August):590–610.

Bernanke, B. S. 1990. "Clearing and Settlement during the Crash." *Review of Financial Studies* 3(1):133–51.

307

Bhattacharya, S., and A. V. Thakor. "Contemporary Banking Theory." *Journal of Financial Intermediation* 3:2–50.

Boyd, J. H., and E. C. Prescott. 1986. "Financial Intermediary-Coalitions." *Journal of Economic Theory* 38(April):211–32.

Bryant, J. 1980. "A Model of Reserves, Bank Runs, and Deposit Insurance." *Journal of Banking and Finance* 4(December):335–44.

Bryant, J. and N. Wallace. 1984. "A Price Discrimination Analysis of Monetary Policy." *Review of Economic Studies* 51(April):279–88.

Cagan, P. 1965. *Determinants and Effects of Changes in the U.S. Money Stock, 1875–1960.* New York: National Bureau of Economic Research.

Calvo, G. A. 1978. "On the Time Consistency of Optimal Policy in a Monetary Economy." *Econometrica* 46(November):1411–28.

Canzoneri, M. B., and C. A. Rogers. 1990. "Is the European Community an Optimal Currency Area? Optimal Taxation Versus the Cost of Multiple Currencies." *American Economic Review* 80(June):419–33.

*Carr, J., F. Matthewson, and N. Quigley. 1994. *Ensuring Failure: Financial System Stability and Deposit Insurance in Canada.* Toronto: C. D. Howe Institute.

Cass, D., and K. Shell. 1983. "Do Sunspots Matter?" *Journal of Political Economy* 91(April):193–227.

Cass, D., and M. Yaari. 1966. "A Re-Examination of the Pure Consumption Loans Model." *Journal of Political Economy* 74(August):353–67.

Champ, B., and S. Freeman. 1990. "Money, Output, and the Nominal National Debt." *American Economic Review* 80(June):390–97.

Champ, B., B. Smith, and S. D. Williamson. 1996. "Currency Elasticity and Banking Panics: Theory and Evidence. *Canadian Journal of Economics* XXIX(4)(November):828–64.

Champ, B., S. Freeman, and W. Weber. 1999. "Redemption Costs and Interest Rates under the U.S. National Banking System." *Journal of Money, Credit, and Banking* 31(August, part 2):568–89.

Cooley, T., and S. LeRoy. 1985. "A Theoretical Macroeconomics – A Critique." *Journal of Monetary Economics* 16:283–308.

*Darby, M. R. 1984. "Some Pleasant Monetarist Arithmetic." Federal Reserve Bank of Minneapolis *Quarterly Review* 8(Spring):15–20.

Diamond, D. W. 1984. "Financial Intermediation and Delegated Monitoring." *Review of Economic Studies* 51(July):393–414.

Diamond, D. W., and P. H. Dybvig. 1983. "Bank Runs, Deposit Insurance, and Liquidity." *Journal of Political Economy* 91:401–19.

Diamond, P. A. 1965. "National Debt in a Neoclassical Growth Model." *American Economic Review* 55(December):1126–50.

Fama, E. 1980. "Banking in the Theory of Finance." *Journal of Monetary Economics* 6:39–57.

*Federal Deposit Insurance Corporation. 1998. *Managing the Crisis: The FDIC and RTC Experience.* http://www.fdic.gov/bank/historical/managing/

Feinman, J. 1993. "Reserve Requirements: History, Current Practice and Potential Reform." *Federal Reserve Bulletin* 79(6):569–89.

Fisher, I. 1926. "A Statistical Relationship between Unemployment and Price Changes." *International Labor Review* 13(June):785–92. Reprinted as "I Discovered the Phillips Curve." *Journal of Political Economy* 81(March-April 1973):496–502.

Fischer, S. 1982. "Seigniorage and the Case for a National Money." *Journal of Political Economy* 90(April):295–313.

Freeman, S. 1985. "Transactions Costs and the Optimal Quantity of Money." *Journal of Political Economy* 93(February):146–57.

Freeman, S. 1987. "Reserve Requirements and Optimal Seigniorage." *Journal of Monetary Economics* 19:307–14.

Freeman, S. 1988. "Banking as the Provision of Liquidity." *Journal of Business* 61(January):45–64.

Freeman, S. 1989. "Fiat Money as a Medium of Exchange." *International Economic Review* 30(February):137–51.

Freeman, S. 1993. "Resolving Differences over the Optimal Quantity of Money." *Journal of Money, Credit, and Banking* 25(November):801–11.

Freeman, S. 1996a. "The Payments System, Liquidity, and Rediscounting." *American Economic Review* 86:1126–38.

Freeman, S. 1996b. "Clearinghouse Banks and Banknote Over-Issue." *Journal of Monetary Economics* 38:101–15.

*Freeman, S., and J. Haslag. 1995. "Should Bank Reserves Pay Interest?" *Economic Review*, Federal Reserve Bank of Dallas, Fourth Quarter:25–33.

Freeman, S., and J. Haslag. 1996. "On the Optimality of Interest-Bearing Reserves in Economies of Overlapping Generations." *Economic Theory* 7:557–65.

Freeman, Scott, and Gregory Huffman. 1991. "Inside Money, Output, and Causality." *International Economic Review* 32(August):645–67.

Freeman, S., and G. Tabellini. 1998. "The Optimality of Nominal Contracts." *Economic Theory* 11(3):545–62.

*Friedman, M. 1960. *A Program for Monetary Stability*. New York: Fordham University Press.

Friedman, M. 1969. "The Optimum Quantity of Money." In *The Optimum Quantity of Money and Other Essays*. Chicago: Aldine.

Friedman, M., and A. Schwartz. 1963a. "Money and Business Cycles." *Review of Economics and Statistics* 45(February):32–64.

Friedman, M., and A. Schwartz. 1963b. *A Monetary History of the United States*. Princeton: Princeton University Press.

Greenwood, J., and B. Jovanovic. 1990. "Financial Development, Growth, and the Distribution of Income." *Journal of Political Economy* 98(October, part 1): 1076–77.

Grilli, V., D. Masciandaro, and G. Tabellini. 1991. "Political and Monetary Institutions and Public Finance Policies in the Industrial Countries." *Economic Policy* 13(October):341–92.

*Hammond, B. 1957. *Banks and Politics in America from the Revolution to the Civil War*. Princeton: Princeton University Press.

Jevons, W. S. 1875. *Money and the Mechanism of Exchange*. London: Appleton.

*Johnson, J. F. 1910. *The Canadian Banking System*, Washington, DC: U.S. Government Printing Office.

Jones, L. E., and R. Manuelli. 1990. "A Convex Model of Equilibrium Growth." *Journal of Political Economy* 98(October, part 1):1008–38.

*Kahn, C. M., and W. Roberds. 1999. "The Design of Wholesale Payments Networks: The Importance of Incentives." Federal Reserve Bank of Atlanta *Economic Review* 84(no. 3):30–9.

*Kareken, J. H. 1983. "Deposit Insurance Reform: or Deregulation Is the Cart, Not the Horse." Federal Reserve Bank of Minneapolis *Quarterly Review* 14(Spring):3–11.

Kareken, J. H., and N. Wallace. 1977. "Portfolio Autarky: A Welfare Analysis." *Journal of International Economics* 7(February):19–43.

References

Kareken, J. H., and N. Wallace. 1981. "On the Indeterminacy of Equilibrium Exchange Rates." *Quarterly Journal of Economics* 96(May):207–22.

King, R., and C. Plosser. 1984. "Money, Credit, and Prices in a Real Business Cycle." *American Economic Review* 74(June):363–80.

King, R., N. Wallace, and W. E. Weber. 1992. "Nonfundamental Uncertainty and Exchange Rates," *Journal of International Economics* 32:83–108.

Kiyotaki, N., and R. Wright. 1989. "On Money as a Medium of Exchange." *Journal of Political Economy* 97:927–54.

Krugman, P. 1979. "A Model of Balance of Payments Crises." *Journal of Money, Credit and Banking* 11(August):311–25.

Krugman, P., and J. Rotemberg. 1991. "Speculative Attacks on Target Zones." In *Target Zones and Currency Bands*, P. Krugman and M. Miller, eds. Oxford: Oxford University Press.

Kydland, F., and E. Prescott. 1977. "Rules Rather than Discretion: The Inconsistency of Optimal Plans." *Journal of Political Economy* 85(June):473–91.

Lacker, J. 1988. "Inside Money and Real Output." *Economic Letters* 28:9–14.

Laidler, D. 1984. "Misconceptions about the Real-Bills Doctrine: A Comment on Sargent and Wallace." *Journal of Political Economy* 92:149–55.

Leamer, E. 1985. "Vector Autoregressions for Causal Inference?" *Carnegie-Rochester Conference Series on Public Policy* 22:255–303.

Litterman, R., and L. Weiss. 1985. "Money, Real Interest Rates, and Output: A Reinterpretation of U.S. Postwar Data." *Econometrica* 53(January):129–56.

Loewy, M. 1991. "The Macroeconomic Effects of Bank Runs: An Equilibrium Analysis." *Journal of Financial Intermediation* 1(June, no. 3):242–56.

Lucas, R. E. Jr. 1972. "Expectations and the Neutrality of Money." *Journal of Economic Theory* (April):103–24. Also in *Studies in Business Cycle Theory*. R. E. Lucas Jr., ed. Cambridge, MA: MIT Press, 1981.

Lucas, R. E. Jr. 1973. "Some International Evidence on Output-Inflation Tradeoffs." *American Economic Review* 63(June):326–34. Also in *Studies in Business Cycle Theory*, R. E. Lucas Jr., ed. Cambridge, MA: MIT Press, 1981.

*Lucas, R. E. Jr. 1976. "Econometric Policy Evaluation: A Critique." *Carnegie-Rochester Conference Series The Phillips Curve* 19–46. Also in *Studies in Business Cycle Theory*, R. E. Lucas Jr., ed. Cambridge, MA: MIT Press, 1981.

*Lucas, R. E. Jr. 1981. *Studies in Business Cycle Theory*. Cambridge, MA: MIT Press.

Lucas, R. E. Jr., and N. Stokey. 1983. "Optimal Fiscal and Monetary Policy in an Economy without Capital." *Journal of Monetary Economics* 12(July):55–93.

Maeda, Y. 1991. "Fiat Money in a Pairwise-Trading Multi-Good, Overlapping Generations Model." *Journal of Economic Theory* 54:84–97.

Metzler, L. A. 1951. "Wealth, Saving, and the Rate of Interest." *Journal of Political Economy* 59(April):93–116.

*Miller, P. J., and T. J. Sargent. 1984. "A Reply to Darby." Federal Reserve Bank of Minneapolis *Quarterly Review* 8(Spring):21–26.

Miron, J. A. 1986. "Financial Panics, the Seasonality of the Nominal Interest Rate, and the Founding of the Fed." *American Economic Review* 76:125–40.

Muth, J. F. 1961. "Rational Expectations and the Theory of Price Movements." *Econometrica* 29(July):315–35.

Persson, T., and L. E. O. Svensson. 1989. "Why a Stubborn Conservative Would Run a Deficit: Policy with Time Inconsistent Preferences." *Quarterly Journal of Economics* 104(May):325–45.

Porter, R., and R. Judson. 1996. "The Location of US Currency: How Much is Abroad?" *Federal Reserve Bulletin* 82(10):245–74.

Prescott, E. 1987. "A Multiple Means-of-Payment Model." In *New Approaches to Monetary Economics*, W. Barnett and K. Singleton, eds. Cambridge, MA: Cambridge University Press.

*Radford, R.A. 1945. "The Economic Organization of a P.O.W. Camp." *Economica* 12(November):189–201.

*Rolnick, A. J., and W. E. Weber. 1989. "A Case for Fixing Exchange Rates." *Federal Reserve Bank of Minneapolis 1989 Annual Report*: 3–14.

*Rolnick, A. J., B. D. Smith, and W. E. Weber. 1998. "Lessons from a Laissez-Faire Payments System: The Suffolk Banking System (1825–58)." *Federal Reserve Bank of St. Louis Review* 80(May/June, no. 3):105–16.

Romer, D. 1985. "Financial Intermediation, Reserve Requirements, and Inside Money," *Journal of Monetary Economics* 16:175–94.

Salant, S. W. and D. W. Henderson. 1978. "Market Anticipation of Government Policy and the Price of Gold." *Journal of Political Economy* 86(August):627–48.

Samuelson, P. A. 1958. "An Exact Consumption-Loan Model of Interest With or Without the Social Contrivance of Money," *Journal of Political Economy* 66(December):467–82.

*Sargent, T. J. 1986a. "The Ends of Four Big Inflations." In *Rational Expectations and Inflation*. New York: Harper & Row, 40–109.

*Sargent, T. J. 1986b. "Interpreting the Reagan Deficits." *Federal Reserve Bank of San Francisco Quarterly Review* (Fall):5–12.

*Sargent, T. J., and N. Wallace. 1981. "Some Unpleasant Monetarist Arithmetic." *Federal Reserve Bank of Minneapolis Quarterly Review* (Fall):1–17.

Sargent, T. J., and N. Wallace. 1982. "The Real-Bills Doctrine vs. The Quantity Theory: A Reconciliation." *Journal of Political Economy* 90(December):1212–36.

Sargent, T. J., and N. Wallace. 1983. "A Model of Commodity Money." *Journal of Monetary Economics* 12(July):163–87.

Schreft, S. L. 1992. "Transactions Costs and the Use of Cash and Credit." *Economic Theory* 2(April):283–96.

Sims, C. 1972. "Money, Income, and Causality." *American Economic Review* 62(September):540–52.

Sims, C. 1980. "Comparison of Interwar and Postwar Cycles: Monetarism Reconsidered." *American Economic Review* 70(May):250–75.

*Smith, B. 1985. "American Colonial Monetary Regimes: The Failure of the Quantity Theory and Some Evidence in Favour of an Alternate View." *Canadian Journal of Economics* 18(3)(August):531–64.

*Smith, B. 1988. "The Relationship Between Money and Prices: Some Historical Evidence Reconsidered." *Federal Reserve Bank of Minneapolis Quarterly Review* (Summer):18–32,

Smith, B. 1991. "Interest on Reserves and Sunspot Equilibria: Friedman's Proposal Reconsidered." *Review of Economic Studies* 58:93–105.

Sprague, O. M. W. 1910. *A History of Crises Under the National Banking System*, Washington, DC: U.S. Government Printing Office.

Tallman, E. W. and J. R. Moen. 1990. "The Panic of 1907: How Trusts Tipped the Scales." *Federal Reserve Bank of Atlanta Economic Review* 75(May/June):2–13.

Tobin, J. 1965. "Money and Economic Growth." *Econometrica* 33(October):671–84.

Tobin, J. 1970. "Money and Income: *Post Hoc Ergo Propter Hoc?*" *Quarterly Journal of Economics* 84:310–7.

Tolley, G. 1957. "Providing for the Growth of the Money Supply." *Journal of Political Economy* 65:447–84.

Townsend, R. M. 1979. "Optimal Contracts and Competitive Markets with Costly State Verification." *Journal of Economic Theory* 21(October):265–93.

Townsend, R. M. 1980. "Models of Money with Spatially Separated Agents." In *Models of Monetary Economies*, J. Kareken and N. Wallace, eds. Minneapolis: Federal Reserve Bank of Minneapolis: 265–303.

*Wallace, N. 1979. "Why Markets in Foreign Exchange Are Different from Other Markets." *Federal Reserve Bank of Minneapolis Quarterly Review* (Fall):1–7.

*Wallace, N. 1980. "The Overlapping Generations Model of Fiat Money." In *Models of Monetary Economies*, J. Kareken and N. Wallace, eds. Minneapolis: Federal Reserve Bank of Minneapolis: 49–82.

Wallace, N. 1981. "A Modigliani-Miller Theorem for Open Market Operations." *American Economic Review* 71(June):267–74.

Wallace, N. 1983. "A Legal Restrictions Theory of the Demand for 'Money' and the Role of Monetary Policy." Federal Reserve Bank of Minneapolis *Quarterly Review* 7(Winter):1–7.

*Wallace, N. 1984. "Some of the Choices for Monetary Policy." *Federal Reserve Bank of Minneapolis Quarterly Review* (Winter):15–24.

White, L. J. 1991. *The S&L Debacle: Public Policy Lessons for Bank and Thrift Regulation*. New York: Oxford University Press.

*Williamson, S. D. 1987. "Recent Developments in Modeling Financial Intermediation." *Federal Reserve Bank of Minneapolis Quarterly Review* (Summer):19–28.

Young, J. P. 1925. *European Currency and Finance*, vols. 1 and 2, Commission of Gold and Silver Inquiry, United State Senate, serial 9. Washington, DC: U.S. Government Printing Office.

Author Index

Subject Index